*Fundamentalist U*

# Fundamentalist U

## *Keeping the Faith in American Higher Education*

ADAM LAATS

OXFORD
UNIVERSITY PRESS

Oxford University Press is a department of the University of Oxford. It furthers the University's objective of excellence in research, scholarship, and education by publishing worldwide. Oxford is a registered trade mark of Oxford University Press in the UK and certain other countries.

Published in the United States of America by Oxford University Press
198 Madison Avenue, New York, NY 10016, United States of America.



CIP data is on file at the Library of Congress
ISBN 978-0-19-066562-3

1 3 5 7 9 8 6 4 2

Printed by Sheridan Books, Inc., United States of America

*Gratefully dedicated to my colleague H.T.D.*

# *Contents*

# *Acknowledgments*

THIS BOOK WOULD not have been possible without the generous financial assistance of the Spencer Foundation. A research grant allowed me to spend the 2014–2015 academic year traveling to the archives of six of the schools central to this story. Without Spencer's help I never would have been able to conduct this sort of ambitious research.

My home institution, Binghamton University, provided a sabbatical leave in the spring of 2017. The release time made it possible for me to revise and polish the manuscript with the help of many mentors and friends.

Those colleagues were extraordinarily generous with their time. Tim Gloege and Dan Williams devoted hours to reading the manuscript and offering invaluable suggestions in several conversations. Ron Numbers, L. Herbert Siewert, John Fea, Jared Burkholder, Michael Hamilton, Chris Gehrz, Bill Trollinger, Brendan Pietsch, Molly Worthen, Tim Lacy, Michael Lienesch, Roger Geiger, Christopher Loss, David Bernstein, and Ethan Schrum all read sections of the manuscript and helped me make big improvements.

Jon Zimmerman and Ron Numbers assisted once again as I shook every tree in my efforts to secure funding.

As with all historical projects, this one relied on the help of a small army of archivists. Patrick Robbins at Bob Jones University, Keith Call at Wheaton, Stacie Schmidt and Sue Whitehead at Biola, Abigail Sattler at Liberty, Martha Crain at Gordon, and Corie Zylstra and Nikki Tochalauski at Moody Bible Institute all hosted me as I waded through their collections. Keith Woodruff at Tennessee Temple helped via long email conversations. The librarians at Clarks Summit University allowed me access to their voluminous collection of periodicals. Robert Shuster at the Billy Graham Center went far above and beyond, generously sharing his vast knowledge and experience. He even kept the room open late for me.

In Binghamton, I relied on colleagues such as Wendy Wall, Lisa Yun, Tina Chronopolous, and Leigh Ann Wheeler in early stages to help me figure out what this book would be about. I benefited from the hard work and sharp eye of research assistant Kelly Gavin. And Ben Andrus, research librarian extraordinaire, put in countless extra hours helping me track down evidence that Catholic undergraduates in Michigan really did call themselves fundamentalists.

My thanks to all.

*Fundamentalist U*

# *Introduction*

## HIGHER (POWER) EDUCATION

IT CAN BE difficult not to get overwhelmed by the soap-opera-like qualities of the stories. Studying the history of fundamentalist and evangelical higher education, one is tempted to lose oneself in its headline-grabbing tales of sex and scandal. Can a fundamentalist school leader insist that his faculty members avoid sex, even with their own husbands and wives? Can leaders fire deans and professors on a whim, declaring the first principle of their schools to be "loyalty"? Can school presidents force tortured confessions from their faculty members, demanding not only orthodox teaching but also impossible proof that professors have never dipped into forbidden knowledge?

All of these stories and more will feature in these pages. We will look at the ways Clifton Fowler hoped to impose an idiosyncratic "continence" rule on his faculty at the Denver Bible Institute in the 1930s. We will delve into the ouster of administrator Ted Mercer at Bob Jones University in 1953. We will listen to the extended apologies of Russell Mixter at Wheaton College in 1961, trying somehow to prove that his love of science did not mean that he was teaching atheistic evolution.

For historians no less than for journalists, alumni, and gawkers, these sorts of stories tend to get an inordinate share of attention. But it is important to remember that, by and large, conservative evangelical colleges—like most institutions—spend most of their time rolling methodically down much tamer tracks. The main questions that occupy most of the school leaders in these pages are not those of sex, rebellion, and impassioned evidences of orthodoxy but rather admissions, finances, and accreditation. Dramatic stories can reveal and illustrate some of the tensions inherent in fundamentalist colleges and universities, but they are, by definition, exceptions to the usual humdrum functioning of such schools.

This book digs beyond the headlines to offer a more complete history of fundamentalist and conservative evangelical higher education. These schools have built a distinctive tradition within the crazy-quilt landscape of American higher education, a network of interdenominational conservative evangelical colleges and universities that has played an outsized role in culture, religion, and politics. Schools such as Wheaton College in Illinois, Bob Jones University in South Carolina, Biola University in California, Gordon College in Massachusetts, Liberty University in Virginia, and Moody Bible Institute in Chicago are often as far apart from one another culturally as they are geographically, but all of them—and many others like them—represent a recognizable family of institutions.

When students choose to attend Wheaton College or Liberty University, they do so for a profoundly complicated mix of reasons. Colleges are not only about classroom education or professional preparation. They are a dream, a fantasy sometimes. Colleges say something about whom students want to meet, whom they want to marry. Attending an evangelical college can be either a badge of orthodoxy or a determined quest to probe the limits of reasonable belief. When people wear their Liberty sweatshirts, display their Wheaton car-window stickers, or write checks to their Biola alumni fund, they are telling the world something about who they are, or who they want people to think they are. This book hopes to figure out what that message is and what it has been since the 1920s.

For many people outside of the evangelical tradition, these schools often first come to our attention for their leading role in national politics. In recent years, for example, Wheaton College has taken its case about sex and health care to the U.S. Supreme Court.[1] The president of Gordon College, outside of Boston, ignited a local firestorm with his reminder that the school does not sanction same-sex relationships.[2] And in the Republican presidential primaries for the 2016 election, candidates flocked to schools such as Liberty University in Virginia to make speeches and praise Liberty's "seven thousand acres of shared conviction."[3] In the twentieth century, too, conservative politicians hoped to establish their conservative credentials by visiting these campuses. Candidate Ronald Reagan, for instance, made campaign stops at both Bob Jones University and Lynchburg Baptist College (the future Liberty University). As historian Daniel Williams points out, the 1970s saw the rise among conservative politicians of "obligatory campaign stops at conservative evangelical and fundamentalist schools."[4]

For people inside the extended evangelical family, these schools have played an even more crucial role. As the late historian Virginia Brereton put it, "To understand fundamentalists . . . it is absolutely necessary to examine their educational efforts."[5] Fundamentalism and evangelicalism are not only religious beliefs; they have always been more complicated identities. We will not get a sense of that complexity unless we examine them in action. In other words, we have to ask not just what fundamentalists believed but also what they did. Evangelical schools can tell us about more than just the religious beliefs of their conservative evangelical leaders and students. They can tell us about the day-to-day functioning of evangelicalism.

It was often a complicated affair. In every decade, at every school, administrators balanced the fuzzy but ferocious religious imperatives of fundamentalism with the unclear and shifting institutional imperatives of higher education. It might have been impossible to pin down precisely what it meant to be a fundamentalist, or to be a "real" college, but school leaders in every generation knew that to survive as schools, they must always do two things at once. They had to protect their reputations as safe places for fundamentalist or evangelical youth, whatever that meant at the time. Yet they also had to offer the best possible modern educations, whatever that meant at the time. These schools, in other words, always had to balance their absolute need for academic legitimacy with their equally non-negotiable need to maintain their reputations for religious purity. By giving us an opportunity to observe those negotiations in all their complexity—the interactions between theology, politics, culture, education, and institutional life—studying these schools as schools gives us our best chance to make sense of conservative evangelicalism as it really is and as it really was.

In addition, looking at these schools during the twentieth century is uniquely important if we hope to make sense of America's continuing culture wars. Evolution and creationism garner the biggest headlines, but conservative evangelical colleges have always taught a profoundly dissenting attitude about more than just mainstream science. Was America meant to be a Christian nation? Which books count as great literature, and why? What is the proper role of a godly woman in regard to her husband? How should teachers in elementary and secondary schools teach their pupils about these things? The family of evangelical colleges and universities has not been at all monolithic in its answers to these questions, but taken as a whole these schools have offered young people a distinctively evangelical environment in which to learn about them. They have also provided scholars with an insulated evangelical setting in which to study and discuss them. If we do not understand that environment, we will never understand the conservative side of sensitive cultural issues such as evolution, homosexuality, and abortion. After all, our culture wars are not between educated people on one side and uneducated people on the other, in spite of what so many pundits like to assert. Rather, our culture wars are usually fiercest between two groups of people who have been educated in very different ways.

Also important is that we will get a stunted and slanted vision of the landscape of American higher education if we fail to include this unique network of schools. Just as other distinctive networks such as historically black colleges and universities (HBCUs) or all-women colleges have shaped higher education as a whole, so have evangelical schools. In some ways, these schools stand out as institutional dissenters. In others, however, we can see the way the ineluctable logic of higher education has steamrolled all schools in its path, even those schools most determined to resist current collegiate trends.

To put it in its simplest form, an examination of this network of schools can offer vital answers to some basic questions:

- What has it meant to be a fundamentalist or evangelical?
- What has it meant to be a "real" college or university?
- How have conservative evangelical colleges functioned as centers for both conservatism and evangelicalism?
- What and how have they tried to teach each new generation?

None of these is a separate question. None can be answered alone. In order to find out what it has meant to be an evangelical or fundamentalist, we need to understand what fundamentalists and evangelicals have done. We need to find out what they have considered important in their schools. Indeed, we need to know why they wanted their own schools in the first place. And if we want to make sense of those schools, we need to know what conservative evangelicals have thought and believed. Why was it wrong to attend movies? How do people know truth from falsehood, science from guesswork? Similarly, we can only understand conservative evangelicals' politics if we can get a glimpse of the schools they hoped to bequeath to their children and grandchildren.

To complicate matters, the most basic terms in these discussions are difficult to agree on. Many of the great-grandchildren of fundamentalist college founders, for instance, no longer call themselves "fundamentalists." The label has become as tricky and turbulent as other keywords in American history, such as "progressive" and "democratic." Even at the resolutely fundamentalist Bob Jones University, historian Carl Abrams has argued that the label no longer works.[6]

What has it meant to be a fundamentalist? There can be no simple answer, and this book is, in large part, an extended attempt to figure it out. In its most basic meaning, however, fundamentalism has been an interdenominational network of conservative evangelical Protestant groups. Certainly not every conservative Protestant is a fundamentalist. Not even every conservative evangelical Protestant is. Moreover, there have been some self-proclaimed fundamentalists outside the boundaries of conservative Protestantism, as we'll explore in Chapter 2. But at its heart, the label is generally used to describe a religious network, an extended family within the wide boundaries of conservative evangelical Protestantism. Fundamentalism has been dedicated to the elusive dream of orthodoxy, dedicated to remaining true to the supernatural truths of real religion as revealed once and for all in the pages of an inerrant Bible. Even as so much of American culture drifted toward secularism and liberalism—*because* it did—fundamentalism emerged as a vague but defiant rock-ribbed insistence on loyalty to home truths. Though preachers and pundits often assumed that fundamentalists and other conservative evangelicals were simply old-fashioned traditionalists, in fact fundamentalists' traditionalism made them something different. As American culture and religion changed in the twentieth century, fundamentalists didn't simply defend the old. They created something new—a modern anti-modernism, a traditionalism that created and venerated its own innovative traditions.[7]

As a label, "fundamentalism" was coined in the 1920s as part of a struggle for control of American Protestant denominations, especially groups such as the northern Baptists and Presbyterians. Fundamentalists wanted to unite across denominational lines to fight against liberalism. Theologically, fundamentalism has been more of an attitude or an affiliation than a rigidly defined system of belief. Moreover, it has always included more than just explicitly religious or denominational controversy.

Conservative politics and cultural attitudes have always played important but imprecise roles in defining fundamentalism.

As we'll see in these pages, on the many campuses of the fundamentalist and evangelical school network, the term was used with an inherently slippery circularity. In practice, fundamentalism was defined by itself. Fundamentalism was what fundamentalists did, what fundamentalists believed. When in doubt—as fundamentalists often were—fundamentalists looked to impeccably fundamentalist thinkers and organizations for guidance. If Bob Jones or the Moody Bible Institute (MBI) embraced something, it must be trustworthy. Of course, this circular game led to endless anxiety about the reliability of its referents. Was Bob Jones too obdurate? Had MBI strayed? And what could one do when authorities disagreed?

And those authorities did disagree. As a coalition of conservatives from different denominations, fundamentalism could never simply impose on itself a single set of permanent boundaries. All fundamentalists valued revivalism, soul-saving, and battling theological modernism. But as we'll see in the chapters to come, some admired the conservative theological rigor of Calvinism, while others emphasized different religious ideas. Some insisted on one specific vision of the coming apocalypse, while others demurred. Outside of theology, too, fundamentalists generally agreed on a vague cultural conservatism, including an emphasis on traditional gender roles, temperance, chastity, and patriotism. But what should a fundamentalist do if her patriotism conflicted with her dispensationalism? Or if his Calvinism disagreed with his teetotalism? The answers were never clear and never could be. Disagreements about definitions were not the exception but the rule in fundamentalist and evangelical higher education. Fundamentalist intellectuals often made their cases for one idea or another, but as we'll see throughout this book, fundamentalist school administrators tended to muddle along in the broad middle, hoping to keep everyone happy as they sorted out their differences.

Those differences were stamped onto fundamentalism from the very beginning. To the endless frustration of evangelical intellectuals and scholars, fundamentalism never recovered from the vagaries of its first formative years. Throughout the 1920s, Americans tended to lump together a variety of conservative ideas and stereotypes into a fluid and amorphous "fundamentalism." Partly as a result, by the 1950s key members of the fundamentalist family abandoned the label, preferring to call themselves instead "neo-evangelicals" or simply "evangelicals." To add even more confusion, since the 1950s people have used the terms "evangelical" and "conservative evangelical" to refer to both the neo-evangelical reform movement and the wider world of conservative Protestant belief. Someone could call herself an "evangelical" in one breath and a "fundamentalist" in the next, and be correct each time. Yet at the same time, self-identified "evangelicals" and "fundamentalists" fought bitterly with one another, each side accusing the other of theological laziness and intellectual cowardice. In light of all these connected and conflicting meanings, as coming chapters will show, the much-vaunted split between evangelicals and fundamentalists is better understood as a bitter and ongoing family feud. Not a single and ultimate "irreparable breach," if we take that to mean a final, once-and-for-all separation, but rather a perennial splitting, cracking, fraying, mending, and resplitting, so common and so heartbreaking in large and fractious families.[8]

Examining the history of conservative evangelicalism and fundamentalism from the perspective of its network of colleges and universities makes those continuing tangled connections clearer. A higher-education perspective also highlights the ways conservative evangelicalism has always considered itself an integral part of mainstream America. Scholars of religion, for sensible reasons, tend to focus on what has defined conservative evangelicalism—what has made fundamentalists different from non-fundamentalists. They have analyzed how evangelicals have stood out from both mainstream culture and close religious cousins.[9] When we look at what evangelicals have done with their interdenominational colleges, however, we are struck immediately by the fact that they are overwhelmingly more similar to than different from the rest of America. In every decade, in every generation, fundamentalist and evangelical colleges have insisted on their status as real American colleges, whatever that has meant at the time. Indeed, time and time again, conservative evangelical schools have sold themselves as islands of the true America, the safe America, the properly Christian America.

As a result, these schools have always existed in a state of peculiar tension. On one hand, they have insisted that they are keeping up with—and exceeding—the changing academic standards of mainstream higher education. Yet on the other hand, they have had to demonstrate to a skeptical evangelical public that they are remaining true to the imprecise spiritual and cultural imperatives that set them apart. Every school in this network has had to prove its continued loyalty to an ill-defined evangelical purity while also proving its continuing mastery of shifting standards of academic excellence. Every generation of college presidents, provosts, deans, faculty members, and students has been subject to withering fundamentalist scrutiny from interested parties. Naturally, alumni and parents have always closely followed the goings-on at any college. In the case of these religious schools, however, even unaffiliated observers and nosy fundamentalist letter writers have felt the right and the duty to intervene. This kind of fundamentalist scrutiny has covered every question of college life in every generation. Are textbooks too friendly to atheistic evolution? Are students allowed to smoke, drink, attend movies, and generally backslide into sinful secular culture? Are professors' heads being turned by academic fashions, slipping into modernism and world-pleasing liberalism? And the question we see over and over again in every archive: is school X or Y still "true"? Just as colleges and universities everywhere frantically chased the elusive allure of "prestige," fundamentalist schools endlessly negotiated the treacherous currents of reputation, rumor, and innuendo to safeguard their status as reliable institutions. This was more than vanity; this was a question of survival.

To be sure, these questions have been asked at many more conservative religious colleges and universities than will play leading roles in the pages of this book. The focus in these pages will be on one network of specifically interdenominational schools, not just conservative evangelical schools in general. Denominational colleges have certainly played an important role in shaping evangelicalism, but they have had a different set of challenges, a different twentieth-century experience. Denominational colleges have worked to provide havens for generations of educated, faithful Nazarenes, or Baptists, or Brethren. As historian Molly Worthen has argued, denominational schools have provided a unique intellectual environment for evangelical scholars, "gilded cages" that protected them even as they sidelined them.[10] And, as historians such as Darren Dochuk and Bethany Moreton have uncovered, at times denominationally affiliated colleges have pioneered influential subtrends within the wider field of evangelical higher education.[11]

The interdenominational schools that form the heart of this book have always experienced a wide variety of connections to denominational colleges. Yet unlike leading denominationally affiliated schools such as Calvin College, Pepperdine University, Harding University, or Goshen College, the schools in this book have not been guided by any one denominational tradition. Rather, they have considered themselves both the guardians and the wards of the broader conservative evangelical impulse.

Of course, the line between denominational schools and interdenominational ones has not always been easy to determine. Many denominational colleges have always attracted students from a wide variety of religious backgrounds, and many interdenominational schools have tended to be dominated by one denominational tradition. In general, however, schools that have conceived of themselves as nondenominational or interdenominational have usually understood themselves differently, even if they themselves were often unsure of exactly what that difference meant. They have not had denominational boards to settle disputes; they have always struggled to define their nebulous goal of broadly evangelical education. It is that broader evangelical education that is the subject of this book.

As I've worked in the archives of these schools over the years, I've heard a friendly but puzzled question time and time again: "Why are you interested?" For those inside the extended family of conservative evangelicalism, it can seem odd for an outsider to spend so much time researching evangelical higher education. I was not raised in any sort of fundamentalist or evangelical family. I don't have happy or bitter memories of evangelical summer camps or college days. There is nothing personal for me about the changing norms of fundamentalism. Certainly some might think that an outsider like me just can't "get it." At least of equal danger, though, is that insiders are too close to their own schools to see them in a broader context. As with any family story, family members can tend to overemphasize differences and dissensions that do not appear as important to those without any personal stake. Family members are in danger of coming to the archives prepared to find proof of truths they already know.

The dangers for me have been different. Researching and writing from an outsider's perspective, I risk missing important subtleties of tone and meaning. Unlike evangelical scholars, I am at risk of overemphasizing the details that loom large in archives but not in real life. I lack the personal connections to aunts or grandparents who lived through the events I'm studying. Yet even acknowledging these significant limitations, I have confidence in the promise of an outside perspective, if it can be done right. I am not interested in vindicating one faction over another. I have no personal scores to settle or axes to grind. Rather, I am interested in the broader questions raised by this network of schools, questions of interest to everyone, regardless of our backgrounds. I come to this study not out of any personal animus, but rather because of the vital importance of these colleges in American culture and politics. To me, the most intriguing historical questions concern the relationships between education and culture, between schools and morals, between institutions and ideas. There is no better way to explore these questions than by examining these flagship schools.

To make sense of this network born in the fundamentalist controversies of the 1920s, we'll need to begin earlier. Chapter 1, accordingly, looks at the real and dramatic changes that took place in American higher education in the last decades of the nineteenth century. Religious schools that fundamentalists had relied on—leading institutions such as the University of Chicago and Yale University—had taken part in a wholesale shift in the nature of higher education. By the 1920s, fundamentalist leaders began founding their own network of schools and converted a few mainstream institutions to their movement. We'll examine those attempts and place them in the context of the ever-changing debate over what it meant to be really fundamentalist. Continuing in the 1930s, the struggle to define fundamentalism was played out, in large part, on the campuses of conservative evangelical colleges. Different schools answered the question in different ways, but leaders agreed that there could be and would be no central authority to confirm fundamentalist legitimacy. By the 1940s and 1950s, progressive fundamentalists at leading colleges yearned to regain their place as respected intellectuals beyond the circles of their own schools. To do so, some schools, such as Wheaton College, embraced the neo-evangelical reform movement, while others, such as Bob Jones University, resisted. The split between fundamentalists and evangelicals also became a split among conservative schools, though the split was not quite as hard and fast as some school leaders—and some historians—insisted. Next, we'll look at the ways the sixties played out in these conservative schools. In some cases, students rallied for their own evangelical versions of the Free Speech Movement and student protests. In others, students and school leaders joined together to promote a very different sort of patriotic, conservative college movement. By the 1970s and 1980s, as the last chapters show, the world of conservative evangelicalism had been dramatically transformed. Though more moderate schools had embraced the neo-evangelical movement, in part, in order to speak to broader political and cultural issues, it was the more steadfast self-identified fundamentalist schools that often became the hotbeds of political influence. Political candidates such as Ronald Reagan flocked to the most conservative schools in the network to shore up their conservative credentials. As we'll see, this sort of conservative activism was not a novelty of the 1970s but rather a consistent part of the tradition of conservative evangelical colleges since the 1920s.

Not only conservative politics but also conservative attitudes about cultural norms have always shaped life at these evangelical colleges. As we move from the 1920s to the 1980s, we'll examine the way these schools have grappled with perennially difficult issues such as race and racism, dating and sexuality, evolution and science, knowledge and belief. We'll also question the ways conservative evangelical commitments have interacted with more prosaic questions of higher education administration: How should these schools admit students? What does it mean to have a "Christian" athletic program? How should evangelical schools pursue accreditation? Finally, of no surprise to anyone who has spent any time in higher education, perhaps the stickiest issue of all: how can evangelical colleges pay for it all?

As we'll see, there has never been a single, unified evangelical or fundamentalist answer to these questions. Alumni of Gordon College these days might be shocked or even horrified to be lumped together with alumni of Bob Jones University, and vice versa. Nevertheless, throughout the twentieth century, this network of institutions has shared a set of debates that has defined them in sharp distinction from mainstream schools. They have formed a self-consciously dissenting family of schools dedicated to the enormously difficult challenge of educating each new generation in a religious and intellectual tradition at odds with mainstream culture. In every case, they have wrestled with questions of theology, politics, education, and nuts-and-bolts administration not merely as colleges but as colleges with a unique mission. It has not been enough, at these schools, for young people to have a transformative college experience. It has not been enough for students to learn the basics of a profession or to ponder the timeless questions of truth, goodness, and beauty. These schools hoped to do all these things, but to do them in a determinedly evangelical environment, one that produced not only educated people but educated Christians in a secularizing society.

# I

# *College and Christ*

*It may come as a surprise to some [fundamentalists] that the very first public and private schools in our country had a traditional approach or philosophy of education. Harvard, Yale, Andover Newton—to name but a few—used to be "our" schools.*

—A. A. BAKER, 1979[1]

## *Revolution and Its Discontents*

Something happened. It wasn't just the overheated imagination of frustrated fundamentalists. By 1920, the landscape of American higher education had gone through a wholesale revolution. Since their foundings, American colleges had taught young men—and for a long time it was only men—how to be Christian gentlemen. At least, that was the goal. From the seventeenth century until the late nineteenth century, the assumption at most American colleges was that learning could not be separated from Christian morality. By the onset of the twentieth century, that assumption had changed radically.

The change in the religious nature of America's leading colleges and universities, though, was only a symptom, a result of more profound changes in American ideas about what it meant to know something and what it meant to learn something. Colleges dedicated to passing along established truths gave way, in general, to universities dedicated to seeking out always-changing knowledge. Sweeping revolutions in the ways colleges and universities taught students resulted from and contributed to sweeping revolutions in the ways students and faculty understood fundamental concepts such as science, truth, and knowledge.

These changes transformed the day-to-day operations of higher education. New universities welcomed new types of graduate students as they strove to keep up with European standards of research freed from the moral and epistemological dictates of revealed religion. Modern universities added professional programs in engineering, business, medicine, education, and agriculture. Faculty insisted more and more stridently on their primary role as researchers and scholars. They fought and generally won the right to think outside the strictures of traditional religion. New fashions in student life, too, elevated the role of sports, clubs, and socializing. The role of college presidents changed. Old-school presidents were supposed to be starchy moralists who taught advanced students to see the divine unity of all knowledge and morality. The new breed of presidents were scholars, scientists, and bureaucrats. Their role was to attract the best faculty researchers and to fund the best college experiences.

There was nothing sudden or conspiratorial about these changes. Nor were they universal or universally acclaimed. From very early days, school leaders worried about slipping orthodoxy. Since at least the middle of the 1700s, some school founders tried to guarantee continued religious faithfulness in their colleges. Those leaders usually added mandatory creeds and earnest declarations of faith without addressing the underlying causes of change. As a result, their attempts to maintain traditional religious attitudes withered.

In the 1920s, American fundamentalists became the latest and most successful religious leaders to create a new network of colleges that resolutely refused to go along with the secularizing and pluralist trappings of the modern academic revolution. Yet even these broadly successful fundamentalist school leaders often eagerly embraced the institutional elements of the revolution that had swept over the landscape of American higher education. They disputed new ideas about science and modern conceptions about the nature of knowledge. Still, fundamentalists did not reject the institutional changes that had gone along with such intellectual and cultural changes. As we'll see in the chapters to come, fundamentalist colleges were racked by acrimonious debates about these questions throughout the twentieth century, but by and large fundamentalist school founders wanted modern schools that engaged in modern research and taught in modern ways, even as they disputed what non-fundamentalists meant by such things. We will not understand the tensions that pervaded the colleges and universities of twentieth-century fundamentalists if we don't make sense of the complicated ways they reacted to the intellectual and academic revolutions of the nineteenth century.

## *Delivering Veritas*

As conservative pundits have long been fond of pointing out, today's elite American universities all began as resolutely Protestant colleges.[2] In their earliest days, schools such as Harvard, Yale, and Princeton really did infuse every educational moment with Protestant theology. Early schools were not merely religious versions of modern institutions, either. They reflected the values and ideas of their communities. From a twenty-first-century perspective, the first generations of American higher education might seem barely recognizable.[3]

Harvard College, for example, was the first college in the British colonies, and one of the first institutions of any kind established in the new Massachusetts Bay Colony. In the words of historian Roger Geiger, the purpose of the school was nothing less than to "uphold orthodox Puritanism."[4] The priority early settlers placed on setting up a college was no accident. Historian George Marsden has demonstrated that higher education formed a central pillar of Puritanism. Harvard was meant as more than a place to study. The school functioned as a "keystone of the edifice of social authority," Marsden argued. Beyond just teaching the next generation of Puritan divines, early Harvard served to define social roles and to organize a relatively rigid social hierarchy. The Puritan colony, indeed, could not function without a college, since it relied on Harvard to identify its leaders and to maintain its "fundamental principles."[5]

Perhaps not surprisingly for a theocratic society such as the Massachusetts Bay Colony in its early years, Harvard demanded strict orthodoxy from its leaders. In 1654, Harvard's first president, Henry Dunster, resigned due to his belief that infant baptism was not acceptable. The colony's General Court agreed that no one who "manifested themselves unsound in the faith" should teach or lead in Harvard College.[6]

Though Harvard had a long head start, other early Puritan colleges assumed similarly theocratic roles. At Yale in 1722, for example, leaders insisted on a faculty creed as a way to guarantee continued religious orthodoxy.[7] What was college for? Yale's charter spelled out its vision: "Every student shall consider the main end of his study to wit to know God in Jesus Christ and answerably to lead a Godly sober life."[8] At the fledgling College of New Jersey—the future Princeton—celebrity Puritan thinker Jonathan Edwards briefly assumed the presidency in 1757, pledging to maintain the college as a redoubt of Puritan learning. At Yale, President Edwards's contemporary Thomas Clap (1739–1766) made similar promises.[9]

In these early generations, Puritan leaders did not merely layer religious ideas onto recognizably modern colleges. Rather, basic attitudes about knowledge and the proper role of education created college atmospheres radically different from modern expectations. In the seventeenth century at Harvard, for instance, faculty and students were not expected to conduct research as we know it. As Geiger argues, "The corpus of knowledge transmitted at Harvard was considered fixed, and inquiry after new knowledge was beyond imagining."[10] Not only did early Harvard hope to teach students in a religious atmosphere, but the school itself was built around Puritan ideas of truth and knowledge. Real knowledge had been delivered by revelation. Students' and teachers' jobs were to decode and understand, not to invent or challenge. The point of higher education was to demonstrate to new generations the abiding truths of Christianity.

By the middle of the eighteenth century, these Puritan assumptions had lost their unquestioned power in American colleges. For years, Harvard tutor John Leverett had encouraged Enlightenment thinking among Cambridge's stuffy ministers.[11] By 1722, Harvard College officially endorsed such notions, establishing Hollis Chairs to attract independent scholars enamored of Enlightenment ideas.[12] By 1750, the modern notion that college was the proper home for exploring and expanding new knowledge had become accepted and expected. For example, before Ben Franklin popularized the experimental study of electricity with his stories of kites and keys, Harvard's John Winthrop used his Hollis funding to purchase equipment to do the same thing. Not just Winthrop but Harvard as a whole became the American home for teaching the new ideas of John Locke, Isaac Newton, and John Tillotson.[13]

Puritan ideas about proper knowledge might have held sway for only a century or so, but their expectations of student life lingered much longer. The daily routines of Harvard's first students might have looked very familiar long into the 1800s. Throughout that period, students had very little freedom in their schedules. They enrolled in a program that dictated a full-day schedule of chapel observance, study, and three recitations. They did not choose a major or even declare a professional interest—at least not in the way today's students might. Early curriculum was limited mainly to the study of Latin, Greek, possibly Hebrew, and mathematics. Students were generally examined orally twice annually and hoped to eventually perform a polished disputation along traditional lines.[14]

Perhaps most famously, in 1828 the leaders of Yale College offered a defense of this style of education. President Jeremiah Day (1817–1846) and his colleagues insisted on the value of recitations and disputations as the heart and soul of higher education. The goal of this style of education, President Day explained, was to build both "the *discipline* and the *furniture* of the mind." Seemingly pointless exercises in memorization and recitation taught young people how to learn. Such exercises strengthened the mind and sharpened the native intellect. Day argued that higher education must never be viewed as primarily a preparation for any specific profession, but rather as building a foundation for cultured life.[15]

Certainly this kind of higher education would be feasible or even attractive only for families of means. In 1869, only about one in every hundred Americans between the ages of eighteen and twenty-four was enrolled in an institution of higher education.[16] In early generations, only well-off families sent their children—or even just some fraction of their male offspring—for this sort of polishing. And it was generally seen as such, as polishing and finishing, not as the most vital part of professional preparation. Perhaps not surprisingly, then, boys and young men from affluent families tended to drop in and out as it suited their schedules. College was seen as an educational experience, to be sure, but not the sum total of one's education. One's time at Harvard, Yale, or Princeton was undoubtedly vital for social success, but not for professional success.[17]

As we might expect, too, today's assumptions about the proper age of college students did not apply. As late as the 1870s, it was not shocking to see William Rainey Harper, future president of the University of Chicago, earn his Ph.D. from Yale at age eighteen.[18] Certainly Harper's academic success was precocious, even at the time, but until the twentieth century students could often complete degrees at relatively young ages. Because admission was based on language exams, talented students from families that could afford tutors managed regularly to enter college at young ages. Around 1800, the median age for entry at Columbia was only fourteen; at Harvard, fifteen; at the College of New Jersey (the future Princeton), sixteen.[19]

Perhaps more important, our modern expectations of a bright line dividing college from secondary school did not exist until near the end of the nineteenth century, and such rules did not become universal until the middle of the twentieth. Before that, it was common, even customary, for much younger students to enroll in a college, even if they had not mastered the language skills needed for admission. Such students would be part of a school's preparatory department, where they would acquire the necessary skills. In many schools, these preparatory departments became the largest parts of the college.[20]

Once they arrived on campus, these young men in America's young colleges did not see themselves as striking out on their own. Rather, their daily schedules remained rigidly controlled for as long as they remained. The goals of their studies were dictated by tradition and teachers. College was not a time for students to find themselves, but rather a time for them to fit into a mold that had been found for them long before.

Of course, in different decades, at different schools, this experience could vary widely. Early colleges often tinkered with these approaches to higher education. At Yale, for example, President Timothy Dwight (1795–1817) insisted on rigid Calvinism as the heart and soul of Yale's curriculum. But he experimented with the normal sorts of discipline meted out to students in his era. Instead of physical correction and public shaming, Dwight relied on private counseling and an early form of report cards. As a result, during Dwight's years Yale became America's leading college and avoided some of the riotous student rebellions seen elsewhere.[21]

Just as important, even as these structures may have seemed timeless and unchangeable to both students and college leaders at the time, American colleges as a whole had always been subject to sometimes imperceptible changes that eventually became revolutionary. As we've seen, the earliest goal of imparting a fixed body of knowledge to students gave way in the eighteenth century to a more recognizably modern goal of incessant research after new truths. During the nineteenth century, the structure of early American colleges was changing as well. Yale's leaders had been prompted to publish their 1828 defense by the alarming success of the new Amherst College (founded 1825), a school that promised "a new and liberal course."[22] As America emerged from its brutal Civil War in the 1860s, long-held assumptions about the nature of higher education and the proper structure of collegiate life underwent another series of slow but ineluctable revolutions.

## *The Academic Revolution*

Between the Civil War and World War I, those conjoined revolutions transformed American ideas about the nature of higher education. Like any successful revolution, the profound changes in higher education became so widely accepted that they came to be seen as natural and obvious to many Americans. When the stupendously wealthy barons of the Gilded Age wanted to start new schools, for instance, they simply assumed that those schools would take the revolutionary new form of the modern research university. As Roger Geiger has pointed out, new millionaires such as Leland Stanford, John D. Rockefeller, and Jonas Clark invested their money in new schools in California (Stanford, c. 1891), Chicago (University of Chicago, c. 1890), and Massachusetts (Clark, c. 1887). When they did so, they did not wonder if their shiny new institutions should reflect the new norms of higher education. For all of them, those new norms seemed to be the obvious way to structure a good school.[23]

Historians have identified a profound triple revolution in higher education during this period. The Morrill Land-Grant Act of 1862 pushed schools to offer more than just liberal-arts education. An academic revolution led to new graduate programs and new ideas about the proper role and rights of faculty. And a collegiate revolution quickly normalized new ideas about the guidelines for student life. Fueling and fueled by this academic triple revolution was a dramatic intellectual revolution. New ideas about knowledge, truth, and scholarship—what we might best call the triumph of modern science and the modern scientific worldview—developed hand in hand with the changes that swept institutions of higher education. As historians have argued, these two revolutions were tied tightly together. Schools changed as ideas changed, and ideas changed as schools changed.[24]

Many of those changes had clearly identifiable causes. For instance, the allure of funds from the Morrill Land-Grant Act proved irresistible to most school administrators. Beginning in the war years, colleges scrambled to provide professional training that could improve their cases for receiving land-grant funding. Agriculture and engineering were usually the first new subjects introduced into university life. Over the course of the second half of the nineteenth century, the notion that colleges should include training in specific professions took deep root. Law schools, business schools, and medical schools, which often had been conducted as independent enterprises, tended to fold themselves into the growing university structure.[25] At a more fundamental level, higher education became the presumed home of such professional training. Of course, college had always been seen in some ways as preparation for the professions, but after the land-grant revolution that training took on a much more precise and technical flavor.

By the late 1800s, American academics looked with envy and embarrassment at the gulf between American graduate education and that of European universities. Many school leaders had themselves taken the ritual tour of leading German schools, and they came back with a sense of the provincial and intellectually stultifying traditions of America's colleges.[26] By the 1880s, academic leaders such as Andrew Dickson White at

Cornell, Charles W. Eliot at Harvard, and especially Daniel Coit Gilman at Johns Hopkins had introduced German-style graduate training into their own schools. In doing so, they instituted a new norm in the goals of American higher education.[27] For many school leaders at the time, the shift was captured by a change in name. Great European "universities" offered graduate research in an array of subjects, unfettered by religious tradition. Backward American "colleges" drilled reluctant youths in crusty old slogans. As Daniel Coit Gilman wrote from the brand-new Johns Hopkins University in 1876, "Our plans look toward the freedom of 'the University,' and not to the restrictions of 'the College.' "[28]

American schools had offered Ph.D.'s in the past, but only in the 1880s did such graduate programs take the form we are familiar with today.[29] At the same time, the expectation for university research decisively repudiated older traditions of religious orthodoxy. This attitude was most pronounced at schools such as Johns Hopkins, Michigan, and Harvard—institutions that considered themselves the cutting edge of the modern research system. However, as George Marsden has argued, the notion that modern universities required intellectual freedom from religious oversight proved irresistible even among religious conservatives. At conservative holdout Princeton, for example, staunch Calvinist president Francis Patton insisted on Princeton's continuing role as a broadly Christian college. Yet even Patton was determined that his modern university must resist intellectual control by any faction, even by his beloved Presbyterianism. Patton thrilled a modern-minded alumni audience in New York City in 1898 when he promised, "I will do what in me lies to keep the hand of ecclesiasticism from resting on Princeton University."[30] Like the initially skeptical group of alumni, Patton recognized that in 1898 a real university, a modern university, must not let itself be governed by denominational or sectarian considerations. Research must be allowed to range beyond the traditional catechism if it was to be considered real research at all.

For students, too, the emergence of the modern university meant a revolution in the college experience. Traditions that had persisted for centuries came to seem ridiculously outmoded and irrelevant. Student life no longer needed to be dictated from morning to night in an endless round of chapel services and recitations. As Roger Geiger explained, by the turn of the twentieth century

> the pillars of the traditional college—the curricular separation of the classes, the fixed course for the AB, required Latin and Greek,

> and routines structured around three daily recitations—were all superseded by a curriculum based on academic disciplines and student choice.[31]

For students, the freedom of the modern higher education system meant more time to spend with student clubs, sports, and social groups. As a result, during this period colleges saw the rise of campus groups such as the Young Men's (and eventually Young Women's) Christian Association.[32] Campuses also welcomed student fraternities and student athletic leagues. By 1900, Geiger argues, student activities such as football had become "too important . . . to be left to the students."[33] This change in student lifestyle became an intrinsic part of university governance. Sports, frats, and clubs were not merely quirky add-ons. Rather, they became a key source of school revenue, as a new breed of active alumni used their financial influence to support such beloved collegiate lifestyles. Even the most popular college administrators failed to limit the growth and influence of athletics. Not only was there too much money involved, but students and alumni also insisted on winning teams as an essential part of a thriving college.[34] Just as new norms of professional programs and faculty research became inherent parts of American expectations and assumptions about higher education, so too did a distinct set of campus activities for students.

Beyond just lifestyle and curriculum changes, the intellectual expectations of students reflected the modern academic revolution. Indeed, the reason daily chapel and daily recitations fell so quickly out of favor largely reflected dramatic cultural changes in ideas about proper knowledge. As Michigan's president, James Burrill Angell, put it in 1905, in the old days students were expected merely to embrace received wisdom. In the new academic dispensation, Angell told them, students must learn "the power and the passion for discovering new truth."[35]

Taken together, this triple revolution utterly transformed the landscape of American higher education between roughly 1870 and 1920. By the end of that period, a new goal of graduate education along European lines had become the norm for any school hoping to call itself a university. The research conducted by those graduate students and their faculty mentors took on a new tone, often under the grand but vague label "science." Of course, American colleges and universities had always included some teaching and scholarship in science. As historian Jon Roberts has argued, already by 1850 almost half of college faculty taught science or math classes. But in those earlier years, the most common collegiate conception of "science" was as a decidedly less rigorous intellectual pursuit, more of a mechanical or even vocational type of education.[36]

At the intellectual heart of the academic revolution was a changing understanding of the meaning and purpose of science. Between the late 1890s and the early part of the twentieth century, at leading universities, prominent thinkers such as John Dewey led a wholesale revolution in attitudes toward knowledge. For Dewey and those of his ilk, "science" was more than just a collection of academic methods and disciplines, more than just ways to pursue knowledge. Ideas about science and the scientific nature of truth, morality, and reality became more of a "personal orientation."[37] As historian Andrew Jewett argues, Dewey's influential ideas took on the shades of a "missionary enterprise," one that hoped to transform both morals and knowledge.[38]

Changing ideas about knowledge—powerfully articulated by scholars such as Dewey—dictated changing structures for academic life. Modern schools no longer considered knowledge to be an inherited body of information. Rather, at the heart of modern scientific inquiry lies the assumption that knowledge must be pursued freely along rational, naturalistic lines. As Jon Roberts has argued, "Truth claims based on alternative epistemologies—tradition, divine inspiration, and subjective forms of religious experience—increasingly lost credibility within the academy."[39]

It bears repeating that these changing notions of truth and science did not reign unopposed in American higher education. Indeed, the fundamentalist dissenters we'll meet throughout the rest of this book might be understood—intellectually at least—as primarily dissenters against this newly dominant attitude in mainstream colleges. But even those most fervent academic reactionaries accepted, by and large, the fundamental structural changes that had swept American higher education between 1870 and 1920.

Talking about an academic revolution in this way can make it sound as if things changed in American culture and higher education on one specific date, for all time. It can make it sound as if these changes were agreed upon at one grand meeting—or perhaps at a secret conclave—hosted by leaders of Johns Hopkins, Cornell, and Harvard. Of course, that was not how it happened at all. Rather, changes in both popular and academic expectations about higher education happened over a generation. The changes transformed schools in profound ways, though popular angst usually focused only on a few of the most obvious surface changes.

## *The Public Reaction*

Some bookend examples might best illustrate this widespread tendency. In the 1860s, for instance, when Andrew Dickson White began promoting his idea of a new type of university, his plan for Cornell embodied the new trends in institutional organization. The school offered a traditional classical course including Latin and Greek for those students who wanted it. But it also offered an array of professional and academic programs for those who did not care to pursue the traditional curriculum. Perhaps most important, the new university rejected the "old style of reciting by rote."[40] Students instead attended lectures, read assigned texts, and took periodic written examinations. White stressed that the new university—counter to the long American tradition of higher education—would not include a preparatory department. In all these ways, Cornell embodied the coming revolution in higher education.

Some of White's changes did not stick. He explained in 1872, for example, that Cornell would be thoroughly modern in its inclusion of mandatory military training, as well as provisions for students to work at the university in exchange for tuition.[41] Neither of these unsuccessful innovations, though, nor any of the successful ones raised the same hackles as did Cornell's religious changes. When White and backer Ezra Cornell first described their new school, they were attacked in the New York legislature—not as academic iconoclasts, not as wild-eyed institutional reformers, but rather as "godless."[42] And White engaged the debate on those terms. He defended the new school as "a Christian institution," though not a sectarian one.[43] White bemoaned the fact that nothing had generated for his school "more bitter enemies" than Cornell's lack of denominational affiliation.[44] Accusations of irreligiosity were self-serving lies, White charged, due to the "persistent . . . misrepresentations" of Cornell's religious rivals.[45] Cornell was indeed a Christian school, White insisted, though it made chapel attendance voluntary and avoided any one denominational tradition. Nevertheless, even that staunch religious loyalty had been attacked—with far more venom than had any of Cornell's other revolutionary changes in college life—by critics White called outmoded pseudo-academics, intellectual pretenders seeking "to gain favor by hanging on the skirts of a sectarian college."[46] Though the structure of the new university was radically new, White wrote, and radically better, small-minded critics focused myopically on surface changes in student religious requirements.

White wrote from the beginning of the period of academic revolution. Concern with student religion persisted throughout the period, well into the twentieth century. By 1909, near the end of the stretched-out triple revolution, journalist Harold Bolce reported in the pages of *Cosmopolitan* magazine the remarkable results of the changes in higher education. Professors and administrators at America's leading schools, Bolce wrote, no longer saw their jobs as the careful cultivation of traditional religious values in America's elite young people. The social issues most in need of moral guidance, Bolce said, issues such as "marriage, divorce, the home, religion, and democracy," were studied and propounded "as if these things were fossils, gastropods, vertebrates, equations, chemical elements, or chimeras."[47]

Bolce and his editors were not interested in the profound structural changes that had led to this change in teaching. Rather, they fretted that leading schools no longer insisted on traditional moral and religious ideas. At Syracuse, for example, a magnificent Methodist school and thoroughly "up to date," Bolce warned that while the trappings of traditional religion had been maintained, the ideas had been discarded.[48] Bolce quizzed Syracuse sociologist Edwin L. Earp, for instance, and breathlessly reported Earp's iconoclasm:

> "Do you not believe, Professor," I asked, "that Moses got the ten commandments in the way the Scriptures tell?"
>
> The professor smiled. "I do not," said he. "It is unscientific and absurd to imagine that God ever turned stone-mason and chiseled commandments on a rock."[49]

Bolce and his editors knew a good scoop when they saw it. In response to popular interest, they expanded Bolce's expose to a series of three articles. They were not interested in why professors had begun to sneer at traditional religious assumptions. They did not look into the profound changes that had changed the underlying structure and purpose of higher education. Rather, they correctly assumed that readers wanted to see shocking truths about the lack of traditional religious teaching at leading colleges.

No headlines screamed that students no longer recited three times daily. No public controversies roiled over the radical change in academic organization into disciplinary departments led by faculty experts. The introduction of European-style Ph.D. programs did not interest many people outside of the academy. But the changing role of religion in higher education did. Throughout the period of academic revolution, bitter arguments about the proper role of religion became the public face of those deeper academic and intellectual revolutions.

On one side, self-appointed modern experts considered themselves the inevitable victors, the champions of science, modernity, and true morality. Syracuse's Professor Earp, for instance, confidently dismissed traditional religious thinking as "unscientific." Similarly, near the end of his career, President White insisted that he was on the side of the angels in a contest between what he called "Science and Theology" or even "Humanity with Unreason."[50]

On the other side, outraged muckrakers such as Harold Bolce denounced the ways modern higher education had abandoned its traditional role of inculcating youth with specific religious moral values. Bolce and *Cosmopolitan* were not alone. In this period, fellow journalists in leading periodicals such as *Atlantic Monthly, The Century, Scribner's,* and *McClure's* filled page after page with titillating exposés of student life.[51] Yet neither Bolce nor the religious conservatives who agreed with him took issue with other elements of the revolutionary changes that had swept over higher education. They did not disparage science; they only lamented the false pretensions affected by some sneering scientific poseurs. They did not dispute new ideas about the structure of higher education; they only wished that it could include traditional religious truths.

## *An Empire in Ruins*

Fundamentalists in the 1920s joined this popular outrage about the religious fruits of the nineteenth century's intellectual and academic revolutions. As George Marsden put it so memorably, in the mid-twentieth century conservative evangelicals looked around at the landscape of American higher education and saw an "empire in ruins."[52] Once-evangelical schools such as Harvard, Yale, Chicago, and Princeton had taken radically new directions. They had embraced modern notions of truth, knowledge, and scientific inquiry. As a result, they had tossed out older structures for student life and study. They had transformed professors' missions from professing an inherited faith to relentlessly pursuing new truths unrestrained by traditional orthodoxies.

Beginning in the 1920s, fundamentalists did not try to rebuild their old empire of evangelical colleges but rather sought to imitate its successful conquerors. The new and renewed universities and colleges founded by fundamentalists in the 1920s did not reject outright the modern academic revolution, even when they protested against the intellectual revolutions at its heart. To be sure, in some cases, such as accreditation at Bob Jones College, fundamentalists held out against certain elements of modern academic life. But as a whole, the schools they created were dissenting modern schools, not restorations of an earlier standard. Indeed, throughout the twentieth century, fundamentalists touted their schools as better, more modern versions of modern American higher education. Even in their fervent dissent against the intellectual underpinnings of the modern academic revolution, fundamentalist leaders and thinkers did not simply deny the value of modern knowledge, science, and academic inquiry. Rather, they insisted that their dissenting forms of science and knowledge represented better science, truer knowledge, and more modern inquiry.

Some critics of evangelical colleges, or those with only a scanty knowledge of them, might think that fundamentalist schools hoped to replicate a far older Puritan notion of higher education, or maybe an antebellum idea of a small sectarian school. That has been true in some cases on the surface. Fundamentalist intellectuals have sometimes echoed their Puritan forebears in their insistence that truths are stable, heritable, and reliable. Institutionally as well, some school leaders insisted on an old-fashioned top-down leadership structure. All schools instituted strict rules for students and faculty, as was the norm for the nineteenth-century religious college. But fundamentalist colleges and universities—even the most conservative among them—embraced the victorious tenets of the modern academic revolution. Fundamentalists, for instance, accepted without demur the radical modern notion of "college" as the proper home for new knowledge, an institution dedicated to groundbreaking academic study by a special class of credentialed teachers who were also pioneering scholars. Of course, not every small evangelical school could afford to free faculty from overwhelming teaching loads, but in principle fundamentalist schools gave at least lip service to modern ideas about the role of faculty as researchers. Even the smallest and most financially unstable schools invested from time to time in various research institutes and programs, encouraging faculty to engage in research guided by evangelical ideas. In principle, at least, schools assumed that faculty would do more than just impart ancient ideas; faculty were expected to be thoroughly modern in their preparation and performance.

Fundamentalist schools also accepted without much fuss other elements of the modern academic revolution. For example, fundamentalist colleges, just like mainstream ones, simply assumed as the twentieth century progressed that their role was to prepare students for specific professions. They simply assumed that students would enroll in majors and select their own courses. They simply assumed that students would attend lectures, complete assigned readings, and write essays or take cumulative exams. In spite of their occasional rhetoric about an older vision of higher education, fundamentalist school leaders never questioned these fundamental structural changes that had swept higher education.

Moreover, when fundamentalist leaders did impose lifestyle rules, faculty creeds, and authoritarian leadership on their colleges, they did so in a conscious effort to revive or retain ideas they acknowledged to be old-fashioned. Students and faculty accepted and often celebrated constraints on their lifestyles or research methods. But such protests against modern academic life became badges of pride precisely because they formed a self-conscious dissent from accepted norms in American higher education.

The twentieth-century career of fundamentalist higher education would be a much simpler tale to tell if these things had been different. If fundamentalist school leaders had rejected more decisively the structure of modern higher education, their network of colleges might have formed merely another curious footnote in the history of American higher education. Instead, fundamentalist and evangelical colleges and universities saw themselves as modern American schools. They expected their students to learn to become doctors, lawyers, engineers, and teachers. They expected their faculty to be academic experts in their fields. Eventually, at least, they expected their students to have completed high school before moving on to their schools. In short, they did not reject the academic revolutions that had made those things seem normal. However, they expected to do all the things that modern universities did without signing on to the fundamental intellectual presuppositions that had dictated those changes in modern university life. Fundamentalist schools wanted to be modern schools, but of a distinctly fundamentalist type. They promised all the modern features of mainstream schools, infused with a commitment to profoundly dissenting ideas about the nature of real knowledge, morality, and belief.

# 2

# *In the Beginning*

*My soul is a starving skeleton; my heart a petrified rock; my mind is poisoned and fickle as the wind, and my faith is as unstable as water . . . . I wish that I had never seen a college.*

—"A MOTHER'S SON," 1921[1]

## *Fundamental Flaws*

This was not what fundamentalists wanted.

Students chanted threats at their school's administrators. They marched outside the administration building and pelted the windows with rocks and rotten eggs. In the end, police waded through the student picket line and whisked the trustees off to jail for their own protection.[2]

The year was 1929, not 1969, and the city was Des Moines, not Madison or Berkeley. The debacle at Des Moines University taught a harsh lesson to its fundamentalist supporters. A few years earlier, Toronto-based fundamentalist activist T. T. Shields had taken over the struggling Baptist school. With the full enthusiastic support of fundamentalist leaders nationwide, Shields introduced sweeping changes that he hoped would save the school from pernicious trends in religion and higher education.[3]

It served instead as an object lesson in what not to do. Shields fired all faculty members and forced them to reapply. He banned fraternities, smoking, dancing, and dating. Perhaps worst of all, he installed his purported paramour, Edith Rebman, to enforce these new rules, rarely visiting campus himself. It did not take long for students and faculty to rebel. When they did, local people had been so offended by Shields's and Rebman's abrasive attitudes that they gleefully supported student demands. Shields and Rebman were pushed out; the school issued diplomas to students who had earned them.[4]

The entire episode was an extreme example of how badly things could go wrong. Though perhaps embarrassed by the humiliating results, most fundamentalists in the 1920s agreed that they needed to do something to save higher education. Too often, they fretted, colleges and universities had abandoned their traditional Protestant guidelines. Too often, students were left on their own to negotiate the murky morality of modern America. Even worse, to fundamentalist intellectuals and activists, many colleges seemed actively to promote a slanted vision of life and learning that would guide students directly to perdition.

What happened in Des Moines was not typical. Throughout the 1920s, fundamentalists successfully established a new network of schools to buck the trends of the recent academic revolutions, as this chapter will explore. But the Des Moines experience did demonstrate that many fundamentalist activists had more zeal than experience when it came to running universities. Not only that, the Des Moines riots were only the most dramatic expression of a dilemma shared by all fundamentalist school founders in the 1920s: it was never clear at the time precisely what fundamentalism was or how fundamentalist schools should be organized. Theologically, fundamentalism was more of a dream than a plan; fundamentalists yearned for an evangelical orthodoxy that could never be clearly defined. Beyond theology, school founders all brought their own idiosyncratic ideas about the meaning of fundamentalism to their schools. They discovered to their chagrin that their grand ideas about establishing truly fundamentalist colleges could be swamped by the institutional demands of American higher education. All in all, such uncertainty dictated the turbulent course of the history of fundamentalism and fundamentalist higher education throughout the twentieth century.

## *Quacks like a Duck*

During the 1920s, the world of evangelical Protestantism fractured. What did it mean to be a faithful Christian in a modern age? Perhaps not surprisingly, the more extreme answers garnered more than their share of attention, both at the time and ever since. A self-described "fundamentalist" movement called itself the side of tradition. Modernists, on the other hand, considered themselves the champions of healthy innovation.

In a nutshell, modernists pushed to free the church from theological blinders, from accreted habits that had taken the form of gospel.[5] Fundamentalists offered a different solution. They often assumed they represented ancient tradition, the "old-time religion," but in fact their insistence on a united-front evangelical orthodoxy represented something new. Beginning in the early twentieth century, fundamentalists wanted to introduce new safeguards against the influence of modernist thinking.[6] As historian Timothy E. W. Gloege has argued recently, instead of traditional orthodoxy, early fundamentalists pushed for "the performance of orthodoxy facilitated by modern promotional techniques."[7]

Compared with the systematic theologies that guided denominational thinkers, fundamentalist theology was eclectic and stubbornly imprecise. But it was not simply haphazard. They didn't agree on the specifics, but fundamentalists generally were in accord that there were a few fundamental beliefs that signified real religion. People who held these beliefs—whatever their denominational background—could be considered true Christians. And true Christians could safeguard their religion by insisting on these fundamental beliefs. What were these beliefs? Fundamentalists generated several lists, most of which included similar basics: the belief that the Bible contained no errors in its original draft; the notion that Jesus Christ truly was born of a virgin; an idea that Christ's death was an epochal event in human history, one that changed humanity and atoned for original sin; and the concept that Jesus really did rise from the dead, not symbolically or spiritually but bodily and significantly. For instance, conservative Presbyterian activists pushed for a five-point list of absolute fundamentals in 1923.[8] Minnesota's William Bell Riley insisted on his nine-point creed as the definition of true fundamentalism.[9] Texan J. Frank Norris offered journalists a five-point list: "First the inerrancy of the Scriptures. Second, the virgin birth. Third, the deity of Christ. Fourth, the substitutionary atonement. And, fifth, the imminent, physical and literal return of the Lord."[10] In each case, fundamentalists hoped their lists would serve as infallible markers of dedication to authentic Christianity. As theological modernists attempted to bring new perspectives to old ideas, fundamentalists hoped to put up new walls to create a safely orthodox religion, open to conservatives from a variety of denominations.

The attention lavished on the battle between Protestant modernists and fundamentalists brought the term "fundamentalism" into widespread use during the 1920s—such wide use, in fact, that the label was soon used as a sort of conservative catchall, a way to sum up a defiantly reverent attitude toward traditional values during a time of rapid social change. Yet by the end of the 1920s, such broad use of "fundamentalism" died away. Members of conservative evangelical factions continued to use the term, but other sorts of conservatives backed away. Fooled by this complicated partial fadeout, journalists and historians from the 1930s to the 1950s often asserted that fundamentalism as a whole had died off by the end of the 1920s.[11]

By the 1950s, the resurgent popularity and influence of fundamentalist evangelists such as Billy Graham proved that fundamentalism was alive and well—one sort of fundamentalism, at least. Conservative evangelicals who had called themselves fundamentalists in the 1920s had established new colleges and taken control of a few old ones, as we'll explore in this chapter. They had established independent churches and parachurch organizations that grew in popularity and influence between the 1930s and the 1950s. Soon new generations of academic historians explored the ways this sort of fundamentalism had, to use the words of historian Joel Carpenter, "not only survived but thrived" since the 1930s.[12]

Just as people in the 1920s struggled to define fundamentalism, so too have historians of religion. Some have offered one definition or another, while others have instead wisely maintained a broad scope of meanings.[13] In order to make sense of fundamentalism and its network of dissenting fundamentalist colleges, we need to understand that there has never been a single "real" fundamentalism and several pretenders; rather, there has been a clamor of claimants to the title, some with better claims than others, but all relying on their own definitions.

It's a messy story, and we will understand it more clearly if we take a closer look at the early career of fundamentalism as a broadly conservative identity, something that meant more than any one sharply defined way of thinking about God or society. After all, those broadly conservative meanings played decisive roles in defining the purpose of fundamentalists' schools. Fundamentalist colleges always wanted to be more than simply religious schools that ascribed to a list of theological or denominational fundamentals. They wanted to be more than merely denominational colleges that taught the traditions of one branch of the evangelical family. They wanted above all to be safe schools, schools in which conservative evangelical students from all denominational backgrounds could be protected from the troubling trends of modern life without giving up the benefits of higher education. In theology as well as culture and politics, fundamentalist schools embraced a new kind of big-tent conservatism based on this non-negotiable but also indefinable goal of student safety.

## *"The Newspapers Make Fun of Us and Call Us 'Fundamentalists'"*

What did they mean?

Throughout the 1920s, a wide array of politicians, activists, and bystanders used the term "fundamentalism" in a wild variety of ways. In some cases, they used it to refer to conservative evangelical Protestants and their campaign against theological modernism. Just as often, though, people used "fundamentalism" as a broad label for conservative thinking and belligerent action.

On the floor of the U.S. House of Representatives in early 1926, for example, Texas representative Thomas Lindsay Blanton urged his colleagues to support an amendment to an appropriations bill for the District of Columbia that contained a provision prohibiting teachers from disrespecting the Bible or voicing unpatriotic ideas. He warned his fellow conservatives, though, that doing so would subject them to the ridicule of liberals. "The newspapers make fun of us," Blanton complained, "and call us 'fundamentalists' whenever we want to inquire into what the children are being taught."[14] Clearly, he did not relish being the butt of journalists' jokes. But when he said they called him a fundamentalist, what did he mean?

A year earlier, ambitious social scientists at the University of Michigan set out to chart students' ideas about their own religious identities. Only 8 percent of all the students called themselves "fundamentalists." But a whopping 18 percent of Catholic students labeled themselves that way.[15] They didn't think of themselves as conservative evangelical Protestants. But what did they mean?

Not even the best-informed theologians and intellectuals could offer a simple definition of fundamentalism. Writing from Princeton Theological Seminary, eminent conservative theologian J. Gresham Machen said that he wasn't a fundamentalist, except for the times that he was. Machen yearned for a true conservatism, a true traditionalism that did not confuse itself with the trappings of "some strange new sect."[16] Yet Machen also insisted that he himself should be considered a fundamentalist in some ways. When Machen made his careful distinctions, what did he mean?

Machen was a theologian's theologian, but Thomas Blanton was certainly not. When Blanton complained to his congressional colleagues that he was being mocked as a fundamentalist, he didn't mean anything about theological modernism or lists of doctrinal fundamentals. To twenty-first-century ears, when he said "fundamentalist," he meant what later generations would often call "conservative." He meant unyielding, aggressive patriotism. He meant vigorous defense of free-market values and opposition to communist subversion in unions and politics. He meant keeping America for 100 percent Americans. And he was not afraid to back up his words with his fists.

He had first come to Congress from Texas in 1916. After an unsuccessful run for U.S. Senate, Blanton remained a loud and proud conservative stalwart in the House of Representatives until 1937.[17] Rather than fighting with theological modernists, Blanton was most famous for battling with leftists, socialists, and unionists. His most ferocious conflicts in Congress were with Representative Marion Zioncheck of Washington. In 1936, the two ideologues nearly came to blows on the floor of the House. They feuded bitterly over issues of unions, Blanton denouncing them and Zioncheck defending them.[18]

When in 1926 Blanton lamented the ways journalists called him a fundamentalist, though, he wasn't concerned with unions or immigration. Rather, he was defending a rider that had first appeared in a 1924 appropriations bill for the District of Columbia and demanded strict patriotism from public-school teachers there. Blanton wanted Congress to again support the provision, which had cut the salary of any DC teacher convicted of teaching "partisan politics, or disrespect for the Holy Bible, or that this is an inferior form of government."[19]

Clearly, when he complained about being called a fundamentalist, Blanton was not interested in denominational controversy. He did not care directly about the inerrancy of the Bible or the historical facticity of miracles. Rather, he wanted the power to restrain teachers who he thought were "teaching disloyalty." He wanted to force teachers to refrain from teaching "partisan politics" when those politics meant criticism of the United States. Students, Blanton thought, must be taught to have "respect for the Holy Bible."[20] When Blanton said people mocked him as a fundamentalist, he was referring to this broad sort of cultural and political traditionalism. He apparently saw fundamentalism as an attitude, a way of thinking about political activism. Part of fundamentalism, the way Blanton used the term, was an unwillingness to go along with the status quo. It connoted a certain belligerence, a willingness to stand up and be counted in the fight to preserve traditional American values.

Similarly, when students at the University of Michigan—including many Catholic students—described themselves as fundamentalists in

1925, they did not mean that they were a certain sort of conservative evangelical Protestant. Or, to be more precise, some of them probably did, but many more seem to have thought of "fundamentalism" as a catchall term for religious conservatism. It is tempting to think that these poor students were just confused, that they didn't understand what fundamentalism really meant. But to dismiss such students as merely mistaken about the nature of real fundamentalism misses the point. Fundamentalism meant something different to those Michigan students, something broader than merely factional Protestant theological disputes.

At Michigan, as far as we can tell from our twenty-first-century perspective, student fundamentalists meant different things by that label. To be sure, the evidence is frustratingly imprecise. We don't know from the published report of the survey what students were asked, or how many of them were interviewed, or how many responded. We don't know if or how the researchers tried to weed out complicating factors. But still we get unmistakable clues that educated young people in 1925 considered it entirely proper to call themselves fundamentalists, whether or not they were conservative evangelical Protestants. In the survey report, only 8 percent of Michigan students called themselves fundamentalists.[21] But as J. H. Ralston pointed out in the pages of the *Moody Bible Institute Monthly*, a much larger proportion of Catholic students identified themselves that way. Perhaps most intriguing, Ralston did not seem at all surprised or put out by the widespread use of the fundamentalist label among Catholic students. Rather, at the staunchly Protestant Moody Bible Institute the more important and lamentable takeaway from the Michigan survey was that so many Protestant students embraced modernism and evolution. As Ralston reported, only 12 percent of Methodist students called themselves fundamentalists, while 33 percent called themselves modernists. Only 6 percent of Congregationalists said they were fundamentalists, while 48 percent said they were modernists. Indeed, the Catholic students seemed friendlier to fundamentalism than did the Protestants, with only 12 percent coming in for modernism compared with 18 percent for fundamentalism.[22]

What could leading theologians make of this religious muddle? For even the most perspicacious and concerned scholars, fundamentalism was not easy to define. From his ivory-tower perch at Princeton Theological Seminary, J. Gresham Machen often ventured forth into the public sphere to explain and defend fundamentalism.[23] In private, however, Machen worried that the inherent vagaries of interdenominational fundamentalist theology was not the best way to defend the doctrines of orthodox Christianity.

Unlike most of his contemporaries, Machen recognized that the fundamentalist label was being applied in a host of different ways. For some, fundamentalism meant primarily a militant defense of Christian tradition, or, as Machen described it to a friend, "all those who hold firmly to historic Christianity based on the Bible in the face of modern unbelief."[24] In that sense, he explained, one might correctly call Machen himself a fundamentalist. And if one meant by "fundamentalism" a ferocious opposition to theological modernism, he wrote, "I am willing to call myself a Fundamentalist of the most pronounced type."[25]

Most people, however, used the term differently, in a "broad, popular sense," to describe a movement against "the spiritual decadence of our age."[26] Machen celebrated such activism, embracing what he called his fundamentalist "brethren,"[27] with whom he stood in "fellowship."[28] As a dedicated Calvinist, however, Machen saw his own work as something different.

For Machen and many other conservative intellectuals in the 1920s, the nascent fundamentalist movement introduced a difficult theological tension. We can see the tension at play in Machen's apology to the founders of Bryan University in 1927. As we'll see later in this chapter, the founders of Bryan University were among the pioneers of fundamentalist higher education. They hoped to create a new kind of school, an interdenominational fundamentalist school that would defend the faith in an age of looseness and liberalism. Like fundamentalists everywhere, they wanted to reach beyond denominational boundaries to unite militant conservatives in their cause. And like school founders everywhere, they looked for a celebrity president to help prove their legitimacy. When they asked Professor Machen to take the role, however, he refused politely but firmly.

The goal of a new fundamentalist university was a good one, Machen agreed. He was honored by the invitation to lead the new school. Interdenominational work was valuable and central "in these days of widespread defection from the Christian faith," Machen wrote. However, theologically, he could never consider himself a fundamentalist. Rather, he was a dedicated Calvinist, devoted not to an interdenominational mission but to his beloved Presbyterian faith.[29]

Machen valued fundamentalism and even at times called himself a fundamentalist. Overall, though, by 1927 he didn't consider himself a fundamentalist. Why not? There's no simple answer, and we'll see in coming chapters how this tension bedeviled fundamentalist thinkers for decades. In short, though, fundamentalist theology was stubbornly unsystematic; it did not insist on any one orthodoxy, but rather defended the idea of evangelical Protestant orthodoxy in general against the perceived dangers of the modern world. For Machen and for many of his students and successors, conservatism needed rigor and system, not just anger and belligerence. Machen could value non-systematic interdenominational partnerships, but he could never compromise his specific Calvinist beliefs.

Fundamentalist institutions never solved this tension between the defense of orthodoxy in general and the defense of specific orthodoxies. Theologically, fundamentalists often revered the systematic rigor of denominational conservative thinkers such as Machen. Fundamentalist schools, however, remained committed to a broader, vaguer theological conservatism.

## *Monkeys and Modern America*

It was not only in the field of theology that the vagaries of "fundamentalism" bedeviled school leaders. It was not only belligerent politicians like Thomas Blanton and conservative Catholics like the students at Michigan who leaped onto the fundamentalist bandwagon. Friends and foes alike tended to equate fundamentalism as a whole with a host of related issues, including the drive to ban evolution from public schools. Among those who hoped to protect and promote the teaching of evolution, the term "fundamentalism" was often used as a simple synonym for anti-evolution sentiment. The leading 1920s pro-evolution pundit Maynard Shipley, for instance, called the anti-evolution movement "the Fundamentalist drive."[30] Many fundamentalists, too, tended to conflate the denominational controversies over proper Protestant doctrine with political controversies over proper public-school teaching. At the Bible Institute of Los Angeles, for example, a cartoon in the monthly magazine illustrated the common tendency among fundamentalists to assume that "modernists" used evolutionary theory to attack "fundamentalists" and the Bible.[31]

Indeed, the anti-evolution movement and the interdenominational fundamentalist movement were so closely linked among both fundamentalists and non-fundamentalists that some fundamentalist intellectuals lamented the connection. Curtis Lee Laws, the Baptist editor who had coined the term "fundamentalism" in the summer of 1920, regretted the stifling closeness of the two campaigns. As Laws wrote five years later,

**FIGURE 2.1** "I defy you to run over that"
Fundamentalism and evolution, 1924. *King's Business*, January–June 1924. Courtesy Biola University Archives.

"The Scopes trial ought never to have been made an issue of fundamentalism. In our opinion the fundamentalists will be wise to major on other matters than evolution."[32] Laws was not the only fundamentalist who had hoped to keep some distance between the interdenominational battle to ban modernist religious changes and the political campaign to ban evolution from public schools. Other fundamentalist commentators such as Moody Bible Institute's James M. Gray, college lecturer Alfred Fairhurst, and anti-evolution activist T. T. Martin agreed that evolution could be taught in schools if it was taught correctly.[33] For these commentators, the proper worry of the fundamentalist was the way evolution was taught, not simply the fact that it was taught. Nevertheless, throughout the 1920s many people assumed that to be a fundamentalist meant to oppose the teaching of evolution in any form.

The equation of the anti-evolution campaign with fundamentalism was not the only widespread misconception about fundamentalism. In spite of the fact that religious fundamentalism had its headquarters in places such as Los Angeles, Chicago, New York, and Minneapolis, fundamentalists and their enemies often agreed that there was something southern about it. Even fundamentalist activists such as John Roach Straton of New York

City and Gerald Winrod of Kansas agreed that fundamentalism was somehow southern.[34]

Perhaps less surprising, southern fundamentalists also insisted that true fundamentalism incorporated a defense of Dixie. From Texas, for example, the flamboyant Baptist fundamentalist J. Frank Norris lauded "our Southland, the boasted home of orthodoxy," as the true home of fundamentalist feeling.[35] In North Carolina, fundamentalists often bundled southern pride together with their theological and educational arguments. They repeatedly blamed liberals for importing "foreigners" from the North to teach evolution and atheism. And when they fought for control of their flagship state university, North Carolina fundamentalists blasted university president Harry Chase as a "damn Yankee," guilty of supporting "modernists, Darwinian apologists, and Northerners."[36]

Wily opportunists also saw a chance to use fundamentalism to line their own pockets. Edward Young Clarke founded the "fundamentalist" Supreme Kingdom in 1926, hoping to capitalize on the popularity and vagueness of fundamentalism. Coming off his morally tarnished but financially rewarding experience of expanding the revived Ku Klux Klan, Clarke hoped this new organization could build on the same vague sense of cultural traditionalism in order to bring in members and their membership fees.[37] His new organization, Clarke promised, would fight against liberalism in religion, but only in a vaguely conservative way. The goal would be to "rebuild in the minds of our children the religion of our fathers."[38] Clarke hoped that his conservative cocktail would prove attractive to joiners. He mixed in opposition to evolution, to atheism, and to communism along with nuts-and-bolts programs such as social centers and life insurance.[39]

To attract attention, Clarke returned to his tactics from the early days of the revived Klan. He made extravagant claims to any journalist who would listen. Evolution promoter Maynard Shipley, for instance, reported in horror that Clarke planned nationwide "bonfires" of "those damnable and detestable books on evolution."[40] Clarke promised "the overthrow of our present form of secular government."[41] In practice, though, Clarke's new group never exerted much influence outside of his home city of Atlanta. Even there it floundered. His membership drive, based on a broad and vague definition of fundamentalism, never attracted the millions of members that his earlier work had done.[42]

As schemers like Clarke made extravagant promises for the reactionary potential of their imaginary fundamentalist armies, worried liberals lined up to offer their own harsh definitions of what it meant to be a fundamentalist in 1920s America. Perhaps the most biting definitions came from journalist H. L. Mencken. Mencken had traveled from Baltimore to Dayton, Tennessee, to report on the Scopes trial. What he saw there only confirmed his disgust at what he thought fundamentalism meant. As he memorably concluded in 1925, fundamentalists were nothing but "yokels" who were "unable to learn" because they had been "degenerating for generations" in the backwoods.[43]

Though few other writers could match Mencken's unique mix of biting humor and ferocious social critique, many agreed with Mencken's angry, dismissive definition. Julian Huxley, evolutionary biologist and grandson of "Darwin's Bulldog," Thomas Henry Huxley, defined fundamentalism as "an anti-biological and anti-scientific movement" that was "virulent" in spite of widespread education.[44] Another liberal pundit agreed that the "menace of fundamentalism" creeped from "the American hinterland," festering in sad locales with a "very high imbecility coefficient." Only the "bigoted and the backward," this writer concluded, could be attracted to fundamentalism.[45] Some anti-fundamentalists offered more humorous dismissals. Writing in the popular magazine *Forum*, one anonymous contributor insisted that "fundamentalism" had as its root words "*fundo*, 'I make solid,' *mente* 'in the head.' "[46]

Throughout the 1920s, as fundamentalists founded their universities and colleges, they took pains to fight back against these widespread slanderous definitions. For instance, in the early spring of 1927, Minnesota fundamentalist leader William Bell Riley told a hometown newspaper that his fundamentalist movement did not represent the sort of anti-intellectualism of which it had been accused. As he told the *St. Paul Pioneer Press*, "Every time I hear the argument that this is a controversy between experts on one hand, and, as someone has said, 'organized ignorance,' on the other, I smile. This is not a debate between the educated and the uneducated."[47] Similarly, Curtis Lee Laws reeled from the hostile definitions of "fundamentalism" that had become so ubiquitous by 1925. "When will sensible people cease to revile and seek to understand fundamentalists?" Laws asked. Though he admitted that the label had been tarnished by "extravagant men who have made of themselves a public nuisance," Laws insisted that real fundamentalism had always been a respectable and respectful religious movement.[48]

By the end of the 1920s, however, not everyone was convinced. Outside of the circles of energetic evangelical activists who tried to unify their fractious conservative allies into an insuperable fundamentalist alliance, fundamentalism lost much of its appeal. By the early 1930s, conservative Catholics no longer referred to themselves as fundamentalists. And conservative anti-communists in Congress no longer insisted that their campaigns were considered part of a fundamentalist movement. The label stuck only among a group of conservative evangelical Protestants, who clung to it even as they disputed its growing negative connotations. But the wider meanings did not disappear. As we'll see in the rest of this chapter, evangelicals who founded colleges meant a host of different things when they called their schools fundamentalist. Fundamentalism meant a defiant defense of orthodoxy in principle, but not any one specific systematic theology. In practice, fundamentalism could include a bundle of different meanings, including opposition to evolutionary science, a fierce southern pride, and a certain ineffable belligerence in the face of sneering modern trends. It could include Representative Blanton's political belligerence. It could include the vague conservative yearnings of Catholic students in Michigan. At the fledgling network of evangelical colleges devoted to the fundamentalist impulse, fundamentalism could mean all these things and more. And, as we'll see throughout this book, the diffuse meanings of fundamentalism remained a perennial problem in the world of fundamentalist higher education.

## *The Kids Aren't All Right*

For many of the fundamentalist intellectuals we've met—men such as Curtis Lee Laws and J. Gresham Machen—perhaps the toughest insult to swallow was also one of the most common. Enemies of fundamentalism in the 1920s often insisted that the essence of fundamentalism was a lack of proper education. Modernist leader Shailer Mathews of the University of Chicago, for example, defined fundamentalism as a "reactionary movement" led by "elderly men, or those who have not had a thorough education along modern lines."[49] From Dartmouth College, President Ernest Hopkins twisted the knife, writing in 1925 that no one could graduate from any "first-class college a Fundamentalist." Indeed, Hopkins insisted, one could define a first-class college as one from which a "Fundamentalist" could not be graduated.[50]

Even fundamentalists who could not claim the academic credentials of a Machen smarted at this sort of accusation.[51] Evangelists such as T. T. Martin, Bob Jones Sr., and J. Frank Norris all valued intellectual work and academic achievement. The problem, fundamentalists agreed in the 1920s, was not with fundamentalism but rather with the sorry state of contemporary higher education. College, as we saw in Chapter 1, really had changed between 1870 and 1920. By the time fundamentalists protested in the 1920s, the ideals of higher education in general had shifted away from a traditional inculcation of Christian morality. By the 1920s, fundamentalists accused, colleges had begun actively undermining true faith.

As was often the case, evangelist Bob Jones Sr. expressed these fundamentalist feelings in the most flamboyant language. In his stump sermons of the 1920s, Jones related a tale meant to terrify fundamentalist parents nationwide. A fundamentalist family had scrimped and saved to send their beloved daughter to college. As Jones told the story:

> At the end of nine months she came home with her faith shattered. She laughed at God and the old time religion. She broke the hearts of her father and mother. They wept over her. They prayed over her. It availed nothing. At last they chided her. She rushed upstairs, stood in front of a mirror, took a gun and blew out her brains.[52]

Throughout the 1920s, fundamentalists told each other similar horror stories. Anti-evolution evangelist T. T. Martin, for instance, warned that many young people attended college at an age when their minds and souls were the most vulnerable. One sad young man, Martin related, had left his fundamentalist family to have his head turned by the ideas on offer at a modern college. By the time he repented of his slanted education, it was too late. "My soul is a starving skeleton," the former student reported, "my heart a petrified rock; my mind is poisoned . . . . I wish I had never been to college."[53]

Fundamentalists wanted more than just scary anecdotes. They devoured scholarly studies of the changing patterns of academic life. Many read with horror James Leuba's 1916 study, *The Belief in God and Immortality*. Leuba, a psychologist from Bryn Mawr College, found that students tended to move away from their childhood beliefs in their college years. To some fundamentalists, this study provided clear evidence of the dangerous teaching that was going on in many schools.[54]

Several fundamentalist intellectuals attempted to assess the true state of teaching at America's colleges and universities. Charles Blanchard, president of Wheaton College, surveyed fifty-four schools in the Midwest and reported to the 1919 founding meeting of the World's Christian

Fundamentals Association that schools were no longer to be trusted. Leaders, even at nominally Christian colleges, had lapsed into a soul-destroying modernism; they now taught evolution and moral decay.[55] Other fundamentalist school surveys came up with similarly sobering results.[56]

In the face of accusations that fundamentalists did not value higher education, leaders in the 1920s resolved to make sure students had schools they could rely on. At first, some activists tried to take back control over both public and private colleges and universities. Even with religious schools, in almost every case fundamentalists found it impossible to insist on orthodoxy. Instead, as we'll see, fundamentalists founded their own network of reliably fundamentalist schools.

Years before William Jennings Bryan drew international attention with his stalwart defense of the Bible in the face of Clarence Darrow's taunts at the Scopes trial, he kicked off the fight for evolution-free schools at the University of Wisconsin. Bryan picked a fight with Wisconsin president Edward Birge in order to publicize the woeful changes that had swept over American higher education. Both Birge and Bryan were evangelical Protestants, but they had very different conceptions of the proper role of religion in higher education. As a longtime professor and university leader, Birge had participated in the transformation of the University of Wisconsin into a recognizably modern research university. Though a devout Protestant, Birge separated his personal beliefs from his administrative duties. The role of the university president, Birge believed, was no longer to inculcate young minds with thoughtful Christian morality but rather to manage finances and support the work of intellectually independent scientists and scholars.[57]

When William Jennings Bryan publicly criticized Birge in 1921 for allowing evolution-friendly speakers on campus, Birge fought back. The university, Birge believed, must welcome the latest advances in science and thinking, no matter where they might lead. Bryan had a very different vision of proper higher education. If a university sponsored religiously dangerous ideas such as evolution, Bryan argued sardonically, it should equip its classroom with warning signs. "Our class rooms," the signs should read, "furnish an arena in which a brutish doctrine tears to pieces the religious faith of young men and young women; parents of the children are cordially invited to watch the spectacle."[58]

It was not enough, Bryan felt, for a university leader to proclaim his personal faith. Public universities should not teach any particular faith,

Bryan acknowledged, but they should at least remain safe places for religious students. They should not cram false science down the throat of unsuspecting young students. In this fight and at other large public universities, Bryan and the fundamentalists lost.[59] The academic revolutions of the past fifty years had established Birge's idea of modern higher education as the only legitimate way to organize a public research university.

With good reason, fundamentalists hoped for better results when they fought for control of private religious colleges. As Curtis Lee Laws protested, "We who send our children away to Baptist schools do not wish them sent back with their faith shattered . . . . Unless our denominational schools prepare our boys and girls for the responsibility of life there is absolutely no reason why they should exist."[60]

At Baptist-affiliated Wake Forest College in North Carolina, fundamentalists put this idea to the test. T. T. Martin charged President William Louis Poteat in 1920 with terrible spiritual failings. Poteat, Martin warned, was part of a "fatal, Bible-warping, soul-destroying" conspiracy that had oozed out of modernist schools to take over Baptist colleges.[61]

Unlike Birge or other leaders of public universities, Poteat did not try to separate his personal faith from his university mission. Rather, he defended himself on explicitly theological grounds. "I accept," Poteat pleaded, "the New Testament as the law of my life and standard of my thinking. To find its meaning and to extend its power have been the business and joy of these forty years."[62] To be Christian, to be Baptist, Poteat successfully insisted, one did not have to be a fundamentalist. Most important for our purposes, Poteat convinced his Baptist brethren that a good Baptist college did not have to inculcate students in fundamentalist religion and fundamentalist virtue. To be a modern college, even a modern religious college, Poteat argued, faculty had to teach students about evolution and other modern scientific breakthroughs. Faculty had to have the freedom to pursue truth beyond the bounds of fundamentalist strictures.[63]

Even when fundamentalists scored some successes—as when J. Frank Norris claimed to have prodded Baylor faculty to sign a fundamentalism-friendly creed[64]—most denominational colleges did not accept fundamentalist definitions of proper Christian higher education. Like Poteat, most college leaders had accepted the basic tenets of the academic revolution. Even at schools founded by religious organizations, modern knowledge had come to imply academic freedom and the pursuit of scholarship without religious restrictions.

## Seminaries and Institutes

Colleges and universities such as Baylor, Wake Forest, and the University of Wisconsin did not absorb all the attention of fundamentalists when it came to higher education. As a religious movement, they also worried intensely about seminaries—institutions to train pastors. In the 1920s, too, fundamentalists could celebrate their continuing influence at a network of Bible institutes (BIs)—schools that did not offer degree programs but rather cranked out missionaries and religious workers.

For obvious reasons, the content and structure of seminary training became a recurring issue in the fundamentalist movement. In order to maintain a network of fundamentalist churches, fundamentalists nationwide needed theologically reliable schools to train theologically reliable ministers. As the fundamentalist movement gained steam in the 1920s, leaders and intellectuals pinned their hopes on a new school in Dallas, Evangelical Theological College.

Founder Lewis Sperry Chafer promised that his new seminary—known these days by the name it took in 1936, Dallas Theological Seminary, or simply as "Dallas"—would adhere adamantly to his vision of the fundamentalist theological impulse. He warned that too many seminaries had become "shot through with a modern paganized philosophy."[65] As did other school founders, Chafer and his associates installed a mandatory faculty creed, in order to guarantee that the school would "teach the fundamental doctrines of the unmutilated Word of God."[66] More precisely, Chafer and his associates hoped to define their school by its devotion to a certain method of Bible reading, the dispensational approach.

Dispensationalism—as we'll see in more detail in Chapter 6—was not universally accepted among fundamentalist intellectuals. Not surprisingly, then, the founders of Dallas fretted over whether or not their dispensationalism meant they were fundamentalists.[67] Chafer disliked the tone and flamboyance of populist fundamentalists such as J. Frank Norris. When it came down to it, though, like J. Gresham Machen, Chafer agreed that his school should be considered fundamentalist in the "accurate" sense.[68] To Chafer, true fundamentalism was a theological position, a commitment to the theology of premillennial dispensationalism. Poorly educated preachers such as J. Frank Norris, Chafer lamented, "very soon will cause the greatest embarrassment and confusion, and the name 'Fundamentalist' will have been utterly ruined, if it is not already."[69]

To counter such unfortunate besmirching of the fundamentalist name, Chafer and his co-founders insisted on both dispensationalism and academic rigor at their seminary. Privately, Chafer promised one backer that his new school would be "the very highest class in every particular."[70] Chafer's brother, Rollin, publicly defended the seminary against the "pitiable superiority complex" of religious liberals.[71]

At Dallas, founders hoped for a new seminary that would give fundamentalist pastors a rigorous and defiantly orthodox academic and theological education. They hoped to distinguish themselves radically from liberal seminaries such as those at the University of Chicago or Yale. They wanted to maintain a fundamentalist movement focused on dispensational theology, not on public controversy or vague cultural conservatism. More than that, though, they also wanted a school that would be different from another success story of fundamentalist higher education, the Bible institute.

After all, though one wouldn't suspect it from reading the endless jeremiads about higher education in fundamentalist magazines and journals from the 1920s, the fundamentalist movement had inherited a thriving network of higher-education institutions. Most four-year colleges and universities had gone along with the mainstream assumptions of the nineteenth-century academic revolution, it was true. And leading seminaries had slid or leaped into modernist theology and liberal social thinking. But in the 1920s, those types of schools were not the sum total of the higher-education options for fundamentalist students. Bible institutes were part of a vibrant American tradition of purpose-driven higher education. And, though the intellectual founders of Dallas and other schools took pains to keep their work separate from the nitty-gritty educations on offer at BIs, those BIs became—for a while—the workhorses of fundamentalist higher education.

A spate of Bible institutes popped up in the late nineteenth century, beginning in 1882 with the Missionary Training Institute in New York, later known as Nyack College.[72] A few years later, the flagship Moody Bible Institute opened in Chicago.[73] The goals of these schools were different from those of four-year colleges or graduate seminaries. Using the language of whirlwind nineteenth-century evangelist Dwight Moody, Bible institutes wanted to train a generation of "gap-men," and soon gap-women.[74] Such folks, BI founders and leaders believed, did not need to read Hebrew or Greek. They did not need long courses of mathematics or European history. With an urgency driven by their belief in the imminent return of Jesus, Bible institute teachers hoped to get the Gospel out to as many people as they could, as fast as they could. They wanted to bridge the gap between overeducated seminary graduates and unlettered city dwellers worldwide.

In the late nineteenth century, Bible institutes were seen as a necessary modern innovation, a response to changing times.[75] BIs taught students how to read the Bible the right way, how to reach people with the Word. As Nyack trainer A. B. Simpson explained in 1888, BIs should be

> institutions less technical and elaborate than the ordinary theological seminary, and designed to afford the same specific preparation for direct missionary work, and to meet the wants of that large class, both men and women, who do not wish formal ministerial preparation, but an immediate equipment for usefulness as lay workers.[76]

Students at Bible institutes might take classes in the "Books of the Bible, the Great Doctrines, Chapter Studies, Homiletics, Church History, Practical and Personal Work, and Missions," as did students at the Bible Institute of Los Angeles in 1910.[77] This was not "college," however. For one thing, students did not expect to enter a program and remain until they had completed it. Rather, at most schools, students popped in and out of courses as they had time and ability. As one 1903 Boston Bible School catalogue pleaded, "It is very desirable to begin the year and stay till it ends. But, when this is impossible, students are welcome to begin the year and stay as long as they can."[78] At many BIs, too, students did not pay tuition.[79] The training on offer was seen as part and parcel of a missionary sacrifice, not a collegiate experience of self-improvement.

Professionally, at least, there would not have been a way to use Bible institutes as a way to move up a career ladder, nor did school leaders want there to be. In early years, there were no degrees, though most schools offered a variety of certificates of completion. The faculty at some schools was entirely volunteer, offering only a few courses such as Bible study, mission preparation, and maybe teacher training. In addition, there was no sense that these schools were only for high school graduates or for eighteen-year-olds. All the students, in early years, were what we might call "nontraditional" students in today's colleges. Older men and women attended Bible institutes to brush up on their knowledge of the Bible or to improve their skills for missionary work.[80]

In the 1920s, however, such things were not as unusual as they may sound today. Between the 1880s and the 1940s, a host of similar institutions of higher education jostled for attention in a crowded marketplace. "Colleges" and "universities" rubbed elbows with "normal schools," "institutes of technology," "female institutes," "teachers colleges," and proprietary professional schools. Outside of the colleges and universities, many of these institutions offered no degrees. They had no four-year programs. Standards for student entrance—even at schools that called themselves colleges or universities—were riotously imprecise. Perhaps most conspicuously, there was not the same moral weight on dropping out. Students dropped in and out as they needed to. Their sights were set on a quick course of training for a specific goal: how to build or run a large mill, perhaps, or how to operate a modern farm efficiently, how to teach a grammar class, or how to spread the Gospel.

Fundamentalists and other religious people might have attended a Bible institute for a week or for years. Similarly, farmers, teachers, and engineers attended various institutes when and where they could. For teachers, for example, this same period witnessed a burst of "normal schools." Students attended these schools when they could, to earn a teaching certificate rather than a college degree. Unlike the colleges that many normal schools evolved into, most of them offered no degree and required no high school diploma. The academic requirements were infamously lax.[81] Farmers sometimes went to "agricultural & mechanical" institutes to improve specific skills or learn improved methods.[82] Like normal schools, many of these "A&Ms" eventually became part of the congealing landscape of higher education in the twentieth century. At technical institutes also, the goals were not usually the same as at later liberal arts colleges or modern research universities. Early technological and engineering institutes focused on specific goals, such as training military engineers or teachers of technical know-how.[83] Some of these "institutes" survived and became universities, with their roots betrayed only by their names, such as the Massachusetts Institute of Technology, founded in 1866. Others closed their doors as these alternate forms of higher education became less desirable.[84]

Casual readers of the history of fundamentalism and Bible institutes might find the early haphazard structure of BIs merely quirky. In fact, such schools emerged as a religious expression of a common impulse in nineteenth-century higher education. And, as the academic revolutions described in Chapter 1 slowly became more and more dominant, Bible institutes joined other institutes in moving toward the now expected college structure. BIs such as Gordon Bible Institute in Massachusetts and Moody Bible Institute in Chicago wrestled with these trends throughout the early twentieth century.

At Gordon, the change came early. The school had begun in 1895 as a fairly traditional missionary training institute. Students did not expect to earn a four-year degree. Rather, they hoped to gain useful knowledge to make them better spreaders of the Word. By 1918, however, changing expectations about higher education led the leaders of Gordon to offer bachelor's degrees. They also changed the institution's name several times, from Gordon Missionary Training School (1895) to Gordon Bible Institute (1914), Gordon Bible College (1916), and Gordon College of Theology and Missions (1921).[85]

The name changes reflected Gordon's attempt to keep up with the latest trends. In this case, the most direct pressure came from the students. As the norms of higher education became more exclusively aligned with those of four-year colleges, students at Gordon requested that the school change its name. They wanted to earn a degree from a "college," not merely an "institute." As an early Gordon College president remembered, "It meant much to them as future Alumni."[86] At Gordon and at all sorts of schools nationwide, by the early decades of the twentieth century, attendance at a "real" college was taking on the forms we're familiar with today: students attend for a four-year span, they take a course of classes aligned around a major focus, and in return they earn a bachelor's degree that will confirm their expertise in a certain field. The graduates of Gordon wanted to be able to say to their peers and to potential employers that they had graduated with a degree from a college, not merely with a certificate from a Bible institute.

At Moody Bible Institute (MBI), students had less luck. In 1931, students petitioned the administration to change the school's name to "college" and to begin granting four-year degrees. As these sixty students put it:

> We desire the degree, not as an end in itself, but as a means to an end, that we might stand anywhere and everywhere, and preach or teach God's living Word, full of the Holy Spirit, and at the same time make men know we can "give a reason for the hope that is within us": not only from a scriptural standpoint, but also as to their own high standards of education and be used of God to win the well-educated as well as the less-educated man to Christ.[87]

Offering degrees, these students insisted, would prove that Moody Bible Institute adhered to the highest educational standards. They believed that MBI needed to make these changes to stay competitive. The leaders of MBI thought otherwise; it would be decades before these students' dream came true.

Most other Bible institutes, however, were not able to resist the competitive logic of American higher education. In order to attract students, Bible institutes during the 1920s, 1930s, and 1940s moved toward the new collegiate norm. Just as many normal schools became teachers colleges or state universities, many agricultural institutes became universities, and technical institutes often transformed into four-year comprehensive colleges, so Bible institutes often moved from quick training programs to four-year Bible colleges governed by the inescapable expectations of modern American higher education.

## *"Our Schools"*

Those emerging Bible colleges often remained part of the growing network of fundamentalist higher education. They were not alone, though. As a result of the bruising battles for control of colleges and universities, by the middle of the 1920s fundamentalist leaders acknowledged that they would need to take more drastic steps to provide truly fundamentalist education for young people. Bible institutes were not enough. They would need their own fundamentalist colleges. Just as fundamentalists had difficulty defining the true meanings of fundamentalism, so fundamentalist school founders did not see eye to eye about what would make a college truly fundamentalist.

In every case, fundamentalist school founders wanted to open or convert colleges that would offer students the very best modern educations. Those educations, though, had to be purged of the influences of liberal modernist theology. Yet theology was not the only thing that distinguished fundamentalist colleges. In every case, for instance, new or renewed fundamentalist colleges banned the teaching of evolution, at least the teaching that human evolution happened without divine guidance. Flawed ideas about human evolution, the thinking went, would lead to a loss of faith and eventual damnation—precisely the dangers fundamentalist colleges wanted to avoid. Plus, schools imposed strict rules about what students could wear and how they could act. As with evolution, these lifestyle rules were explained and defended as an inherent part of proper fundamentalist upbringing for young people. As we'll see in more detail in Chapter 4, fundamentalists believed immodest dress, dancing, drinking, attending movies, and smoking would lead to improper, unchristian sexual behavior. Bad behavior would also send out the wrong message about the morality of fundamentalist youth. In addition to these universal strictures, however, each new fundamentalist school added some idiosyncratic rules and requirements that had far less direct connections to religion. As we've seen, during the 1920s friends and foes alike offered a dizzying array of competing connotations for the term "fundamentalism." School founders themselves were no different. Each insisted on his or her own quirky components of proper fundamentalist higher education.

At Des Moines University, fundamentalist dreams soon turned into nightmares. The goal and promise of fundamentalist leader T. T. Shields was to purge the school of all liberal theology. Along the way, however, the day-to-day realities of higher education and the personal failings of Shields and fellow administrator Edith Rebman got in the way. Most fundamentalist schools did not implode the way Des Moines did, but every school found itself in a similar situation: among students, faculty, administrators, and bystanders, the quirks of a unique situation were understood as something inherent in fundamentalism itself.

Shields promised great things. When he took over the school in 1927, he promised "a great Christian school of higher learning which will be absolutely free from the taint of modernism."[88] As fundamentalist leader William Bell Riley crowed, Shields's policy of interrogating all faculty before they could reclaim their jobs meant that "New Theology professors" would have no chance to "pussyfoot it" past Shields's inquiries.[89]

Many faculty members had no desire to pussyfoot anything. The entire departments of chemistry, biology, physics, and mathematics refused to return, disgusted by Shields's tactics and by the reputation of the fundamentalist movement.[90] In addition, rumors soon circulated that the faculty purge only went so far. The football coach, for example, was allowed to stay on in spite of his open cynicism about fundamentalist religion. When asked if he had been converted, "born again," the coach reportedly answered, "Yeah, lots of times."[91] A fundamentalist school could do without its science faculty, critics sneered, but it had to have its football coach.

As did the leaders of every new and renewed fundamentalist school, Shields and Rebman explained all their new rules as part of fundamentalist orthodoxy. Students were forbidden from drinking, smoking, and dancing.[92] Even these rules, however, seemed erratically enforced. At one point, though there had been no rule imposed, Rebman punished female students for doing cartwheels. Such exuberant behavior, Rebman sniffed, was not fundamentalist, and certainly not ladylike.[93]

Rebman was widely accused of mixing theology with personal vindictiveness. She established snitch squads of informers, for example. When she did not like a professor, faculty charged, she instigated a whispering campaign that he was theologically liberal.[94] On one occasion, she got up and left a chapel talk by a hostile administrator. The reason for her dramatic departure, she explained, was that she was disgusted with his liberal-leaning "ministry." It seems more likely, however, that she was nonplussed by his repeated inquiries into her rumored sexual relationship with Shields.[95]

As the dream disintegrated in 1929, Shields blamed the blow-up on a "wide, wide conspiracy" of "devilish elements," hidden theological liberals among the leadership at the college. Of course, Shields himself had hired all the leaders by that point, and upon doing so had insisted that they were all tried-and-true fundamentalists.[96]

Even with such extravagant goings-on in the name of fundamentalism, Des Moines University might have had more success if it had been able to carry out the basic tasks of modern higher education. By the 1920s, the pressure on four-year traditional colleges like Des Moines was moving in the same direction as the pressure on normal schools, Bible institutes, and technical institutes. Students had come to expect that a real "college" would award degrees in exchange for a four-year course of study. The straw that broke the students' backs was not the harsh and erratic new lifestyle rules in the name of proper fundamentalism. It was not even the rumors of the sexual relationship between Shields and Rebman. Certainly such things were widely unpopular among both students and faculty. But the students rebelled outright only when they heard that Shields planned another faculty purge, one that would leave students unable to complete their degrees. When it came right down to it, students—along with their families and their lawyers—were prepared to fight tooth and nail to receive their earned degrees, whatever fundamentalist hanky-panky threatened to get in the way.[97]

A different dilemma confronted the founders of Bryan University (now Bryan College) in Tennessee. As the name suggests, the school was founded as a memorial to William Jennings Bryan, the hero of many fundamentalists for his dramatic stance against evolution at the Scopes trial in Dayton, Tennessee. When Bryan died quietly in his sleep a few days after the 1925 trial, fundamentalist leaders immediately began planning what William Bell Riley breathlessly described as a "a great Fundamentalist University, erected in his memory and destined to wear his name while time should last."[98]

After J. Gresham Machen turned down the offer to be president of the new school, the veteran fundamentalist Bible teacher George Guille took on the role.[99] He promised "a high-grade institution of learning" that would become "internationally known for its belief in the Bible as the inspired Word of God and for its devotion to the Lord Jesus Christ."[100] At first Guille's job seemed simple. Fundamentalist leaders from around the nation—some with deep pockets—raced to sign a 1925 statement of support for the new school.[101]

However, Bryan College's founders soon ran into a fundamentalist roadblock. As we've seen, given the inherent vagaries of fundamentalist theology, it had become standard practice at fundamentalist colleges to enact a mandatory statement of faith for faculty. Without such an ironclad creed, many school founders believed, faculty members might slide into liberal theology and unchristian ideas. In the absence of denominational doctrine, the creed was the key to guaranteeing continuing fundamentalist fidelity.

At Bryan University, the founders soon agreed on a fairly typical eight-point mandatory creed. Faculty members were required to agree that the Bible was inerrant in its original "writings." They had to believe in a triune God, in the virgin birth of Jesus, and that all humans were born sinful and in need of a savior. That savior, faculty agreed, was Jesus and he died for humanity's sins. Faculty also had to believe that Jesus would return to earth and that there was an eternal heaven and hell. They had to agree that humans were created as described in Genesis.[102]

Bryan University's creed echoed other fundamentalist lists, such as William Bell Riley's nine-point statement of faith for the World's Christian Fundamentals Association. But it left out a few key ideas. Whereas Riley asked fundamentalists to believe in " 'that blessed hope,' the personal, premillennial and imminent return of our Lord and Saviour Jesus Christ,"[103] Bryan College's founders could only agree on " 'that blessed hope,' the personal return to this earth of Jesus Christ."[104]

For those outside of the fundamentalist fold, these statements might sound nearly identical. To those inside, however, leaving out the words "premillennial" and "imminent" meant a great deal. Christians have always wondered about the promised return of Jesus. Premillennialists have thought that He must return to establish a thousand-year reign of peace on earth. Postmillennialists, in contrast, have interpreted the Bible to say that Jesus would return at the end of the thousand years of peace. During the 1920s, fundamentalist intellectuals such as James M. Gray and Curtis Lee Laws insisted that issues of the millennium were of only secondary importance. If one was opposed to theological modernism, they thought, one could be a fundamentalist, regardless of one's belief about the timing of Jesus's return.[105] Among many conservative evangelicals, too, the precise meanings of premillennialism had been left politely vague.[106] Nevertheless, the idea has been such a central part of fundamentalist thinking that some historians have emphasized the doctrine of the premillennial return of Jesus as the very definition of fundamentalism.[107]

For Guille and the leaders of the new Bryan University, however, premillennial belief presented a unique dilemma. Many of them agreed with Riley that a real fundamentalist should be a premillennialist. Their namesake, however, hadn't been. William Jennings Bryan had been proud of his postmillennialism. When they opened their new school—ironically using rented space in the very high school in which John Scopes had claimed to have taught evolution—they did not insist on premillennial belief for their faculty.[108] Their struggles showed once again how difficult it could be to agree on a theological definition of proper fundamentalism. At Bryan University as at every fundamentalist college, unique circumstances forced founders to impose their own vision of true fundamentalism.

Perhaps no other fundamentalist college was stamped quite so deeply by the quirks of its founder than was Bob Jones College (BJC). Evangelist Bob Jones Sr. had become in the 1920s one of the most passionate fundamentalist leaders in the drive for new fundamentalist colleges. When he opened his successful new school, Jones promised a school that would purge any liberal theology. In addition, he promised parents a school that would be ferociously conservative about things that had very little to do with theology but everything to do with Jones's vision of proper fundamentalism.

Bob Jones College built a mandatory faculty creed into its original charter. All members of the Bob Jones community would pledge to battle "all atheistic, agnostic, pagan and so-called scientific adulterations of the Bible." This charter, Jones promised, could "never be amended, modified, altered, or changed."[109] The goal, he explained, was to guarantee the faith of all students. "Fathers and mothers," Jones wrote in 1928, "who place their sons and daughters in our institution can go to sleep at night with no haunting fear that some skeptical teachers will steal the faith of their precious children."[110]

The fear of creeping Protestant liberalism was not the only worry Jones hoped to allay. Just as at other fundamentalist schools, students had to follow a strict set of rules. They were not to listen to "jazz" or to dance, play cards, or drink. At BJC, however, the rules went further than at other places. Women students at the new school were not allowed off campus without a chaperone.[111] More than that, women students at BJC were expressly forbidden from sharing clothes. As Bob Jones Sr. wrote in an open letter, "There is one regulation which we wish our girls to thoroughly understand. WE DO NOT ALLOW OUR GIRLS TO WEAR EACH OTHERS CLOTHES." The goal, apparently, was to promote a general attitude of modesty, to avoid worldly temptations of fashion and jealous competition.[112]

The college's leaders made it clear that these rules were not to be merely winked at. To be a fundamentalist, Bob Jones style, one had to be willing to stand by what was right, regardless of possible public outcry. In 1927, for instance, Bob Jones Sr. claimed that he had expelled seventeen of eighty-five students. When local parents complained, the remaining students rallied to Jones's defense. A large majority of the remaining students wrote and signed a resolution pledging not to support any local business that had criticized the college.[113] Doctrine was not enough. At Bob Jones College, true fundamentalism was also measured by such ineffable factors as loyalty and steadfastness.

Other ideas, too, became part and parcel of Bob Jones's brand of fundamentalism. The school opened in Florida in 1926, moved to Cleveland, Tennessee, in 1933, and made its final move to Greenville, South Carolina, in 1946. For its entire existence, Bob Jones College (Bob Jones University since 1946) incorporated a fierce southern regionalism into its fundamentalist identity. As Bob Jones Sr. told audiences during 1920s, "We are not going to deliver the South to this rationalistic, atheistic leadership."[114] As the school matured, its leaders tended to defend traditional southern values with the same tenacity and obstinacy as they did their religious beliefs.

Beyond insults to southern pride, Jones warned of a host of other dangers in modern America. Young people, he preached, were at risk every day from "paved highways, automobiles, and modern travel."[115] Fundamentalist young people, in particular, had to contend with sneering modern attitudes and know-it-all pseudo-experts, folks who assumed that "if a person believes in what is usually called the 'old-time religion,' he must, so to speak, have a greasy nose, dirty fingernails, baggy pants, and he mustn't shine his shoes or comb his hair."[116] As a whole, the promise of fundamentalist higher education at Bob Jones College in the 1920s was far broader than just safely orthodox religious teaching. Students at Bob Jones, the school promised, would be taught firmly but fairly to avoid the looming dangers of life in modern America. They would be taught the dangers of liberal theology, but they would also be drilled in the values of southern pride and heroic loyalty. They would be kept safe from the temptations of modern music, flashy clothes, and unmarried sex. They would be smarter, cleaner, purer, and more loyal to fundamentalism and to Bob Jones than any other group of young people in the world.

At Bob Jones College as at every other fundamentalist school, these aspects of fundamentalist higher education had only tenuous connections to precise theological debates. As we've seen, even the most careful fundamentalist theologians could not offer a simple theological definition of fundamentalism. Fundamentalism was defined in practice, not on paper. At the emerging network of fundamentalist colleges, definitions were shaped by leaders' vague, shifting, and idiosyncratic beliefs about the true meanings of fundamentalism, as well as by the day-to-day exigencies of running a modern college.

## *By Their Fruits*

It might be tempting for those who know the later history of schools such as Bob Jones University to think that there was a sort of fundamentalist spectrum at these schools—a range of schools from more fundamentalist, with more and stricter rules, to less fundamentalist, with fewer. During the 1920s and for decades to come, however, the notion of a spectrum of more and less fundamentalist schools doesn't match the historical record.

In the 1920s, for example, the leaders at Wheaton College took a backseat to no one in their claims to the title of true fundamentalism. And in some cases, Wheaton had stricter student rules than Bob Jones College. At Wheaton, for example, students were not allowed to perform dramatic plays until the middle of the 1960s.[117] At BJC, however, students in the 1920s performed ostentatiously non-fundamentalist plays such as *The Importance of Being Earnest*, by Oscar Wilde.[118] Other fundamentalist school leaders took notice. J. Oliver Buswell, president of Wheaton between 1926 and 1940, later publicly questioned the use of drama at Bob Jones College. Such "theatricals and grand operas," Buswell warned, "lead young people . . . into a worldly life of sin."[119] How could a school consider itself fundamentalist if it allowed and even encouraged young people to engage in such worldly pursuits?

Instead of a spectrum of fundamentalist practice, such quirks were due to the fact that the definition of fundamentalism in the 1920s remained impossible to pin down. Founders and early leaders of each college put their stamps on what it would mean to be properly fundamentalist. In Iowa, Des Moines University crashed and burned largely because Edith Rebman caused fundamentalism to be equated with erratic, vicious, amoral, and inefficient management. In Tennessee, Bryan University struggled to figure out a way to establish a fundamentalist college without insisting on one of the signature theological tenets of modern fundamentalism. And in Florida, Bob Jones College felt the heavy imprint of its founder's hand: fundamentalists at Bob Jones College were free to love drama and art but less free to disagree with the school's southern-fried traditionalism.

In every case, these idiosyncrasies of the 1920s continued to inform fundamentalism at its leading colleges and universities. As we'll see, in coming decades Bob Jones Sr.'s southern loyalties eventually pushed Bob Jones University out of the evangelical mainstream on issues of race and racism. At every fundamentalist college, uncertainties about the outer boundaries of proper fundamentalism plagued leaders for generations. Every move, every major decision was plagued by questions of how it would be received by the wider fundamentalist public. Leaders of fundamentalist colleges knew that every choice they made would be subjected to withering fundamentalist scrutiny. Precisely because there was no clear and binding definition of true fundamentalism, leaders at these schools had to define it as they went along.

# 3

# A Mote in the Eye

*It simply never occurred to me that I was not free to express my opinions and I did express them. How was I to know that loyalty meant dictatorship?*

—JOSEPH FREE TO BOB JONES SR., May 25, 1938[1]

## A Question of Authority

The Great Depression was surprisingly good to America's colleges and universities. Budgets were tight, but young people with fewer job options often turned to higher education in their attempts to beat the economic hard times. Fundamentalist colleges enjoyed bumper crops of students as the nation tightened its belt and stumbled through the lean years of the 1930s. The network of fundamentalist schools, however, faced some challenges that mainstream institutions did not.

The jumbled legacy of the 1920s meant that fundamentalist schools could never establish beyond doubt just what it meant to be truly fundamentalist. They could never relax and assume that their fundamentalist credentials would be recognized by all. And, as interdenominational schools rather than denominational colleges, they had no governing boards, conventions, or presbyteries they could turn to in order to settle disputes and establish bona fides. They had no historic denominational orthodoxy they could rely on, but rather the far more slippery goal of generic evangelical orthodoxy. As a result, colleges in this network were forced constantly to prove their continuing fidelity to an ill-defined fundamentalist standard. Most often, they turned to one another for affirmation. As historian Michael S. Hamilton explained:

> As a popular religious movement whose institutions and ethos existed outside the main channels of the American religious establishment, fundamentalism faced a continual need to set boundaries

> so that its constituency would know who was in the fundamentalist tent, and who was not.[2]

Throughout the 1930s, schools such as Wheaton College, Bob Jones College, and Denver Bible Institute struggled to figure out exactly how to prove their status as "real" fundamentalist schools. At their heart, these questions became questions of authority. On the national scene, who decided if a school was reliably fundamentalist? And within schools, who decided what fundamentalist education looked like? Presidents? Trustees? Zealous alumni? Nosy fundamentalist neighbors?

This peculiar tension created one of the most striking ways fundamentalist schools stood out from mainstream institutions of higher education. At most colleges and universities, the 1920s witnessed a dramatic restructuring of campus authority. As Roger Geiger has explained, in that decade "faculty power was making inroads against autocratic presidents." Building on the intellectual and institutional revolutions of the past fifty years—as we explored in Chapter 1—faculty members at elite universities claimed a measure of independent power through a competitive job market and through bodies such as the American Association of University Professors.[3]

At fundamentalist schools, in contrast, anxiety over slipping orthodoxy meant that neither faculty nor administrators could ever be sure of their independent authority. Fundamentalist faculty remained the subject of constant scrutiny by students, alumni, school leaders, and the broader fundamentalist public. It was those teachers, many fundamentalists believed, who had so often turned reliable religious schools such as the University of Chicago or Yale into havens of skepticism. Instead of establishing independent power over academic programs, as faculty members increasingly did at mainstream colleges, at fundamentalist schools faculty had no independent authority, no way to insist on their intellectual freedom if it ranged outside the boundaries of fundamentalist orthodoxy (or even if it was merely rumored to do so).

As we'll see in this chapter, questions about evolution and creation continued to be among the touchiest. Throughout the first half of the twentieth century, fundamentalist scholars agreed that God must have created life as the Bible described, but they disagreed about what that meant. Fundamentalist colleges and universities agreed that they must not teach the pernicious doctrine of evolution, but they never could agree about precisely how not to teach it. As they did throughout the twentieth century, these tensions often pitted faculty against administration, with earnest fundamentalist scientists probing the merits of mainstream science and anxious fundamentalist administrators scrambling to reassure parents and donors that their schools remained resolutely evolution-free.

Each school processed these challenges about evolution and institutional authority in its own way. At Denver Bible Institute, for example, rumors of sexual and theological malfeasance by a dictatorial leader forced the school to appeal to outside fundamentalist evaluators. At Bob Jones College in Tennessee, founder Bob Jones Sr. rammed through a top-down policy of loyalty to avoid unanswerable questions of fundamentalist boundaries. And just outside of Chicago, President J. Oliver Buswell of Wheaton College was shown the door for crossing an invisible line. President Buswell discovered to his chagrin that he had violated unwritten—indeed, unspoken and not even agreed-upon—rules of school leadership. These stories are of more than merely local interest. The struggles of these three schools to define their structures of authority represent similar struggles at fundamentalist institutions of higher education nationwide. The particulars of each case were unique, of course. Taken together, these three episodes help illustrate the ways all fundamentalist schools responded to their universally shared problem of authority.

## *Booms and Busts*

The national attention paid by fundamentalists to their new colleges made things difficult in some ways for school leaders and faculties. It also provided one enormous benefit. During the late 1920s and 1930s, planting a flag for fundamentalism could be very good for a small college. During the 1930s, some of the leading fundamentalist schools changed from regional schools to national and even international hubs for evangelical learning. At the brand-new Bob Jones College, for instance, between 1928 and 1944 students came from every state except Nevada and New Mexico. Students arrived in large numbers from Michigan (190), Pennsylvania (122), and Ohio (108), drawn by the fundamentalist promises of Bob Jones's new school.[4]

The same was true for Wheaton College, near Chicago. Before it declared itself for fundamentalism, a majority of students came from Illinois. By the late 1930s, a great many more students traveled much farther for the opportunity to attend a top-notch fundamentalist school. In

1917, for instance, 60 percent of students came from Illinois. By 1938, that number had dropped to only 25 percent, where it remained throughout the twentieth century.[5]

In Dallas, a similarly bold fundamentalist experiment in seminary education experienced similar national success. Evangelical Theological College, which became Dallas Theological Seminary in 1936, attracted students from around the nation and around the world. It offered a niche education in the dispensational premillennial theology so near and dear to so many fundamentalist intellectuals. As a result, Dallas thrived, becoming what one historian called the "academic and theological 'Vatican'" of fundamentalism, America's "most important training ground for dispensational teachers and pastors."[6]

The worldwide draw of fundamentalist schools was not just for traditional students. From Chicago, Moody Bible Institute reached followers around the nation and around the world. In 1927, the school began a Radio School of the Bible, which had more than ten thousand registrants by 1940. The listeners came from all over. In 1942, WMBI broadcast its programs through 187 radio stations in forty-five states, plus in Canada, China, and throughout Latin America.[7]

Of course, students showed up in person, too. One survey from the late 1940s found that enrollment at seventy evangelical colleges doubled between 1929 and 1940.[8] Evangelical leaders may have liked to think of this growth as a sign of God's stamp of approval on their work, but it was also part of a wider trend throughout American higher education during the period. At most colleges and universities, the first years of the 1930s were very tough. But by the end of the decade the total number of teaching faculty expanded by more than a third.[9]

Not every fundamentalist school experienced the same sort of expansion, but for those schools that managed to capture the fundamentalist imagination, students came in ever-growing numbers during the first few decades. At Dallas, for instance, a modest first class of sixteen matriculated in 1924. By 1930, that number had grown to fifty and the school desperately needed new buildings to accommodate them.[10]

In 1936 alone, Wheaton's undergraduate population jumped 17 percent. As Michael Hamilton points out, even in a time of rapid expansion in higher education, Wheaton's growth was remarkable. Between 1916 and 1928, the college had grown by more than 400 percent in terms of student attendance. In contrast, a group of twenty-seven Methodist liberal-arts colleges also grew during that period, but only by 46 percent.[11]

The 1930s could also bring a share of financial anxiety. In 1933, the fledgling Bob Jones College (BJC) had to declare bankruptcy and move from Florida to Cleveland, Tennessee. Even during such touch-and-go financial times, however, the school's student body continued to expand. In its first year, 1927, BJC enrolled eighty-eight students. The next year, more than double that number showed up.[12] In the school's new Tennessee home, three hundred students enrolled in 1933, four hundred in 1936, and more than a thousand in 1946.[13]

At Bob Jones College, the explosive growth in student enrollments allowed, even forced, a similarly explosive growth in programs. When the school opened, it offered only a two-year associate's degree. By 1929, however, it had expanded to offer its first students a full four-year program with a bachelor's degree. In the early 1930s, BJC instituted undergraduate programs in elementary education and secondary education, as well as a master's degree program in religious education.[14] During its years in Tennessee (1933–1946), Bob Jones College grew into five schools: an academy that offered elementary and secondary education, a four-year liberal arts college, an undergraduate business school, a graduate school of religion, and a graduate school of fine arts.[15]

Like most small colleges in the period, fundamentalist colleges in the 1930s raised their money through tuition and alumni donations. At Wheaton, for example, nearly a third of operating income in the early 1930s came from one-time individual donations.[16] Though private foundation money had come to exert considerable influence in American higher education during the 1920s, only elite research universities benefited. For instance, between 1924 and 1929 the Rockefeller-funded General Education Board (GEB) funneled $12 million to research universities. Most schools, however, did not benefit from this new largesse. During the 1920s, just six schools—Caltech, Princeton, Chicago, Cornell, Stanford, and Harvard—monopolized more than three-quarters of GEB funding.[17] So while the landscape of university research funding changed enormously during this period, fundamentalist colleges found themselves in the same position as the vast majority of colleges and universities, schools that had to pay their bills the old-fashioned way.

## *He Said, She Said*

At some fundamentalist schools, financial solvency was the least of leaders' worries. At Denver Bible Institute, for instance, during the 1930s authoritarian leader Clifton Fowler and his estranged wife, Angie, stood accused of sexual sins, insanity, heresy, and cultishness. The example of Denver Bible Institute demonstrates the anxiety inherent in the fundamentalist movement: without any outside regulatory body, fundamentalism could degenerate into a personality cult or a heretical enthusiasm. These sorts of generalized and loosely defined fears often found their fullest expression in fundamentalist investigations of their institutions of higher education, because such schools were often the most prominent institutional hubs of the movement. At colleges, universities, seminaries, and Bible institutes, fundamentalists worried that theological idiosyncrasies could be elevated to school policy and sexual appetites transformed into scriptural absolutes.

Similar to other tangled community scandals, the details of the Fowler case may never be resolved with absolute certainty. However, due to the nature of the emerging network of fundamentalist institutions of higher education, we have a remarkably complete record of the goings-on in Denver throughout the 1930s. In 1936, President Fowler appealed to national fundamentalist school leaders in an attempt to clear his name. As part of the resulting investigation, a wealth of statements and affidavits survived in the archives of Wheaton College. So, though we may never know exactly what transpired, we have a better-than-usual collection of source material to tease out the story of the Fowlers and Denver fundamentalism.

According to that record, the basic outline of the story seems clear. First, in early 1933, Clifton Fowler had his wife declared insane.[18] In May 1933, Angie Fowler fled her home, staying nearby with a fundamentalist friend.[19] She showed up at the church associated with the Bible institute and disrupted services. She plopped herself down in the very front, booing and hissing during Mr. Fowler's sermon. She stood outside at the end of services and shouted out denunciations of her husband and his school. She tried to gather dissidents to her, nurturing grudges against Mr. Fowler and Denver Bible Institute. Worse yet, in the eyes of the deacons, she denounced the sexual transgressions of her estranged husband, "endeavoring to fill the minds and mouths of our people with nauseating, disgusting sex talk, producing a most unhealthy indelicacy in matters that should be kept sacred and private."[20]

Such accusations did not put Angie Fowler off. Mrs. Fowler produced a statement from a medical doctor affirming that *Mr.* Fowler suffered from a "Perverted Sex Complex."[21] She submitted to a separate, friendlier examination by a doctor who agreed that she had suffered at her husband's hands, but not to the point of insanity. The problem, rather, was that "her normal sex life" had been "frustrated" by her husband's homosexuality.[22]

With such rumors and accusations rampant in Denver and throughout the network of concerned fundamentalists nationwide, the reputation of the Fowlers' Bible institute suffered. In 1936, Clifton Fowler applied to the Evangelical Teacher Training Association to be readmitted as a member school. Association leaders balked. To clear his name, Fowler approached President J. Oliver Buswell of Wheaton College, pleading with him to appoint a commission that could fully investigate the matter. Because there was no local way to satisfy fundamentalists of the school's legitimacy, President Fowler hoped a national blue-ribbon panel could do the job.[23]

Soon the committee was in place, and reluctantly Buswell agreed to serve. He secured the day-to-day assistance of Wheaton administrator George V. Kirk. Also on board were President Will Houghton of Moody Bible Institute, President Paul Rood of the Bible Institute of Los Angeles (the future Biola University), and Wendell Loveless of Moody Bible Institute's radio division.[24] It was a tricky task. The committee hoped to get as much information as possible without further besmirching the names of Fowler, fundamentalism, or Bible institutes.[25] Fowler promised his full cooperation, but as the principal target of the rumors, he was of course an unreliable source.[26]

The committee's investigation revealed upsetting truths. Something, it seemed, was indeed rotten in Denver. But the amorphous nature of American fundamentalism left Buswell and his fellow panelists unable to do more than offer an ineffectual and ambivalent statement that solved nothing. Fowler's crimes may have been execrable, but Buswell and the other fundamentalist school leaders wanted only to wash their hands of the affair.

The committee's procedure was cautious and familial. As Robert C. McQuilkin of Columbia Bible College advised a close colleague at Moody Bible Institute, it would be best for fundamentalism as a whole if the entire investigation could be kept quiet, so as not to sour the reputation of Bible institutes and fundamentalism in general.[27] And indeed the committee proceeded tentatively. Instead of broadcasting an appeal for testimony, committee members instead submitted short lists of trusted fundamentalists in Denver and the region. The committee inquired confidentially of these vetted locals for details and recommendations.[28] The goal, as Buswell wrote to these targeted advisors, was to keep the entire affair "a strictly private matter among Christian brethren."[29]

The testimonials that emerged were damning. One local pastor advised, "I would do anything within my power to see the DBI closed up, because of the affect [*sic*] that the training is having on the Christian testimony of the young people who attend."[30] Another Denver-area fundamentalist, a graduate of Denver Bible Institute, told the committee, "I regret to say that there is a certain stigma attached to anyone coming from this institution. I never mention the fact that I graduated from DBI. I find it hard to live down."[31] One local warned Buswell, "All who enter within the confines of the school as students or casual visitors come under a peculiar 'hypnotic' spell." In Denver, this informant explained, "the strong Fundamental Pastor's of the city, almost to a man," had broken ties with Fowler and Denver Bible Institute.[32]

Fundamentalists in Denver took the investigation very seriously, sending in long letters full of excruciating detail to confirm the rumors against Clifton Fowler. It was true, some said, that Fowler taught the heretical doctrine of "Bullingerism," or hyper-dispensationalism. Fowler, that is, taught that baptism had been a rule for Christians in earlier dispensations, but that it no longer applied to people living in the present age.[33]

Insiders confirmed that Fowler forced a "Life Work" policy in which teachers committed to staying at Denver Bible Institute for life.[34] He demanded full and lascivious confessions from students, then used their admitted sexual sins against them.[35] In general, as one former colleague charged, Fowler tried to "set up a little 'Papacy' with himself as Pope."[36]

But not every Denver fundamentalist denounced Clifton Fowler. Many correspondents blamed Angie Fowler for the troubles. An alumna who had moved to California insisted that the odd Fowler rule of sexual continence even among married couples came not from Mr. Fowler but from Mrs. Fowler. Back in the early 1930s, this writer told the committee, Mrs. Fowler had told her in confidence that Mr. Fowler had wanted children but that she refused to "submit to the marriage relationship." It was Mrs. Fowler, this writer insisted, who thought the verse from 1 Corinthians 7:29—"they that have wives be as though they had none"—could mean that Christian workers must abstain from sexual relationships with their spouses.[37]

Another Clifton Fowler loyalist compiled a list of outrageous charges made by Angie Fowler, going back years. In the early thirties, this loyalist wrote, Mrs. Fowler had been the first to defend her husband against accusations of sexual "uncleanness." Only when Mr. Fowler had castigated his wife righteously for her many sins did Mrs. Fowler join in the accusations, telling all and sundry that he could be "called a SODOMIST from North to South, East to West."[38]

One informant told President Buswell that he had conducted his own two-week investigation of the Denver school. He was given complete liberty to go anywhere and talk with anyone, he wrote. His conclusion? "If anything 'undesirable' obtains at DBI I did not see it." As did other Clifton Fowler loyalists, this writer blamed any disturbing rumors on Mrs. Fowler, whom he called "mentally unbalanced." While he was visiting, Angie Fowler stood vigil outside of church services, denouncing the church and the school in a loud voice and, perhaps out of a desire to appear more profoundly humble, aggressively polishing the shoes of passers-by.[39]

Yet even Clifton Fowler's supporters admitted that he could be extremely hard to work with. As a fundamentalist, though, and more specifically as a fundamentalist educator, he was performing an invaluable service, in their view. The students who came out of Denver Bible Institute, one Colorado fundamentalist leader told Buswell, "showed remarkable understanding of the Fundamental Truths of the Word."[40]

Such earnest defenses did not sway the committee. To a person, they agreed that the activities and teachings of Clifton Fowler could not be recommended to the fundamentalist community.[41] Beyond that, they were utterly unsure what to do.

One thing they agreed upon was to follow up on rumors whenever possible. George Kirk of Wheaton College tracked down letter writers and asked them in person about the Fowlers and their school. Such reports, Kirk informed the committee, were even more damning than were the letters.[42] President Will Houghton of Moody Bible Institute also met with many of those involved. Houghton was disturbed by a repeated story of a young man whose "morals were corrupted in an unmentionable manner by Dr. Fowler."[43] Houghton tracked down leads until he located a witness he trusted, a Denver Bible Institute insider who claimed to have heard the "very unsavory story" from the boy himself.[44] Other insiders, too, confirmed accusations of sex abuse by Clifton Fowler.[45]

What to do? President Buswell thought the situation was impossible. He and the committee could not possibly "commend this man or this work to the confidence of the Christian public," Buswell wrote to a confidant. However, there was nothing else they could do, since they had no official power to take any action. In addition, if Fowler maintained the confidence of his trustees, he was in effect impervious to outside criticism.[46]

In its official report, Buswell's committee cleared Fowler of charges of the Bullinger heresy. The other charges, though, had merit. Fowler may have been an able teacher. He clearly generated much loyalty within the fundamentalist community of Denver. However, his management of the schools was "unsound," collecting far too much authority in his own hands. Fowler, the committee warned, used "unwholesome confession methods." His rule of continence among married couples was also "unwholesome." The report made no mention of Fowler's apparent sexual predation on students and young teachers at his school. The omission seems to have been not a mere oversight but rather part of the committee's plan to avoid ruining the good name of Bible institutes and fundamentalism as a whole. Nor did the committee claim to be offering any "final judgment" on the narrow question of Fowler himself. Rather, the committee limited itself to a bland statement that they were "not convinced that President Fowler is competent to be the head of a Bible Institute, and we cannot recommend him or his work to the confidence of the Christian public."[47]

With a nearly audible sigh of relief, the committee members passed any further responsibility to Denver-area fundamentalist leaders.[48] Such a handover, thought committee member Wendell Loveless of Moody Bible Institute, was "the happy solution" to the entire situation.[49] As long as the locals agreed to remove the names of the committee members from any further deliberations, the committee could wash their hands of the entire ordeal.[50]

Clearly, the main concern of this fundamentalist investigation was not the safety or security of Fowler's victims. At no time did committee members articulate any sort of responsibility for students and teachers drawn into the Fowlers' intrigues. Rather, the committee wanted first and foremost to maintain the legitimacy of fundamentalist higher education, and of Bible institutes in particular. They could not stop Fowler's depredations, they thought. What they could and did do was to remove his school from the implicit list of trusted institutions.

Certainly Fowler's howls of outrage and public protest at the committee's report indicates that he, at least, took this removal very seriously.[51] In spite of Buswell's assumptions that Fowler was impervious to criticism within the walls of his institutional fortress, Fowler himself felt excruciatingly vulnerable to the committee's decisions. Indeed, the entire episode demonstrated the inherent difficulties of authority in fundamentalist schools. Within his realm, no matter how shocking and well-founded the accusations, President Fowler's authority could not be simply overruled. However, national fundamentalist leaders did have the power to remove Denver Bible Institute from their lists of approved institutions. The Evangelical Teacher Training Association had the right and duty to refuse Fowler's application. Individual fundamentalist leaders in Denver and around the country had similar duties to inform unwary fundamentalists of Fowler's "unwholesome" ideas. Such denunciations, whether active or passive, did indeed have some limited power to assert authority at a distance.

## *Dirty Griper*

But only if the local fundamentalist school cared. As our second example shows, a fundamentalist leader who was willing and able to dismiss outside criticism could exert virtually unlimited authority within the local school community. At Bob Jones College, for example, during the 1930s Bob Jones Sr. and his son, Bob Jones Jr., answered these questions of authority very differently than Clifton Fowler had. Students and faculty who disagreed with the Joneses' ideas about proper fundamentalism found themselves removed summarily. Their stories, former faculty knew, would be used in Jones's legendary chapel talks as grim warnings to the remaining school community about the perils of "griping."[52] Jones would never appeal to outside fundamentalist authorities to condone or approve his policies. Rather, every new case of internal dissent seemed to push the leaders of Bob Jones College to stronger and sterner declarations of their own ability to decide such matters themselves.

As a result, the tradition of purges and housecleaning at Bob Jones College went on long past the 1930s. As we'll see in coming chapters, the history of the school has been marked by periodic defections of faculty, students, and even top administrators. It was in the 1930s, though, that founder Bob Jones Sr. established his ironclad principle of loyalty. Theological differences—some of them, at least—could be discussed among friends. Political differences—within reason—did not necessarily mean an end to fellowship. But at Bob Jones College, the question of authority was answered repeatedly in unmistakable tones. Fidelity to fundamentalism meant fidelity to the school and its leaders. Any perceived disloyalty was treated with steely intolerance, since it meant at one and the same time a betrayal of Bob Jones and treason against fundamentalism itself.

Even sympathetic writers have noted the power of Bob Jones's principle of personal loyalty. As Bob Jones University professor Daniel Turner wrote in his in-house history, "Bob Jones was the sole controlling personality in the early days of the College and made all decisions relative to the cultural, religious, and academic life of the school."[53]

This personal authority extended to all spheres of college life. In the 1930s, for instance, even desperate economic difficulties were explained in terms of personal disloyalty and treachery. Due to the economic structure of the new school, Bob Jones Sr. was forced to default on his interest payments in 1930. In 1933, the college filed for bankruptcy.[54] Bob Jones Sr. explained these unfortunate events not as a struggle against prevailing economic trends but rather in terms of the perfidy of a resentful ex-professor. W. J. Hall had been a history professor at the college for its first two years. He stood accused, however, of referring to anti-fundamentalist theologian Harry Emerson Fosdick as a "great Christian man." After repeated warnings, Hall was fired.[55] In 1932, according to President Jones, Hall took his revenge. He teamed up with financial backers of the school to call in their investments. Bob Jones Sr. insisted that he had plenty of pledges from other investors, but since the Depression left everyone cash-strapped, Jones was unable to meet Hall's demands. More than just a result of economic hard times, Jones explained, the school's 1933 bankruptcy was the result of a conspiracy between disgruntled modernists and their lackeys at the bank.[56]

Threats from such faculty dissenters became a repeated theme at the college. On its own, individual faculty grumbling was manageable. In the 1937–1938 school year, however, Bob Jones Sr. and his son and heir, Bob Jones Jr., became convinced that a hostile faculty clique had taken root, dedicated to overthrowing the school and all it stood for. The Joneses purged it ruthlessly. Just as they had explained their financial troubles as the result of a deadly blend of theological heresy and personal disloyalty, so they explained this episode of spreading faculty dissent as the fruit of deadly satanic disloyalty.

Ruth Flood was the first. She had been at the college since 1929, near the very beginning.[57] In those early years, she was beloved by the Bob Joneses, who affectionately referred to her as "Floodie."[58] In 1937, however, she asked for a raise. She hated to ask, she explained, because she valued the Bob Jones principle of "absolute loyalty." However, though she might be able to scrape by at present, she worried about her precarious financial future.[59]

Bob Jones Sr. fired her immediately. It wasn't the money, he explained. He had already planned to give her a raise. But in 1937, in particular, the request proved to Jones that Floodie had fallen under the "subtle, hypnotic powers of associates."[60]

Students, too, came under the spell of this sinister faculty conspiracy. In the same year, Marjorie Foster was expelled for stealing $12 from the school's office. Why had she done it? According to her, at first, she hadn't. Under repeated grilling, however, she confessed.[61] And when she confessed, it was about more than the money. She admitted to having come under the "hypnotic spell of satan," working through the sinister influence of those same disloyal faculty members.[62] In her self-abasement, she named names. She confirmed the Joneses' assertion that an ungodly clique had been operating underground at the school, spreading sin and disloyalty in equal measure.[63]

Who were these sinister presences on Bob Jones College's campus? How did they get there? What did they do to undermine Jones's loyalty principle?

If it had only been the murmurings of French teacher Dorothy Seay, the elder Jones thought, he could have handled it.[64] She was soon joined, though, by drama teacher Joseph Free. United in discontent, the two of them reinforced each other and spread subversive dissatisfaction among students and faculty alike. By the end of 1938, they were out. Both protested loudly and publicly, but unlike Clifton Fowler in Denver, the Bob Joneses in Tennessee did not care much about outside pressure. Indeed, the Joneses used the incident as a chance to underscore their unshakeable equation of fundamentalist fidelity and personal loyalty.

Dorothy Seay had come to Bob Jones College in 1936. She had a master's degree from the University of Chicago and was working on her Ph.D. Bob Jones Sr. had sent her a copy of the school's religious creed and Seay embraced it.[65]

Her first few months, though, did not go very well. By December 1936, Bob Jones Sr. had already called her in for three meetings. If she could not get on board with the Bob Jones College approach, Jones warned her, she would be out on her ear. The first principle of the college, Jones explained, was

> absolute loyalty to the administration. If something happens in the administration which you do not like, your protest is your resignation. If you stay here you must not under any circumstances criticise the administration.

Seay had been too friendly with students, Jones wrote. That sort of "hobnob[bing]" led to dangerously relaxed relationships. In addition, Seay had criticized the administration to the students and had criticized some teachers to other teachers. Worst of all, in Jones's opinion, she had strayed beyond her role as a teacher. "You are not employed," Jones warned Seay, "to philosophize about life in the classroom, nor are you employed to comment about things and people. You are employed to teach languages."[66]

The choice was clear, and Seay had one week to make her decision: either she could accept these non-negotiable rules or she could clear out by Christmas.[67]

Seay stayed, but not for long. The next academic year, Joseph Free joined the faculty of the school's thriving drama department. He had taught at three other colleges before coming to Bob Jones.[68] When he first arrived, he remembered, he had hoped to deepen his relationship to Christ by working in a fundamentalist environment.[69] According to the Bob Joneses, however, he joined with Dorothy Seay in a persistent criticism of the school and its leadership. By the end of the year, he was out, resigning and getting fired at the same time.[70] Dorothy Seay, too, was fired the next day.[71]

Unlike the whispering and rumor-mongering that had racked Denver Bible Institute, at Bob Jones College this incident was not swept under the rug. On the contrary, the Bob Joneses carried out an elaborate community inquisition. The perfidy of Seay and Free became an object lesson highlighting the rigid and unshakeable authority of the leaders of Bob Jones College.

In the case of Dorothy Seay, the Joneses conducted a detailed and public inquisition. They asked her students an array of pointed questions. Boys were asked if Seay had invited them up to her room. All students were asked if she had suggested that it was sometimes okay to go to the movies. Had Seay made positive comments about popular singer Dorothy Morrow?

Students' answers were damning, in the eyes of the Bob Joneses. Perhaps worst of all, Seay had reportedly told students in class not to tell anyone at the college about what she was saying. She told students that other professors also doubted the firm authoritarian rules of the school. One woman, for example, taught at the college during the day but "played jazz and sang blues" at night. It was silly, Seay reportedly told students, for faculty loyalists to criticize such behavior, because it was entirely normal and healthy.[72]

The last week of May 1938 must have been a tense one on the Bob Jones College campus. Not only did Jones fire Seay and Free, but he also informed the school community of the decision and asked for their support. The two of them, Bob Jones Sr. told the community, had been at the heart of a dangerous faculty conspiracy, an attempt to subvert the religion, morals, and spirit of the school. At a student body meeting, Jones asked students to identify anyone on the faculty that students thought might be a danger to the school and to their souls. Eighty students, Jones wrote, wrote Seay's name on their secret ballots. Others later told Jones the same thing. The faculty, too, agreed that Seay had become a danger, a "spiritual liability."[73] A majority also called Joseph Free's influence bad for the "spiritual development of the institution."[74]

Both Seay and Free left, but not without firing some parting shots. Free penned a long letter in which he denounced the Bob Joneses and their school. In all his teaching jobs, Free complained, he had never been treated in such a shockingly disrespectful manner. He had worked at several schools,

> two of them orthodox. (But not obnoxious.) My loyalty was never questioned . . . . It simply never occurred to me that I was not free to express my opinions and I did express them. How was I to know that loyalty meant dictatorship?

Free admitted that he had encouraged students in his debate class to critique Bob Jones Sr.'s chapel talks. He admitted that he had twice called the elder Jones conceited.[75]

He vehemently denied any sort of conspiracy, however. He had been accused of coaxing student Marjorie Foster into stealing school money. Nonsense. What he had done, he wrote, was listen sympathetically to her claims of innocence. He had been accused of planting seeds of disloyalty in the minds of long-term faculty members such as Ruth Flood. Ridiculous. He had had one conversation with Flood, Free wrote. If her attitude toward the school changed, it must have been a long time coming.[76]

Bob Jones Sr., Free charged, had been warped by his "lust for power and publicity." The school had degenerated into teaching a "dogmatic pseudo-religion." The overblown chapel talks were more than just the effusion of a conceited braggart, Free warned. They had become a deadly mantra of self-obsessed religious and educational jingoism.[77]

Seay published her denunciation in the pages of the *American Mercury*. Though Seay officially remained "Anonymous," and though she referred to Bob Jones College as "Blank College," there was no doubt among the Bob Jones community about the author or the target. At Bob Jones College, Seay wrote, students and faculty were twisted into a "Gestapo"-like culture of "intricate intrigue." Bob Jones Sr. worked students and faculty into a "religious fervor," resulting in "mass confessions of wrongdoing, mostly imaginary, of course." The rules were so ridiculously strict and the enforcement mechanism so viciously personal that many students took a "certain perverse adolescent relish in the exercise, including the discovery and denunciation of the minute lapses of their classmates."[78]

Unlike the mess at Clifton Fowler's Denver Bible Institute, these swirling accusations did not lead the Bob Joneses to seek outside affirmation of their continuing status as trustworthy fundamentalists. Rather, the episode seemed to have convinced them to insist more firmly on their principle of absolute institutional and personal loyalty.

The central principle of loyalty at Bob Jones College did not result merely from an accident or a personality quirk of the Bob Joneses. Rather, it worked as an effective, if turbulent, answer to the question of fundamentalist authority. Unlike at Denver Bible Institute, the Joneses' leadership style was not open to outside fundamentalist scrutiny. If students or faculty did not like it, their only option was a humiliated exit. As Bob Jones Sr. expressed the principle in a chapel talk:

> We are not going to pay anybody to "cuss" us. We can get "cussin'" free from the outside . . . . We have never been a divided college . . . . Gripers are not welcome here. If you are a dirty griper, you are not one of us.[79]

Bob Jones Jr. seemed to think this loyalty principle was embraced by other schools as well. When the University of Michigan wrote to ask for a reference for Joseph Free, the younger Jones replied that he could not oblige. Free, after all, "was not loyal to this organization and . . . he did a great deal toward disturbing the entire Speech Department." If the University of Michigan valued loyalty or "harmonious organization," Jones warned, they must not hire Free.[80]

In the early years of Bob Jones College, the top leadership used examples of student misbehavior and faculty dissatisfaction as evidence of such sinister conspiracies, not as evidence that the rules were too strict or the pay too low. When it came to hiring, the leadership at Bob Jones College insisted even more firmly that degrees and credentials were not the most important qualifications for a good fundamentalist teacher. Even the most accomplished applicants, even those who claimed to embrace the religious mission of the school, might prove to be satanic agents dedicated to promoting disloyal conspiracy. As a result, from the 1930s onward the college gave top hiring priority to loyalty. In 1934, for example, only three of twenty-six faculty members had graduated from Bob Jones College. By 1946, that number had increased to almost half, thirty-two of sixty-six.[81]

Students, too, were praised as much for their loyalty as for their talent or academic accomplishment. The Bob Joneses learned this lesson not only from unpleasant experiences with Dorothy Seay, Joseph Free, Ruth Flood, and Marjorie Foster but also from what they saw at other fundamentalist colleges. In 1940, for instance, Bob Jones Jr. told a friend that his school would never have the sort of turbulence that Wheaton had recently experienced. Why? Because, Jones explained, "we have a loyal crowd of students."[82]

## *Poison Pens*

The students at Bob Jones College may not have been as uniformly loyal as Jones hoped, but there was no doubt that Wheaton really had experienced some tough times. During the 1930s, the Wheaton community wrestled with the same questions of authority and leadership that had bedeviled Denver Bible Institute and Bob Jones College. The challenges proved just as difficult at Wheaton, though the details of Wheaton's problems were unique and were resolved in the college's unique way.

Unlike the top-down structures in Denver or Cleveland, Tennessee, authority at Wheaton was diffused haphazardly. Officially, during the 1930s final decisions about school leadership and direction were made by the board of trustees. As the complicated case of ousted President J. Oliver Buswell demonstrated, however, those trustees juggled many competing sources of influence. They had to consider input from administration, students, faculty, alumni, and the broader national fundamentalist community. They were influenced by rumors throughout the Wheaton community and by rumors from across the international network of fundamentalism. They took into account personal friendships as well as the school's financial bottom line. Because they could not rely on any established once-and-for-all definition of proper fundamentalism, they had to draw—uncertainly and tentatively—on all these things in order to come to any sort of important decision. In the end, Buswell's ouster set Wheaton firmly on the course it followed for the rest of the century. Buswell sought to define fundamentalism narrowly as a strident defense of Presbyterian orthodoxy, but the rest of Wheaton's leadership insisted on something different. Fundamentalism at Wheaton would mean an impossibly inclusive big-tent conservative evangelicalism, one that would stoutly if quixotically resist giving offense to any influential members of the far-flung fundamentalist community.

Just as the single definition of fundamentalism had never been adequately established, so it was never quite clear in those early years what criteria would be used to judge a fundamentalist school leader. Critics of Buswell threw everything they had at him, from athletics to evolution, Presbyterianism to popularity. Those who had the ear of anxious trustees whispered that Buswell had lost the confidence of the alumni and that donations would wither. In the end, the sheer weight of innuendo was enough to remove Buswell, especially when combined with his own combative attitude.

He might have seen it coming. After all, Buswell had been hired on the spot in 1926, after Charles Blanchard died. As a visitor, Buswell had given a series of chapel addresses in February 1926 and had impressed several trustees as the kind of leader Wheaton needed. As the leading scholar of Wheaton's history explained, "The board hired [Buswell] without a search process and without any philosophical discussion about the kind of person they would like to preside over the college."[83] With similar brusqueness, Buswell was out in 1940, though he went on to a long career in fundamentalist higher education as leader of New York's National Bible Institute.[84] With both the hiring and the firing, the leadership of Wheaton College demonstrated its utter lack of an institutional process to handle evolving questions of leadership and authority. There were no explicit criteria for finding or judging effective leadership during the 1930s; the process was a wrenchingly personal one. Trustees went with gut feelings, and when enough of them felt Buswell should go, he had to go.

Most of those gut feelings concerned the reputation of Wheaton among the national fundamentalist community. Before they offered Buswell the job, the trustees gave Charles Trumbull the opportunity to reject him. Trumbull was the hugely influential editor of the *Sunday School Times*. His implicit stamp of approval would signal the continuing faithfulness of Wheaton's leadership to fundamentalists nationwide.[85]

By the late 1930s, rumors of dissatisfaction with Buswell's leadership began to pile up. One student who was there in 1937 later remembered that year as a tense one, with Wheaton's campus fraught with an atmosphere of debate. Among students, he remembered, "there was real arguing going on." At least to this student, the arguing concerned not only the direction of Wheaton College or the leadership of President Buswell but also a broader "sort of a conflict . . . within the Christian church, and in the Christian campuses." Wheaton's leadership was about more than just Wheaton; it was a question of the meaning of fundamentalism as a whole.[86] Another student remembered similar "rumors on campus." As a result, when Buswell finally exited, "there seemed to be a sigh of relief."[87]

According to all observers, part of the problem resulted from Buswell himself. There was no clear consensus about his strengths and weaknesses. There was agreement, however, that Buswell reacted to the growing rumors by leaping in headfirst. As historian Michael Hamilton put it, Buswell was "drawn to controversy like a bear to a beehive."[88]

But that was not all. The uncertainties surrounding the nature of fundamentalism that Wheaton had inherited from the 1920s lingered. To President Buswell, the central issue for all true fundamentalists was denominational purity. Buswell had become active in a controversy between Presbyterian factions. He had urged fundamentalists to separate themselves from mainline Presbyterian churches and form purer breakaway ones.[89] As Buswell remembered, this denominational activism was the "principal item of complaint against him."[90]

It was true, to some degree. Members of the board did not share Buswell's zeal for separatism. They did not agree that true fundamentalism required such institutional separation. Moreover, they likely recognized that many of their students and potential students remained part of mainline churches. If Wheaton came to be associated with this separatist definition of fundamentalism, it would lose much of its support within the national fundamentalist community.[91]

As a community, the leadership at Wheaton decided that Buswell's separatism could not be allowed to represent Wheaton as an institution during the late 1930s. But at least as important as such religious and denominational questions were questions of educational administration that could have happened at any small college in the same era. For instance, the brewing tensions about denominational activism came to a boiling point in 1939 over the intractable issue of athletics. Wheaton's football coach, Fred Walker, was accused of swearing at players, of conducting himself in an unseemly, unchristian manner. Buswell resisted firing him, provoking the animosity of other leading administrators at the school. When Buswell finally agreed to let Walker go, those administrators changed their minds and kept Walker on.[92]

Alumni discontent fueled the developing storm. Just before a momentous board meeting in January 1940, a report to the trustees from a group of Chicago alums detailed the charges against Buswell. Buswell had alienated the faculty, the alumni group accused. His Presbyterian come-outism had "antagonized" most alumni. Athletics, too, were suffering. Student enrollment had dropped. In short, this alumni group urged the trustees to take action against Buswell for a variety of reasons, including disputes over the proper nature of fundamentalism, day-to-day difficulties with keeping faculty and coaches happy, and failure to keep tuition dollars coming in.[93]

Such charges were the final pieces of evidence that spurred the trustees to confront the tricky question of Buswell's performance as president, but there had been underlying tensions as well. Buswell, to a large degree, had embraced the developing standards among mainstream higher education to a greater degree than had his fellow administrators at Wheaton. As was occurring in other colleges and universities, Buswell hoped to encourage more scholarly publication among faculty members. Buswell wanted to pay higher salaries, to join the competition for top academic talent that had become the norm at many colleges and universities.[94]

Other administrators, including dean of students Wallace Emerson, vice president of academic administration Enock Dyrness, and vice president of business affairs George Kirk, pushed for a more traditional view of the proper role of fundamentalist faculty. As had been the tradition at small religious liberal arts colleges, these other administrators might have described proper faculty priorities as faith first, teaching second, and research maybe.[95]

Emerson, Dyrness, and Kirk had the ear of influential leaders on the board of trustees, which was unfortunate for Buswell. In addition to the complaints of alumni, the anti-Buswellians brandished evidence of student dissatisfaction. In late 1939, one student penned an open letter complaining about Buswell's performance in the classroom. She had hoped that Buswell's ethics class would help her to "fight the good fight" against the encroaching secularism of her day, but in spite of her efforts and prayers, it had not. She studied hard and prayed hard, but Buswell's class still taught her nothing.[96]

Other students agreed. One wrote that Buswell's ethics class was cruelly organized and intellectually unfair. One book that they had not even discussed had been used as the basis for the exams. "I am convinced," he complained, "that it is unfair to require all Seniors to take this course."[97]

If he had been willing to stoop to self-defense, President Buswell might have given the trustees evidence to the contrary. He had asked students to complete evaluation forms for his ethics class, and in spite of the ferocious complaints from the students above, most students seemed very satisfied. As a group, they appreciated the way Buswell's class combined information with spiritual value. They rated Buswell as a fair grader, a fair teacher in his presentation of opposing views, and a fair listener.[98] As one student who had taken his class explained years later, Buswell was "well-liked by many of the students."[99]

Faculty, too, seemed to have a mixed opinion of Buswell's performance. In June 1939, Buswell had circulated a questionnaire to all faculty. Of course, many faculty members might not have felt free to voice their dissatisfaction directly to Buswell himself, so we need to be cautious in our interpretation of the results. Overall, however, of those who responded, only six said they were dissatisfied "with the work of the president of the college." Five gave no vote, and thirty-four said they were not dissatisfied. Twenty-three did not reply at all.[100]

Perhaps the most dramatic episode in this agonizing back-and-forth came with an intensely awkward denunciation of Buswell by chemistry professor L. Allen Higley. Higley had written anonymous letters to members of the board, signed "An Alumnus." In his letters, Higley repeated the many charges laid against Buswell. "Scores and scores of alumni," Higley wrote,

> are withholding their support in disapproval of the way things are managed. The athletics is a disgrace to any college even to one not making Christian Professions . . . . His ethics class was formerly regarded a joke, but now that the result is seen it is deemed mostly false teaching and exploitation of personal dogmatism, and pet theories. He teaches the very foundation of evolution and Modernism . . . . Mr. Buswell will soon make a modernistic college of Wheaton . . . . Real scholars call him stupid. In his pride, he forsakes his most loyal supporters in order to have his own way . . . . Wheaton needs a *new head.*[101]

Unfortunately for Higley, evangelist and board member Harry Ironside confronted Buswell with Higley's letter. Were those charges true? What did Buswell intend to do about them?

Buswell recognized Higley's handwriting. He confronted Higley and forced him into a humiliating retraction. Higley wrote back to the board members, admitting that he had written the letter. Buswell made Higley add a new postscript: "I withdraw the above as the statements of others, and offer my apology for them." In spite of the retraction, Buswell fired Higley.[102]

The board met in January 1940, girded for an ugly debate in this poisonous atmosphere.[103] Even at that late date, their decision could have gone either way. The charges against Buswell seemed serious indeed, but no one on the board or elsewhere could assert with convincing certainty that Buswell had violated any explicit rules or guidelines. Such guidelines did not exist. Since the tumultuous 1920s, not even the most perspicacious fundamentalist intellectuals could define the boundaries of fundamentalism. Did Buswell defend true fundamentalism by leading the Presbyterian come-outers? Or did the board do so by maintaining Wheaton's connection to mainline denominations? No one knew. Nor could anyone in the late 1930s assert for sure that Buswell's leadership did not meet the standards of leadership for an institution of higher education. Should a school president remove an effective but erring football coach? Should he push for higher faculty salaries and demand more faculty publication?

In the event, two things swayed the trustees against Buswell. First, he demonstrated his usual pugnacity. "The trustees," Buswell demanded at the momentous January meeting, "must back me up or fire me."[104] One trustee remembered Buswell insisting that if they wanted him gone, they would have to fire him, as he refused to resign quietly.[105]

Second, just as the board had deferred to fundamentalist editor Charles Trumbull when they hired Buswell, so they took their cues from him in Buswell's firing. Trumbull had pointedly instructed trustee Philip Howard Sr. to stay away from the January meeting. To other board members, the move signaled Trumbull's neutrality. It told them that he would not make any move to defend Buswell. By implication, board members recognized that the national fundamentalist community would not condemn them for getting rid of Buswell. So, by a vote of nine to three, they did.[106]

Administrator George Kirk thought that the students approved. When they were told of Buswell's removal, he wrote to a confidant, there was a vast silence that seemed like approval.[107] But neither Kirk nor Buswell nor anyone else had any real way to gauge what the silence meant. None of the pressing questions of authority was really settled by Buswell's ouster. Wheaton College—students, faculty, administrators, and alumni—still did not have a clear sense of what real fundamentalist higher education leadership must look like.

Certainly the leadership crisis at Wheaton in the late 1930s played out very differently than did those at Denver Bible Institute and Bob Jones College. J. Oliver Buswell had none of the dictatorial power of Bob Jones Sr. or even of Clifton Fowler. Instead of investing authority in one authoritative leader, Wheaton College did the opposite, removing its leader in an impossible quest to avoid offending any potential fundamentalist donors or students. Taken together, however, these three cases demonstrate the profound uncertainties about authority in the developing network of fundamentalist higher education.

## *Gaps and Gorillas*

One thing fundamentalist school leaders agreed upon was that their schools must somehow oppose the teaching of evolution, at least as it was taught in mainstream colleges. At Wheaton, for example, one of the accusations made by Allen Higley was that Buswell "teaches evolution and some say he doesn't have head enough to know it."[108] Beyond the vague consensus against it, however, the question of evolution education remained intensely controversial throughout this school network. Before the 1960s, as we'll see in Chapter 9, not even the most fervently conservative schools insisted that fundamentalist science must believe in a young earth or a recent, literal worldwide flood. In the first half of the twentieth century, "gap theorists," "day-agers," and "flood geologists" argued and debated, but until the 1960s, none of them was able to claim exclusive status as the only reliable fundamentalist belief.

They all agreed on one thing, though: evolution was dangerous. Opposition to the alleged atheistic implications of modern evolutionary theory had been a bedrock principle of all fundamentalist colleges in the 1920s. As Wheaton president Charles Blanchard argued at the founding conference of the World's Christian Fundamentals Association in 1919:

> In our colleges, especially, the teaching that man has descended or ascended from brute beast is not only unsupported by any unquestioned facts and therefore totally unscientific, but is a distinct denial of the Bible account of the creation of man, the beginning of sin, the plan of salvation and the extension and triumph of the Christian religion in the world.[109]

A few years later, Dean Lowell H. Coate of Marion College in Indiana issued a similar warning about the perils of evolutionary theory. Coate thought a new type of evangelical college was needed, one that would "oppose evolution, destructive criticism, and liberalism as taught by the modernists."[110]

Such promises of an evolution-free (or, more precisely, evolution-safe) college remained prominent throughout the 1920s. Before the experiment at Des Moines University failed so dramatically, fundamentalists nationwide imagined a new school shielded from the implications of evolutionary theory. One fundamentalist fan reported that at Des Moines "evolution will never be taught, and considered only that its fallacy may be exposed."[111]

At the new Bob Jones College, too, opposition to prevailing trends in evolution education had been one of the first reasons for the school. In its original charter, Bob Jones pledged that the new school would fight "all atheistic, agnostic, pagan and so-called scientific adulterations of the Gospel, unqualifiedly affirming and teaching the inspiration of the Bible (both Old and New Testaments); the creation of man by the direct act of God."[112]

Similarly, Moody Bible Institute had always placed primary emphasis on the goal of protecting young minds from the implications of evolutionary theory. In the mid-1920s, President James M. Gray encouraged fundamentalist parents to send their children to Moody Bible Institute for a Bible course before they attended a traditional college. Why? Because the Moody course "renders [a student] immune to the evolution and modernistic germs, while it enables him to examine them in the light of Christian revelation as he could not have done before."[113]

Throughout the 1920s, 1930s, and 1940s, such insistent but loosely defined anti-evolutionism remained a key element of fundamentalist higher education. In the mid-1940s, for example, Bob Jones Jr. clarified his school's position on evolution education. Bob Jones College, he reported, taught evolution—in a way. At Bob Jones College, Jones explained, students learn to "believe in the creation of man by the direct act of God." That did not mean that students wouldn't learn about evolution. Students at Bob Jones College would read the works of Darwin, Spencer, and Huxley. However, Jones explained, "we tell them that these men were just guessing."[114]

Throughout the 1940s, opposition to mainstream scientific ideas about evolution remained a hallmark of all fundamentalist colleges. At least, that was the assumption of the editors of the *Sunday School Times*. In 1946, they wrote a circular letter to leaders of fundamentalist schools, asking whether their institutions taught evolution, and if they did, whether they

FIGURE 3.1 "Rearranging his library"
The most threatening idea of all. *Biola Chimes*, June 1939. Courtesy Biola University Archives.

taught it as a "tenable theory, or is it exposed as fallacious, from a scientific point of view, and opposed to the bible?"[115] As we've seen, nationally respected fundamentalist watchdogs such as the editors of the *Sunday School Times* could never simply order schools to get in line. But they could and did publish lists of recommended schools. As they made clear in this query, opposition to evolution remained a central qualification for that recommendation.

Between the foundings of fundamentalist schools in the 1920s and the middle of the century, such colleges served as institutional headquarters for the anti-evolution movement. For one thing, the schools themselves taught and disseminated fundamentalist ideas about evolution. They taught generations of evangelical students that they could be educated, they could be scientific, without abandoning the idea that God remained the best, most scientific explanation for the emergence of humanity. Just as important, this network of schools provided institutional homes for anti-evolution scholars and activists.

Moody Bible Institute, for example, taught both students and its wider community about the dangers of evolutionary theory. Readers of its monthly magazine could read the latest anti-evolution science from flood geologist George McCready Price.[116] They could also peruse theological denunciations of evolutionary theory from scholars such as Leander S. Keyser.[117] They might also read lower-brow anti-evolution fare, such as a poem written firmly with evangelical tongue in cheek:

> Why the missin' link's still missin'?
>     Kind o' curious, don't yer say,
> Why all natur' has forgotten
>     This here evoluti'n way?
> Peers like God might jest be sayin',
>     Back a long, long time ago,
> In the days of His creatin',
>     What He meant that yer should know.[118]

Students at Moody Bible Institute itself would be encouraged to learn about evolution, but to be careful with it. If a "mature student" at the school wanted to learn about evolutionary theory, James M. Gray argued in 1929, such a study would be most welcome. However, proper evolution education must be limited to biology, not to any possible religious implications.[119] When push came to shove, Gray always sided with those who denounced evolution. For example, he refused to run any article in his monthly magazine that might confuse readers by suggesting that fundamentalists could also be "evolutionists." Fundamentalists must be united, Gray thought, in their explicit and repeated denunciation of any atheistic implications of evolutionary theory.[120]

For their part, students in this era remembered evolution as a central part of their educational experiences. One Wheaton student in 1937, for example, recalled that L. Allen Higley's class gave the student "my first real touch with evolution." Everything he had learned before, he said, had been simple denunciations of evolution. From Higley, he heard "all the evolutionist's side of it, but then [Higley] knew the Word of God well enough that he was able to present what the Word of God said too on the thing." According to this student, Higley taught "pure science," but he did it in a way that did not trouble the student's earnest faith.[121] Other Wheaton students from the 1930s had similar memories of learning about evolution from faculty members such as Russell Mixter and John W. Leedy.[122]

Into the 1940s, too, students at Wheaton studied evolution, but took away a creationist message. One student who went on to a tragic but productive evangelical career—as we'll see in Chapter 4—remembered a biology lab in 1945. The experience, she wrote home to her mother, was "really thrilling." Each student had his or her own microscope and studied directly the constructs of life. One day, she wrote, "I saw the cutest little bacterium tearing around in some water! He looked like a turtle." What lesson did she take away from this eyes-on scientific study? As she told the folks at home, "Truly we are fearfully and wonderfully made."[123]

The faculty likely would have been delighted to hear of this student's enthusiasm and of her ultimate conclusion about the development of life. However, at Wheaton and elsewhere, evangelical scholars themselves fought ferociously about their visions of proper creationism. Did real Christian faith suggest that God had created life in different time periods, with long "gaps" of time between creations? Or did the "days" in Genesis really refer to long geological ages? Each evangelical scientist had his preference, and as with all academic controversies, different opinions led to strained professional relationships. For example, during the 1920s, President Buswell at Wheaton did not shy away from publicly denouncing the gap theory, though he knew many of his own faculty members embraced it, including his old enemy L. Allen Higley.[124]

On Wheaton's campus, indeed, Buswell was not the first of Higley's worries. During the 1930s, Higley had a tougher time handling challenges from a different school of creationist thought, the flood geologists. At the time, Higley served as the president of the Religion and Science Association. The group as a whole firmly denounced Buswell's preferred day-age creationism.[125] They could not agree, however, on other important questions. For his part, Higley embraced a "ruin-and-restoration" gap model, which posited a long stretch of geologic time between the initial creation of the universe and the later creation of Adam & Eve. The flood geologists, in contrast, embraced the notion of a radically recent appearance of life on earth, with no gaps of geologic time, no equation of biblical days with geologic ages. For flood geologists, the apparent great age of the earth could be best explained by the worldwide flood described in the Book of Genesis.[126] Just as with any other academic controversy at any university or research institution, this debate was no less vicious just because it largely went unnoticed and unremarked by the wider evangelical community.

In 1936, Higley organized a conference on these issues at Moody Church in Chicago. In his efforts to maintain unity among creationists and to maintain the scientific respectability of creationism as a whole, Higley invited creationists of all camps as well as a mainstream non-creationist geologist from nearby Northwestern University. Perhaps due to Higley's efforts at inclusive creationism, flood geologists in the Religion and Science Association worked to undermine his influence. According to the leading historian of creationism, Ronald Numbers, the flood geologists worried that Higley might use his prestige as a collegiate scientist, part of the "Wheaton crowd," to move the organization away from a young-earth position. As Numbers put it, Higley's 1936 conference revealed "the deep fractures running through the creationist community."[127]

They needn't have worried. As we've seen, Higley's bitter machinations against Buswell cost Higley his job. There was no doubt, though, that having such a job remained hugely important among early anti-evolutionists, many of whom lacked the scientific credentials to hope for such a position. Perhaps the example of Harry Rimmer can best demonstrate the importance of fundamentalist colleges as homes and headquarters to the anti-evolution movement in the interwar years. As Ronald Numbers has argued, "No antievolutionist reached a wider audience among American evangelicals during the second quarter of the century than Harry Rimmer."[128] And Rimmer's enthusiastic preaching of gap-theory creationism was possible only with the enthusiastic help and support of college leaders.

Rimmer himself never underestimated the power of higher education in the fight against evolution. Back in 1925, he argued that the number of colleges who turned good evangelical students into "practically infidels" was "appalling."[129] Students in college, Rimmer believed, must be reached early with the anti-evolution message. If scholars and teachers waited until after the impressionable college years, Rimmer wrote with his customary exuberant capitals, "IT IS TOO LATE TO SAVE THE SOULS OF THOSE WHO IMPLICITLY BELIEVED THE TESTIMONY OF SOLEMNLY AUTHENTICATED LIES!"[130]

During the mid-1930s, President Nathan Wood of Gordon College lured Rimmer to Gordon's campus to teach classes in evangelical science. The purpose, Wood believed, would be twofold: Gordon students would benefit directly from the classes, and Rimmer could offer anti-evolution revival services in the New England area under Gordon's auspices.[131] In order to make the offer more attractive, Wood offered to book a full schedule of revival events during Rimmer's tenure at Gordon, paying between

$25 and $50 per address. If that was not enough money, Wood assured Rimmer, Wood could ask for more.[132]

Doubtless, this sort of logistical and financial support proved vital to Rimmer's continuing anti-evolution crusades during the 1930s. It also proved irresistibly attractive for college leaders such as Wood. Association with Rimmer's hugely popular creationist presentations allowed Gordon College to promise students the very latest in evangelical celebrity faculty. More than that, by associating its name so prominently with Rimmer's regional revivals, Gordon College cemented its position as the leading regional evangelical college more firmly in the minds of New England's fundamentalists.

During the 1940s, a new generation of creationist intellectual ferment began brewing among conservative evangelicals. Just as they had for decades, evangelical institutions of higher education proved central to these developments. For example, one of the most influential creationist organizations of the postwar era had its roots in 1941, at the instigation of Moody Bible Institute president Will Houghton.[133] As we'll see in coming chapters, the American Scientific Affiliation promoted its brand of intellectually respectable creationism throughout the rest of the twentieth century. And it did so, to a large degree, by relying on the support and leadership of its "inner circle" of leaders based at Wheaton College.[134]

## *"Because I Said So"*

Just as debates over the proper nature of evangelical thinking about evolution would continue for decades and generations, so too did deeper divisions about the proper structure of authority at fundamentalist schools. The three examples we've seen in this chapter have demonstrated the very different ways such divisions could manifest themselves. The difficulties plagued fundamentalist schools throughout the twentieth century.

Some schools experienced tensions similar to those at Wheaton College. At these schools, as at Wheaton in the 1930s, authority was never firmly housed in any single person or office. At Wheaton, as at similar schools, top leaders stoutly resisted any attempt to wedge fundamentalism into a narrow definition. School leaders were loath to alienate any influential members of the far-flung fundamentalist community. As a result, muddled and sometimes contradictory visions of proper fundamentalism awkwardly rubbed along together.

At Bob Jones College and schools like it, authority was established as a prerogative of the top leadership. Decisions made by the Bob Joneses became authoritative statements of proper fundamentalist belief and behavior. As a result, Bob Jones College—and eventually Bob Jones University—found it enormously difficult to change policy positions once they had been established. For instance, early opposition to accreditation and intercollegiate athletics became implicit articles of faith, not just humdrum questions of administration. Perhaps most explosively, 1920s positions on race and racism were elevated into tests of loyalty, leaving the school far outside of the evangelical mainstream in coming generations.

Crises like the one at Denver Bible Institute continued, too. Schools and churches continued to be roiled by competing streams of rumors and innuendo; they continuously reached out to the wider fundamentalist community to secure stamps of approval, legitimacy, and purity; and they never settled once and for all how to handle ferociously independent leaders who might also be sexual predators, theological mavericks, or greedy con artists. These episodes were not accidents or merely unfortunate exceptions but rather part of the foundational structure of independent fundamentalist institutions. With authority vested in personalities and charismatic leaders, it would be surprising not to see a consistent record of abuse.

Fundamentalists never knew whom to trust. Both legitimate schools and scams would appeal to uncertain fundamentalist credentials. Fundamentalist school leaders were aware of the difficulties, but none of the possible answers ever seemed satisfying. As we've seen in this chapter, the variety of solutions only sidestepped the ultimate dilemma of authority in fundamentalist higher education. In practice, fundamentalist schools became addicted to celebrity and reputation. They appealed to famous fundamentalists such as Harry Rimmer and Charles Trumbull to help pin down the vague and shifting boundaries of proper fundamentalism. In the end, though, such celebrity vouchers were only valuable opinions, not decisive rulings.

Whatever the issue—from proper creationism to proper athletics; from acceptable theological positions to acceptable student fashions—there was never a single "fundamentalist" answer. This was not because fundamentalists were somehow a more fractious and fickle bunch than non-fundamentalists. Certainly, mainstream colleges in the same era experienced similarly tumultuous debates, though about different topics and with a different cast of characters. At fundamentalist colleges, the challenge was defined in large part by the very uncertainty surrounding the many possible meanings of fundamentalism itself. When there were disagreements and disputes, there was never a clear authority to whom one might appeal. Indeed, the very question of authority itself was the most contentious of all, and remained so for the rest of the twentieth century.

# 4

# "I Came to Be Went With"

*I came to be went with, but I ain't yet.*
—A "little country girl from Alabama," explaining why she came to Bob Jones College, c. 1931[1]

## *Flaming Fundamentalist Youth*

How did fundamentalist college students know they were in love? For at least one young woman in the mid-1940s, it had as much to do with Jesus as it did with her future husband, Jim. Born into one of the first families of early fundamentalism, Elisabeth Elliot (still Betty Howard at the time) wrote weekly letters home to her parents during her time at Wheaton College. She included detailed descriptions of her forays into righteous romance. When she finally met the perfect match, she knew. Unlike her feelings for her former beaus, she did not feel an immediate physical attraction for Jim. Rather, when she was with him she felt closer to Jesus. As she wrote in the summer of 1948, Jesus "gave His strong hand to us" as she and Jim spent time together. The two of them were never alone, Betty confided. Rather, "the interflow of spirit was as a triangle, with Christ at the apex."[2]

Perhaps we shouldn't be surprised by Betty's frank and meticulous reports of her budding romance to her mother. After all, it wasn't only fundamentalists who viewed the primary goal of college to be the pursuit of a proper mate. Before the radical social changes of the 1960s, as historian Beth Bailey has noted, American women of all religions were encouraged to think of college as the right place to get both "an education and a man."[3] For parents and earnest students alike, fundamentalist colleges added the extra draw of finding a mate with similar religious and cultural beliefs. Young fundamentalists hoped for a better chance of finding a reliably fundamentalist life partner if they attended Bob Jones College,

Bryan University, or Moody Bible Institute than if they went to Furman University, the University of Tennessee, or the University of Chicago.

In the first half of the twentieth century, fundamentalist colleges and Bible institutes did more than just offer a congenial meeting place for like-minded fundamentalist youth. Schools did more than simply welcome students who viewed courtship through the developing sexual standards of fundamentalism. The schools themselves worked hard to create an environment that bucked emerging social trends concerning courtship and sexuality. During the 1920s, 1930s, 1940s, and 1950s, fundamentalist colleges moved from traditional assumptions about proper courtship and sexuality to ferociously traditionalist insistence on such expectations, because—unlike Betty Howard—many students at fundamentalist schools fought back. As colleges, universities, and Bible institutes defined tighter rules about the acceptable limits of fundamentalist behavior, plenty of students found ways to engage in those behaviors—sexual and otherwise—that the schools were working so hard to prohibit.

It was not only courtship and sexuality that worried fundamentalist school administrators. Throughout that same period, fundamentalist schools imposed draconian rules on all types of student activities. It is important to remember, however, that before the lifestyle revolutions of the 1960s and 1970s, fundamentalist colleges were not the only schools to impose onerous rules on their students. In the late 1920s, for example, students at Florida State College for Women (now Florida State University) were expected to abide by strict rules and regulations. Alcohol was banned. Male visitors were banned from rooms. Students were required to check out if they left campus and check back in when they returned.[4]

Such rules were a standard part of student life for many decades at all sorts of schools. At the University of Michigan, for instance, as late as 1947 students gathering in groups of three or more to listen to school football games on the radio had to register their "party" with school authorities.[5] A new administrator at the University of Virginia in 1959 enforced strict rules against student drinking.[6] At Winthrop College in South Carolina, female students in the early 1960s were still required to wear dresses in public places and were not allowed to walk in unchaperoned couples or groups to the campus lake.[7] As late as 1965, on the tradition-minded campus of Vanderbilt University, women students had to check in at the dorms by eleven o'clock on weeknights.[8]

From the 1920s through the 1950s, fundamentalist schools joined in this tradition of controlling student behavior, but with their own unique challenges. As a general rule, the student lifestyle codes at fundamentalist schools were stricter and more invasive than the ones at mainstream colleges. Students at fundamentalist colleges were not usually allowed to smoke, drink, gamble, put on dramatic plays, or even attend movies. Interactions with the opposite sex, especially, were subjected to detailed and intrusive institutional oversight. In the period before the 1960s, all colleges controlled student behavior more than do most schools today, but fundamentalist colleges pushed that control far past the limits of most non-fundamentalist schools. For instance, the couple at Bob Jones University who got in trouble in 1952 for sneaking into and out of an abandoned office at midnight probably would have been in trouble at any college of that era.[9] But few mainstream colleges posted spies outside the movie theater downtown to discourage student attendance, the way Wheaton did in the 1920s.[10]

Fundamentalist schools stood out, too, for trumpeting their strict student rules as an intrinsic part of true fundamentalist education. School leaders often assumed—though, as we'll see, thoughtful fundamentalists sometimes challenged the notion—that strict lifestyle rules were a necessary part of raising truly fundamentalist youth. In addition, fundamentalist administrators justified and enforced those rules in explicitly fundamentalist language.

That language—along with a widely shared attitude toward proper control over students' sexual and social behavior—can tell us a great deal about the day-to-day meanings of fundamentalism in practice. With good reason, as we saw in Chapter 2, some historians have tended to focus on the distinctive theological elements of fundamentalism in their search for a workable definition of what it meant to be fundamentalist in the twentieth century.[11] The enforcement of fundamentalist lifestyle rules on college and Bible-institute campuses, however, shows how circumscribed a role such theological distinctiveness played in passing fundamentalism along to the next generation.

In general, misbehaving young fundamentalists on college campuses were not told that their behavior would put them on the wrong side at the Day of Judgment. Nor were they often quoted inerrant Bible chapter and verse to explain the error of their ways. Such warnings and threats happened from time to time, of course, but far more common were stern but vague circular arguments that bad behavior violated fundamentalist ethics because good fundamentalists did not engage in bad behavior. Students were more often warned that they must act like "Christian gentlemen" and "ladies" than that they must watch out for their eternal souls. Students were told repeatedly—at all sorts of fundamentalist institutions of higher education—that sexual dalliances, smoking, and sloppy attire would take away their ability to evangelize, would dilute their "Christian witness." Even more commonly, students were scolded with warnings familiar to every sort of school—college and high school, fundamentalist and mainstream—that bad behavior was bad because it would lead to direct, worldly punishments, including suspension and expulsion from school.

Students, too, sometimes viewed their fundamentalist schools first and foremost as distinctly *strict* institutions, not distinctly fundamentalist ones. One appreciative student in the late 1920s, for instance, described Bob Jones College as "a strictly disciplined Christian school." For her, at least, the thing that made her alma mater special was not its attitudes toward an inerrant Bible or about the coming apocalypse but rather its frantic and ruthless discipline.[12]

Within the world of fundamentalist higher education, different types of institutions developed different lifestyle traditions and expectations. Speaking broadly, Bible institutes established and maintained stricter expectations for student behavior. Such students, after all, were preparing specifically for vocations as soul-winning missionaries. Their behavior could never be considered incidental to their higher educations. At fundamentalist liberal-arts colleges and universities, on the other hand, the traditions of American colleges tended to carry more weight. Students tended to think of themselves as college students, albeit of a certain fundamentalist type. As such, they often expected more opportunity for faddish, youth-oriented fun as an inherent part of their college experience.

## *The Keen and the Miserable*

The goings-on at many fundamentalist colleges in the pre-hippie era often looked and sounded much like those at any mainstream school. And, just as different students had very different experiences at mainstream schools, so too did young fundamentalists. Some students enjoyed every minute. Years before she met her future husband, for example, Betty Howard loved everything about Wheaton College. Her first school-sponsored social event, she told her mother, had been "*really* keen!"[13] For students who didn't fit in, however, fundamentalist college life could be quite the opposite. A few years before Betty Howard arrived at Wheaton, Eddie Kindstedt told his mother that he was "just miserable all day" at Bob Jones College.[14]

Everyone else, he lamented, seemed to know just what to do, but he "went through *hell*" in gym class because "I did not know what to do so I just stood there and all the fellows laughed at me and thought I was nuts." Like many miserable new college students before and since, Eddie only wanted to go home.[15]

Just as at non-fundamentalist schools, colleges like Wheaton and Bob Jones College offered their students a universe of official and semi-official activities to fill their time outside of class. Unlike at mainstream colleges, campus social life at most fundamentalist schools remained dominated well into the twentieth century by the "lits," or literary societies. At mainstream institutions, these student organizations had had a long and illustrious career, beginning in the pre-Revolution era and ruling campus up through the Civil War.[16] At most schools, though, the emergence of semi-secret fraternities in the mid-nineteenth century spelled the end of the literary societies.[17]

The lits lasted much longer at fundamentalist schools, perhaps because fraternities were prohibited or discouraged on most campuses and students were barred from many other social activities. At Bob Jones University, they lasted through the 1980s.[18] Perhaps their longevity was due to the fact that they were in fact called "fraternities" and "sororities" at BJU, although, as one student remembered, they were really "more like study clubs."[19] At Wheaton the lits petered out in the late 1950s due to lack of student interest.[20] In the earlier years of the fundamentalist movement, however, lits dominated the social scene at many fundamentalist colleges and universities. One Wheaton student in the 1920s remembered that "practically everyone" joined one of the student societies. Every Friday night, one of the societies would put on a "program," featuring songs, readings, and other student performances.[21] Through the 1930s and into the 1940s, it remained standard social practice at Wheaton for many students to join a lit and to participate in the programs put on by all the societies.[22] As Betty Howard told her mother in 1944, "lit night" offered a chance for students to dress in fancy dinner clothes and enjoy a group meal with "candlelight and music."[23] Unbeknownst to Betty and many of the other enthusiastic participants, not every student felt included. The lit societies were technically open to all, but in practice only students with extra spending money were able to participate. As one student remembered from his time at Wheaton in the 1930s, "my money went for tuition and books and the necessities rather than blazer jackets and tuxedos, and dinner parties and dates."[24]

Students at fundamentalist schools also engaged in such typical college activities as student newspapers and yearbooks. At Gordon College, for example, students published a range of newspapers and bulletins, including seat-of-the-pants publications such as the short-lived *Broadcaster* as well as more polished student newspapers such as the *Gordon Herald* and eventually *Tartan*, and the *Hypernikon* yearbook.[25] At Wheaton, students worked in a variety of media, including the *Record* (newspaper), *Tower* (yearbook), *Kodon* (literary journal), and WETN (radio station).[26]

Beginning in the 1960s, as we'll explore in Chapter 7, students at fundamentalist and evangelical colleges pushed hard to exert more control over their publications. Before then, at most schools, administrators did not hesitate to dictate content and style to student writers and editors. At Biola College, for example, President Samuel Sutherland thrust himself into the middle of student disagreements in the offices of the *Chimes*. In 1953, when student leaders could not agree about the proper way to run the paper, Sutherland quashed the festering feud—by kicking out both squabbling leaders.[27]

Student writers, too, always had to keep in mind that they represented more than just themselves. In 1954, Sutherland vetoed a student essay in the *Chimes*. Sutherland didn't deny that the student had submitted an "accurate" and "well written" review of a book by Presbyterian fundamentalist leader Carl McIntire. However, the review pressed a few uncomfortable buttons for American fundamentalists in 1950s. Was McIntire nothing but a "religious racketeer"? Sutherland worried that the review could be "offensive" to fundamentalist friends of McIntire, so he yanked the piece without a second thought.[28]

Administrators worried about more than just student publications. In addition to yearbooks and newspapers, most fundamentalist schools sponsored a variety of student musical groups. Such groups varied widely in style and makeup, from gospel choirs to traveling orchestras to brass bands. Those musicians, however, played under the same sort of strict scrutiny that ruled student newspapers. In 1932, for example, the faculty of Bob Jones College disbanded one student orchestra for playing "inappropriate music."[29] As more student missionaries hoped to use their musical gifts to spread the Word of God, schools found themselves struggling to supervise them all. At Biola in the 1950s, a new faculty committee was charged with making sure that every student musical group was a good fundamentalist representative of the school. If not, the committee would have full authority to punish or disband the group.[30]

Not surprisingly, fundamentalist colleges also featured a full range of Christian clubs. At Bob Jones College in the 1930s, students who wanted more Christian activity in their lives could join the Pioneer Club. Members gathered every day to pray for the school, to plan and support the annual school banquet, and to help organize and run school activities of all sorts. In the spirit of Bob Jones Sr., the Pioneers also pledged to root out "any atheistic or modernistic teacher" who had managed to sneak into the faculty. The Pioneers promised to close the school itself if they ever suspected the institution had begun a slide into modernism.[31]

At Gordon, the religious clubs were less interested in rooting out school apostasy but no less earnest about organizing students to evangelize. In the early 1950s, Gordon students could join academic honor societies, the student council, the Theaetetus Society (for philosophy majors), the Greek Club, the Forensic Society, or even the Canadian Club. In addition to such secular fare, Gordon students might join the Commuters' Fellowship for additional prayer, the Foreign Missions Fellowship for those thinking of heading to foreign fields, the Highway Crusaders for on-the-road missionary outreach, the Friendship House for those interested in spreading the Gospel among children, and the After Dinner Fellowship for evening group prayers.[32]

Schools also offered students a range of less formal activities. At four-year colleges and universities, these activities tended to echo traditions from mainstream higher education. At Bible institutes and schools that had begun as Bible institutes, life in the 1920s, 1930s, 1940s, and 1950s tended to harken back to earlier traditions of tightly controlled student calendars.

At Wheaton, for instance, traditions continued from pre-fundamentalist days. One student arriving in the 1920s found that all freshman were required to wear green beanies for a couple of days. The school took each incoming class on a hayride in nearby Glen Ellyn. Students sang songs by a bonfire and slept in a hayloft.[33] Arriving in the 1940s, Betty Howard found those traditions alive and well. For Howard, college life was a delightful mix of wholesome fun activities and challenging fundamentalist academic work. As she told her mother a week after she arrived on campus, "Last night we had a hike over to Glen Ellyn. Stopped at a lodge and sang around the fire, ate, etc. It was lots of fun. Well, I've got to read 20 chapters of Genesis now, so I'll have to stop."[34] In 1944, freshmen at Wheaton were compelled to walk barefoot along certain campus paths until late October. When accosted by any older student, they were to respond, "Hail, Snail!"

They still had to wear beanies and were expected to carry a copy of the student handbook on a lanyard around their necks.[35]

Similarly, new students at Gordon College in the mid-1940s found themselves subjected to semi-official hazing rituals. One night, the entire freshman class was shaken out of bed in the wee hours and forced to wear wrong-side-out clothes, mismatched shoes, and "cake-batter mud packs." They were marched to a nearby river, where they held a tug-of-war contest against the sophomore class. Years later, students remembered those rituals fondly, as a delightful part of their college experience.[36]

Students at Bible institutes and colleges with a recent Bible-institute past more often found themselves occupied morning, noon, and night with school rituals. At Biola in 1940, for example, resident students woke up every morning for early prayers. On Mondays and Tuesdays, students gathered for evening devotions. On Wednesday evenings, female students attended the King's Daughters prayer club while males learned to be "fishers of men" in the Fishermen's Club Room. Thursday evenings were devoted to world missionary outreach, led by the Student Missionary Union. On Friday evenings Biola students relaxed a little bit at Home Night, with "fun and Christian fellowship" directed by a variety of student groups. On Saturday evenings, students directed their prayers toward their gospel outreach plans for the next day. Sundays, Biola students fanned out around the Los Angeles area, "preaching, teaching, or singing, the gospel of grace." On Sunday evenings, students gathered back on campus, congregating in the auditorium for a final prayer and song service.[37]

Not every school imposed this sort of day-to-day, minute-to-minute prayer schedule on their students. Indeed, even at Biola in 1940, not every student participated in every one of the scheduled activities. Unlike earlier generations of college students, as we saw in Chapter 1, students in the twentieth century expected to control much of their own schedules outside of class. At most fundamentalist schools, as at an earlier generation of mainstream colleges, some chapel services were mandatory for all students. Yet even at fundamentalist colleges, by the twentieth century most activities outside of class had come to be seen as voluntary. Of course, the level of control exerted by schools over their students' schedules varied. At Bob Jones University, for example, even in 1960 students had a tightly controlled daily schedule of chapel service, meals, and classes. BJU employed student monitors to check every dormitory room every morning. Students were not allowed to opt out.[38]

As one might expect, with so much control of student life, schools found themselves struggling to handle all the details. As at many non-fundamentalist schools, students often complained that the school was failing. One student wrote to Wheaton president J. Oliver Buswell in 1926, for example, to complain about the atrocious food in her dormitory. The meals, she said (apparently too angry to bother correcting her spelling), "are very poorly balanced, very poorly cooked, very unapetizingly served, and thoroughly repulsion to me."[39] With so many moving parts involved, the best President Buswell could tell her was that his administration was looking into the problem.[40]

Furthermore, the increasing demand for housing sometimes led to cracks in the walls of fundamentalist lifestyle rules. As Betty Howard remembered in the 1940s, Wheaton's options for student housing were overstretched. As a result, some students rented rooms in private houses nearby, where a jaded "house mother" could not be bothered to impose rules. As a result, these students could do "anything they want."[41]

In spite of their many flaws in providing adequate room and board, fundamentalist higher education was still too pricey for many students. Even at schools from the Bible institute tradition that traditionally had not charged tuition at all, many students struggled to pay fees and nominal tuition bills. At Chicago's Moody Bible Institute, for example, the archives bulge with records of delinquent student accounts from the 1920s through the 1950s.[42] At Biola, too, school administrators refused to give penurious students a break on board bills. In 1942, one anxious mother wrote to Dean Samuel Sutherland (he would become president in 1952) to try to work out a financial settlement for her daughter. The daughter was barely scraping by as a Biola student. Would it be possible, the mother asked, for her to skip breakfasts and get a break on her bill?[43] Sorry, Sutherland told her. Biola needed to keep the rules—and the bills—equal for all students, or else the school would be flooded with an unmanageable load of individual requests.[44]

At Wheaton, administrators enforced a rigid billing system. In the 1920s, for instance, students who had not paid their tuition bills were barred from classes.[45] Even into the 1950s, some students remembered a financially defined hierarchy at Wheaton. The dining hall system, one student remembered, was "stratified." Some places were cheaper, so "all of us poor kids and missionary kids" ate there.[46] Even students from more well-off families felt the financial pinch. As soon as she arrived in 1944, for example, Betty Howard complained that "every time you turn around you are charged another $10 for something."[47] Unlike the Bible institutes, colleges like Wheaton did not hesitate to charge fairly hefty tuition bills. For Betty Howard, that meant a first-semester bill amounting to more than $350. In addition to the tuition of $150, the Howards owed $10 for "matriculations," $63 for a dorm room, $125 for food, $1 for a key deposit, and a radio fee of $1.35. Young Betty apologized for the huge bill. As she told her mother, "I nearly fainted when I saw it."[48]

Most fundamentalist schools—four-year colleges and Bible institutes alike—assumed that their students would participate in all sorts of athletic competitions. In 1937, Wheaton inaugurated an athletic program, hoping to keep up with trends in mainstream higher education.[49] For Betty Howard, at least, it worked. By the time she arrived on Wheaton's campus in 1944, the athletic program had become more proof that Wheaton fit in with the non-academic traditions of American higher education. As she got ready to cheer for her school against a local rival, North Central College in nearby Naperville, Illinois, she explained to her mother the importance of the big game. "You see," Betty wrote, "Wheaton is to N.C. what Army is to Navy, or Harvard to Yale."[50]

The nearby fundamentalists at Moody Bible Institute soon glowered at the relative athletic successes of their Wheaton rivals. In 1945, one MBI student lamented that their teams should be able to put on a better showing on the basketball court. After all, he wrote, MBI had at least three hundred men to recruit from, as well as a good practice court and even "a regularly hired athletic coach." Yet despite such appurtenances, the MBI "A" team still lost to the Wheaton "Bs."[51]

In its first years, Bob Jones College also fielded intercollegiate teams, the Swamp Angels. In 1933, however, Bob Jones Sr. eliminated all non-intramural athletic programs.[52] Many years later, Bob Jones Jr. remembered that his father had worried about the lifestyle dangers posed by traveling sports teams. In the 1920s, the younger Jones recalled, "we found the people were betting on our games, littering our campus with whiskey bottles."[53]

In other aspects of campus life, too, Bob Jones College stood out. Whereas most fundamentalist schools banned student productions of plays and musical theater, Bob Jones College encouraged them. By the 1940s, the Bob Jones College theater program was drawing ferocious criticism from the wider world of fundamentalist higher education. In 1949, for example, former Wheaton president J. Oliver Buswell, now leading New York's National Bible Institute, published a scathing indictment of the Bob Jones program. "Your own educational program," Buswell accused Bob Jones Sr., "is reeking with theatricals and grand opera, which lead young people . . . into a worldly life of sin."[54]

Again and again, the Bob Joneses fielded similar accusations that their drama program did not fit into fundamentalism.[55] As usual, when challenged, Bob Jones Sr. and Jr. insisted all the more strongly on having their way. In 1955, one student's parents complained about the mandatory drama program. Bob Jones Sr. told them in no uncertain terms that if the student remained, he would have to participate. "On Bob Jones University campus," Jones explained,

> life is not divided into the secular and the sacred. The Shakespearean programs open with prayer and close with prayer just like any other programs. We are not training people for the stage. We are training them for Christian work, and this is part of the training.[56]

And though almost all other fundamentalist schools disagreed, the Bob Joneses maintained their idiosyncratic rules in spite of all complaints.

At most schools students could not participate in dramatic plays the way Bob Jones University students did, but they were allowed, and even expected, to engage in some forms of mildly wacky behavior. At Wheaton, for example, students in the 1920s snuck a cow into the bedroom of one of their favorite professors.[57] Years later at Moody Bible Institute, students reported with glee that one popular student had had a full bucket of ice water dumped on him while he was napping.[58] In 1947, at Gordon College at least, administrators were likely to wink at some violations of the rules. At the fall reception that year, many students stayed out past their twelve-thirty curfew. They were punished, to be sure, by losing all their remaining curfew exceptions, but their chastisement was done more in a spirit of humorous indulgence than as serious scolding.[59]

In most cases, students at fundamentalist schools engaged in an unscripted back-and-forth with administrators and rulebooks. Even at fundamentalist Bible institutes, students were expected to have some fun during their studies. School leaders seemed to understand that building school spirit often included the occasional tweaking of the rules and even mockery of school leaders. Yet administrators looked askance at the possibilities of students going too far off the rails. At Moody Bible Institute in 1947, for example, buttoned-down President William Culbertson warned students that some had recently crossed the line. "We are not against wholesome fun," Culbertson intoned during a chapel talk. "We are not even averse to playful and good-natured quips and actions being perpetrated against ourselves, so long as they are within bounds." A recent episode in which the president of the senior class was locked in a closet, however, was not within those bounds. For this prank, one student was expelled summarily and six others were punished.[60]

When it came to student behavior and misbehavior, fundamentalist schools found themselves caught in a higher-education trap. On one hand, every fundamentalist college from the 1920s to the 1950s insisted on rigid and sternly enforced lifestyle rules as an inherent part of proper fundamentalist education. Fundamentalists in that era understood themselves to be something different from mainstream Americans. While other youth flamed or rocked around the clock, fundamentalist youth were meant to take a different path. The fundamentalist credibility of any school relied on its ability to squash behavior that fundamentalists saw as loose, secular, and immoral. On the other hand, fundamentalist families expected that their colleges would be real colleges in every aspect. And, as historian Helen Lefkowitz Horowitz has argued, by the 1920s some sorts of student hijinks had come to be expected as part of any college experience.[61] Like President Culbertson in 1947, fundamentalist school students, faculty, and administrators walked a fine line in their efforts to satisfy contradictory implicit expectations of the expected behavior of fundamentalists who were also college students.

## In Loco Parentis

As historian Christopher Loss has pointed out, fundamentalist colleges were not alone in their struggles to find a pragmatic balance between administrative control and student misbehavior. In many cases, during the 1920s mainstream schools created or tightened *in loco parentis* rules in an attempt to handle their increasing responsibility for students' entire college lives.[62] At fundamentalist colleges, even the thickest student handbooks could not handle every possible question about proper student behavior, and leaders often struggled to give case-by-case rulings. In each new generation, new issues came up that required decisions. For instance, in 1950 administrators at Moody Bible Institute wrestled with a new challenge from the ever-changing world of non-fundamentalist popular culture. Was it legitimate, students asked, for young fundamentalists to go watch roller derby? Students suggested that it should be treated like other sorts of athletic competition—well within the boundaries of acceptable fundamentalist socializing. The school's leaders disagreed. Roller derby, the administration decided, tweaked customary gender rules too much. With its aggressive female stars and its celebratory mix of violence and lewdness, a committee decided, "the practices, spirit, and appeal of the Roller Derby are contrary to Christian principles."[63]

If the proper rules for students at fundamentalist schools could never be set down once and for all, it was not for lack of trying. Colleges, universities, and Bible institutes offered students and the wider fundamentalist community thick rulebooks to guide their behavior. The *Gordon Handbook* in the mid-1940s gave students both general guidelines and specific rules. In general, students were enjoined to act in ways such that they did not bring "the name of Christ they serve into disrepute." Naturally, the handbook explained, rules at a fundamentalist college would be different from those of "secular colleges." It was their rule, students were informed, "that all of our activities, even our purely social events, should be of such a nature that we would be happy to invite the presence of the Lord Jesus Christ there at any time."[64]

This mid-1940s Gordon rulebook also spelled out the usual list of fundamentalist prohibitions. Students were not allowed to drink, smoke, or swear. They were not allowed to go to theatrical or cinematic productions, at least not worldly ones. The leaders of Gordon had had some difficulty deciding on a precise dividing line between acceptable and unacceptable films, and the dense prose of their 1940s student handbook showed it. As they told students, certain films might be acceptable, but it was not okay for students to attend

> public entertainments that are prepared and presented in an atmosphere of worldliness and sins, and by men and women who do not have the interests of the Kingdom at heart and who in general fail to manifest its principles in their lives.[65]

Clearly, rules like these left plenty of wiggle room for interpretation and dispute. Who could say if a certain film was prepared in the proper atmosphere? Who could rule on whether or not the actors had Christian ideas in mind?

In their personal appearance, too, wartime Gordon students were required to maintain a respectable appearance, as befit their roles as "ambassadors of Christ." For women, that meant modesty in dress, jewelry, and makeup.[66] As with all these rules, Gordon's administrators stressed that the big picture of Christian missionary outreach must be kept in mind. With stakes so high, the handbook reminded students, the school retained every right to kick out any student who seemed to be reluctant to take the spirit of the rules to heart.[67]

Similarly, the history of the student "pledge" at Wheaton shows how difficult it was for school leaders to maintain rules that were both clear and sensible. In its first incarnation, students in 1925 were encouraged to abstain from tobacco, cards, dancing, and theaters. The next year, school leaders toughened the language to be sure students knew they were "expected to abstain" from such things. In 1930, the Wheaton pledge added a specific ban on alcohol. As applications boomed in the 1930s, the school insisted that all applicants sign a copy of this pledge, to be sure that every potential new student understood the expectations of the school. In the 1950s, the pledge evolved to encourage students to maintain the spirit of this pledge when it came to selecting television programs to watch.[68]

Between the 1920s and the 1950s, fundamentalist colleges did not hesitate to punish students who violated these rules. Often, administrators reacted most harshly to those students who seemed to dispute the propriety of the rules themselves, resulting in punishments that sometimes felt lopsided. Students caught drinking alcohol or playing cards, for instance, might be allowed to apologize and offer sincere pledges of repentance and reformation. Students who seemed to kick against the fundamentalist spirit of the rules themselves, however, were usually expelled, even if they had not broken any specific rules.

At Bob Jones University, administrators took pride in their willingness to get rid of problem students. As Bob Jones Sr. recalled, in only the second year of the school he decided to expel nearly a quarter of the total student body. It was not an easy decision, he explained to an alumnus, but it was the right one. "The reason we do not have the problems they have in other schools," Jones wrote, "is because we put on tremendous evangelistic emphasis and have strict discipline." Breaking the stringent lifestyle rules at Bob Jones University often meant a one-way ticket home.[69]

For fundamentalist school administrators, the stakes were high. If the wider fundamentalist community—along with other conservative Protestants who often sent their youth to fundamentalist schools—felt that a certain college or institute was not strict enough, they might decide to send their students and their tuition dollars elsewhere. In the mid-1940s, the editors of the popular fundamentalist magazine *Sunday School*

*Times* conducted a mini-inquisition into the rules at colleges. Did a given college permit students to attend movies? To smoke? Drink? Play cards?[70] Gordon's president at the time, T. Leonard Lewis, made it clear to the publication's editors that his school allowed no such things. After all, Lewis concluded, "we are not simply a Christian liberal arts college and seminary."[71] To Lewis, at least, and to the satisfied editors of the *Sunday School Times*, proper fundamentalist higher education was meant to be something more than simply college in a Christian environment.[72] The lives of students were meant to be shaped by more than just doctrine. Students were expected to conform to strict but imprecise behavior patterns as well as strict but imprecise doctrinal beliefs.

At Biola in the 1950s, too, President Samuel Sutherland found himself besieged by inquisitions and complaints from the fundamentalist community. When a student article in the *Chimes* implied that Biola students often attended secular entertainments such as "light opera, the Russian Dance Company, or even the Ice Capades," Sutherland complained, he heard about it.[73] One angry letter, from "A Grieved Donor of a Quarter of a Century," informed Sutherland that a recent *Chimes* article had caused him or her to throw the paper angrily in the trash. "Are we to gage the spiritual depth of the Bible Institute," the angry former donor asked, "by the articles in these student papers?"[74]

President Sutherland warned the *Chimes* editor that she must keep the big fundamentalist picture in mind when she decided on the content of the paper. Biola, Sutherland told her, needed to be something different, something better than mainstream colleges. As he put it, "in our effort to become 'collegiate,' we have gone clear beyond the bounds of BIOLA's standards and emphasis. We must be careful not to confuse the term 'collegiate' with popular worldly standards."[75] Like President Lewis at Gordon and other school leaders nationwide, Sutherland worried that it was too easy for fundamentalist colleges to forget their fundamentalist roots as they strove to conform to hardening expectations about college life.

## *Kicking Against the Pricks*

Understandably, many students resented the intrusive rules. One Wheaton student in the 1920s later remembered that most students would "sort of gripe" because "the control was rather tight."[76] Much of the time—from the 1920s to the 1950s, at least—student complaints were strident but phrased politely in the language used by fundamentalist school leaders themselves. In 1946, for example, a student at Moody Bible Institute argued in the pages of the student paper that male and female students should be allowed, "even encouraged," to eat together in the dining room. It would be more pleasant and fun, true, but this student reasoned that the real goal of such integration would be to improve students' ability to evangelize in the jumbled world beyond the institute's walls. How could they practice their skills of talking to diverse groups, he asked, if they had no practice?[77]

Many students were most upset by the inconsistencies that seemed an inherent part of student lifestyle rules. Rulebooks that gave administrators wide latitude to decide if behavior was done with the proper attitude also gave administrators power to act in arbitrary and unpredictable ways. At Wheaton in the early 1950s, for instance, students asked why the sophomore class could screen the movie *Bambi* on campus, yet students could not attend movies of their own choosing.[78] The rules might seem "arbitrary," President V. Raymond Edman told the Wheaton community, but they were part of the same "great underlying purpose." The school hoped to encourage the good and discourage the bad. Although no rules could "guarantee spirituality," Edman conceded, a strict set of rules helped young people figure out the proper goals for their own behavior.[79]

It was not only students who worried about the rules. Thoughtful fundamentalist leaders noticed that fundamentalism in practice had come to be understood as a simplistic code of banned behavior. As one frustrated fundamentalist businessman put it in 1960, the strict rules in fundamentalist institutions of higher education had come to make fundamentalism seem like only a ban on the "big five." That is, students were taught too often that they could be good Christians by not smoking, not drinking, not dancing, not playing cards, and not attending movies. The positive theological depths of true fundamentalism, he complained, had been lost in the shuffle.[80]

Not all students, however, disliked the rules. According to Bob Jones Sr., when he kicked out students for misbehavior in the first years of the school, the remainder of the student body cheered.[81] At Wheaton in the 1930s, too, students remembered that many of their fellows seemed to embrace the rules. At chapel services, for example, students often voluntarily confessed their rule violations.[82] One student who arrived on Wheaton's campus in 1938 thought that all students, like him, appreciated the "Christian atmosphere." Along with many of his peers, this Wheaton student appreciated the fact that strict rules guided his behavior.[83] That same year, a student opined in the pages of the Biola *Chimes* that the rules might not make Biola "easy, or pleasant, as the world and flesh see it." However, once students understood the purpose and effectiveness of strict rules, he wrote, they would "ever rejoice at the privilege . . . knowing that every lesson is given only to make you fit instruments for His use."[84]

Perhaps not surprisingly, many student rule-breakers were not just misbehaving. For some earnest students, their behavior represented religious dissent, not merely hedonistic excess. The most unusual case involved student Ralph Parce at Moody Bible Institute. In 1934, Parce admitted that he was a socialist. But to the consternation of the MBI community, Parce insisted that there was no conflict between his political beliefs and the doctrinal platform of the Bible institute.[85] Parce's evangelical socialism put the MBI administration in a pickle. On one hand, faculty leaders were concerned that harboring an openly socialist student would wreck MBI's carefully built reputation as a citadel of unyielding fundamentalism. On the other hand, teachers worried about establishing a precedent for vetting students merely on the basis of their political beliefs. In the end, the faculty voted to let Parce remain, but only with a razor-thin one-vote majority.[86]

As the faculty had predicted, anti-communists howled. Celebrity Red-hunter Elizabeth Dilling was outraged at the school's decision. No one, she warned President James M. Gray, could be both a socialist and an earnest Christian. In her fury, Dilling conducted some personal investigations on the MBI campus and found that Parce was not only a socialist but also a chain smoker.[87] Parce himself was willing to give up his membership in the Socialist Party of Wisconsin, but he found he could not give up smoking.[88] By the end of the decade, a new faculty committee interviewed Parce and found him still committed to both socialist ideas and smoking. For both reasons, they decided not to allow him to reenroll.[89]

Parce was unusual among fundamentalist students in his commitment to socialism, but not unusual in his principled dissent from school rules. More commonly, students found themselves enamored of non-fundamentalist ideas from the kaleidoscopic world of Christianity itself. For example, while Moody Bible Institute wondered what to do with its evangelical socialist, it also clamped down on student interest in the preaching of the Reverend J. C. O'Hair. O'Hair was the pastor of the nearby North Shore Congregational Church in Chicago. He had reached out to some MBI students, welcoming them to his services and giving them books and promotional materials to share with their fellow students. Among other controversial topics, O'Hair preached to MBI's fundamentalist students that they must not engage in water baptism and that the Christian church did not begin until the time of chapter thirteen of the Book of Acts.[90] Students caught propagating O'Hair's ideas on campus were forced to surrender all his books and promise not to "converse nor cause any controversy or doubt in anyone's mind by talking on these subjects" in the future.[91]

At Wheaton College, too, students often broke theological boundaries. In 1949, for example, one of the student clubs invited Professor Lewis Irwin from the nearby University of Chicago to speak on campus. His talk, "Why I Do Not Believe the Bible Is Verbally Inspired by God," sparked predictable outrage among conservative trustees. In his own defense, the student leader who had issued the invitation, Charles B. Bass, told President Edman that his group was not hoping to flout fundamentalism. On the contrary, Bass insisted that he and his fellow students hoped only to flesh out true fundamentalist education by learning the best arguments of "liberal teachers in seminaries and graduate schools." Bass and his fellows wanted to strengthen their faith, he told Edman, by hearing firsthand this "subtle teaching" and learning how to answer it.[92]

Trustee David Otis Fuller was not impressed by such arguments. Speakers such as Irwin were "a gross violation of the principles for which Wheaton stands," Fuller told Edman in an angry letter. Nor was Lewis's talk an isolated event. Students had also welcomed a group of Catholic nuns to give a talk recently. This sort of "inclusive, compromising policy," Fuller warned, was "clearly destructive of every foundation principle for which Wheaton has stood."[93]

In spite of Fuller's emphatic protests, such religious dissent remained strong on Wheaton's campus into the early 1950s and beyond. One student who arrived in 1953 found himself falling in with a famously contrarian prayer group. His small band, led by "our campus radical" Richard Shrout, became known and apparently grudgingly tolerated in spite of its proud reputation as "spiritually radical."[94]

Religious dissent took on a lonelier and more idiosyncratic form for some fundamentalist students. At the same time that Richard Shrout led Wheaton students in radically Protestant directions, a student at Gordon College mounted a different sort of spiritual protest. Samuel Hart frustrated both school administrators and his parents by his earnest devotion to his own vision of religious purity. Young Samuel refused to sit for his exams. He refused to complete his school assignments. And in spite of his father's repeated efforts to find Samuel a paying job, he refused to work for mere money. Instead, Samuel spent all his time and efforts exclusively in street-corner evangelism in nearby Boston. Samuel was "so sure that the Lord is coming within the next four years," Gordon president Leonard Lewis noted, that he scorned all efforts to get him to be "regular in his work."[95]

Such fundamentalist dissent, however, was a relatively rare problem for fundamentalist school administrators. Much more commonly, students broke school rules for decidedly different reasons. At Wheaton, for example, one student remembered a group of fellow students who kept a barrel of liquor in the attic of their boardinghouse. At raucous parties, women moved unsupervised from room to room. "It was as bad," the student remembered, "as anything in a fraternity at a state university."[96] Within the strict confines of Bob Jones University, too, students perennially broke the most basic rules. As dean of men William Liverman remembered, from the early 1950s through the early 1980s the school always had problems with student theft. At times, Liverman recalled, he felt as if he were running a detective agency, marking money with dye, extracting confessions, and dealing with a student body that suffered from "serious weaknesses."[97]

The disciplinary folders of fundamentalist schools were overstuffed with a litany of run-of-the-mill student misbehaviors. At Moody Bible Institute in 1932, for example, one student was caught in a "recent delinquency." He had been keeping the wrong company and taking money from his parents for tuition but not paying the school. He frequented "shows, pool halls, etc."[98] His father was heartbroken. "I have did every thing in my power," the father wrote to MBI, "to bring him up a Christian boy but now I only see failure."[99] The MBI's leaders sympathized, but they still expelled the student and demanded full payment of arrears.[100]

The administrators at MBI expelled students for a dizzying array of mundane transgressions. One student was expelled in 1932 for skipping chapel and lying about it.[101] Another was tossed out for smoking and lying.[102] One was forced to leave for cheating on exams,[103] and another for drinking and having an "untidy room."[104] Students were expelled for unspecified outbursts of "moral delinquency"[105] or for the "wrong attitude."[106]

In some cases, MBI administrators went to astonishing lengths to root out student misconduct. In the mid-1930s, MBI supervisor James W. Davis was not merely willing to hear accusations against student Benjamin Kolton. Instead, Davis hit the streets in search of confirmation. Had Kolton really passed bad checks? Had he really engaged in a lifestyle of drinking and gambling? Davis accompanied Kolton to a saloon, where the bartender greeted Kolton with a friendly "Hello, Bennie, what are you doing around here?" Davis was understandably suspicious after that, but he found to his frustration that none of the "underworld" types he confronted was willing to squeal on Kolton. When Davis accosted one Harry Sherman, owner of a "cabaret," about Kolton's moral deficiency, Sherman "professed sudden disinterest in the case" and refused to speak further with Davis. Without solid evidence, and despite the fact that Kolton often smelled of alcohol and tobacco, MBI kept him on. In the end, Kolton went on to a spotty career as a missionary, eventually accused of misappropriating mission funds.[107]

Even given MBI's extraordinary dedication to rooting out all student misbehavior, their earnest administrators apparently only captured a fraction of the whole. One student in 1931 confessed that he had cheated in every examination throughout his first years at MBI. He had never been caught or even accused, but unlike the brash and brazen Benjamin Kolton, this "conscience stricken" student begged to have all his class credits taken away.[108]

Along with all the cheating, lying, drinking, stealing, smoking, and theater attending, students at fundamentalist institutions of higher education consistently sought to evade the strict rules on sex and courtship. As one frustrated administrator wrote of a female student at Moody Bible Institute in 1938, in spite of repeated efforts at counseling, confession, and redemption, the student eventually had to be kicked out. As the administrator put it, in spite of her own best efforts and those of the MBI staff, this student just "could not let boys alone."[109] She was not the only one. Wheaton College found itself pressed to hire guards to keep women students from sneaking out of their rooms at night for romantic assignations.[110] Clearly, not every student at Wheaton or at any of the fundamentalist institutions embraced the fundamentalist ethos of courtship the way Betty Howard did. For many of them, just as for many students at non-fundamentalist schools, their schools' insistence on chastity outside of traditional marriage simply did not match their own vision of proper college life.

## *Forbidden Fruit*

Fundamentalist schools were not alone in enforcing strict rules about dating and sexuality. As late as 1962, for instance, the University of Michigan had long and precise rules about curfews and sexual behaviors. Just as fundamentalist schools did, Michigan administrators listed detailed penalties for violations.[111]

Similarly, just as at non-fundamentalist universities, fundamentalist institutions grappled with a wider range of sex-related questions than simply those of dating and courtship. In the first half of the twentieth century, fundamentalist leaders struggled to define proper gender roles as a whole. Since its inception in the 1920s, fundamentalism had always seen itself as the hard edge of traditional cultural attitudes about gender and family structure as well as sexuality.[112] Yet even within those insistently traditional roles, women found wiggle room in fundamentalist institutions, as they did in non-fundamentalist ones. As historian Margaret Bendroth has argued, in the 1920s, 1930s, and early 1940s, many fundamentalist women assumed leadership roles in the very same organizations that fought for traditional gender hierarchies.[113] It was not at all unusual for women to assert control of fundamentalist outreach efforts based explicitly on their status as women. At Biola, for example, in the first decade of the twentieth century the president's wife led a group of "Bible Women" in neighborhood evangelism. They took responsibility for teaching young children the Gospel, for helping sick women keep their homes tidy, and for making and distributing clothing to indigent Angelenos.[114] For fundamentalists as much as for other Americans, such nurturing roles were considered the proper sphere of women's leadership and influence.

Fundamentalist colleges, too, sometimes showed little desire to restrict women from influential teaching positions. In 1929, for instance, nearly half of Wheaton's faculty were women. By 1955, that number had dropped to a third, but Wheaton still found itself squarely in the middle of all private liberal arts colleges when it came to numbers of women faculty.[115] At Wheaton, at least, the relative decline in women faculty members was not part of a conscious effort to reduce the number of women professors. Rather, like many other fundamentalist institutions, Wheaton likely mirrored trends in the wider culture. After World War II, speaking broadly, fundamentalists participated in a widespread tendency to put more emphasis on male-dominated gender hierarchies and on the proper role of women as homebound mothers.[116]

Even before the war, however, fundamentalist schools were intensely gender-segregated institutions. Among faculty and students, schools insisted on different rules and standards for men and women. Sometimes these rules were official, but often they took the form of implicit, unquestioned assumptions about the proper roles of women and men. In practice, for example, it could be more difficult for qualified female students to get admitted. At Wheaton College, women applicants needed better academic records than did men, because the school had a policy of keeping each class balanced between men and women. Because so many more women applied, they found themselves at a decided disadvantage.[117]

Potential women faculty members, too, could face higher hurdles. In 1937, for example, a Gordon College official told one highly qualified applicant for a teaching position that the school was hiring only men. The applicant had a stellar academic record. Her evangelical credentials were impeccable—a Wheaton alumna with a solid record of excellent teaching and Gospel service. It was not enough. "Some of the trustees," the Gordon official informed the applicant, "feel strongly that we have too many women on our staff already."[118]

Every school imposed a longer list of rules on female students. In the early years of Bob Jones College, the evangelist-founder apparently assumed that women naturally required such rules. He assumed, further, that women would share his patronizing assumptions about the petty nature of feminine vanity. At his school, women students were required to wear only "simple dresses," and those dresses must reach at least two inches below the knee. Most important, Bob Jones warned potential students, they must understand that women were never allowed to share clothes. It seems Jones worried that inevitable feminine squabbles over clothes would lead to dissension among the student body. Even with all these restrictions, however, Jones gave potential applicants the assurance he assumed they required: BJC students, he told them, had "the reputation of being the most attractive group of girls in the country."[119]

Indeed, many fundamentalist school leaders worried mainly that their "girls" were far too attractive. In spite of its location near the sunny beaches of Southern California, the leaders of Biola tried to keep their students from visiting the shore. Once students left campus, President Sutherland worried, it became too difficult for administrators to control potential sexual threats. All his attempts to keep groups of male and female students separated at the beaches had not worked. Even when he could keep men and women students separate, beach visits could expose students to sexual risks. At those beaches, Sutherland explained, some women, non-students "who frequented the beaches for their own purposes," acted in decidedly non-fundamentalist ways by "actually ma[king] advances to the fellows." Women students, too, found themselves the targets of "strange young men" at the beach. The solution, Sutherland thought, was to keep "our

Christian young people . . . intact as a group." That way, the school could make sure that they had only opportunities for "more normal association with each other."[120]

It was not just school leaders who imposed strict segregation of male and female students. Students, too, often enforced gender norms with one another. Male freshmen who broke the complicated new-student traditions at Wheaton in the early 1940s, for example, found themselves forced to wear lipstick and curlers. And one fellow, the "college comedian," was able to bring down the house by dressing as a girl at a pep rally and flinging flowers up into the grandstands.[121] Women students also entertained their peers by inverting gender assumptions. At one pep rally, Betty Howard remembered, "some girls put on a mock football game." Wheaton students did not need the joke explained to them, nor did they wonder about the strictures of fundamentalist gender ideology. Instead, "kids simply howled."[122]

Gender rules were not only for fun, however. Betty Howard, at least, took her role as a fundamentalist woman very seriously. She agreed with her grandmother that women must respect their "highest calling." For Betty as much as for her grandmother, it was nothing short of "tragic" for young women to slip into "all this career business nowadays." Far better to remember women's proper and exalted role in "making a home."[123]

Not every student was as earnest as young Betty Howard, and all fundamentalist schools made extensive efforts to guide and police student courtship. As historian Beth Bailey has argued, beginning in the 1920s new trends in courtship among mainstream Americans "removed couples from the implied supervision of the private sphere . . . to the anonymity of the public sphere."[124] Instead of courting in the family parlor, twentieth-century couples tended to date at movie palaces, dance halls, and restaurants. Among the non-fundamentalist mainstream, Bailey argued, courtship moved out the range of family and community supervision. Fundamentalist colleges promised to move it back.

In the 1920s at Moody Bible Institute, for example, male students who found themselves attracted to female students had a few steps to follow. First they asked the girl for a date, never the other way around. Then the women students would ask their "lady supervisor" for permission. If the supervisor approved, the date could go ahead.[125]

Bob Jones College took this sort of romantic supervision one step further. In the 1920s, every student was required to attend school dances and every student was required to secure a date. Those unlucky few who couldn't find a partner would have a date assigned to them by school administrators. As one student remembered, at times those school-selected dates "blossomed into romances."[126] Even when and if they did so, however, young people at Bob Jones College were not allowed to express their romantic feelings physically. At official school dances students were never allowed to touch.[127] Nevertheless, the chance of meeting a reliably fundamentalist future spouse was promoted as one of the central attractions of the new fundamentalist college. As Bob Jones Sr. promised one prospective student, at his new school students could be confident they would have only "fine Christian boys and girls for associates."[128]

At Bob Jones College as at other fundamentalist schools, leaders and students often put as much emphasis on the "fine" as on the "Christian." The goal of the BJC approach in the early years, as Bob Jones Sr.'s wife, Mary Gaston Stollenwerck Jones, explained later, was not just to protect young people from worldly trends and liberal theology. Many of the college's students, she recalled, had come recently from "rural" backgrounds and had no idea how to behave in more refined settings. Taking them to dances at "a hotel with elevators and all that," Mrs. Jones believed, was an important part of their fundamentalist education, an important way to show them and the wider American populace that fundamentalism was a high-class affair.[129]

At Moody Bible Institute, too, part of the rigid insistence on proper courtship resulted from administrators' assumptions that many students had not had the benefits of a middle-class upbringing. As one student in the 1920s remembered, "A lot of chaps . . . were raw farm boys." They had no conception of middle-class norms of courtship and dating. For those reasons alone, it was "very, very wise" for the school to impose rigid restrictions on courtship, this student believed. After all, a student from a lower-income background might be fully dedicated to fundamentalist theology while having absolutely no clue about "etiquette and that kind of thing." Left to their own devices, such students would revert to their disreputable working-class courtship traditions. "It was easy," the student later explained, "for some of those fellows to go too far."[130] In his opinion, at least, strict courtship rules served to socialize fundamentalists into the vanishing middle-class world of parlors and chaperones.

In the late 1940s, Moody Bible Institute president William Culbertson relied at least as much on class snobbishness as on fundamentalist theology to make his case for rigid sexual self-restraint among students. He reminded students of two rules for such self-restraint. First, students should be "continually aware" of their duty as Christians to set an example to each other and to non-Christians. Just as important, when it came to the "conduct of couples," Culbertson insisted that students must follow standards "that are accepted by people of good taste."[131] The official rules at Moody Bible Institute had long reinforced Culbertson's desire for middle-class norms. The student handbook during the late 1930s, for example, warned students that they must "deport themselves at all times as behooves a Christian gentleman or Christian gentlewoman."[132]

As the twentieth century progressed, fundamentalist schools doubled down on their strict rules for guiding and controlling student love. In the eyes of some sympathetic fundamentalists, at least, those efforts seemed to work. In 1945, John R. Rice celebrated the strict environment when he visited the campus of Bob Jones College. "I felt like thanking God," Rice gushed in his popular fundamentalist newspaper *Sword of the Lord*, "that young love could blossom in a Christian environment without the tawdry license and necking and looseness so customary among worldly young people."[133]

Such hothouse flowers required a huge amount of supervision and care. Into the 1930s and 1940s, fundamentalist schools not only maintained but also tightened their strict rules for courtship and social interaction. At Moody Bible Institute, for example, the student handbook in the late 1930s offered detailed rules for proper mixing with the opposite sex. Men and women students, the handbook warned, would inevitably come into contact with one another. It was vital for all students "to exercise care so to conduct themselves as to indicate that their primary purpose in being a student is train for Christian service."[134] First-term students at MBI needed special permission in order to "visit" with students of the opposite sex. All other students were free to mingle on Sunday afternoon until three-thirty, as well as on Monday afternoon and on Monday evening until ten. All students, other than first-termers, could also accompany each other to church on Sunday evenings. If things got serious and a couple wanted to spend more time together, they could seek permission for "special social hours" from their superintendents.[135]

At MBI and most other Bible institutes, though, even such specially permitted courtship was expected only to go so far. Because all students at Bible institutes were supposed to be preparing from some form of Christian work, they were often not allowed to get married or even engaged without additional formal permission. In the 1930s, for example, Moody Bible Institute kicked out several students who had surreptitiously gotten married or engaged without leave from the school.[136] In the 1940s, too, Gordon College reflected its roots as a missionary training school by insisting that students could get engaged only with special permission.[137]

In the late 1940s, MBI administrators added additional rules in an apparent effort to eliminate some loopholes exploited by libidinous MBI students. Henceforth, the new rules stated, students would no longer be able to hold hands in public. Nor could couples linger together at the entrances to the gender-segregated dining room before meals. Most important, male students would be required to produce a formal letter of invitation before staying at "a home other than his own in which his young woman friend is living or staying." Too many students, it seems, had figured out that they could find sympathetic third parties to host couples at off-campus houses.[138]

Similarly, at post–World War II Biola, administrators decided on new and stricter rules for couples. From 1948 on, no students could hold hands or demonstrate any sort of romantic affection. This was true even of married couples. The administrators reasoned that observers would not be able to tell immediately if couples were married. To avoid any potential confusion, all hand-holding was simply banned.[139]

Some students embraced these rules and appreciated their schools' efforts to connect them with suitable mates. Future Bob Jones University administrator William Liverman, for instance, was able to meet his future wife only due to the matchmaking efforts of the school administration. As a student in 1948, Liverman and the other BJU students received new seating assignments at meals every three weeks, in an effort to help students mingle in the tightly controlled atmosphere. For Liverman, it worked. At one new dining table, he found himself placed next to the woman who would become his wife. Nor did the earnest young William Liverman let the school's strict rules get in the way of courting her. He may not have had many opportunities to take her on unsupervised dates—as many non-fundamentalist young people were doing in 1948—but the world of fundamentalism gave him different chances to woo her. Once the school helped him find a girl he liked, he finagled an invitation to preach at her church and wowed her with his polished, heartfelt sermon.[140]

Certainly there was no lack of enthusiasm among students for courtship. In addition to official school rules and social functions, students developed their own traditions. In the first years of Bob Jones College, for example, students found ways to bend the strict rules against male-female interactions. As one student later recalled, every student eagerly rushed to the campus post office for the mail call—not because they were eager to receive letters or packages but because, as she remembered,

> it was a legitimate way to break the "no loitering" rule on campus and to converse with people of the opposite sex without being given demerits . . . . In truth, we girls were looking for some special *male* that we hoped would be there.[141]

For this student, the "male-call" tradition worked. She first caught a glimpse of her future husband as they both conspicuously didn't loiter outside the post office.[142]

Indeed, for many students, all other aspects of higher education paled in the face of the race for the best marriage partners. In Betty Howard's opinion, at least, several women leaped too hastily into engagements. And they symbolized those engagements in the same way as non-fundamentalist Americans at the time, with a diamond engagement ring. As Betty told her parents:

> One of the kids in the dorm got her diamond last night. She went caroling with her man and of course came home sparkling in more ways than one. She is only a soph and seems so young![143]

At Wheaton and many other schools, though, students developed their own traditions to announce their romantic status to the public. Students might date at official events such as caroling and group trips to local restaurants. They could attend sporting events without raising eyebrows. Going to chapel together, however, served as an acknowledged symbol that they were engaged to be married.[144]

Students also developed their own methods to figure out which courtship rules were serious and which might be winked at. At Biola, for example, the student newspaper in the late 1930s ran a gossipy regular feature called "The Gong." Week after week, "The Gong" gently satirized the dating patterns of the Biola community. Someone, apparently, had been secretly sending roses to a popular student. Everyone wanted to figure out the mystery. And another student won praise, not censure, for his mildly aggressive sexual jokes. As "The Gong" related, the jokester stood agog as he watched a "general exodus of fair young ladies from the elevator." He turned to his friend and asked, "If we stand here do we get our pick?" At the time, the stakes were fairly high. As students were well aware, Biola administrators could and did kick students out for holding hands on campus.[145] What else might be punished severely? Were students permitted to send roses? Was it acceptable to make jokes about girls coming out of an elevator? Students can be forgiven for feeling some tension about these gray areas in the world of fundamentalist courtship and sexuality. By poking fun at the ways Biola students were fascinated with courtship and the opposite sex, the student newspaper helped the community figure out what sexual and romantic behavior would be considered acceptable and what would not.[146]

Just as at any school, at fundamentalist institutions of higher education some students wholeheartedly embraced the school's rules, while others concocted plans to evade them. Still others—perhaps a large majority—muddled along, following the rules with varying degrees of resentment or enthusiasm. When it came to love, sex, and courtship, all the schools had some students who struggled to understand and define what it should mean to fall in love and get married for fundamentalist and evangelical men and women. What should young women do to attract men? What should they not do? What sexual feelings were properly Christian and which were merely carnal? How could young people sort through their feelings of attraction to discern the will of God in their romantic lives?

As we've seen, during her student days at Wheaton College Betty Howard gave serious thought to all these questions, for herself and for her fellow students. Of course, during those years, no one could have known that she would go on to a remarkable career as a writer on the meanings of evangelical love. After she left Wheaton, she followed her future husband, Jim Elliot, to Ecuador to work as a missionary. Once there, the two were married. Only a few years later, Jim Elliot was killed by suspicious locals.[147] Elisabeth Elliot went on to a long career as a missionary and author, eventually writing several books about evangelical gender roles and romantic love, including *Let Me Be a Woman* (1976), *Passion and Purity* (1984), and *Quest for Love* (1996).

As a student in the 1940s, she was already groping toward the ideas that would define her later career. When she first met her future husband, Jim, she felt attracted to him in a novel sort of way. She had had plenty of dates in her years at Wheaton, and she had liked plenty of men. But her feelings for Jim were different. Initially, Betty was attracted to him as someone who "knows the Lord in an unusual way." As she wrote to her parents, she "really enjoyed" being with him, because he was so connected and accomplished spiritually.[148]

Unlike with her earlier suitors, Betty found that Jim helped her deepen her relationship with Christ. When the two of them spent time together, she wrote in the summer of 1948, she could feel Christ's presence more profoundly, more directly. "How He sustained and gave us His strong hand," Betty wrote, "we alone can understand." The feelings of love and affection she felt for Jim, Betty explained, were utterly beyond anything merely carnal. Their connection was not direct but rather was mediated through Christ. As a result, Betty and Jim were able to connect on a much higher plane. As she struggled to explain to her mother, "What passed between us during those last moments was not in words . . . . The interflow of spirit was as a triangle, with Christ at the apex."[149]

Nor was theirs just an evangelical summer fling. As the fall of 1948 rolled around, Betty was still utterly enraptured by the new sort of love she shared with Jim. As she told her mother in September, "What else can I write than of Jim?" He seemed to be far more than merely physically attractive, far more than merely clever or fashionable. The more time she spent with Jim, Betty wrote, "the more awed I stand at the vast reaches of his soul." She worried that her own Christian devotion might not be able to keep up with Jim's spiritual attainment. She felt, she fretted, like nothing but a "clogged channel" for the divine. Her love for Jim helped her clear that channel, just as it helped her focus her desires on becoming closer to God. Her only wish: "O to be holy!"[150]

Jim and Betty did not create their notions of proper evangelical love on their own. Both of them found friends at school who shared their desire to define some sort of properly evangelical romantic love. One of their school friends shared his dream of finding a "girl he loved when here at Wheaton." He had been frustrated with every relationship, since no matter how ardent at first, "his feelings seemed to ebb at times." Luckily for him, through his earnest and diligent prayer God's plan for romantic relationships was made clear. There were two forms of love, he discovered, "the natural love and the divine." Men and women were meant to find each other and help communicate God's love to each other. Of course, natural love would ebb and flow, grow and fade with time. But heterosexual married couples could embody for each other "God's love, in Christ." It would never change, never fade. Rather, it would remain a vibrant living soul at the heart of pure romantic relationships. For Betty Howard, this friend's story came as nothing short of a "revelation!"[151]

Clearly, Elisabeth Elliot was far from typical. Not many fundamentalists or evangelicals shared her eloquence or her experiences with love and loss. In her ideas about love, courtship, sex, and marriage, however, Elliot had plenty of company. At fundamentalist schools around the nation, young fundamentalists struggled publicly to define what it should mean for fundamentalists to search for a mate. Just as Jim, Betty, and their Wheaton friends helped each other define proper evangelical romance, students at nearby Moody Bible Institute shared their ideas in the pages of their student newspaper.

In November 1945, one graduating man told the MBI community what he wanted "in a Christian Young Woman." Far and away at the top of the list, this student wanted a romantic partner who "seeks God's will first." There were other important attributes, to be sure. This senior wanted a mate who had friends that he liked, who was "neat and orderly in her appearance," "practical," and a "deep thinker." The perfect woman would be thoughtful and wise. She would never seek to be merely "agreeable at the expense of righteousness."[152]

Another MBI student shared a similar list of desirable qualities in a future spouse. The "worst predicament," he told the MBI community, "would be an unhappy marriage." Therefore, he took care to look out for the proper sort of mate. As he put it:

> Take away the nagging neurotic, the giggling no-account, the gossiping gadabout, the spendthrift socialite, or the painted plutocrat.... Give me a strong, sound, sociable, serious, sensible servant of our Saviour, burdened for souls and selected for the same field of service as I. Give me a champion cook, a child-cherishing, cheerful, chary, charming, capable, compassionate companion and I'm certain of continual contentment.[153]

It was not only men at MBI who offered lists of desirable qualities. One new student offered her non-negotiable list of qualities in a future husband. First of all, she clarified that she was not looking for a mate on her own, but rather was eager to discover "God's choice for my mate." Her ideal partner would love "the Lord with his whole heart." He would be a "servant of mankind for Jesus' sake." Her perfect partner would be both serious and humorous. He would be aggressive in business while also "fervent in spirit." This young woman offered a promise to her future mate. "I'll be a busy help mate," she concluded cheerfully, "for I'll be everlastingly patching his clothes, especially the knees of his trousers!"[154]

Another MBI student wanted something slightly different. Her perfect man, she agreed, would always "put God first in everything, not merely in theory, but in practice." And he would also be an energetic and optimistic soul-winner. He would have to be hardworking and frugal, fearless and neat. Yet this young woman was not willing merely to be a helpmate. She fully expected a husband to consider her a "co-partner." She would settle down, she wrote, only when she found a partner who had a "teachable spirit."[155]

Often the qualities students looked for were tied to traditional gender expectations. For instance, one young man insisted first and foremost that a woman could be attractive only if she was "chaste and unbending . . . [with] simple, childlike faith in Christ."[156] At other times, though, MBI students worried that their partners might be too traditional, too bound by old-fashioned gender expectations. One woman, for example, fretted that too many young fundamentalist men turned up their masculine noses at important questions of home decor and personal hygiene. As she put it, she needed a husband who would not think "it's sissy to regard neatness and color-harmony."[157] In every case, men and women at MBI—at least in the public pages of the *Moody Student*—put godliness at the top of their lists of necessary qualities in a potential future spouse. Just as did Jim, Betty, and their Wheaton friends, MBI students wanted to be sure to disregard merely worldly qualities in their quests for love.

At Bob Jones University, too, at least some portion of the student body worked hard to embody true fundamentalist attitudes about love, courtship, and marriage. When William Liverman finally proposed to his future wife in the late 1940s, he found the perfect romantic setting. They had been visiting her family in Wisconsin, and he managed to find a spot on the shore of Lake Michigan. It was a beautiful night, he remembered, and she wanted to say yes. But she didn't. Not right away, at least. She was worried that she was being swayed by the waves and the moon. She was worried that she was being influenced by her merely bodily feelings of attraction for William. It was important to her that she consider the proposal clearly in the cold light of divine reason. Luckily for William, she found her feelings for him to be pure, Christian, and properly fundamentalist, so she eventually agreed to get married.[158]

## *The Love That Dared Not Speak Its Name*

The Livermans, Betty Howard, and thousands of other evangelical students had plenty of questions about proper fundamentalist courtship and romance in the decades between 1920 and 1960. But there was one thing they didn't wonder about. At fundamentalist schools in this era, homosexuality was considered so far beyond the pale of acceptability that it was not even mentioned in the thick rulebooks that tried to dictate so many aspects of student behavior. Students were presumed to be heterosexual, and the many rules about sexual behavior regulated only male-female contact.

We might think that fundamentalist schools were merely naive about homosexuality, that they simply did not imagine that their students could be anything but heterosexual. The archival record, however, hints at a much more complicated historical truth. Among school administrators, there was a tacit recognition of the fact that homosexuality was not impossible among fundamentalist students. Tracking down fundamentalist attitudes toward homosexuality, though, is a difficult task. As did their contemporaries at non-fundamentalist schools, fundamentalist school leaders wrapped all their discussions of homosexuality in thick layers of cold silence, angry denunciation, and hateful euphemism.

To be sure, fundamentalist school leaders at least matched the ruthlessness and vindictiveness of their peers at mainstream schools. Before the 1960s, we must remember, homosexual students were relentlessly persecuted and prosecuted at all sorts of institutions. At the University of Wisconsin in 1948, for example, four students were arrested and punished for their "abnormal sexual activities." Throughout the 1940s, as historians Margaret Nash and Jennifer Silverman have demonstrated, students suspected of homosexuality were systematically purged at similar state universities.[159]

At fundamentalist schools, homosexuality among students and faculty was often discussed only in carefully indirect language. Clifton Fowler, for instance, the obstreperous leader of Denver Bible Institute during the 1930s, was accused of homosexuality repeatedly, but in elaborately vague terms. One Denver local told fundamentalist investigators that Fowler "corrupted" a young student's "morals . . . in an unmentionable manner."[160] Even the follow-up investigations by concerned fundamentalists referred only to a "very unsavory story" concerning Fowler and a young man.[161] Other Denver fundamentalists accused Fowler vaguely but unmistakably of giving "young men such a prominent place in your home."[162] One doctor hired by Fowler's estranged wife accused Fowler of having an undefined "Perverted Sex Complex."[163] Another concerned Denverite told the fundamentalist investigators—using an unintentionally apt foggy metaphor—that there had been a "cloud charging perversion" around Clifton Fowler for some time.[164] When it came to accusations of homosexuality, only the estranged and bitter Mrs. Angie Fowler left an explicit comment in the record, warning her former husband, "You can be called a SODOMIST from North to South, from East to West."[165]

Clifton Fowler was inarguably a unique case in the world of fundamentalist higher education between the 1920s and the 1950s, but not because he was accused of homosexuality. Careful and confusing language to describe accusations of homosexuality and homosexual behavior was common at all fundamentalist schools in that era. From Biola, for example, one student was expelled in 1942 for an undefined "unspeakably abominable sin."[166] Two other students were exhorted in 1955 to spend less time together in their "unusually intimate clique." The women were so close, Biola administrators worried, that "rather ugly rumors were started concerning their attitudes and conduct." Perhaps they were not homosexuals, President Sutherland admitted. Yet he still pushed them apart "for the sake of avoiding the appearance of evil."[167]

In a dramatic case from the early 1950s, one former Biola student faked his own death and fled to Texas to avoid exposure as a homosexual. In his 1951 apology, the student did not call himself a homosexual, though he referred to himself as a "filthy so-and-so." He promised that his renewed relationship with Jesus would save him in the future whenever he felt the "perverted urge."[168] The student was no more cruel to himself than were Biola's administrators. When the story finally came out, Biola issued an official statement to the student body condemning the student. For many years, the school explained, this student had "been a victim of a vicious condition of inherent baseness and depravity." Such a condition, Biola warned, "may even lead to more vicious acts, including murder."[169]

Fundamentalists did not take accusations of homosexuality lightly. Yet they did not shy away from making them, even with very limited evidence. As we'll explore in detail in Chapter 5, for instance, when administrator Ted Mercer was purged from Bob Jones University in 1953, he was accused of homosexual activity, among other charges.[170] In Dean Mercer's case, as for all other accused homosexuals, discussion of purported homosexuality was wrapped in thick layers of euphemism and indirection. In every usage, though, fundamentalists agreed on a basic truth: they considered homosexuality to be the ultimate sexual sin, the ultimate disgrace. It was never discussed as a type of sexuality, and instead it was always being treated as a damnable behavior, a perverted choice. At the same time, it was recognized as a common if lamentable form of sin. Fundamentalist school administrators may not have codified rules against homosexuality in their student handbooks, but among themselves they assumed that some fraction of their student body would engage in homosexual behavior.

## *As the Good (Rule) Book Says*

Just as with other rules about student life in the years before the 1960s campus revolts, it might come as a shock to discover how similar non-fundamentalist colleges could be to fundamentalist ones in the persecution of homosexual students. At the University of Texas in Austin in the 1940s, for example, homosexuality on campus was presumed to be a dire and immediate threat—such a threat, in fact, that the campus president was punished for not acting quickly enough to purge a "nest of homosexuals" from campus.[171] Certainly fundamentalist schools were not alone in using vicious and dehumanizing language to persecute homosexuals.

As with all questions of sexuality and student behavior, however, fundamentalist schools tended to impose stricter rules on students and to enforce them more vigorously. Unlike those at some mainstream schools, for instance, no administrators at fundamentalist colleges would wink at student drinking or at unsupervised heterosexual romance. At fundamentalist schools, indeed, rigid lifestyle rules and energetic enforcement of those rules often came to be taken to be a central defining element of fundamentalism itself. By the 1940s and 1950s, as we'll explore in more depth in Chapter 5, many thoughtful fundamentalists worried that fundamentalism itself was in danger of being swamped by a legalistic mentality of mere rule-following.

As we've seen in this chapter, fundamentalist colleges usually tried to regulate nearly every non-academic aspect of student life. Drinking beer, smoking tobacco, playing cards, and attending movies were nearly universally banned. The rules were most strict and were most strictly enforced when it came to regulating courtship and sexuality, especially female sexuality.

Even so, students at even the strictest schools found plenty of room around the margins of their thick rulebooks. In some cases, misbehavior took the form of collegiate hijinks such as throwing water balloons or ritual cross-dressing. In other cases, it involved finding ways to drink beer or have unapproved, unregulated sex. In still other cases, breaking the rules resulted from conscious, disciplined dissent, including listening to banned liberal theologians or forming study groups dedicated to radical spirituality.

Yet we must remember not to be fooled by the ubiquity of misbehavior in the archival record. Obviously, students who misbehaved generated more administrative headaches and more administrative memos than those who did not. Those students who embraced the rules and the spirit that guided them left less archival traces of their college years. Yet that does not mean there weren't lots of them in every generation. Like Betty Howard, many students not only embraced the rules but also pushed themselves far beyond the demands of any student handbook. Not many students were as eloquent or as prolific as the future Elisabeth Elliot, but for every student who sparked investigations and accusations by administrators and parents, there were many more who appreciated their schools' efforts to keep them on the right spiritual track. Many students—maybe the vast majority—never found their way into the disciplinary record of their college, likely because they would have agreed with one student at Wheaton in 1938. As he remembered, "There was constantly the Christian atmosphere, which I appreciated, and which sort of held me together with the College."[172]

# 5

# *Billy Graham Was a Transfer Student*

*I am not against you, Billy. I love you . . . . but I must be true to my God. I haven't much time left.*

—BOB JONES SR. TO BILLY GRAHAM, January 17, 1956[1]

## *America's Preacher Boy*

William Franklin Graham Jr.'s career started out like those of so many fundamentalist evangelists before him. Young Billy Graham wanted to save souls. His mother dreamed of sending him to Wheaton to learn how, but Chicago was far away from their home in Charlotte, North Carolina, and Wheaton was expensive. There was a new fundamentalist school closer to home, though, so in 1937 Billy trooped off to Cleveland, Tennessee, to learn the evangelistic ropes from Bob Jones.[2] For a while, he was one of Bob Jones Sr.'s favorite "preacher boys."[3] But Billy wasn't happy at Bob Jones College. Bob Jones Sr. didn't like Billy's best friend, who Jones thought had a "subtle, peculiar type personality."[4] And Billy hated all the rules. As he remembered later, "It shocked me. There were demerits for just about everything."[5] When Billy left for the Florida Bible Institute (now Trinity College) and eventually Wheaton College, Bob Jones Sr. warned Billy's father that the move would "demoralize" the young preacher.[6]

It didn't. By 1960 Billy Graham had done much more than simply prove Bob Jones wrong. He had built a career as the kind of preacher fundamentalists had always dreamed about. He had returned fundamentalist religion to its place on America's center stage; he became "America's Pastor."[7] But he didn't do it without pushing the boundaries of fundamentalism itself. To a great extent, Graham came to define and embody a new sort of fundamentalism calling itself "neo-evangelicalism," or simply "evangelicalism."[8]

For some fundamentalists, Graham's style of stadium evangelism crossed a line. To draw in more souls, Graham sometimes accepted the local sponsorship of liberal Protestant churches as well as conservative ones. Fundamentalist critics worried that anyone who accepted Jesus's call during one of Graham's emotional rallies might join the church of one of those liberal sponsors. Once there, converts would learn the soul-destroying doctrines of theological modernism instead of the tried-and-true fundamentals of the faith. Fundamentalists, some members of the conservative-evangelical family insisted, must maintain their unyielding separation from mainline ideas about the Bible and the faith. Billy Graham and his neo-evangelical fans disagreed. An evangelical could maintain his steadfast fidelity to fundamental doctrine while accepting the help of people who disagreed.

During the years that Graham built his career as a new sort of fundamentalist, the extended family of fundamentalist colleges had to wonder if they fit in better with the new branch of the family or the old. Were they forward-looking "evangelical" schools? Or resolutely "fundamentalist" ones? Given their history, it might come as no surprise that different schools reacted in starkly different ways. A few schools embraced one side or the other. Bob Jones University, for example, doubled down on its promise to remain a purely fundamentalist institution. In California, the new Fuller Seminary welcomed a role as the leading theological school of the new evangelical movement. In Illinois, Billy Graham's alma mater, Wheaton, became the flagship evangelical liberal arts college, just as it had earlier been the flagship fundamentalist institution. From the perspective of the evangelical intellectuals who pushed their institutions to embrace one side or the other, the emergence of a new type of fundamentalism appeared as a "decisive break"[9] and an "irreparable breach."[10]

However, even those schools most closely associated with one side of the family or the other continued to attract students from both sides. For a long while, they continued to think of themselves as belonging to the same fundamentalist family of schools. More commonly, most of the schools in the network muddled through in the middle, perhaps leaning one way or the other but hoping to remain attractive to students from all sorts of evangelical and fundamentalist families. After all, as struggling institutions, they had little choice. They could not afford to write off potential students and potential tuition dollars from any branch of the conservative evangelical family, whether they called themselves "fundamentalists" or "evangelicals." Students, too, seemed less aware than school leaders that any sort of decisive split had occurred. Long into the 1970s, students continued to think of schools like Bob Jones University and Wheaton College as part of the same fundamentalist family, often with the encouragement of school administrators.

As with any family estrangement, the split between fundamentalists and evangelicals left hard feelings and bitter memories on all sides. In the day-to-day functioning of the schools themselves, however, life in the 1950s and 1960s went on much as before. As they had since the 1920s, faculty members at evangelical and fundamentalist schools continued to live under intense scrutiny from the entire community of fundamentalists and evangelicals. As we'll see in this chapter, the tradition of headline-grabbing faculty purges continued. Such collegiate witch hunts were relatively rare, but the furor caused by each case echoed throughout the wider world of evangelical higher education for decades. Even those faculty members who never felt the sting of being kicked out of their institutions still found themselves cut off in important ways from some of the emerging traditions at non-evangelical colleges. Unlike their peers at pluralist schools or liberal religious schools, faculty members at evangelical and fundamentalist colleges remained painfully aware that their administrators could brook no wandering—nor even any appearance of wandering—from the implicit truths of evangelical or fundamentalist life. Academic freedom at evangelical and fundamentalist schools came to mean something very different from what it became at non-evangelical institutions.

## *Under the Microscope*

Teachers at fundamentalist colleges never hoped to get rich. Most of them viewed their work—both teaching and any publishing they might find time to do—as an expression of their own mission to spread the Gospel among their students and communities. Faculty members had to endure more than just low pay and heavy teaching loads, however. At fundamentalist and evangelical colleges, universities, Bible schools, and seminaries in the middle of the twentieth century, administrators and trustees often believed that low pay was a positive good, not just an unfortunate side effect of limited institutional funds. Many school leaders insisted that faculty members constituted both their schools' greatest strength and greatest liability. Higher salaries and better working conditions might only encourage teachers to think of their jobs as cushy sinecures rather than as self-sacrificing missions.

At some schools, ambitious faculty members continually prodded administrators for conditions similar to those at mainstream research universities. Paul Jewett of Fuller Seminary, for example, warned the school's board of trustees that a sabbatical program was not a vacation for faculty. Rather, any school that hoped to "rank with the best institutions of its kind" had to invest in faculty research. An improved sabbatical program was the cheapest and most practical way to do so.[11]

Trustees' and administrators' reluctance to improve conditions for faculty members often resulted from more than just tight budgets. At Wheaton, for example, during the middle of the twentieth century faculty tended to be poorly paid in relation to other schools.[12] And in the opinion of the leading historian of the college, "Wheaton's leadership believed it was good for the college's religious character to have a poorly paid faculty."[13] Teaching, they believed, should be seen as a missionary enterprise. Only with relentless self-sacrifice could missionary work achieve its true goals.

Leaders of other schools were equally suspect of faculty ambitions. At Bob Jones College, Bob Jones Sr. liked to share a story of one interview with a potential teacher in 1941. The whole thing seemed to be going wonderfully, Jones related. Near the end, she asked, "'How much do you pay?' And I said, 'Not one cent, sister.' . . . She had a hireling heart."[14] For Jones, even an expression of interest in salary and benefits was a betrayal, evidence of an unclean, mercenary spirit. Most of the teachers at Bob Jones College in the 1940s could never be accused of such an attitude. Even the most sympathetic historian of the school has called faculty pay "meager."[15] At its cramped campus in Cleveland, Tennessee, two or three faculty families might share a house. Married couples might even be forced to live in their classrooms.[16]

Generally, the Bob Joneses frowned on public discussion of teacher salaries. By the mid-1950s, they had actively and explicitly banned such talk.[17] Teachers were expected to display their loyalty by never questioning the haphazard and inadequate pay scale. The archives, however, include glimpses of faculty pay. One faculty member hired in 1938, for example, received free room and board plus $100 per month. Bob Jones Sr. promised a bonus if possible.[18] In the mid-1950s, a top administrator at BJU was paid $225 per month during the nine-month teaching year, in addition to campus housing and board.[19]

Bob Jones may have insisted that he didn't care about pay scales, but school leaders at other fundamentalist and evangelical colleges often compared faculty pay to other institutions. In general, even those evangelical schools that most wanted to meet the academic standards of mainstream colleges could not—or simply did not—keep up financially. In 1958–1959, for example, Gordon College paid faculty members an average salary of $5,000. Associate professors averaged $4,400, assistants only $4,000.[20] In contrast, in 1960, full professors at Brooklyn College earned between $10,300 and $16,000 annually. At Columbia University, full professors made at least $10,000 per year. Assistant professors at Brooklyn College earned between $7,000 and $9,900, while crosstown at Columbia assistant professors earned between $5,500 and $7,000.[21] Across a spread of forty-four land-grant institutions in the academic year 1959–1960, assistant professors earned an average salary of $7,000. Full professors at those schools took home an average of $10,210.[22]

By the late 1960s, some evangelical and fundamentalist school leaders began to wonder if their lagging pay scales were hurting faculty morale. In 1969, Biola administrator J. Richard Chase conducted a comparative study of colleges in his region. His school paid a range of salaries: Biola's thirteen full professors commanded salaries ranging from $12,000 annually to just over $14,000. Associate professors earned between $8,700 and $11,400. Assistants received between $7,600 and $10,300.[23] Such faculty pay, Chase concluded, was far below the average for colleges of similar size and ambition.[24]

Even if administrators wanted to improve pay and decrease teaching loads, the tenuous financial position of their schools often mitigated against it. In the first years of Liberty University, when it was still Lynchburg Baptist College, one member of the English faculty's standard teaching load included 225 students each semester. It was an unmanageable number, she thought, but there was not much chance she could expect relief. The school, she recalled, had not been able to hire enough new faculty to keep up with expanding student enrollment.[25]

Low pay and heavy teaching loads were not the most notable difference between evangelical and non-evangelical schools, however, as most small private colleges paid low salaries and demanded lots of teaching. In addition to such challenges, faculty members at evangelical schools remained painfully aware of their need to conform to never-quite-clear and always-changing standards of belief and behavior. Administrators could accuse faculty members of failing to live up to such standards, basing their charges on vague rumors circulating among the evangelical and fundamentalist community. Certainly the general atmosphere at fundamentalist and evangelical colleges was different from the atmosphere at non-evangelical schools. As sociologists Christopher Jencks and David Riesman noted in a widely read 1968 book, most mainstream colleges had witnessed a decisive shift, an "academic revolution" in the relationship between administrators and faculty. By the late 1960s, Jencks and Riesman concluded, administrators were "more concerned with keeping their faculty happy than with placating any other single group."[26] At evangelical and fundamentalist colleges, the situation was always much different. Faculty members were both celebrated and suspected, underpaid and overly supervised.

Of course, faculty members at all types of schools experienced various sorts of ideological pressure throughout the twentieth century. Liberal or Left-leaning faculty members at all colleges had good reason to worry about Red hunts.[27] By the end of the twentieth century, conservative or Right-leaning professors often complained about being squeezed out.[28] The pressure on faculty members at evangelical colleges was similar, but far more intense and far more typical of professional life. It was not odd or unusual, in other words, for a faculty member at an evangelical school to feel pressure to conform. Indeed, it was an annual, weekly, and even daily ritual on most campuses.

As we've seen, such scrutiny of faculty attitudes and lifestyles had always been a part of life at fundamentalist schools. Many of the network's first generation of administrators did not hesitate to hector and chastise faculty members. In 1926, for example, James M. Gray of Moody Bible Institute sent an unapologetically harsh memo to the entire faculty. Too often, Gray warned, "officials and employes" were showing up late for meals. As a result, they missed the saying of the prayer and disrupted the meals. This behavior, Gray wrote, was not acceptable and would not be tolerated.[29] Such top-down browbeating continued for decades at MBI. In 1947, for example, staff and faculty were reminded that they were obliged to maintain the school's "traditional policies" in terms of "attitudes, conduct or appearance."[30] At fundamentalist institutions, it wasn't just students who were kept to a strict checklist of behavioral and theological imperatives.

All the schools in the network maintained similar sorts of attitudes toward faculty members. In 1952, at Biola, for instance, President Sutherland dismissed faculty complaints about short notice for afternoon meetings. All faculty members were required to be at school all day, mornings and afternoons, Sutherland reminded them. They were expected to be available for meetings at any time. Too many of them had recently taken too much liberty in leaving campus after their classes had been taught.[31]

Long into the 1950s, 1960s, and 1970s, fundamentalist and evangelical schools maintained their iron grip on faculty schedules and lifestyles. At most schools, this policy reflected the deep distrust that school leaders felt toward their faculty, many of whom had earned graduate degrees at non-fundamentalist institutions. At Wheaton College, for example, trustees consistently worried—in the words of historian Michael Hamilton—that "the faculty represented the single greatest danger to maintaining the college's Christian character."[32]

Administrators and trustees often enforced faculty rules through more than just memos and harsh reminders. Because of the many connections between fundamentalists and evangelicals in overlapping networks of church groups, missionary bodies, school administrations, and a variety of publications, every administrator heard plenty of talk about the alleged goings-on among his faculty. Those rumors about faculty malfeasance often played a leading role in sniffing out suspicious thoughts and behavior on the part of faculty members. In 1966, for example, a trustee at Wheaton College passed along a rumor to President V. Raymond Edman that a new faculty member held iffy, "amillennial" beliefs about the second coming of Christ—in other words, he was accused of believing that Christ was currently ruling on earth through the church and of not embracing the premillennial view, which held that Christ would return in glory to usher in a thousand years of peace and prosperity. As we've seen, most fundamentalists were premillennialists, though it had always been a theological bone of contention among fundamentalist thinkers. Nevertheless, rumors of faculty amillennialism were enough to propel President Edman to action. Were they true? Edman investigated immediately, hoping to reassure the anxious trustee that "every prospective faculty member is closely questioned on the premillennial view and signs the doctrinal platform."[33]

The rumor mill among the "evangelical network" allowed many school leaders and concerned evangelical and fundamentalist bystanders to point fingers at faculty foibles. At Fuller Seminary in California, for instance, rumors played a role in uncovering suspect faculty activities in 1966. President Ockenga "got wind" that faculty member James Daane smoked cigarettes and held amillennial views.[34] Similarly, in 1978 an influential Boston preacher warned a friend of rumors he had heard circulating among Boston's evangelical community. It was whispered that seminary professors at Gordon-Conwell Seminary had embraced liberal views of scripture and salvation. He had no idea whether it was true, but fretted nonetheless. "Even if it is only partially true," he explained, "we do indeed have a problem."[35]

How could faculty members prove their fidelity to evangelical and fundamentalist truths? How could they decisively demonstrate, in the face of scandalous rumor, that they had not strayed from evangelical and fundamentalist expectations for their behavior and belief? Time and again, faculty members repeated the words of their annual school pledges. As we've seen, since the 1920s these pledges had been a standard requirement at fundamentalist schools. In some cases, too, faculty members and even top administrators offered occasional informal reminders of their loyalty. At Bob Jones University, for example, where the principle of faculty loyalty had always been given top priority, administrator Gilbert Stenholm felt a need to prostrate himself occasionally before the Bob Joneses. In 1968, for instance, Stenholm promised Bob Jones III that he would "rededicate myself to carry out the purposes for which this school was founded." It had been standard practice, Stenholm told the grandson, for the grandfather to stop by Stenholm's office occasionally to deliver "words of encouragement, admonition, and sometimes rebuke."[36] Again in 1975, Stenholm worried that his loyalty might be under suspicion. He promised once again that Bob Jones Jr. and III should feel "assured of my loyalty . . . I hope that I may be forgiven, and that my future actions will cause the past to be forgotten."[37]

## *Purge*

Even with annual pledges and occasional rebukes, the heady mix of indistinct orthodoxy, in-group whisper campaigns, low faculty pay, and constant suspicion and onerous supervision led to occasional faculty purges. Each case was different. In every case, however, purged faculty members were accused of a mix of theological and behavioral sins. And in every case, the explicit charges and countercharges were swept along by roiling undercurrents of rumors, unspoken accusations, personal grudges, and competing cliques. And though each case at each school seemed outrageous and unpredictable at the time, in fact such purges had always been and would continue to be a regular part of faculty life at evangelical and fundamentalist colleges.

At Wheaton College, for example, 1948 became another year of tense controversy. In July, history professor and department chair C. Gregg Singer quit. Why? He complained of the low pay, the cold climate, and the fact that he was overlooked for a promised promotion to full professor. He had been insulted repeatedly, he declared, by trustee inquisitions into his theological orthodoxy. Worst of all, though, Singer felt that President V. Raymond Edman had created an unhealthy academic environment. All in all, Singer concluded, "the nervous strain and confusion make it impossible to do one's work."[38]

Professor Singer had been unhappy for a long while. According to a co-conspirator, Singer had gathered a group of disgruntled faculty members into a powerful secret clique. The faculty group planned to save Wheaton by taking over the presidency and kicking President V. Raymond Edman upstairs to a ceremonial public relations position. With their own man in the president's office, the faculty group would cut back enrollment from 1,500 to 1,200 in order to reduce teaching loads. They would raise faculty salaries and separate the undergraduate college from the secondary academy and the graduate school. They had included the head of the alumni association in their plans. Perhaps more important, each man had tested the waters among his extended network of evangelical friends and confidants. As a result, they had confidence that the ouster of Edman would be well received. Based on their discreet inquiries among the people they knew and trusted, they concluded, "Christian people all over the country had lost confidence in [President Edman]."[39]

Unfortunately for the closet revolutionaries, Edman had the board of trustees on his side. Trustee Herman Fischer lamented the fact that Wheaton had adopted tenure protections for faculty members like Singer. It made it much more difficult for the board to get rid of such a troublemaker. Fischer liked Professor Singer personally, he insisted. The two men were neighbors. Nevertheless, Fischer confessed that some trustees—Fischer didn't name names—did indeed feel that it was time for Singer to go.[40]

At the start of 1948, Professor Singer gave the trustees an opening. As did all faculty members, Singer signed the college's statement of faith at the start of every year. This year, however, he made a tiny change. At the time, the school's pledge included the following article:

> We believe in "that blessed hope," the personal, premillennial and imminent return of our Lord and Savior Jesus Christ.[41]

Singer agreed that Christ would be returning in person. He agreed that Christ would be returning imminently. But he lined out the word "premillennial." His Calvinist beliefs, he explained, led him to distrust "fundamentalism with its emphasis on dispensationalism."[42] As we've seen, and as we'll explore in more detail in Chapter 6, some Calvinist intellectuals had always shared Singer's distaste for the innovative dispensational methods of biblical interpretation that had long been popular among many fundamentalists.

The board of trustees smelled blood. Professor Singer's theological punctiliousness gave them the excuse they needed to get rid of him. At heart, however, the problem with Professor Singer was not his insistence on amillennialism instead of premillennialism. After all, as Singer pointed out, he had made his distaste for premillennialism clear to President Edman upon being hired in 1945.[43] Moreover, by April, Singer was even willing to sign the statement of faith again, this time leaving in "premillennial."[44]

It would not be enough. Wheaton was a small town. The circles in which fundamentalist faculty and administrators moved were tight and laced with interconnections. For too long, President Edman had been hearing whispers that Singer had been making "unrestrained and prejudicial remarks" about Edman to students and faculty alike. In an angry and heated one-on-one meeting, Singer had threatened to sue the school and even launch a "student strike."[45] Singer's principled disagreement with premillennial theology was only an excuse. President Edman wanted Singer out. With the backing of the board of trustees, Edman got his way. The only concession Singer could wring out of Wheaton's administration was an official statement that Singer had done no wrong. Holding his nose, President Edman pronounced that Singer "stands *fully vindicated* of all charges against him."[46] In the case of Professor C. Gregg Singer, the dispute over premillennialism was only the theological wallpaper spread hastily and patchily over a long-simmering dispute about the role and power of faculty members at a fundamentalist school.

## *Authority and Accreditation*

When Singer decamped in 1948 to a position at Salem College in North Carolina, he left alone.[47] But a few years later, Bob Jones University experienced the most tumultuous faculty purge in its purge-laden history. By the time the dust had settled in the fall of 1953, more than a hundred faculty and administrators had quit, no longer willing to put up with the Bob Joneses' intense and never-ending demands for loyalty.

Ted Mercer stood at the center of the storm. He had come to Bob Jones College years earlier as an undergraduate. He stayed for graduate school, then for a dozen more years as a faculty member, as dean of men and registrar, then as a special assistant to the president.[48] By the summer of 1953, by all accounts, Mercer was one of the top administrators at Bob Jones University. Yet that summer, he was summarily fired. Why? According to Bob Jones Sr. and Jr., Mercer had schemed to overthrow their authority. He had become too friendly with students. He even might have engaged in abusive sexual relationships with students. Mercer offered a different explanation. He was ousted, Mercer protested, for finally blowing the whistle on the Joneses' deeply dysfunctional cult of personality.

As we've seen throughout their history, fundamentalist institutions recognized no higher authority to settle such disputes. No human one, at least. Neither Mercer nor the Bob Joneses could appeal to an accrediting agency or a denominational council for a ruling. Instead, both sides engaged in a flurry of charges and countercharges. Each side produced letters, pamphlets and speeches to students, alumni groups, and influential fundamentalists. Each side hoped to define this purge in its own terms. Was this a healthy dismissal of satanic forces? Or was this another sign that the university had devolved into an authoritarian cult?

The exact numbers are disputed, but it seems clear that huge numbers of faculty and administrators left the school between 1951 and 1953. At the end of the 1951–1952 school year, some seventy faculty members departed, citing a variety of personal and professional reasons. When Ted Mercer left at the end of the 1952–1953 year, another fifty-three went with him, including three other top administrators.[49]

Most of the departing faculty members went quietly, but not Ted Mercer. Officially, Mercer was fired for becoming too friendly with students.[50] In a public statement just after the firing, Bob Jones Sr. explained that he had an obligation to fire anyone "who is not loyal." All employees, Jones said, including himself, had always been "employed provisionally." Mercer, Jones suggested, had been fired for "griping."[51]

Privately, Jones offered more details. To one friend, Jones explained that he had received "unimpeachable" evidence that Mercer had been engaged for years in "digging into the foundations of this institution." Mercer's crimes, Jones implied, included some sort of unspecified abuse to students, causing them "untold harm."[52] To a parent, Jones explained that Mercer had almost succeeded in his devilish plan. "If God hadn't been here in power," Jones confided, "[Mercer] would have destroyed the school." The way Jones told the story, Mercer had even admitted in a talk just before he was fired that he had come under the influence of some evil power:

> "Ted, [Jones said] there [is] something wrong with you. You are crazy, you are living in sin, your emotional life is twisted and disturbed, or you are under the power of the devil. Something is wrong with you. What is it, Ted?" [Mercer] looked down and then looked up at me and asked me, "What *is* the matter with me?"[53]

Bob Jones Sr. didn't expect the fundamentalist community merely to take his word for it. He produced letters from students describing Mercer's dangerous behavior.[54] One former student, Matthew Welde, described the ways Mercer had shown him inappropriate attention. Mercer had sent daily call slips to Welde to force Welde to report to Mercer's office. Mercer bought the student clothes and books and asked Welde to call him "Ted." Mercer wrote letters every day and became angry if Welde didn't write back. All in all, Mercer exerted a "physical attraction [that] was revolting to me, [but] he had such a strange hypnotic mind that I was held under that kind of a spell." All the while, Welde explained, Mercer had been scheming to get rid of Bob Jones Sr. If they could remove him, Mercer had told Welde, "the university would be a Utopia." In Welde's telling, Mercer changed after Welde proposed marriage to his girlfriend. Instead of a clingy, inappropriate friend and mentor, Welde charged, Mercer suddenly became a vengeful enforcer, looking for chances to have Welde and his fiancée kicked out of school. "He even," Welde wrote, "gave us a book on sex."[55]

It wasn't only Welde, Jones insisted, who had been pushed by Mercer toward sexual sin. Jones produced another student letter detailing the experiences of a student night watchman. One night, just after midnight, this student had caught two students crawling out of Mercer's office window. When the student watchman reported the incident, Mercer seemed to want to have it hushed up. At the least, Mercer seemed to want to undermine the school's rigid rules about sexuality and courting. At worst, Mercer might have been actively encouraging and abetting sexual relationships among the students, maybe even having sexual relationships himself with students.[56]

To those familiar with the history of Bob Jones University, the language of this 1950s purge often sounded strangely similar to that of the purges we saw in Chapter 3. Just as Dorothy Seay and Joseph Free were in the 1930s,

Ted Mercer was officially charged with "hobnobbing" with students.[57] As with Seay and Free, Mercer's "hobnobbing" implied more than just a forgivable overfriendliness. At Bob Jones University, to hobnob implied a never-specified sexual inappropriateness. Dorothy Seay, for example, had been accused of luring male students up to her bedroom, and Joseph Free of having at least two female students under his influence. Moreover, just like Seay and Free, Mercer was charged with cobbling together a "satanic attack on the institution." Mercer was supposed to have been able to exert the "strangest hypnotic power" over naive students.[58] In the tight-laced world of 1950s fundamentalism, specific sexual crimes were never spelled out, not even in private correspondence. Instead, the merest implication of an older man exerting a hypnotic influence over young students was enough for fundamentalist audiences to fill in the salacious details.

For his part, Mercer protested both his firing and the smearing that went on afterward. The insinuations and vague allegations of predatory homosexuality, Mercer insisted, were all part of the oppressive spirit of punishment and ostracism that hung over the heads of all members of the Bob Jones University community. In spite of the way he had been treated, Mercer wrote in a pamphlet he published just after his firing, "I *do* love the school and I *am* loyal."[59] Right up to the end, Mercer explained, he had had no inkling that he was to be fired.[60] The real roots of his ouster were far more prosaic than Jones had suggested. First and foremost, in Mercer's telling, he had incurred the founder's wrath by choosing a doctor for his very pregnant wife that Jones did not approve of.[61] And Mercer had openly sympathized with the seventy-plus faculty members who had departed in 1952.[62] Perhaps worst of all, Mercer had become a popular leader at the school, perhaps more popular than Bob Jones Sr. and definitely more popular than Junior.[63]

Mercer disputed each of Bob Jones's accusations. He had never confessed any sort of sin or problem, Mercer insisted.[64] Nor could the vote of the board of trustees have been unanimous against him, Mercer claimed, in spite of Jones's repeated assertion that it was. Two of the trustees were not present at the June meeting at which the allegedly unanimous vote took place, Mercer wrote, and even if they had been present, they had told Mercer privately that they did not support the firing.[65]

As for the most damning insinuations against him, Mercer explained, they were never made openly, but only by hint and infamous suggestion. That was because, Mercer argued, there was never anything to such rumors. Yes, Mercer admitted, he had been friendly to students. He never would deny it. He disputed the notion "that to like your students and to be liked by them or to do any kindnesses for them is a sin of deep dye."[66] No charges about his relationship with Matthew Welde had been made, Mercer explained, until after Mercer had been fired.[67] In fact, Mercer had helped Welde and his fiancée, Millie Cox, handle the onerous regulations at Bob Jones University. They had come to Mercer for help, struggling to develop their romantic relationship under the strict campus rules. Mercer insisted that he had always enforced those rules, but that he also helped students to understand why the rules were in place. His goal had always been to help students see the ways the rules were not problems to be avoided but spiritual guides to be embraced.[68]

In August, Mercer offered a follow-up open letter to alumni and the board of trustees. He had been fired and then viciously smeared because he had objected too loudly to the unhealthy and unsustainable leadership structure at the school. When it came to vital issues of faculty pay, accreditation, and leadership structure, according to Mercer, the school had become trapped in a deadly downward spiral.[69]

The situation had become painfully obvious in 1951, Mercer wrote. A group of top leaders, including Mercer as well as Bob Jones Jr., agreed that the school needed to improve living standards for faculty. With low pay, backbreaking teaching loads, and cramped campus housing, no teacher would take a job at Bob Jones, and the ones already there wouldn't stay. Instead of listening to calm reason, Mercer wrote, Bob Jones Sr. only increased his "belligerence" if anyone mentioned this important topic.[70]

At the same time, the school's faculty and administration found themselves trapped by an uncertain authority structure. Deans found themselves in the impossible situation of having to fulfill contradictory orders from both Senior and Junior.[71] The tensions were exacerbated at one meeting when a group of deans "tittered" at Junior's comment that he was in charge.[72] Both Bob Joneses felt obliged, Mercer thought, to assert and demonstrate their authority, and faculty members were leaving in droves because of the father and son's "wrathful caprice."[73]

Part of the bluster of the Bob Joneses, Mercer believed, resulted from their stubborn refusal to consider the pressing question of accreditation. Whatever the Joneses thought, Mercer argued, the school needed to seek accreditation in order to survive.[74] The quest for accreditation, though, challenged the Joneses' tradition of out-and-out falsification of the school's records. For years, Mercer charged, both Senior and Junior had padded the reports about faculty salaries. They had inflated enrollment numbers and school statistics.[75] The school needed accreditation, Mercer argued, but the Bob Joneses refused to allow outsiders—or even most insiders—to see the profoundly disturbing difference between the school's inflated claims and its struggling reality.

Mercer wasn't alone in his charges. Dean Karl Keefer left at the same time and made similar charges. Keefer, like Mercer, had been at the school for a long time, fifteen years in Keefer's case. He insisted that he still loved the school. But he could no longer go along with the school's mercurial leadership "and still live at peace with myself." Keefer had seen the ill effects of faculty workloads in his own household. His wife, Sue, had been worked far too hard, threatening her health and eroding her soul. Yet Keefer's complaints had gone unheard. Nor did the top leaders listen to the many similar complaints by all the faculty members who left in 1952. The principles of leadership and loyalty, Keefer argued, were too much to bear. "In Bob Jones University," Keefer complained, "no tiniest facet of the Founder's thought can be considered non-essential, and . . . one must either actively or tacitly agree with all decisions and actions of the administration or leave the organization." Keefer no longer agreed, so he felt the time had come for him to leave—reluctantly.[76]

As with so many disputes in the world of fundamentalist higher education, Mercer's firing quickly evolved into a many-sided effort to control the flow of rumors and accusations. Keefer, for example, repeated his charges in an open letter to the Bob Jones University faculty. The faculty members who had left, Keefer explained, had not done so on good terms, in spite of what most of them had said publicly. The real reason was the "atmosphere of mental and spiritual coercion" that ruled the campus. Keefer had kept silent at the time, but he felt he could do so no longer. How many faculty members, Keefer wondered, had had experiences similar to those of his suffering wife, who had been compelled for years to engage in "forced labor" without any acknowledgment or compensation? He still loved the school, Keefer concluded, and that was why he had to leave. The current policy of utter top-down control would kill the school. True loyalty meant speaking out.[77]

Both sides tried to control the stories of all parties involved. Both Bob Jones Sr. and Ted Mercer's wife, Alice, wrote to Matthew Welde in the aftermath of the firing. Jones warned Welde not to speak with other members of the board of trustees. They didn't really want information. They only wanted to make Jones look bad, Jones insisted.[78] Alice Mercer warned Welde that Jones was using him as a pawn, showing his private letters around and trashing his reputation. More important, Alice Mercer wanted Welde to see the truth of life at Bob Jones University. "Life in the *reddest* of Russia," she wrote, "could not have been made more miserable for anyone than it was for us."[79]

Bob Jones loyalists flooded alumni mailboxes with letters. The head bookkeeper informed alumni that Mercer had been charging the university for lavish travel and luxurious accommodations.[80] Another administrator wrote to insist that the university could earn accreditation at any time if it chose to.[81] Still another asserted that the Bob Joneses had always been punctilious about keeping and reporting absolutely precise and correct statistics about the school,[82] and another produced faculty testimony that they never felt bullied or mistreated by the Bob Joneses.[83]

For his part, Mercer insisted that the charges against him rested mainly on "deep and dark inferences about me and hints of unimpeachable evidence from far and near." The Bob Joneses relied on a "barrage of letters" to make these vague charges because they wanted to distract the university community from the truth.[84] That truth, Mercer wrote, was far more prosaic than the Bob Joneses led the community to believe. Why were so many longtime faculty members and administrators shown the door? Because they wanted higher salaries.[85] Worst of all, those who left were damned in the crudest terms, denounced by Bob Jones Sr. as "crooks" and "instruments of the devil."[86] They would hear it all, Mercer told the university alumni and board of trustees, but none of it was true. Only by spreading rumors and lies could the Bob Joneses hope to maintain their unhealthy iron grip on the faculty and community.

As we might expect, with stakes this high the dispute became decidedly personal. Perhaps most heartbreaking, Ted Mercer's college roommate and lifelong friend Roy Mumme denounced him. Mercer had been disloyal, Mumme told him, and they could no longer be friends.[87] Nor did Bob Jones Sr. take a detached attitude. As Ted Mercer looked for a new job, Jones condemned him in no uncertain terms. Jones felt he could never "recommend Ted Mercer anywhere under any circumstances any time. He is the most malicious and most cruel betrayer of a trust I have ever known in my life."[88]

It took Mercer a few years to land a position as president of Bryan College, where he thrived for decades.[89] Bob Jones University, too, paid a steep price for the purge. Not only faculty but a group of students left as well. From 1953 to 1957, enrollment declined from 2,022 to 1,893.[90] The

Bob Joneses themselves only increased their insistence on their loyalty principle. In 1954 and 1955, Bob Jones Sr. wrote a harsh letter to all faculty and administrators insisting on the continuing need for loyalty above all. Every employee, Jones wrote, was expected to contribute to his or her maximum capacity. Spouses and even children must do their part to further the mission of the school. Any criticism by a faculty member, unless done in the proper spirit and to the proper authority, meant instant discharge. As Bob Jones put it, "You are not to criticize the institution to anyone except the proper executive, and even this criticism is to be made in a constructive, Christian way."[91]

Faculty members and administrators, Jones reminded the community, did not always have as much information about students as did the top administration. For that reason, faculty should restrict themselves to teaching, not "to give students advice about life's problems."[92]

For a while at least, the remaining faculty apparently accepted the lesson of the Mercer purge. At other evangelical and fundamentalist schools, however, the pattern repeated itself. As we've seen, Wheaton College experienced regular ousters of top faculty and even a president. Across the country, evangelical institutions saw repeated waves of faculty purges. At Pepperdine College, to cite just one example, 1958 saw the resignation of nearly half the active faculty. New president M. Norvel Young hoped to move the school into accord with conservative influences in the Church of Christ denomination, and, as at Bob Jones and other evangelical institutions, faculty members voted with their feet.[93]

## *A New Evangelical*

During the 1940s and 1950s, fundamentalist intellectuals worried about more than just low pay, heavy teaching loads, and institutional bullying. Fundamentalism, some believed, needed drastic reform. The legacy of the 1920s had left fundamentalists with a public reputation as cranky anti-modern witch-hunters, out of touch with mainstream values and trends. Why couldn't fundamentalism hold tight to its theological seriousness, some intellectuals asked, while abandoning its self-destructive suspicion of everyone besides trusted fundamentalist insiders? Why couldn't fundamentalists take back their former role as America's conscience, as America's force for good? In 1947, for example, Wheaton alumnus Carl Henry pleaded for a profound reform, for a "progressive Fundamentalism with a social message."[94]

By the time Henry made his plea, fundamentalists—including many faculty members and administrators from colleges, seminaries, institutes, and universities—had created new organizations to assert their role as leaders in mainstream politics and culture. Most notably, the National Association of Evangelicals (NAE) hoped to bring together fundamentalists and other conservative evangelicals to speak with a united voice and to coordinate shared efforts at evangelism.[95]

As always, unity proved elusive. In 1943, Bob Jones Sr. fretted about the difficulties of holding together "our fundamental crowd." If "England, America and Russia can get together" to win a war without jeopardizing their own unique forms of governments, Jones asked, why can't "our fundamental groups" do the same?[96]

As we'll see, Jones's desire for unity wouldn't last long. Even in the early 1940s, other fundamentalists disputed the NAE's right to speak for fundamentalism as a whole. Carl McIntire, a fiery Presbyterian fundamentalist from New Jersey, had recently formed the American Council of Christian Churches, hoping to be "the voice of evangelical Christians."[97] Unlike the wayward NAE, McIntire promised, his organization would preserve itself staunchly separate from apostate Christians in mainline denominations.[98]

For a while, it seemed a safe bet that that the NAE's inclusive big-tent evangelicalism had trumped McIntire's separatist grumbling.[99] Throughout the 1940s, even some of the most irascible fundamentalist leaders remained convinced that the NAE could deliver on its promises for a more powerful united fundamentalism without swaying from orthodoxy. Indeed, in the case of the Bob Joneses, the eventual split from the NAE resulted mainly from personal slights and bruised egos rather than from theological differences or organizational disputes.

At first, both Bob Jones Sr. and Jr. were enthusiastic leaders of the NAE. Senior chaired the first commission on evangelism. Junior was elected to a three-year term on the NAE board of administration, beginning in 1947. By 1950, Junior was elected one of two vice presidents.[100] As a clearer sense of the meanings of a "new evangelical" identity emerged in the late 1940s, however, the fundamentalist Bob Joneses felt increasingly snubbed and underappreciated by the new organization. In 1947, for example, one reader of the NAE magazine insulted the anti-intellectual environment of Bob Jones College. "Can you imagine," this reader sniffed, "any serious academic work being done in an atmosphere of that kind?" Evangelical colleges such as Wheaton, Houghton, and Calvin, the reader noted, had turned out "dozens" of students who had gone on to make names for themselves in mainstream academia, but stuck-in-the-mud fundamentalist colleges like Bob Jones only turned out intellectually stunted, closed-minded preachers, "ridiculous imitations of educational leaders."[101] The NAE, too, neglected to ask Bob Jones College to send a representative to a new committee on education. And when Bob Jones University invited the NAE to hold its 1949 convention on the BJU campus, the offer was refused. As Senior put it in 1949, "Certain brethren connected with the NAE look on us as if we were a liability rather than an asset."[102] The Joneses would not accept a perceived insult for long. In 1951, Junior officially cut ties with the NAE.[103]

By that time, some fundamentalist intellectuals had gone further than simply calling for a new, progressive fundamentalism. They called their new fundamentalism by a new name, or more precisely, by a revived old name. School leaders such as Harold Ockenga, president of Fuller Seminary, preferred to label themselves and their schools "new evangelical."[104] Unlike fundamentalists, new evangelicals hoped to work together with other conservative Protestants to foster nationwide and worldwide revival. Unlike fundamentalists, new evangelicals promised to examine all of their beliefs critically. They remained fiercely committed to the theological basics of fundamentalism, such as an inerrant Bible, a real atonement by Jesus Christ, and real profound miracles, for example. But they allowed more wiggle room on the cultural accretions that had grown up around fundamentalism. Perhaps students could go to the movies after all. And perhaps students should read the works of non-fundamentalist theologians. Above all, a new evangelical would have a more open attitude toward the rest of American society.

Of course, a definition and an identity that seemed perfectly clear in the seminar rooms of Fuller Seminary did not always seem so in the wider world of evangelical and fundamentalist higher education. After all, someone who thought of herself as a "fundamentalist" would likely also consider herself part of a wider "evangelical" tradition. And many "evangelicals" at the time recognized that they were part of a movement that had called itself "fundamentalist" since the 1920s.

The distinction between the two would remain fuzzy and contested for a long time at institutions of higher education. As we've seen, since the 1920s it had never been possible to offer a single, precise definition of fundamentalism. And just as they had since the 1920s, different fundamentalists and evangelicals asserted competing definitions and distinctions about what it meant to be a "fundamentalist" or an "evangelical." As the

1940s progressed, however, the tones of the two sides distinguished themselves ever more clearly. By the time Billy Graham completed his degree at Wheaton College in 1943, for example, Wheaton's faculty had already moved decisively toward an embrace of the neo-evangelical attitude. As one historian put it:

> Wheaton turned Graham aside from the powerful fundamentalist temptation to sectarian separatism, propelling him towards the common American longing for a Christian fellowship that transcends denominational lines.[105]

In turn, over the course of his meteoric successes in the 1950s, Graham himself would further clarify the differences between evangelicals and fundamentalists. As with all things in the world of fundamentalist higher education, the distinctions were often fiercely fought over, and the battles involved an irreducible mix of hurt feelings, theological niceties, old grudges, and unanswerable questions about the proper relationship between fundamentalist faith and mainstream American culture.

By the end of the 1950s, Billy Graham came to embody the new spirit of fundamentalism, the new openness of the evangelical reform. As historian George Marsden has argued, by that time one could get a rough idea of the difference between fundamentalists and evangelicals based on "what one thought of Billy Graham."[106] As we'll see in this section, Graham's blockbuster 1957 crusade in New York City delighted evangelicals and horrified fundamentalists. In that campaign, Graham accepted the sponsorship of both liberal and conservative Protestant organizations. For fundamentalists, the notion that Graham could work with liberal Protestants meant that he was potentially sending new Christians to perdition. More and more, the old idea of separation from all things non-fundamentalist became a defining element of what it meant to be a fundamentalist.

Among the family of fundamentalist colleges and universities, Bob Jones University insisted on its status as the leader of the staunchly separatist, unapologetically "fundamentalist" branch of the evangelical family. By the time Graham packed Madison Square Garden in New York City in 1957, the Bob Joneses had separated themselves and their school from his brand of evangelical outreach. More than that, the Bob Joneses extended their principle of separation to several other organizations that had embraced the neo-evangelical reform. That prospect was not at all clear when Graham was a young student at Bob Jones College in the 1930s. Even back then, Bob Jones Sr. saw Graham's talent for soul-winning. As Jones told Graham's father, "I have ambitions for Billy."[107]

Graham's career took off after his stint at Florida Bible Institute and Wheaton College. By 1947, Graham had become a fundamentalist boy wonder, taking over the presidency of Northwestern Bible College in Minnesota at the tender age of thirty. Northwestern had been founded by the crusty old culture warrior William Bell Riley, the self-declared leader of the fundamentalist movement in the 1920s. As Riley lay on his deathbed in 1947, he hoped to pass the mantle to Billy Graham. Graham wasn't so sure he wanted the responsibility, as he wished to head full-time into evangelical work with the thriving Youth for Christ organization. It was a tough decision, and Graham wrote to Bob Jones Sr. for advice. "I look up to you as a father," Graham concluded his letter, "and appreciate your counsel and help more than you will ever know."[108]

The relationship between the two men, and the two schools, continued for years in the spirit of close cooperation.[109] In just a few short years, however, as Graham's evangelical crusades became a sensation, the relationship between the two men soured, to the point that Jones denounced Graham as worse than a fraud and Bob Jones University refused to host a Graham revival meeting. What happened?

It is difficult to miss the tone of hurt feelings and professional jealousy that took over Jones's letters. In 1951, for example, Jones responded to a short two-paragraph note with an anguished five-page letter to Graham, typed single-spaced and packed with accusations and laments. Graham's campaigns, Jones accused, were not built "on the right foundation." Graham was not thinking first about spreading the difficult truths about salvation; rather, his "love for glamour and your ambition . . . and your desire to please everybody are so dominant in your life that you are staggering from one side of the road to the other." Graham was beginning to believe his own promotional materials, Jones charged. In fact, Graham wasn't really converting people, just holding big feel-good parties. "You are popular," Jones wrote, in words surely calculated to pierce the heart of any revivalist, "like any showman is popular, but you have no real grasp upon the hearts of the people." Had Graham forgotten, Jones wondered, that back before his revivals took off Graham had begged Jones to "call you one of my boys" and tell people that Graham represented the Bob Jones tradition? Now that he was on the front pages, Jones wrote, Graham no longer told people he had attended Bob Jones College. He said he graduated from

Wheaton and implied that Bob Jones was "trying to hang on to your coat tail."[110]

In 1952, Graham assured Jones that he still cherished the older man's "lengthy counsel." He always encouraged fundamentalist young people, he told Jones, to apply to Bob Jones University. And though he occasionally accepted the support of liberal churches, he never had a man on his revival committee "that denied the virgin birth, the vicarious atonement, or the bodily resurrection."[111]

Jones wanted to believe him. But as always in the world of fundamentalism, rumors flew. By the end of 1953, Jones complained that "a rumor has come to me in a round about way to the effect that someone has told you . . . that I have been unfriendly to you and your evangelistic work." It wasn't true, Jones insisted. He still personally liked Graham. Indeed, he hoped for the best, for a true fundamentalist revival. But big headlines usually spelled trouble for untempered young revivalists. It was easy to have one's head turned by the flattery and attention and become too friendly with liberals and modernists.[112]

The Bob Joneses always insisted that they held no personal grudge against Billy Graham. In spite of the unmistakable tones of jealousy and betrayal in his letters, Bob Jones Sr. himself always insisted that his problem with Billy Graham was a theological one. As Graham's revivals grew, Graham accepted help from church leaders outside the world of fundamentalism. His citywide campaigns were organized by committees that included representatives from liberal Protestant churches as well as conservative ones. Working together with non-fundamentalists was fine, Jones argued, if the goal was a non-religious one. But if converts at Graham's crusades were being sent to liberal churches after they pledged their faith in Jesus, those converts would be taught a woefully degraded form of Christianity. His growing opposition to Graham's popular crusades was not a question of personal animosity, Jones insisted, but a much more vital question of salvation.[113]

By 1956, Jones was warning that Graham's crusades had turned into a negative force for true Christianity. "The larger crowds you have," Jones hectored Graham, "the more publicity you get, and the more traveling you do, the more harm you are doing to the cause of evangelism." Evil must be rebuked and reproved, Jones insisted. It must never be cajoled and appeased. Yet that was exactly what Graham was doing with his flattery of liberal Protestantism. And in so doing, Jones warned, "you are selling down the river God's faithful servants."[114]

By 1956, the Bob Joneses refused even to have their school affiliated with Graham's revival campaigns. "It is our sincere conviction," Bob Jones Jr. wrote to one of Graham's revival planners, "that in the long run Billy is going to wreck evangelism and leave even orthodox churches, if they cooperate, spineless and emasculated."[115] The answer at Bob Jones University was clear: fundamentalism now meant separation from new evangelicals and any who might cooperate with liberal or modernist churches. And it tended to enforce that separatism in a particularly aggressive and prickly way.

In 1958, for example, the Bob Joneses hoped to use their usual full-page ad in *Moody Monthly* to proclaim their new status as the true fundamentalist choice, often called the "ultra-fundamentalist" choice, not cowed by the promises of "modernists, infidels and the disciples of the so-called 'New Evangelicalism.'" The leaders of Moody Bible Institute hesitated and eventually decided against running the ad. MBI president William Culbertson wrote in a friendly note to Bob Jones Sr. that they had chosen not to run it because it seemed unnecessarily harsh toward the new evangelicals. True, Culbertson agreed, it was a good thing to be called "ultra-fundamentalist." No one in 1958 doubted Bob Jones University's record as ultra-fundamentalist. Indeed, Culbertson liked that label for Moody Bible Institute as well. But why lump together "new evangelicals" with fundamentalism's traditional enemies? That didn't seem fair or right to Culbertson. After all, Culbertson reasoned, people used the label "new evangelical" in a host of different ways, most of them synonymous with "fundamentalism."[116]

Talk of a divide between the two flagship schools shuddered throughout the fundamentalist family. In 1959, a nervous donor wrote to Bob Jones Jr. for clarification. She wanted to make her annual donation to both BJU and MBI. But she had heard through the grapevine that MBI had refused to run BJU's ad. Was it true? She promised Jones not to send any more money to the Chicago fundamentalists unless and until Jones gave his approval.[117]

As always, that kind of dollars-and-cents activism hit schools hard. President Culbertson wrote back to Bob Jones Jr. in 1959, no longer friendly. Culbertson had heard that the Bob Joneses were spreading the word through fundamentalist circles that MBI no longer represented true fundamentalism. That was too much, Culbertson warned. He threatened that his school would never in the future endorse or support Bob Jones University. Both schools, Culbertson lamented, stand for "the fundamentals of the faith," but the Joneses' bizarrely and unnecessarily hostile style had cut them off.[118]

Moody Bible Institute wasn't the only institution from which Bob Jones University cut ties. In 1960, the school separated from the wildly successful Youth for Christ organization.[119] They also took Charles Fuller's enormously popular *Old-Fashioned Revival Hour* off the campus radio station.[120] By 1960, as the fundamentalists at Moody Bible Institute protested, it was still not entirely clear to most conservative evangelicals what the differences were between "fundamentalists" and "evangelicals." In Greenville, on the BJU campus, it was crystal clear. Fundamentalism—Bob Jones University style—meant ferocious and unyielding separation from any organization that disagreed with the Bob Joneses.

From the other side of the family, fundamentalism looked much different. In the pages of the student newspaper at Wheaton, for example, writers took potshots at fundamentalism's grim insistence on holding itself separate from modern trends. One student bid "Farewell to Fundamentalism." As he put it, "I hereby resign [fundamentalists] to their slow, convulsive death in both peace and isolation."[121] On Wheaton's campus, the label became distasteful to many, a reminder of darker days.

Fuller Seminary, too, firmly embraced an identity as an "evangelical" school. In the late 1940s, Fuller's president, Harold Ockenga, claimed his school was the "main fountain" of the new evangelical movement.[122] By the late 1950s, Fuller's scholars felt free to denounce fundamentalism's outdated ideas. One faculty member, for example, blasted fundamentalism as nothing but "orthodoxy gone cultic."[123]

Fuller's leaders paid a steep price for their aggressive embrace of the new evangelicalism, both in personal and institutional terms. As John Huffman of Indiana's Winona Lake School of Theology (WLST) remembered, WLST's earnest fundamentalist network of churches and revival organizations began hearing "reports back from the field" that Fuller students were not upholding fundamentalist belief in an inerrant Bible. In the case of Fuller and WLST, these rumors led to a breakup, with fundamentalist WLST on one side and evangelical Fuller on the other. Nor could the two seminaries simply go their separate ways. Back when they had both been fundamentalist institutions, the two seminaries had merged. As in any divorce or family feud, they found it agonizingly difficult to agree on the division of property. In addition, President Huffman was confident that Fuller's abandonment of fundamentalism cost it a great deal of donations, "hundreds of thousands of dollars of money that didn't come in any longer." Perhaps more agonizing, Huffman recalled, the split between fundamentalist and evangelical seminaries also cost Charles Fuller "some of his closest, lifelong friends, board members and faculty members."[124]

For some scholars and historians from the extended fundamentalist family, Fuller Seminary's declaration for new evangelicalism and its split from its fundamentalist partners marked a decisive break.[125] However, most other schools that had their roots in the fundamentalist movement moved less decisively, less clearly. In most cases, fundamentalists and evangelicals could not place schools precisely on one side of the family or the other, though by the end of the century evangelical and fundamentalist scholars offered an array of guides.

In 1973, for example, fundamentalist historian George Dollar of Bob Jones University offered lists of remaining "militant Fundamentalist" colleges and universities, "moderate" ones, and the "modified or new-evangelical group." None of his lists were exhaustive or definitive, Dollar explained. In each category, though, Dollar felt confident he could offer a few representative names. Fundamentalist schools, in Dollar's telling, included institutions such as Bob Jones University, naturally, but also several Baptist Bible colleges in Pennsylvania, Colorado, and Missouri, as well as Calvary College in Kentucky, Central Baptist Seminary in Minnesota, Clearwater Christian College in Florida, Faith Theological Seminary in Philadelphia (now in Maryland), Indiana Baptist College, Maranatha Baptist Bible College in Wisconsin, and Midwestern Baptist Bible College in Michigan.[126] Dollar's list of representative "moderate" schools included Biola, Cedarville College in Ohio (now Cedarville University), John Brown University in Arkansas, Moody Bible Institute, Tennessee Temple University, Philadelphia College of the Bible, and Westminster Seminary in Pennsylvania.[127] Even at the schools he called "modified or new-evangelical," Dollar pointed out, it was important to note that the faculty included "some hard-line Fundamentalists who take good stands individually." Dollar included Fuller and Wheaton on this list, as well as Gordon College, Barrington College in Rhode Island (soon to merge with Gordon), King's College in New Jersey, Oklahoma's Oral Roberts University, and Houghton College in western New York.[128]

Even the most well-informed and critical scholars of evangelical and fundamentalist higher education, however, couldn't agree on exactly where and how to draw these lines. In the early 1980s, historian William Ringenberg offered another guide to evangelical and fundamentalist colleges. He agreed with Dollar on some of the "generally acknowledged leaders today" of the fundamentalist side of the family, such as Liberty, Bob Jones, and Baptist Bible of Missouri. But Ringenberg also put Tennessee Temple University in this category.[129] Fundamentalist schools, Ringenberg advised, could be distinguished from other sorts of conservative evangelical institutions by their emphasis on "soul-saving" evangelism,[130] their tendency toward authoritarian leadership styles,[131] their emphasis on religious purity over intellectual freedom,[132] and their tendency to hunker down behind conservative political ideas.[133]

At a conference of prominent evangelical historians in 1985, Timothy Smith agreed that Bob Jones and Liberty could be defined as "independent fundamentalist" schools. But unlike Dollar or Ringenberg, Smith also put Biola in that category, as well as Grace College in Indiana and William Bell Riley's Northwestern College in Minnesota.[134] Like other evangelical and fundamentalist scholars, Smith did not sort his schools according to any hard-and-fast rules, but rather according to reputation, tradition, and personal connections. By the end of the twentieth century, some colleges, universities, and seminaries had come to represent the evangelical reform. Others stood for fundamentalist separatism. At least as many, however, stood for both. Fuzzy and imprecise college rankings based on academics, athletics, and unmeasurable factors of prestige could be joined, in evangelical and fundamentalist circles, by fuzzy and imprecise rankings of evangelical openness or fundamentalist purity.

## *Anyone Who Likes Billy Graham*

If the definitions of "fundamentalist" and "evangelical" seemed unclear, it was not due to any shortage of attempts by school leaders and intellectuals to clarify matters. As we've seen, the Bob Joneses hoped to convince the evangelical and fundamentalist public that "new evangelicalism" was nothing more than warmed-over modernism and infidelity. From the other side of the family, *Christianity Today* editor Carl Henry offered his own wordy definition of the opposition. "Fundamentalism," Henry insisted in 1966,

> is considered a summary term for theological pugnaciousness, ecumenic disruptiveness, cultural unprogressiveness, scientific obliviousness, and/or anti-intellectual inexcusableness . . . extreme dispensationalism, pulpit sensationalism, excessive emotionalism, social withdrawal and bawdy church music.[135]

Clearly, the Carl Henrys and Bob Joneses of the extended conservative-evangelical family wanted people to think the difference between an evangelical and a fundamentalist was stark and striking. Other school leaders and intellectuals weren't so sure.

For example, on the campuses of schools such as Moody Bible Institute and Gordon, the uncertainties surrounding the emergence of Billy Graham, a new evangelicalism, and a renewed fundamentalism caused no end of storm and stress. Certainly each school had a different experience in the 1950s and 1960s, but they shared a number of common traits. At all schools, for instance, the debate over whether the school remained true to fundamentalism or had embraced evangelicalism was fueled by ceaseless rumors and innuendo. Someone heard from someone else that a certain school welcomed neo-evangelical thinking, or that a seminary was trapped in outdated fundamentalist traditions. At all schools, too, administrators faced intense and contradictory pressure from alumni, students, and faculty. Energized new evangelical professors insisted that crusty fundamentalist thinking must be stripped away. Horrified trustees and wealthy alumni donors fretted that schools leaped into new evangelicalism before they looked carefully enough at the consequences of abandoning fundamentalist verities. Students took their tuition dollars from school to school, hoping to find a school in which they could feel at home, without necessarily defining whether they felt at home as evangelicals or as fundamentalists.

Administrators, as always, struggled mightily to keep everyone happy. Most of them wanted to benefit from the burst of evangelical energy represented by Billy Graham's vibrant neo-evangelical attitude. At the same time, they hoped their campuses might remain attractive to fundamentalist families as they considered their college choices. It seemed like an impossible balancing act, but as some fundamentalist and evangelical scholars noticed, the broader fundamentalist public often did not notice the distinctions that loomed so large in the eyes of intellectuals.

Writing from the staunchly fundamentalist Bob Jones University, for example, historian George Dollar lamented the fact that so many neo-evangelical schools still masqueraded as fundamentalist ones. "They go on getting money and students," Dollar complained, from fundamentalist "churches and groups because they have not announced their new-evangelical character." Colleges and universities that had moved toward a neo-evangelical identity, Dollar warned, could often get away with luring unwary fundamentalist students, since "most of their followers do not know of the differences which exist among evangelical people."[136]

At the storied Moody Bible Institute, top leaders such as President William Culbertson certainly would have disputed the notion that they tried to fool any fundamentalists. Culbertson, for his part, seemed honestly nonplussed by the emergence of Billy Graham's reformed vision for fundamentalism. As Graham's career was peaking in the mid-1950s, for example, Culbertson worried that Graham did not spend enough time publicly trumpeting the positive aspects of fundamentalism.[137] When Graham accepted the support of liberal Protestants in his crusades, Culbertson worried as much as anyone that Graham might be sending his thousands of new converts straight into the arms of theological imposters. To Culbertson, his school's official position in 1955 held true in 1957 as well: "The worst sin today is to say that you agree with the Christian faith and believe the Bible, but then make common cause with those who deny the basic facts of Christianity. Never was it more obviously true that he that is not with Christ is against Him."[138]

Yet Culbertson did not agree that Graham and the neo-evangelicals were so far removed from true Christianity, from the fundamentals of the faith. In 1959, at least, Culbertson believed that the neo-evangelical movement continued to uphold fundamentalism's theological truths.[139] Into the 1960s, Culbertson continued to believe that the neo-evangelical movement included "no deviation from the fundamentals of the faith."[140]

Moody Bible Institute, Culbertson insisted, would continue its policy of fundamentalist purity. It would never cooperate with liberal Protestants who had abandoned the fundamental truths of Christianity. But MBI would also continue to do everything in its power to spread Christ's gospel. As Billy Graham prepared one of his blockbuster revival tours of Chicago in 1962, Culbertson tried to spell out his school's complicated perspective. Billy Graham was "God's servant," Culbertson announced, and Culbertson was happy to have Graham as his "personal friend." Furthermore, Graham had promised not to include any liberal Protestants in the planning committee for his Chicago crusade. If anyone in the MBI community felt he or she could not participate in the revival meetings, Culbertson respected the decision. Such decisions, though, should never be made in a spirit of bitterness and controversy. In the end, MBI students were free to participate in the neo-evangelical crusade if they felt led to do so. They also were free to stand aloof in fundamentalist protest if they thought it necessary.[141]

For his part, Billy Graham and other neo-evangelical leaders worked hard to convince Culbertson that their revival and reform did not represent a betrayal. When he worked with liberal Protestants, Graham asked Culbertson in 1958, how was that different from Bob Jones making a sermon on CBS? Wouldn't the network host a liberal preacher the next week? And couldn't viewers get confused? What about Moody Bible Institute itself? When it showed its evangelistic films to the public, it welcomed any sponsor, including those of liberal and modernist backgrounds. How was any of that different, Graham challenged, from what he was doing in his crusades?[142]

In the end, as did most other fundamentalist and evangelical institutions of higher education, Moody Bible Institute waffled. It embraced Billy Graham personally. It encouraged MBI students and faculty to work together for revival success. But it could not and would not ignore the theological roadblock symbolized by Graham's cooperative attitude toward liberal Protestants. The neo-evangelical revivals were terrific, but they were also dangerous. Students were encouraged to attend the blockbuster rallies. They were also encouraged to stay away. Culbertson himself went to the revival meetings—twice.[143]

Yet Culbertson always insisted that his support for Graham's neo-evangelical popularity did not imply that Culbertson was no longer a fundamentalist. In 1966, for example, Culbertson insisted that Moody Bible Institute included all those who were working "as orthodox, as Evangelicals, as fundamentalists" to bring worldwide revival.[144] More than anything, Culbertson hoped that his school could somehow continue to bridge the ever-expanding gap between the two sides of the conservative-evangelical family.

Even colleges and seminaries that loudly and proudly embraced the neo-evangelical reform and Billy Graham's cooperative revival policies did not always deny or denounce their fundamentalist heritage. The leaders of Gordon College experienced the same sorts of conflicting pressures from evangelicals and fundamentalists within their extended community. As had other school leaders, Gordon president James Forrester tried to be all things to all people. On one hand, Forrester took an active role in organizing Billy Graham's 1964 Boston crusade.[145] Forrester eagerly, if unsuccessfully, tried to lure Graham to campus to deliver a commencement address in 1965.[146] And Forrester fielded calls from Gordon's supporters to move the school in ever more liberal directions. One local pastor, for instance, wrote of his dismay that Forrester had not done more to distance the school "from the fundamental theology which had so characterized the school in previous years."[147]

At the same time, however, Forrester disputed rumors among Gordon alumni, outraged that Forrester and Gordon "have left fundamentalism and are now following new evangelicalism." Gordon, one fundamentalist alumnus warned, had lost both his trust and his financial support.[148] In words that might have shocked the evangelical and fundamentalist intellectuals who insisted that Gordon had moved decisively and irreparably away from the fundamentalist branch of the family and into the evangelical one, President Forrester assured the alumnus that Gordon remained true. "Gordon," Forrester wrote in 1967, "has not moved from [its] fundamentalist position" or its focus on saving souls. The school, Forrester explained, continued to earn the enmity of "the liberals of our generation . . . [who] repudiate us and I think this in itself is testimony to our position." All in all, Forrester insisted, Gordon remained a fundamentalist college and continued to "affirm the separation of the believer from the world."[149]

Forrester was not alone in insisting that the supposed break between evangelical and fundamentalist schools was not as sure and stark as some people assumed. Forrester's successor at Gordon's helm, Harold Ockenga, had done as much as any evangelical school leader to define and promote the neo-evangelical movement.[150] When Ockenga assumed Gordon's leadership in 1969, at least one alumna worried that the new president was too liberal for Gordon. She had heard rumors, she wrote, that "disturbed her greatly." For his part, Ockenga made no secret of his disdain for fundamentalist troublemakers such as Carl McIntire. But he pointed to his record as a long-standing leader of "the evangelical and conservative cause," noting that he had never supported "liberal or modernist" positions.[151]

At least one fundamentalist member of the extended Gordon community agreed. This supporter, who defined himself as "one of those who takes a fundamental approach to the Bible," wrote to offer Ockenga his fundamentalist vote of confidence. Every Sunday morning, this listener enjoyed his dose of fundamentalist preaching from Ockenga's radio talks.[152] Ockenga, in his opinion, was an evangelical who was true to fundamentalist faith. Of course, this enthusiastic listener simply might have been unaware of the growing split between the two. He might not have known that fundamentalists at Bob Jones University opposed the evangelical belief that had come to dominate Fuller Seminary and Gordon College. He might not have been aware that neo-evangelical sentiment at schools like Wheaton led evangelical students to poke fun at stuck-in-the-mud fundamentalists. And no one might have told him that the evangelical branch of the family was no longer on good speaking terms with their fundamentalist cousins. To his mind, there seemed to be no conflict between holding on to fundamentalist faith while enjoying the preaching of one of America's leading evangelical reformers.

And he was not alone. Across the network of evangelical and fundamentalist institutions of higher education, alumni, students, faculty, and administrators often tried politely to ignore the growing divide, or to explain it away. Fundamentalists worked to find a way to support Billy Graham. Evangelical administrators hoped to continue to attract the tuition dollars of fundamentalist students. Alumni accepted awkward assurances that schools remained on both sides of the fence at the same time. Even at those schools that came to embody the two sides the most sharply, the widely proclaimed divorce between evangelicals and fundamentalists often looked instead like a messy, awkward, and unresolved family feud.

## *One Big Happy Family*

In many ways, Bob Jones University became the flagship school of the separatist fundamentalist branch of the family, and Wheaton College served that role for the evangelical side. Given the bitterness of the growing division between evangelicals and fundamentalists, we might expect these two schools to have experienced a decisive split, a once-and-for-all separation. In fact, throughout the 1950s and 1960s, the two schools continued their decades-long tradition of both cooperation and competition, of ferocious opposition along with friendly feelings.

For years, students from fundamentalist and evangelical families continued to attend both schools, though some fundamentalists in the BJU orbit worried that Wheaton's growing evangelical liberalism put fundamentalist students at risk. In 1961, for example, Paul Jackson of the fundamentalist General Association of Regular Baptist Churches (GARBC) warned of persistent rumors that Wheaton had fallen into "doctrinal error." It was bruited about, Jackson wrote, that Wheaton's faculty included "alarming 'soft spots' . . . of the science department." According to Jackson, many fundamentalist GARBC young people "continue to go there, and we do have a responsibility to help protect them!"[153]

Jackson's guess that fundamentalist students continued to attend Wheaton was not an isolated one. Throughout the 1960s, fundamentalist parents and students continued to believe that Wheaton and Bob Jones were both still fundamentalist schools of the same mold. One parent worried in 1963 about "unsuspecting parents" who continued to send their children to Wheaton "without realizing the dangers that are there."[154] Another fretted in 1968 that fundamentalist families were still being told to send their children to Wheaton for a fundamentalist higher education.[155]

For their part, Wheaton's leaders did not do much to disabuse fundamentalist families of their continuing trust in Wheaton. In 1962, for example, President V. Raymond Edman assured a concerned parent that Wheaton was indeed true to the fundamentalist faith and that she should not listen to any rumors she might hear. Wheaton's faculty remained pure, and the school would always continue to be loved and led by "convinced fundamentalists."[156] Wheaton's alumni, too, continued to embrace Wheaton's tradition as a fundamentalist school. Writing in 1963, for example, one alumnus took pride in the fact that Wheaton was not only *a* fundamentalist college but, as he put it, "*the* fundamentalist college."[157]

In spite of all the hard words and hurt feelings, into the 1960s both Wheaton and Bob Jones continued to think of each other as part of one family of conservative-evangelical schools. In 1964, for example, a sharp secretary in Bob Jones Jr.'s office noticed that BJU's coding system did not have a category for Wheaton. For years, the school's administrators had labeled groups, individuals, and organizations according to a stark and simple system. Everyone who worked for the same fundamentalist goals as Bob Jones University was labeled "F" for "friendly." Everyone else—and this was the far larger category—was tagged "U" for "unfriendly." In 1964, Bob Jones Jr.'s secretary asked where Wheaton belonged. Bob Jones Jr. scrawled back a quick note: "Code F (I thought they had been)."[158]

Some measure of official friendliness made institutional sense. Not only students and tuition dollars straddled the evangelical-fundamentalist divide between the two schools; alumni donations did, too. In 1970, for example, Wheaton's treasurer, H. G. Faulkner, sent along a check for $500 with the explanation that an anonymous donor had asked him to send the money to BJU's scholarship fund.[159] The leaders might have seen their schools as sharply divided, but at least some alumni thought otherwise.

In the early 1970s, however, Bob Jones III worked harder to discourage this sort of inter-evangelical cooperation. In 1973, for example, he fielded an inquiry from a Wheaton alumnus who was thinking of applying to BJU for graduate work. Bob Jones III minced no words. If a student had been happy at Wheaton, Jones wrote, "he would not be happy at Bob Jones

University." The two schools had simply grown too far apart. The faculty at Wheaton, Jones explained,

> teach evolution as a fact in their classes; their rules are not enforced; their campus is a hippie colony; and they are no longer even thought of as a Christian school among Fundamentalists in this country. On the campus of Wheaton, Bob Jones University is looked upon with scorn and constantly ridiculed, made fun of openly by the students. They do not believe what we believe; they are not going in the direction we are going.[160]

For Jones, these differences had grown so stark and so decisive that Wheaton and other "New Evangelical or morally eroded" institutions could no longer be coded as friends. In 1974, he officially changed Wheaton's designation to "U."[161]

## *Focus on the Family*

Jones's furious 1973 denunciation of Wheaton helps us make sense of the ways the evangelical-fundamental feud unfolded on the campuses of colleges, seminaries, institutes, and universities. By that date, it seemed painfully obvious to some school leaders that the two types of schools had grown hopelessly apart. Evangelical colleges allowed or even encouraged their faculty to explore the boundaries of creationist thinking. They welcomed new ideas about faith and scripture, if only as better ways to cement students' faith. They loosened their draconian rules for student life and behavior. Students and faculty often looked down their noses at their fundamentalist cousins.

Fundamentalist leaders, meanwhile, no longer considered their evangelical rivals to be part of the same mission. Just as an earlier generation lamented the way Yale and Harvard had slipped away from Puritan certitude into modern skepticism, so did fundamentalist school leaders in the 1950s, 1960s, and 1970s bemoan the way evangelical colleges had succumbed to puffed-up worldly ambitions. Bob Jones Sr. could agree in 1950 that schools such as Bob Jones University, Wheaton College, and Fuller Seminary were "all in the same fight, and the opposition to you is the same opposition we have."[162] Twenty-four years later, his grandson felt obliged to change twenty-six evangelical organizations from "F" to "U," in an attempt to make clear the insuperable division that had grown between evangelical and fundamentalist institutions.[163]

Even at that late date, however, the division that seemed so clear to intellectuals and school leaders never seemed quite as obvious to the broader evangelical and fundamentalist public. Bob Jones III, after all, had slashed the list of "F" schools only after a student assumed that Wheaton and BJU were similar sorts of schools. And at the many other evangelical and fundamentalist schools, the distinctions were even less clear. Was Tennessee Temple University obviously fundamentalist, as some scholars and students believed? Or might it be better characterized as moderate or even evangelical? Was Biola a fundamentalist school, as some of the school's leaders and later historians have insisted? Or was it evangelical, because it had supported Billy Graham's 1969 crusade in Orange County?[164] How about Moody Bible Institute? Had the "West Point of Fundamentalism" shifted over to the evangelical side? Was Gordon really evangelical, even if its president insisted that it remained fundamentalist?

These questions piled up during the 1950s and 1960s. Instead of insisting on a clear and simple division, the way some intellectuals, historians, and school administrators hoped to do, it is much more helpful to think of the division between evangelical and fundamentalist schools as part of an ongoing family feud. Some members of that extended family became more firmly estranged than others, and that estrangement often grew as time marched on. As we've seen, for example, by the 1970s Bob Jones III was eager to denounce Wheaton College in the harshest terms. Most family members, on the other hand, hoped to keep connected to both evangelical and fundamentalist sides of the family in as many ways as possible. This was especially true on the campuses of evangelical and fundamentalist institutions of higher education, where administrators could usually not afford to write off the potential tuition dollars of either fundamentalist or evangelical students.

If there had ever been a clear and simple definition of the outer boundaries of fundamentalist belief, a forthright and obvious division between "fundamentalist" rules and "evangelical" ones, life at both fundamentalist and evangelical colleges would have been much simpler for faculty members. Time and again, however, at schools throughout the extended family, faculty members found themselves kicked out for a mishmash of reasons: theological heterodoxy, behavioral improprieties, institutional plots, and personal grudges. At Wheaton College, for instance, Professor Singer was accused of improper beliefs about Christ's return as well as incompetent plotting to remove the school's president. At Bob Jones University, faculty members left in droves, unhappy about low pay, long hours, and capricious leadership. In all these cases, the fuzzy and imprecise definitions of fundamentalism and new evangelicalism allowed schools to kick out faculty members who challenged the institutions' leaders, just as they expelled students for a wide variety of misconduct and misbelief. In the end, the growing split between fundamentalist and evangelical schools only added to the unclear definitions of proper fundamentalist belief and behavior that had always been a central fact of life on fundamentalist and evangelical campuses.

# 6

# *What Is College For?*

*So I said, Man, get with it. What guy in his right mind would waste a college education by being a missionary? And he said, Paul.*

—AD FOR SUDAN INTERIOR MISSION IN THE PAGES OF THE *MOODY STUDENT*, May 1967[1]

## *A School of Our Own*

Fundamentalist institutions were fundamentalist, but they were also institutions. To stay alive, schools had to attract and keep students. To do that, as the 1940s flowed into the 1950s, 1960s, and 1970s, institutions of higher education had to satisfy hardening expectations about what it meant to be a "real" college or university. At the same time, however, to stay alive as specifically fundamentalist or evangelical institutions, they had to distinguish themselves from mainstream schools and even from other evangelical schools. In short, fundamentalist and evangelical institutions of higher education could not simply wonder what college was for. Administrators, alumni, faculty members, and students had to answer a more difficult question: what was fundamentalist or evangelical college for?

School leaders wondered how to ensure that their schools were the best schools they could possibly be without simply adopting wholesale the ideas that seemed to animate mainstream higher education. How could a school be different, evangelical scholars asked, without being worse? Most often, evangelical and fundamentalist schools tried to create an alternative intellectual world for their students. For example, many school leaders believed that mainstream schools had swallowed whole the flawed assumptions of evolutionary materialism. As we saw in Chapter 3, during the 1920s, 1930s, and 1940s, fundamentalist schools worked hard to become institutional homes for dissenting creationist thinking. In Chapter 9, we'll examine the ways this creation tradition continued in later decades. The creationist protest has always attracted the most attention from those outside the world of evangelicalism, but on the campuses of evangelical and fundamentalist colleges, it was not the most important issue. For most evangelical scholars, evolutionary thinking was only a symptom of a deeper intellectual malaise. If students could be educated in the true meanings of the Bible, many evangelical educators believed, they would be immune from crass evolutionism and other materialistic errors. If they could learn the proper method of Bible reading, they would be equipped for a lifetime of evangelical activism. And the real reason to teach young people how to read and interpret the Bible, evangelical educators often assumed, was not only to make them better people but also to make them better missionaries. If mainstream schools trained students for the world, evangelical schools could train students to reach the world with the Gospel. In addition, if mainstream schools seemed to abandon old-fashioned notions such as patriotism and free enterprise, evangelical colleges could become homes for those dissenting ideas. Students and faculty, too, often created their own countercultural intellectual traditions. In the face of the determinedly imprecise theological principles of their interdenominational institutions, some scholars yearned for a more rigorous systematic theology. When their schools promoted an inclusive, vague evangelical orthodoxy, for example, some evangelical intellectuals insisted instead on the rigorous and systematic orthodoxy of Calvinism.

## *A Real College*

Something happened. It happened at different times and in different ways, but across the twentieth century, the names all changed.[2] A quick look around the map shows the trend: Northwestern Bible and Missionary Training School in Minneapolis (founded 1902) added Northwestern College of Liberal Arts in 1944.[3] In New York, the National Bible Institute (founded 1907) became Shelton College in 1953,[4] and the Nyack Missionary Training Institute (founded 1882) became Nyack Missionary College in 1956.[5] In 1958, the Philadelphia Bible Institute (founded 1914) became Philadelphia College of the Bible.[6] Some schools changed late: Multnomah School of the Bible in Oregon (founded 1936) did not become Multnomah Bible College and Seminary until 1993.[7]

It wasn't only names that changed. By the middle of the twentieth century, new expectations about the structure and role of higher education had hardened. More and more students assumed that higher education should lead to a bachelor's degree, an essential credential that would allow them to enter the ranks of professional careers. And more and more students assumed that any legitimate college or university would have some form of accreditation to prove its status. Like all schools, fundamentalist and evangelical ones scrambled to keep up.

As historian Roger Geiger and others have shown, the crazy-quilt landscape of American higher education in the nineteenth century became increasingly standardized by the middle of the twentieth century. In earlier years, American students expected to drop in and out of higher education as they needed to. There was no single set of admissions criteria, nor was there a standard set of professional expectations about the nature or importance of higher education. As we explored in Chapter 2, well into the twentieth century America's higher-education landscape was littered with colleges, universities, institutes, normal schools, proprietary schools, and technical schools. By the middle of the century, more and more of these alternate sorts of higher education aspired to the status of a college or university. Instead of offering a buffet of courses or programs, capped with certificates of completion or vaguely defined diplomas, more and more institutions offered four-year undergraduate programs leading to bachelor's degrees and a variety of graduate programs leading to master's degrees or doctoral degrees. To claim legitimacy, schools insisted on similar standards for admission. Even those schools that had long offered bachelor's degrees and graduate degrees tightened their expectations for future students. Instead of simply passing language exams or graduating from well-known preparatory schools, incoming students now had to graduate from a standardized high school program, one that included a relatively uniform transcript of courses in literature, math, science, and history. By 1940, today's rough outlines of higher education had acquired a new prestige, with other sorts of educational institutions racing to show a variety of accrediting bodies that they met the requirements of a "real" college or university.[8]

Though they often disagreed with many other directions of modern American higher education, fundamentalist and evangelical institutions participated in this shift with great enthusiasm. As historian Molly Worthen has noted, by the middle of the twentieth century "evangelicals were no different from many other Americans, succumbing to a national mania for the advanced degrees."[9] For schools that had histories as degree-granting colleges or universities, this shift mostly meant clarifying and systematizing existing admissions requirements, accreditation processes, and academic program requirements. For Bible institutes, however, this shift toward four-year programs and bachelor's degrees—and maybe eventually graduate programs and advanced degrees—required a wholesale structural overhaul.

Since their inception in the late nineteenth century, as we saw in Chapter 2, Bible institutes had seen themselves as a different sort of educational institution. Generally speaking, they did not grant degrees; they did not charge tuition, or at least not very much; they did not refuse students admission because of previous academic records; and they did not offer traditional collegiate four-year programs. Bible institutes were not supposed to be colleges. They were meant instead to provide quick and helpful training to adults—to give them tools to pursue their missions, not to give them credentials to pursue professions. By the middle of the twentieth century, it was obvious to everyone in the world of fundamentalist higher education that the Bible institute model no longer fit the needs of students and families. It was not at all clear, however, what those schools should do.

Some of them, especially the larger and better-established ones, transformed themselves into colleges and universities. They expanded their academic offerings to include traditional liberal arts degree programs. They upgraded their facilities and the credentials of their teaching faculties. They did whatever they needed to do to secure accreditation. Many more schools, however, could not afford all that. Some folded. A few survived as Bible institutes, even if they added degree programs. More commonly, Bible institutes scraped together enough classes to offer a very limited array of degree programs. These schools, usually calling themselves "Bible colleges," offered bachelor's degrees, but mostly only for pastors or missionaries, and sometimes for teachers or church musicians.

As we've seen in Chapter 2, some schools had wrestled with these structural questions in the early years of the twentieth century. At Gordon, for example, by 1918 students could earn a bachelor's degree at a college, instead of earning a certificate of completion at a "missionary training school" or "Bible institute." At most other schools, these changes happened later. At the Bible Institute of Los Angeles, for example, the shift to Biola College was made only in 1949. As President Samuel Sutherland remembered, school leaders felt they had no choice. Sutherland did not dispute the value of the old-fashioned model of Bible-institute training. However, as he put it, "in the academic-minded world of today, it is simply recognized that Institute training is not sufficient to meet the needs."

Students demanded a college degree that would serve as a professional credential.[10]

And though it may have seemed obvious and inexorable to Sutherland in hindsight, throughout the middle of the twentieth century it was by no means clear to evangelical educators what exactly students wanted. Might they continue to attend a school that stuck to its institutional guns just as it stuck to its theological guns? Had the Bible-institute model really become only a relic of a quaint and anti-intellectual fundamentalist past? Did all schools need to add a collegiate program and accreditation, or was there some other institutional model that might work? During the middle years of the century, leaders at Bible institutes came up with different answers to these difficult questions.

During his presidency at Moody Bible Institute, for example (1934–1946), Will Houghton pondered the shifting realities of American higher education. Houghton noted that the label "institute" had come into some disrepute. The country, he noted, was "full of little 'institutes.' " These were not reputable schools, Houghton warned, but rather only "temporary little affairs" that turned the label into an "unfortunate classification." What should Moody do? Houghton did not want to abandon the label, as so many other Bible institutes were doing. He had another idea. Instead of calling itself a "college" or "university," MBI could tap into the prestige of a different sort of institution. If MBI changed its name to Moody Educational Center, Houghton believed, it could appeal to popular esteem for medical centers.[11] Despite Houghton's best efforts, his suggestion went nowhere.

Around the same time, some school leaders offered a different solution: the Bible institute could be preserved as a sort of theological junior college, an inoculation against trends in mainstream higher education. In 1938, for example, young readers of the *Moody Monthly* were advised to attend a Bible institute in order to get some "steadying." Once they were thoroughly trained in fundamentalist intellectual traditions at a Bible institute, they could safely attend a state university and remain "militant" Christians.[12]

In the late 1930s, other evangelical college leaders suggested a similar continuing role for the traditional Bible institute program. President J. Oliver Buswell of Wheaton, for example, advised Biola students that their Bible institute program would prepare them well to transfer to a college like Wheaton. Bible institute training, Buswell argued, meant putting on the "whole armour of God." "We find," Buswell wrote, "that Bible institute graduates make the very best college students."[13]

Long into the 1940s, evangelical leaders made similar arguments for the continuing relevance of traditional Bible-institute training. In 1948, for instance, Clarence Mason of the Philadelphia School of the Bible pleaded with the evangelical public to continue to send their children to Bible institutes. No matter what professional course a person planned on, Mason argued, the training offered at Bible institutes would cement young people in their faith. It would also get them ready for their real life's work. Evangelical students had an extra responsibility to prepare not only for a job but also for God's work as a missionary. The Bible institute, Mason insisted, was the perfect institution to provide that sort of training.[14]

By the time President Mason made his case, however, the handwriting was clearly on the wall. Fewer and fewer students were willing and able to postpone their collegiate careers to spend time putting on spiritual armor. Fewer and fewer students saw the need to, because they could attend an evangelical or fundamentalist college that would provide both armor and an academic or professional degree. By the late 1940s, those Bible institutes and missionary training schools that were financially able to do so had begun offering bachelor's degrees and had changed their names to claim status as a college or university, or had at least begun planning their transitions.

Most, but not all. As in all things in the world of Bible institutes, Moody Bible Institute in Chicago stood out. Into the 1960s, the far-flung MBI community continued to debate the notion of changing the structure and name of the flagship institution. As one student wrote anxiously in the pages of the student paper in 1964, MBI should never change its name. Yes, she agreed, most Bible institutes were becoming Bible colleges. They had to, in order to attract students. But MBI was different. Attending such a prestigious, one-of-a-kind institute remained attractive, she thought. "In evangelical circles," she insisted, "this diploma is gold."[15]

Some students thought MBI could offer bachelor's degrees without tampering with its established name. After all, one student wrote, other unique "institutes" remained uniquely prestigious. Massachusetts Institute of Technology, for example, never needed to change its name to remain attractive to students. The proper plan, he suggested, was simply to "elevate Moody to the same academically respectable, intellectually satisfactory, and educationally effective level as these technical institutes." Like MIT, MBI could offer everything other colleges offered without abandoning its unique and storied label.[16]

It was not only students who wondered about the issue. Longtime MBI general manager H. C. Crowell wondered in 1959 what to do in light of changing trends. There was no need to lose either the name or the Bible institute program, Crowell thought. It would be both prudent and possible, Crowell argued, to "move to a four-year, degree-granting curriculum," yet still "maintain the Bible Institute emphasis."[17]

In the end, that is exactly what MBI did. As he did in all things, President Culbertson consulted the far-flung MBI network before he came to any conclusion. In 1962, he sent a questionnaire to all alumni since 1954, asking them for their feelings about moving to a degree-granting program. By early 1963, he was convinced. MBI, Culbertson told the conservative trustees, had always kept up with changing times. In the 1940s they had begun requiring high school diplomas for admission. In the 1950s they had switched to an increasingly standard semester schedule. The time had come, Culbertson argued, to offer both a traditional Bible-institute training program and a bachelor's degree option. By 1963, Culbertson believed, there was no other viable option. "Evangelical young people and . . . Christian organizations," Culbertson insisted, "demand . . . degrees as the hallmark of academic preparation."[18] Even if MBI kept the "institute" label and training program, it recognized the need to offer the sort of undergraduate college education that students and their families demanded. There was simply no longer room in America's higher-education landscape for schools that could not do so.

Yet many smaller schools did not have the financial ability to create expensive new college programs, nor could they simply remain "institutes." The leaders of several smaller schools found themselves, as usual, forced to think on their feet. By the middle of the twentieth century, many Bible institutes had added a few academic programs and began calling themselves Bible colleges instead.

To make things more confusing, some educators had long used the terms "Bible college" and "Bible institute" interchangeably.[19] By the middle of the century, however, the two sorts of institutions had largely clarified their roles. To Dean Maxwell Coder of Moody Bible Institute, by 1960 the differences were clear. Both Bible institutes and Bible colleges were specifically "professional schools." They did not attempt to do what "liberal arts colleges" did. Rather, Bible institutes and Bible colleges focused on "training . . . Christian workers, teachers, ministers, missionaries, musicians and others." At an institute, Coder explained, students attended for three years. At a college, students tacked on an extra year of "general education."

An institute could offer a diploma or certificate. A college could offer a bachelor's degree.[20]

Unlike larger liberal-arts colleges, Bible colleges tended to offer only a few degree programs. By the later decades of the twentieth century, the limited programs and cramped facilities of many Bible colleges had given them something of a bad reputation among evangelical intellectuals. Even the most fervent advocates of the Bible-college model admitted that most people viewed them as "inferior and only partially evolved as an acceptable type of college education."[21] By 1982, even the largest and best-known Bible colleges felt a need to defend their continuing existence as unique evangelical institutions. Columbia Bible College (CBC) in South Carolina advertised itself as a better option for evangelicals. Some evangelical students, CBC warned, thought it was sufficient to add only "a little Bible" to their higher education. "But if you're serious about a direct involvement in getting God's big job done," the CBC ad explained,

> it takes more than a few Bible courses. It takes a whole education centered around the Bible. You need to know it. You need to live it. You need to communicate it. That's Columbia Bible College.[22]

Columbia's bravado barely masked its deep existential insecurity. By 1980, evangelical educators and intellectuals were not at all assured that students really did need a Bible-college experience. As Kenneth Gangel, professor and former president of Miami Christian College in Florida, argued in 1980 in the pages of *Christianity Today*, the prospect for Bible colleges was "gloomy." If they could join the ranks of the few "progressive Bible colleges" that secured "the highest possible levels of accreditation," engaged faculty and students in academic organizations, and joined other evangelical institutions in helpful consortiums, Gangel concluded, then perhaps they might survive. Any school that hoped to rest on its Bible-institute laurels, however, could not hope to fare so well.[23]

## *The Lure of Accreditation*

Professor Gangel was not the only evangelical school leader to emphasize the importance of accreditation. By the time he wrote, evangelical and fundamentalist colleges had long felt the need to come to grips with the questions of accreditation: To whom should schools apply? Would accreditation force schools to slide toward theological liberalism? Could evangelical schools set up their own accrediting bodies? Most schools viewed accreditation as a valuable and attractive thing; something to work for and brag about. As in so many other things, Bob Jones University bucked the trend. While most schools scraped and saved to satisfy accrediting bodies, the Bob Joneses elevated their anti-accreditation attitude into a quasi-theological principle. Their refusal to seek accreditation, the Bob Joneses insisted for decades, should be seen as a core value of true fundamentalist higher education.

A few other fundamentalists agreed. But on non-fundamentalist campuses, regional accreditation had come to seem like an obvious requirement for respectable institutions. At most schools, accreditation was used as proof that the school satisfied minimal institutional requirements. Independent accrediting agencies investigated the numbers of books in a school's libraries, the numbers of faculty members with advanced degrees, teaching loads, and financial reports. To secure accreditation, colleges and universities had to prove that they met such standards. The process required significant financial investment, but school leaders realized that gaining or losing accreditation was often a life-or-death proposition. Most students would avoid an unaccredited school. After all, credits from unaccredited schools could not usually be transferred to accredited schools. Students graduating from unaccredited schools could not usually apply to graduate schools. To the school-shopping public, accreditation became a seal of approval, a sign that a school was an authentic college or university.

And all fundamentalist school leaders had always insisted that their schools were authentic. Throughout the twentieth century, institutions large and small boasted about their various forms of accreditation. During the 1930s, for example, the letterhead of the Colorado School of the Bible proudly proclaimed, "Accredited Member Evangelical Teachers Training Association."[24] And in the early 1980s, the future Liberty University told potential students that it was one of the few fundamentalist liberal arts colleges that could claim to be "regionally accredited."[25]

It made sense for school leaders to boast. Fundamentalist and evangelical students in all decades worried about accreditation. One student wrote to Fuller Theological Seminary for advice in 1950. He knew he wanted to go to a "conservative Christian College." But he didn't know how important it was for a school to have accreditation. He liked the reputation of Bob Jones University but wondered, "Would it be advisable to go to an unaccredited college?"[26]

Schools that weren't accredited often felt obliged to justify their status as real schools. In 1955, for example, President John Huffman of Winona Lake School of Theology in Indiana explained his school's unaccredited status to a curious correspondent. The correspondent had read that Winona Lake claimed to be "fully accredited."[27] Was it true? "We often use the term 'accredited courses,'" Huffman replied defensively, but Winona Lake had never claimed to be "fully accredited." His school, Huffman explained, never sought any accreditation other than the "high recommendation to innumerable institutions by students and professors who have delighted in reporting the high grade work done in our institution."[28]

The biggest problem, as Huffman recognized, was that even a "high recommendation" did not mean that other colleges, universities, and graduate schools would accept credits from unaccredited institutions. For some unaccredited fundamentalist schools, students and graduates faced a severely limited choice of graduate schools and transfer opportunities. One student in the 1930s, for instance, completed his undergraduate degree at Wheaton College because at the time it was one of the few schools in the country that would accept his credits from CBC in South Carolina.[29] Before Wheaton earned its own regional accreditation, its students had some trouble transferring, too. In 1925, the University of Illinois gave Wheaton only a B rating. That meant that graduates from Wheaton could attend the university's graduate schools only if they first did additional undergraduate course work.[30]

The implied insult stung. Wheaton's leaders worked hard in the 1920s and 1930s to improve their reputation and secure regional accreditation and graduate-school accreditation. It wasn't easy, and it wasn't cheap. In 1925, the University of Illinois's graduate-school inspectors had found Wheaton mostly satisfactory in those departments, with the exception of Wheaton's teaching load. Too many Wheaton professors, the grad-school inspectors concluded, taught more than sixteen semester-hours per week.[31]

As historian Michael Hamilton has pointed out, Blanchard's successor as president at Wheaton, Oliver Buswell, put a high priority on accreditation. Accreditation meant more than simply institutional survival, in Buswell's eyes. As Hamilton explained, Buswell

> passionately believed that one of the best ways to earn intellectual respect for fundamentalist Christianity would be to make certain that Wheaton achieved the highest standing possible in the eyes of secular educators.[32]

Unlike most fundamentalist colleges, Wheaton's long history had given it significant experience with the reefs and shoals of accreditation. It had earned regional accreditation with the North Central Association of Colleges and Schools in 1912, but it had lost it in 1914. By 1916, the school's leaders had pushed through a major restructuring in order to get their accreditation back. College and academy were separated, faculty were split into eight departments, courses were cut into credit hours, and new faculty hires needed more credentials. Until the 1930s, the North Central Association also required a minimum endowment, which Wheaton's leaders struggled to secure. In every decade, the leaders of Wheaton took extraordinary measures to keep their regional and graduate school accreditation. By the 1930s, Wheaton had proven that it would never be called a B-grade institution again.[33]

Other fundamentalist schools worked just as hard to get regional accreditation, even if they did not have the same resources as Wheaton. Gordon's leaders sought for years to secure accreditation from the New England Association for Colleges. In 1944, Gordon's leaders first applied. The accreditors rejected them, as they did again in 1948, 1953, and 1956. The accreditors' reasons were always the same: Gordon required too much teaching from its faculty and paid them too little; Gordon did not have enough money in the bank; Gordon had not had a four-year college program for long enough. Finally, in 1961, the New England Association approved Gordon's programs and facilities.[34]

Accreditation was expensive. It favored established schools with extensive facilities. It's not surprising, therefore, that schools tended to boast about their status. Biola had first earned regional accreditation in 1961.[35] In 1967, Biola bragged about its double accreditation status in advertisements in *Christianity Today*. These quarter-page ads made no claims about fundamentalist orthodoxy or lifestyle rules. Rather, they listed Biola's accreditation with both the Western Association of Schools and Colleges and the Collegiate Division of the Accrediting Association of Bible Colleges. In these ads, at least, Biola emphasized not its theology or fundamentalist credentials but rather such institutional credentials as its large library.[36]

Biola was not the only school to brag. In the 1970s, for example, the new Lynchburg Baptist College prioritized accreditation. In 1974, school leaders admitted, the school had not yet earned regional accreditation. But it had done more to move toward accredited status than any other "'fundamentalist' college in America."[37] By 1982, earning regional accreditation with the Southern Association of Colleges was only part of what had made the new school nothing short of a "Miracle on Liberty Mountain." No other "fundamental, separatist, local-church affiliated" school, Liberty's leaders boasted, could claim regional accreditation.[38]

Liberty's leaders were correct: not many fundamentalist and evangelical schools could afford the facilities required to earn regional accreditation. But that did not leave them entirely out in the cold. In 1931, leaders at Moody Bible Institute had established the Evangelical Teacher Training Association (ETTA), which functioned as a sort of accrediting body.[39] Members of ETTA could earn "gold seal" status by requiring high school graduation for admission, mandating college degrees for faculty, and maintaining a library with at least a thousand volumes. By 1942, ETTA claimed more than one hundred members.[40]

In the mid-1940s, Bible-school leaders established a similar organization along the lines of regional accreditation organizations. Beginning in 1948, the Accrediting Association of Bible Institutes and Bible Colleges welcomed twelve member schools. By the late 1950s, recognizing the shifting currents of higher education, the body shortened its name to the Accrediting Association of Bible Colleges (AABC), with a full-time executive secretary and official recognition as an accrediting agency with the United States Office of Education. As did regional accrediting boards, the AABC established minimum institutional standards for membership and offered both prestige and transferability of school credits.[41] By the end of the twentieth century, AABC member schools maintained a student/faculty ratio no higher than 25:1, required graduate degrees for faculty members, and made high school graduation a minimum requirement for admission.[42]

Not every fundamentalist and evangelical school could meet these standards. Indeed, some school leaders insisted they never wanted to. L. H. Maxwell of the Prairie Bible Institute in Alberta scoffed at the growing pressure to earn accreditation. "God has given us a special method of Bible study second to none," Maxwell insisted, "and we are content to do what God wants us to do without having to adjust to that which others feel led to do."[43]

The most famous fundamentalist dissent from the trend toward accreditation came from Bob Jones University. In its earliest years, Bob Jones College had claimed to be seeking accreditation.[44] As late as 1939, Bob Jones College claimed to be an "accredited" institution.[45]

By the late 1940s, however, the Bob Joneses had taken a stand against accreditation. In 1947, Bob Jones Sr. insisted that accrediting organizations tended to be "not only modernistic and radical but in some ways pagan and atheistic."[46] By that time, Jones knew his policy made his school stand out. As he fulminated in 1950:

> Bob Jones University is probably the only one in America that could join an association that does not join, and we refuse to join. We believe . . . that a Christian institution should make its own policies in line with the purposes it has in view and that no association of any kind should dictate the administrative policies of the institution.[47]

As they did with so many other issues, the Bob Joneses elevated their position on accreditation to near-sacred status.

By the end of the twentieth century, Bob Jones Sr.'s grandson Bob Jones III celebrated the school's continuing refusal to seek accreditation. It was not due to lack of facilities. It was not due to weakness of programs or faculty credentials. Rather, refusal to seek accreditation became at Bob Jones University yet another marker of true fundamentalism, of true purity in a world of higher education that had long since begun its slide into sin. As Bob Jones III explained in 1991:

> Accrediting associations will not approve our educational process if it does not include the worship of their gods. All education is brainwashing. We wash with the pure water of God's word, and they wash with the polluted waters of the New Age.[48]

For the Bob Joneses, accreditation became not merely an inevitable requirement for a modern university but yet another attempt by the secular sinful world to smother those few true fundamentalists willing to stand up to it.

Not surprisingly, this idiosyncratic position put the leaders of Bob Jones University at odds with most of the rest of the network of evangelical and fundamentalist higher education. Since at least 1942, Bob Jones College graduates had a difficult time gaining admission to graduate seminaries.[49] The Southern Baptist Seminary in Louisville, Kentucky, for example, earned the ire of Bob Jones Sr. by telling Bob Jones College graduates they could not attend without catch-up academic work. Bob Jones Sr. huffily insisted, "There must have been some mistake." Bob Jones College graduates, Jones told the Louisville registrar, were accepted and welcomed at great graduate seminaries all over the country, including prestigious schools such as Princeton.[50] Perhaps, Jones threatened darkly, he would simply open his own seminary, drawing students away from Louisville.[51]

Bob Jones College's fight with graduate seminaries didn't end there. Other schools, too, warned the Bob Joneses that they could not admit BJC (and eventually BJU) grads. Carl Henry, for instance, at the time representing Fuller Seminary in California, warned Bob Jones Sr. that Fuller Seminary would be imperiling its own eventual accreditation if it admitted BJC graduates.[52] And leaders in Louisville continued to cross swords with Bob Jones over the question of accreditation. In 1947, seminary president Ellis Fuller found himself utterly flabbergasted by the Bob Joneses' intransigence. Accreditation had nothing to do with theology, Fuller insisted. Rather, it was nothing more than "the best measuring rod for academic standing." He hated to fight about it, Fuller told Jones, yet Jones seemed to be, at best, "confused."[53]

Confused or not, the Bob Joneses continued to tie their opposition to accreditation to their larger vision of proper fundamentalist higher education. As they had done since their founding and would continue to do throughout the twentieth century, the Bob Joneses elevated their idiosyncratic opinions about the institutional structure of their school into theological necessities. Once they had done so, their school often found itself alone and exposed, unable to climb back easily from their hard-and-fast positions. For most evangelical and fundamentalist schools, however, accreditation was only a question of money, not morality. Accreditation, for most colleges, served as more proof that evangelical institutions had satisfied the requirements to call themselves "real" colleges. As those requirements shifted during the middle decades of the twentieth century, fundamentalist and evangelical schools scrambled to shift along with them.

## *The Fundamentalist Multiversity*

In the mid-1950s, some evangelical leaders were hoping to do more than just keep up with changing trends in higher education. Beginning in 1955, Hudson Armerding pushed a plan for a "Christian university" that would help evangelical and fundamentalist colleges leapfrog over non-evangelical schools and reclaim their role as academic innovators. Long before he moved to Wheaton in 1961, Armerding hashed out his plans from his position as dean at Gordon College. Armerding imagined a formal network of evangelical schools that would allow them to make a more profound political, cultural, and educational impact. As Armerding originally conceived it, his plan would encourage participating colleges to adopt a relatively uniform curriculum for the first two years of student attendance. Then every campus would specialize. Some would offer majors in the liberal arts, others in the sciences, and yet others in education, business, law, or medicine. The entire collegiate network would combine to offer outstanding graduate programs, located either at a central graduate campus or spread among the participating colleges. The main result, Dean Armerding predicted, would be an evangelical intellectual powerhouse that would have "nation-wide impact upon the social and cultural life of the nation."[54]

At first Armerding laid out his plan confidentially to President Leonard Lewis of Gordon College. By the end of the year, Armerding made his proposal public. The graduate programs in theology, arts and sciences, education, and business would be located at Gordon's campus. The total cost of hiring new faculty and preparing new facilities would come to roughly $2.5 million per year and would require a total endowment of $65 million.[55] Perhaps most important to evangelical intellectuals, Armerding promised that this pricey endeavor was a modern evangelical necessity. Only by investing in a "Christian university," Armerding argued in 1955, could evangelical scholars confidently raise their voices in all the academic fields, "always with the confidence that truth is one, that there is perfect harmony between God's natural revelation and His written revelation, the Scriptures." Modern academic life required increased specialization, Armerding insisted. Only by combining resources in a multi-campus university could smaller evangelical colleges find faculty members who had both impeccable academic credentials and sincere evangelical belief.[56]

Even after Armerding left Gordon in 1961 to take a job at Wheaton College, the leaders at Gordon remained enthusiastic about Armerding's plan. In late 1961, new Gordon president James Forrester privately enthused about the idea. As Forrester pictured it, Armerding's plan could create a new sort of evangelical intellectual institution, a "great Christian university." The new institution could enjoy similar prestige and structure to "Oxford, Cambridge, the University of Toronto, Claremont College, and other associated programs." Too often, Forrester lamented, "the limited assets available to Christian higher education . . . are divided." Instead of cooperating to offer students and society a compelling intellectual alternative, evangelical colleges often suffered from their "fractured effort." As a result, evangelical students and intellectuals could not hope to match "the consolidated interests of educators committed to the philosophical position of a naturalistic humanism in the university field."[57]

From his post as the editor of the widely read evangelical magazine *Christianity Today*, Carl Henry agreed. The world of evangelical higher education needed some sort of "federated campus," Henry argued in 1962. Too many small evangelical colleges, he lamented, wasted too much effort in their "almost hopeless struggle for accreditation." By combining resources, the network of evangelical colleges could "overcome much of its present fragmentation and lift its academic achievements."[58]

From his new post at Wheaton, Hudson Armerding continued to promote his pet idea of a "national university" that would combine the resources of the network of evangelical colleges. At the annual meeting of the National Association of Evangelicals in 1966, Armerding repeated his belief that such a program could offer graduate programs "of breadth and depth not now available at any one of the potential participating colleges."[59]

In spite of optimistic promises, the notion of a multi-campus evangelical university seemed a tall order. Carl Henry, for one, worried that traditional rivalries would always get in the way. In the Northeast, for example, in spite of their geographical proximity and doctrinal affinity, Gordon College and Barrington College in Providence, Rhode Island, had always seen themselves as rivals, not collaborators. In the early 1960s, Henry told President James Forrester of Gordon privately that the leadership of Barrington would always see its best interests as "stressing its differences from Gordon."[60]

Perhaps due to these stubborn inter-school rivalries, Armerding and other leaders took a measured approach. In the late 1960s, they began planning a consortium of evangelical schools. As Armerding envisioned it in 1969, this Christian College Consortium would establish a permanent institutional center at one school, with a permanent staff to identify and collect academic resources that all the participating schools could use. The proposed consortium would establish commissions on missionary training, scholarship, cooperative programs, and research. To thrive, the consortium would need to recruit at least twenty evangelical Christian colleges.[61]

The Christian College Consortium was officially born in 1971. Charter members included Seattle Pacific College, Oklahoma Christian College, Asbury College in Kentucky, Taylor University in Indiana, Messiah College in Pennsylvania, Eastern Mennonite College in Virginia, Bethel College in Minnesota, Greenville College in Illinois, Gordon, and Wheaton. At first, each school pledged to contribute $1,500 to the consortium, though a few schools balked at the steep price. The first goal of the group was to invest in expensive technological equipment that none of the schools could afford on their own, especially "computer systems for management information systems."[62] By the end of the year, Armerding had convinced his skeptical colleagues that one of the primary goals of the fledging organization must be to "explore the feasibility of a university system of Christian colleges."[63]

The organization thrived, but not in the ways Armerding had fantasized about for so many years. By the mid-1970s, a new sister organization, the Christian College Coalition, had begun to move in different directions. Instead of academic combination, the new coalition stressed political lobbying to secure influence for evangelical schools.[64] The broader goals of protecting religious freedoms for member schools allowed coalition leaders to cast a wider net. By 1980, President John R. Dellenback had sent out more than a hundred invitations to potential members. Evangelical and fundamentalist schools such as Pepperdine, Liberty, and Bob Jones were invited, but so were two Catholic colleges, a Missouri Synod Lutheran school, and a Seventh-day Adventist school.[65]

The fast-growing coalition proved that Christian schools could work together. It also proved, however, that they would not combine into Armerding's dream university. In 1976, the consortium officially gave up its dream of forming a great Christian university. Instead, the Christian College Coalition would provide a political voice for evangelical colleges.[66]

## The Good (Text) Book

Though they were not able to combine into a multi-campus research university, all conservative evangelical institutions of higher education agreed on one thing: higher education must focus squarely on the Bible. They might not have agreed on the details of what a properly biblical higher education entailed, but they never disputed the notion that the Bible must somehow be at the center of all learning. They agreed, too, that however they taught the Bible, doing it right meant going against the grain of mainstream higher education.

In early years, fundamentalist school leaders simply assumed that all they needed were Bible courses taught by reliably fundamentalist teachers. Yet studying the Bible was never so simple for fundamentalists. Since even before the emergence of the fundamentalist movement in the 1920s, conservative evangelical intellectuals found themselves confronting the "two-edged sword" of Bible study.[67] By the middle of the twentieth century, fundamentalist and evangelical scholars came to recognize that merely studying the Bible was not enough, even if they could figure out how to do it correctly.

The Bible and a certain reverent attitude toward it have always been the hallmarks of conservative evangelicalism. Indeed, as the first generation of fundamentalists realized their desire for their own reliable schools, it was generally assumed that such schools would make the Bible their central textbook. A reliable school, that first generation assumed, could be recognized by its attitude toward the Bible.

At the founding meeting of the World Christian Fundamentals Association in 1919, for example, the committee on higher education reported that too many schools had slid away from fundamentalist higher education. How did they know? Because students were losing their "reliance in the Bible as a divine revelation." A new network of "colleges, seminaries, and academies" was needed, the committee concluded, in order to restore the Bible to its proper role as the revered book to guide higher education.[68]

Similarly, as Charles Blanchard of Wheaton College surveyed his neighbor schools in the 1910s, one of the questions he asked was whether those schools considered the Bible to be the "inspired Word of God." Too many schools, Blanchard worried, no longer focused on the Bible.[69] Bob Jones, Sr., promoting his new college during the 1920s, encouraged parents to "be sure to send your son and daughter to an institution that stands for the Bible, unqualifiedly."[70]

True to the hopes of early leaders such as Blanchard and Jones, students at evangelical and fundamentalist schools have always studied the Bible. At Bible institutes and Bible colleges, especially, students began and ended their studies with the Bible. As historian William Ringenberg put it, "Every Bible college from the beginning of the movement to the present has made the English Bible the heart of its curriculum."[71] Schools such as Biola proudly claimed in 1920, "The Bible is the only text book of the Bible institute."[72] At liberal-arts colleges and universities as well, studying the Bible has always been a key element of evangelical and fundamentalist higher education.

Yet from the beginning of the fundamentalist movement in the 1920s, studying the Bible has never been the simple cure-all that fundamentalist intellectuals often assumed. As Timothy Weber has pointed out, fundamentalists have always struggled with an irreconcilable tension when it came to studying the Bible.[73] Fundamentalism, especially in its early years, defined itself as a reverent and populist attitude toward biblical interpretation. Everyone must read the Bible, fundamentalists assumed. And everyone could understand it. No special higher critical methods were needed, no expertise in Hebrew or Greek. Too often, fundamentalists argued, liberal critics found their heads turned by their own fancy methods and had strayed from the home truths available to all in the Bible, properly read.[74]

Yet fundamentalists recognized early on that correct Bible reading must be taught, and taught properly. Left on their own, as historian Brendan Pietsch has argued recently, too many regular readers might be overwhelmed by the seeming inconsistencies in the biblical narrative. They might wonder why so many of the rules laid down in the Old Testament were no longer followed by American Christians. They might struggle to understand why the Bible tarried so long on seemingly endless lists of genealogies. Worst of all, unwary readers might find the answers of the new biblical critics convincing. They might agree that the mishmash of biblical stories and prescriptions resulted from its compilation by merely human editors, prone to all the foibles of fallen humanity.[75]

In response, many conservative evangelicals embraced a different sort of innovation in biblical interpretation. Dispensational methods promised a more scientific, more exact way to understand the Bible. Dispensationalists solved the apparent problems of consistency by dividing up sacred history into discrete dispensations. But dispensationalism was more than just a way to divide time. Once the method was grasped, the miraculous unity and divine beauty of the Bible as a whole could be seen and understood in its full glory. Without it, hapless readers might certainly find convincing the claims of theological modernists and liberal critics.[76]

As in all things, there was never unity among fundamentalist and evangelical thinkers about the propriety of dispensational methods of Bible reading. The influence of dispensational thinking, however, was enormous in the network of evangelical and fundamentalist higher education, especially among schools that emerged from the Bible institute tradition. At Moody Bible Institute, for example, longtime school leader James M. Gray had built his career on teaching readers how to read the Bible through a dispensational lens. Gray's popular "synthetic" approach to Bible study consisted of several steps. First, readers should read an entire book in one sitting. From Genesis through Revelation, readers should begin by reading each book in its entirety. They should not worry about chapters, or verses, or even commentaries. People should read the whole Bible through in this way before going back and reading individual books several times until themes and feelings emerged.[77]

Gray insisted that his synthetic method would allow every reader to experience the Bible as God intended. The message was there; God wanted everyone to understand it. And Gray believed that his every-reader-for-himself method served as the way to clear away any obstacles between text and reader. The Bible needed no help. It only needed prayerful and earnest reading, free from soul-destroying skepticism. As Gray explained, "The facts must come first and interpretation afterwards. To a great extent, if we get the facts, the interpretation will take care of itself."[78]

For students at Gray's Moody Bible Institute and at other fundamentalist schools, studying the Bible often meant learning the dispensational system. In every generation, students such as Gladys Porter spent a good deal of their study time learning to read the Bible properly. For Porter, the most arduous task was learning the intricacies of the system. As a student at Moody Bible Institute in the early 1940s, Porter pored over detailed charts of each dispensation, memorizing names, facts, and meanings. As Gladys Porter did, generations of students—especially at Bible institutes and colleges—sweated out the lists of names, dates, places, and dispensational interpretations. They read the Bible, to be sure. But they never simply read the Bible on their own, free to come up with interpretations that made sense to them. Bible education at many fundamentalist schools meant teaching students how to read the Bible through the lens of God's dispensations.[79]

The evangelical world was never united in its love for dispensational approaches to the Bible.[80] Indeed, by the 1960s evangelical and fundamentalist scholars often agreed that simply learning how to read the Bible—even if it was done right—was not enough. As historian Molly Worthen has argued, building on the "presuppositionalist" thinking of an earlier generation of scholars such as Cornelius Van Til and Gordon Clark, popularizers such as Francis Schaeffer demanded that true Christian education required a far more profound commitment to biblical thinking. In order to live as a real Christian believer, Schaffer argued, evangelicals must do more than simply learn the Bible and master the intricacies of the dispensational method. Biblical presuppositions must guide every aspect of evangelicals' lives. Were schools teaching these deeper truths? Or were they allowing students to wallow in secular presuppositions and worldviews even as they learned to mouth hollowed-out biblical phrases?[81]

By the later 1960s, fundamentalist and evangelical school leaders often worried that these sorts of questions had bite. In 1969, for example, veteran evangelical educator Frank Gaebelein spent the summer at Wheaton College. Together with faculty members there, he hoped to figure out "the relationship of various fields of knowledge with the biblical world view."[82] Students needed to learn the Bible, true, but they needed to do more than that. They needed to learn everything from the proper biblical worldview, examining their presuppositions and bringing them into line with truly evangelical ways of thinking. Otherwise, school leaders worried, they might simply paper over secular ways of thinking with incompatible evangelical and fundamentalist ways of reading the Bible.

From Wheaton College, philosophy professor Arthur Holmes articulated this new need for a more profound intellectual commitment to a biblical worldview. It was not enough, Holmes argued throughout the 1960s and 1970s, for evangelical colleges merely "to offer a good education plus biblical studies in an atmosphere of piety."[83] In order to fulfill their mission, Holmes argued, evangelical colleges needed to differ more radically from secular or pluralist ones. Any truly evangelical school, Holmes thought, must put "biblical and theological studies . . . at the heart of a Christian's thinking."[84] Any true higher education must do more than just encourage students to read the Bible, or even to read the Bible in a specifically evangelical or fundamentalist way. The ultimate goal, at least in Holmes's opinion, was to help all students "develop a Christian world-view."[85]

## *Earthen Vessels*

However they did it, evangelical and fundamentalist students in every decade wanted to do more than merely learn the Bible for its own sake. They often viewed higher education mainly as preparation for life as a missionary, and that focus transformed their understandings of the nature and purpose of higher education. As William Ringenberg concluded in his study of evangelical colleges, "It is difficult to exaggerate the extent to which the early Bible schools emphasized foreign missionary activity."[86] Yet, as historian Joel Carpenter has argued, "this story has been neglected" by historians.[87] If we want to understand fundamentalist higher education and fundamentalism itself, it will be vital to note the ways preparation for missionary work was often seen as the most important role of colleges, universities, institutes, and seminaries. This impulse to preparation for missionary work was particularly dominant on the campuses of Bible institutes and those colleges that had their roots in the Bible institute tradition. At every school, however, the presumption was strong that the main point of higher education—or at least one possible main point of higher education—was to prepare students to win souls for Christianity.

As the Bible Institute of Los Angeles turned itself into Biola College and then Biola University, it never abandoned its emphasis on the call to missions. In 1940, for example, one anonymous student explained the way she had come to enroll as a student at Biola. She had grown up as a child of missionaries in China. Among her social circles—all the "fundamental Church groups in California"—Biola was touted as the best school to help future missionaries. She knew she needed some sort of preparation. A college education, she wrote, would be the perfect way to learn how to "tell . . . the millions of lost and dying souls [in the world] . . . of the matchless wonders of His grace." Once she decided to become a missionary, she prayed about her decision to go to school. "When I thought of Biola," she said, "a great joy swept over my soul." She considered Biola the perfect place to learn the things missionaries needed to know.[88]

This student was correct in thinking that Biola had always emphasized preparation for missionary work. Since its opening in the early years of the twentieth century, Biola, like most Bible institutes, required students to engage in "Christian Work."[89] And, just like students at the other Bible institutes, many students at Biola embraced the requirement. The pages of the student newspaper were filled semester after semester with detailed lists of student evangelical efforts. In 1938, for example, readers of the *Chimes* would discover that in the past semester, male students at Biola had distributed 176,418 tracts and 7,276 gospels throughout the region. Most important to earnest evangelical students, they had converted 891 souls.[90]

Like students at most schools, Biola's students did not have to labor alone.[91] Since 1923, Biola students could join the Student Missionary Union (SMU), or they could simply tag along on SMU trips or listen to the guest speakers SMU brought to campus.[92] Students' efforts were supported institutionally. Biola established a missionary branch in China in 1916, keeping it running for three years even after the 1949 revolution.[93] Students at Biola could enroll in specific missionary majors. For instance, the school opened its School of Missionary Medicine in 1945.[94]

We probably shouldn't be surprised, then, that so many graduates leaped into full-time missionary work. Of forty-five graduating students in 1938 who identified their next steps, only two mentioned secular goals.

One got a job as an engineer, and the other went back to school. The rest simply noted a region or population with whom they planned to work. Some headed to "South America," while others announced their intention to engage in "children's work," "Jewish work," or "home field" evangelism. Some headed for the "Kentucky mountains," "Africa," "China," or "Mongolia" to begin their missionary careers.[95]

During World War II, according to the Biola Alumni Association, it became difficult for graduates to head to battle-torn missionary fields. Nevertheless, between 1937 and 1945 well over three-quarters of alumni were either doing full-time missionary work or getting more "training" for missionary work.[96] This emphasis on missionary training and work remained central at Biola throughout the twentieth century. In 1962, the alumni association claimed that 47 percent of graduates planned to head into full-time missionary work, complemented by another 41 percent who entered evangelism-friendly careers as teachers, counselors, pastors, or youth workers.[97] As the school's director of missions put it in 1969, the school worked hard to "make every student aware that he is a missionary."[98]

Not surprisingly, this steady emphasis on missions and missionary work allowed Biola and other Bible institutes to punch far above their institutional weight when it came to preparing missionaries. As historian Virginia Brereton has pointed out, by 1962, a full 50 percent of all Protestant missionaries were graduates of the network of Bible schools.[99] Colleges and universities that did not have a Bible-institute past, however, also put a strong emphasis on missionary preparation.

Wheaton College, for instance, sent approximately a quarter of its 1950 graduating class into full-time missionary work.[100] At Fuller Seminary in California, preparation for missionary work enjoyed status as the primary reason for higher education.[101] Bob Jones University also maintained a steady focus on missionary preparation. In some cases, that meant welcoming students outside of traditional degree programs. In 1957, BJU opened its Institute of Christian Service. Entering students did not plan to earn a degree, but rather sought to improve their ability to preach the Gospel around the world.[102] Students who wanted both a degree and an intense preparatory course for mission work could enroll in a bachelor's program in medical missions beginning in 1966, or major in missionary aviation beginning in 1970.[103] Though a relative newcomer to the field of fundamentalist higher education, Liberty Baptist College also assumed that missionary preparation was the most important reason for its existence. Throughout its first decades in the 1970s and 1980s, the fledgling school employed a full-time missions director to help students prepare for missionary careers.[104]

At all the schools in the network of fundamentalist and evangelical higher education, the emphasis on missions dictated different structures for student life both inside and outside the classroom. One student at Moody Bible Institute in the 1920s remembered that he hadn't originally planned a career as a missionary. It didn't take him long to feel the call. As he remembered later, "You can't be in the Moody Bible Institute very long before you'll have to face that."[105]

Another MBI student in the 1930s simply assumed that her educational experience should be evaluated by its effect on her work as a missionary. She thought the MBI program was generally good, because it emphasized a thorough familiarity with the Bible, along with basic medical training and cooking classes. It would have been even better, she remembered later, if it had included more language classes.[106]

Like most students at Bible institutes, she took it to be an obvious truism that the purpose of higher education was preparation for mission work. As one student at Wheaton in the late 1930s remembered, he felt "a sort of innate inclination to be in missions or in the ministry." Because of that call, he felt obliged to pursue a college education, in order to be able to bring God's Word to the world.[107] Another Wheaton student from the same era had always planned a secular career as an engineer and intended to head to a state university after high school. However, a church talk by Isaac Page of the China Inland Mission turned his life around. After that, he was inspired to head off to foreign fields to spread the Gospel. Before he did so, though, he headed to Wheaton to learn how.[108]

The preparation they received went beyond rallies and chapel exhortations. The classes themselves taught students both that they should yearn to be missionaries and how to be effective ones. One student at Moody Bible Institute remembered fondly the inspiring academic work of Professor R. A. Glover. Glover was active with the China Inland Mission. His courses at MBI focused on the history of missions, helping students see the inspiring tradition they could join of selfless outreach. For this student, at least, Glover's combination of academic achievement with missionary fervor was "very convincing."[109]

By the time Gladys Porter arrived at MBI in the 1940s, Professor Glover no longer taught The Progress of World-Wide Missions, but Porter's teacher still used Glover's textbook. As had earlier generations of MBI students, Porter learned about the various regions of the world that needed to hear the Gospel. What were the unique features of Africa? China? Japan? The "most neglected fields among the Jews"? She learned about the heroic history of Protestant missionaries, often persecuted for their efforts yet persevering. She also learned of the central importance of mission work to anyone who hoped to call herself a real Christian. As she recorded in her notes for the class, "The duty and ideal of carrying the gospel to the whole world MUST BE brought home to the CONSCIENCE AND HEART of the church."[110]

The emphasis on missionary work changed more than just the curriculum. The goal of preparing each new generation to spread the gospel to the four corners of the globe made the structures of evangelical and fundamentalist higher education look different from those of mainstream schools in significant ways. For example, most schools considered missionary potential to be a leading characteristic when it came to admitting students. In the 1930s, Moody Bible Institute specifically asked recommenders if a potential student "has . . . a genuine love for souls."[111]

When Wheaton College first systematized its admission process in the 1940s, it instituted several characteristics common to all colleges in the era. Applicants would have to have completed fifteen high school academic units, the equivalent of four years of full-time study. They would have to be ranked in the upper third of their high school graduating classes. They would need a decent letter of recommendation. If they were on the bubble, a good college aptitude test score could help. And, like any mainstream college, they decided in the 1940s to give extra points for special abilities. Did a student demonstrate "special artistic, musical, journalistic, or athletic ability"? If so, he or she would have a better chance of getting in. Unlike non-evangelical schools, though, Wheaton also gave bonus points for "demonstrated ability as an outstanding soulwinner."[112]

Once they were admitted, students at evangelical colleges and especially at Bible institutes were evaluated based on their missionary potential. At Moody Bible Institute, for example, students in the 1930s were required to complete a minimum number of hours of missionary outreach. If they failed, they risked expulsion.[113] At Biola, students who did not demonstrate the proper attitude or aptitude for missionary outreach could be in danger of getting kicked out. In 1952, for instance, President Sutherland warned one student that he was at risk of expulsion because one faculty member "doubted that [the student] will ever be fit for Christian service."[114]

## *Markets and Missions*

At most evangelical and fundamentalist schools, higher education implied preparation for a life of work as an evangelist of some kind. It did not necessarily mean a commitment to full-time missionary work in foreign fields or among targeted populations in the United States. It might mean working as a pastor or teacher, or adding to one's role as a wife and mother by sharing the saving power of the Gospel with young people. For many students, it could simply be a vocation one practiced alongside one's profession: every lawyer could proclaim the Good Word with every action. Every doctor, every accountant, every salesperson could spread the Gospel by word and deed. Every scholar, too, could view his or her work in economics, say, or history as a special sort of evangelical endeavor.

As we've seen, the heart of the uniquely evangelical approach to higher education resulted from these kinds of complicated missionary assumptions. However they worked their evangelism into their lives and careers—it was universally assumed—students needed to know the Bible; they needed to know how to read it and how to share it. Even among schools and scholars who disdained the dispensational methods so popular among fundamentalists, it was taken for granted that students must learn how to read the Bible. But that was not the only sort of distinct intellectual tradition that evangelical and fundamentalist schools developed during the twentieth century. At a variety of schools, intellectuals and activists experimented with a variety of ways of tying evangelical Protestantism more tightly to a small-government, free-market ideology.

As historians Darren Dochuk and Bethany Moreton have noted, the principles of free-market conservatism had a long history at a few conservative evangelical colleges. Since the 1940s, schools such as John Brown University and Harding College in Arkansas, as well as Pepperdine College in California, had been intellectual centers of "Christian free enterprise" and conservative "American studies" programs.[115] At those schools, programs such as "freedom forums" and "Students in Free Enterprise" taught students the healthy and strong connections between small governments, free markets, and evangelical theology.[116] During the 1960s and 1970s, a few energetic evangelicals tried to spread the gospel of the market more widely among interdenominational evangelical colleges, with mixed results.

The most notable center of this movement among interdenominational evangelical and fundamentalist colleges was The King's College in New York. In the mid-1960s, administrators Carleton Campbell and Emmett R. Lehman transformed their school's National Freedom Education Center into an aggressive American studies program.[117] At The King's College, "American studies" meant grafting conservative political and economic ideas onto evangelical ones. Campbell and Lehman hoped to combine reverence for an inerrant Bible with a push for smaller government and a freer capitalist marketplace. To help promote their cause, they enticed leaders of evangelical colleges to schools such as John Brown University to see the program in action.[118]

In 1964, for instance, President James Forrester of Gordon College accepted a $300 honorarium to visit John Brown as part of an "educators' conference." Campbell had high hopes that Forrester might enlist his school in the American studies crusade.[119] It was vital, Campbell told Forrester privately, that "we evangelicals" unite to apply Christian beliefs beyond the narrow confines of theology.[120]

Forrester was originally enthusiastic.[121] Together, Forrester and Campbell planned a blockbuster conference at Gordon to help spread the message. The conference organizers invited a line-up of conservative celebrities from both evangelical and free-market circles, including Bill Bright of Campus Crusade for Christ, George S. Benson of Harding College in Arkansas, former congressperson Walter H. Judd, and Leonard Read, head of the Foundation for Economic Education. The goal would be to encourage evangelical campuses to host American studies programs along the lines laid out at The King's College. Such programs promised to teach students "a pervading high regard for Freedom in its spiritual, economic and political dimensions." Faculty could be encouraged to explore "our traditionally motivating intangibles . . . reverence for God, total human concern for the individual, an abiding dedication to preservation of our Constitution and a cherishing regard for personal Freedom."[122]

When Forrester brought the idea home to Gordon's campus, though, his interest quickly cooled. He found that students and faculty at Gordon were not convinced of the evangelical power of this particular brand of free-market conservative thinking. As one faculty member put it, Gordon could not stomach leaders of the "extreme right" such as George Benson. In short, in the view of some influential faculty members, Gordon wanted to remain more committed to evangelical education than to pushing students through "a program of education in conservative thinking." Professors such as Leymon Ketcham were suspicious that the American studies approach was merely old-fashioned secularism disguised in free-market clothing.[123]

Other evangelical leaders took the "American studies" idea in different directions. Just as there have been different visions of American studies at non-evangelical schools, so too did some evangelical school leaders create American studies programs that differed significantly from the strident free-market gospel on tap at Harding, John Brown, or The King's College. In the mid-1970s, for example, the fledgling Christian College Consortium established an American studies program with a different focus. Instead of drilling students in the principles of free-market ideology, the CCC's program brought students from member schools to Washington, D.C., for a semester. Participants would engage in street-level politics in the nation's capital, learning the ropes of public life. Instead of only spreading the intellectual message of free markets, this program hoped to encourage top evangelical students from a variety of colleges and universities to enter politics, bringing their values to their leadership. Those values, it was assumed, might include a yen for smaller government and freer markets, but more important was the evangelical message of larger churches and freer religion.[124]

## *The Opium of the Evangelical Intellectuals*

Small-government conservatism was one sort of unofficial intellectual enthusiasm that sometimes caught on among students and faculty, but it was not the only one. As we've seen, the theology of interdenominational schools was guided by an inherently vague and unsystematic set of principles, rather than any single denominational orthodoxy. It had to be. Fundamentalist and evangelical schools valued intellectual rigor, but they also valued popular methods of biblical interpretation such as dispensationalism. They cherished orthodoxy, but they also insisted on evangelical soul-saving results. From time to time, as we can see in the turbulent career of Calvinism on conservative evangelical campuses, these goals came into messy conflict.

In every generation, the embrace of Calvinism by a faction of students and faculty placed schools and administrators in a difficult position. Since the 1920s, Calvinism had acquired a reputation among fundamentalist institutions of higher education as both compelling and disruptive. Calvinists often demanded greater theological consistency than school leaders wanted to endorse. And they sometimes disparaged important elements of American evangelicalism, including the emotional revivalism and dispensational Bible-reading methods beloved by so many evangelicals. In addition, school administrators remained painfully aware of the fact that their interdenominational schools needed to remain friendly to a relatively wide variety of denominational backgrounds. The big tent of American evangelicalism often included groups that considered Calvinism a foreign imposition. As in all things, school administrators balked at the idea of embracing any idea that would drive away students and their tuition dollars. In effect, Calvinism served as a perennial reminder of the unresolvable tension in fundamentalist and evangelical institutions between the demands of theological purity, interdenominational viability, and institutional pragmatism.

The implicit connection between Calvinist consistency and institutional fragmentation was cemented in the 1920s by the career of Princeton Theological Seminary's J. Gresham Machen. During the 1920s, as we saw in Chapter 2, Machen often acted as the intellectual representative of the nascent fundamentalist movement. Time and again, however, Machen insisted, "What I prefer to call myself is not a 'Fundamentalist,' but a 'Calvinist'—that is, an adherent of the Reformed faith."[125] For Machen, the key to remaining truly Christian during the denominational and cultural tumult of the 1920s was to remain unapologetically true to Calvin's principles. As he told one confidant in 1925, "We must not in these difficult days forget our Calvinism."[126]

During the 1920s, Machen enjoyed a reputation as one of the most accomplished Calvinist theologians of the era.[127] And in the minds of many school leaders, Machen's Calvinism became inextricably linked to his institutional separatism. By the end of the decade, Machen had led a revolt from the Princeton Theological Seminary. The conservative Princeton Seminary, Machen and his come-outer colleagues finally decided, was hopelessly pragmatic, in thrall to liberal theology and its inevitable moral compromises. In protest, Machen and some colleagues founded the rival Westminster Theological Seminary, a school to be devoted to unadulterated Calvinism.[128]

The lesson for other evangelical school leaders was clear: to have a thoroughly Calvinist school, one could brook no disagreement on foundational theological principles. A Calvinist school required theological consistency—a consistency that the leaders of the relatively diverse interdenominational schools could ill afford. Some Calvinist thinkers hoped to convince their friends and colleagues at fundamentalist and evangelical colleges to embrace the challenges posed by Calvinistic thinking. In the early 1930s, Loraine Boettner of Pikeville College in Kentucky hoped to lure President Nathan Wood of Gordon College to an appreciation of the unique relevance of Calvinist theology in modern America. Wood agreed that Boettner's forceful Calvinism could offer some liberal Christians "a tonic and should help to bring back the swing of the pendulum from that [liberal] extreme." Wood wasn't ready to call himself a Calvinist, but he appreciated Boettner's "candid, devout and virile statement of that great system."[129]

Wood was not alone in admiring Calvinism from a distance. As one disgruntled Calvinist accused in 1951, too many "religiously orthodox" colleges fell into a doubly damning muddle. On the one hand, because an evangelical but not Calvinist college "had no vital organizing and patterning principle of its own," it was "content to reduce the Christian element in higher education to Christian 'atmosphere,' together with at most a negative criticism here and there of offensive popular doctrines (Darwinianism, for example) or an ignoring of such topics." On the other hand, in his opinion, such conservative schools lulled evangelical parents into a false sense of theological security by pretending to provide a profoundly Christian education.[130]

For their part, fundamentalist school leaders—even those friendly to Calvinist principles—worried that Calvinist ideas left out vital elements of proper fundamentalist higher education. In 1936, for example, President Buswell of Wheaton College remonstrated with Machen about troubling elements of Machen's new Calvinist seminary. Was it true, Buswell worried, that seminary students were allowed to drink alcohol, even with the apparent connivance of faculty members? Could it be true that Machen's seminary allowed students to attend worldly movies? It was, and they did. To Machen, such starchy fundamentalist prohibitions carried no theological weight. To Machen, Calvinism meant a rigid adherence to theological consistency, even when that consistency flouted fundamentalist traditions.[131]

Most fundamentalist school leaders had to consider broader concerns. If they allowed students to drink alcohol or attend movies, as we saw in Chapter 4, they risked losing their carefully built reputations as fundamentalist schools. And if they insisted on only one theological tradition, they risked the tuition dollars of a broad range of non-Calvinist evangelical families. Even if school leaders themselves admired the intellectual rigor of Calvinism and the intellectual accomplishments of Calvinists, they could not allow their schools to become mere outposts of Calvinist intellectualism.

This institutional dilemma became apparent again in the career of philosopher Gordon Clark at Wheaton. Clark was a follower of Machen and a fabulously accomplished scholar.[132] His was exactly the sort of academic resume that fundamentalist school leaders in the 1930s coveted. He had studied in Europe and earned an Ivy League Ph.D. Yet when he brought his Calvinist rigor to Wheaton's campus, he soon found that even the most ambitious fundamentalist college could not accommodate the demands of Calvinist orthodoxy.

Clark came to Wheaton in 1936. He started a Creed Club for students who wanted to explore the rigors of Calvinist theology.[133] Clark soon realized that his vision of Calvinist intellectual rigor rubbed many of Wheaton's leaders the wrong way. For one thing, Clark tended to disparage the emotionalism of the revival tradition. It made no theological sense, Clark taught his students, to expect an all-powerful and all-knowing God to put the ultimate decision about salvation in the hands of sinners themselves. When Wheaton students swooned in a campus-wide revival in 1943, Clark dismissed the phenomenon as mere "mass psychology," not real salvation.[134] Nor, in the light of Calvin's severe and predestined theology, did it make sense to devote so much time and energy to missionary work. At least, that was the lesson many ardent student followers picked up. As the future theologian Carl Henry attested in 1942, Clark's severe and rigorous Calvinism had "prompted a dwindling of missionary interest among a number of students."[135]

Intellectual rigor was good. Student theological enthusiasm was good. Having an accomplished scholar on the faculty was good. But Wheaton could not survive if the broader fundamentalist community thought its leaders looked down their ivory-tower noses at revivals. Nor could it survive if fundamentalists whispered that Wheaton no longer cared about missionary work. In 1942, Gordon Clark was forced out.[136]

Calvinism itself, however, never was. As we've seen, Calvinist thinking caused other faculty members such as C. Gregg Singer to tangle with Wheaton administrators. Yet in spite of the ambivalence of administrators at schools such as Wheaton, students at fundamentalist and evangelical colleges continued to rediscover the intellectual excitement of Calvin's ideas in every generation. Some fraction of intellectually hungry evangelical students would continue to dig up Calvin's *Institutes* as a refreshing palliative to the emotionalism and intellectually inconsistent jumbles inherent in the many-headed evangelical big tent. At Gordon College, for example, students in 1969 published excerpts from Calvin in an exasperated attempt to teach their fellow students "What True Faith Is."[137] Calvinism itself was never disparaged or banned at most evangelical and fundamentalist schools. However, it became something of an awkward perennial enthusiasm among students and faculty, something to be tolerated and perhaps even quietly encouraged, while school leaders officially distanced themselves and their institutions.

## *In the World of Higher Ed, but Not of It*

In the end, rigorous intellectual Calvinism became yet another answer to the impossible question, "What is fundamentalist college for?" For most schools, some of the other answers were easier to agree on: fundamentalist and evangelical colleges were meant to raise up every new generation of thoughtful, dedicated evangelical Protestants. Such colleges would focus on teaching the Bible. And they would teach students how to spread the Gospel, whether they did it as full-time missionaries or as part of their lives as professionals, parents, and politically active citizens.

None of these agreed-upon answers was as simple as many school leaders hoped. At some schools, part of becoming an educated evangelical meant embracing a religion-friendly brand of small-government, free-market conservatism. At other schools, it meant focusing on imbibing a certain dispensationalist vision of true biblical literacy. At yet others, it might mean overhauling the entire curriculum to make sure it embraced a truly biblical worldview, not just a smattering of secular studies thinly overlaid with passages from Scripture.

Just as ardent Calvinists like Gordon Clark discovered, fundamentalist schools could never be wholly defined by any single orthodoxy or any single enthusiasm. Fundamentalist and evangelical administrators found themselves bound by many of the same institutional imperatives that dictated decisions at non-evangelical schools. In fits and starts across the middle of the twentieth century, the outlines of desirable higher education became more rigidly defined. More and more students demanded a college program that led to a bachelor's degree. Students and employers expected, with greater and greater regularity as the decades rolled along, that higher education would prepare students for a variety of specific professional positions. As a result—as a general rule and not a single dramatic transformation—other sorts of schools turned themselves into colleges and universities. For fundamentalists, that often meant that Bible institutes became Bible colleges, or simply colleges or universities. It also meant that almost all schools, except a few stubborn holdouts, scrambled to prove their higher-education legitimacy by earning some sort of official accreditation.

What was fundamentalist college for? It had to be a real college, and it had to be really fundamentalist or evangelical. No one disagreed on that, but the details were always devilishly difficult to determine.

# 7

# *Nightmare on College Avenue*

*We are not rebelling against Christianity, but against make-believe.*

—WESLEY EARL CRAVEN, student protest leader at Wheaton, 1962[1]

## *The Evangelical Sixties*

Long hair, sit-ins, bombings, and protest after protest—for many college students and observers in the late 1960s and early 1970s, it seemed the world of higher education was being shaken to its core. Left-wing students protested against racism, against stultifying in loco parentis rules, and against the war in Vietnam. Students occupied deans' offices, destroyed science buildings, and dropped out of budding careers. In the decades since then, real and imagined scenes of unyielding leftist politics and unwashed hippie excess have come to define a raucous period of campus unrest known vaguely as "the sixties."[2] As historians have demonstrated, however, there was another sixties experience in American higher education as well, with buttoned-down conservative students protesting in favor of the war and against leftist policies.[3] On college campuses just as in the broader society, the sixties weren't simply a burst of flower-child idealism; they were a clash between two very different visions of proper American culture, and between two very different ideas about the proper role and structure of higher education.

Throughout the 1960s and early 1970s, the campuses of fundamentalist and evangelical colleges and universities experienced their own sort of "sixties." Writing from the safe distance of 1978, one evangelical observer concluded that evangelical colleges experienced "delayed, videotape replays" of the "unrest that rocked the nation in 1968." Though evangelical students sometimes protested "in slow-motion and with lower volume," this evangelical pundit argued, the campus sixties at evangelical schools was essentially the same as that on mainstream campuses.[4]

With forty extra years of hindsight, it's clear he was wrong. In many ways, the evangelical sixties were far more "evangelical" than they were "sixties." The fights were not the same; the protests were not simply quieter or more polite versions of clashes on pluralist campuses. The battles on evangelical campuses may have sounded similar on the surface to those at other types of schools, with protests about the war, civil rights, and oppressive lifestyle rules, but below those protests ran a uniquely evangelical current. The issues that roiled fundamentalist and evangelical campuses were driven by the never-clear and always-contested meanings of fundamentalism and evangelicalism; they were exacerbated by the continuing feud between branches of the evangelical family.

Of course, just as at non-evangelical institutions, evangelical and fundamentalist campus disputes in the late 1960s and early 1970s were also fueled in part by broader changes in culture, demography, and higher education. On evangelical campuses, just as on mainstream ones, the gusts of unrest blew in many directions at once. Some students protested against strict rules and against the fundamentalist mind-set that begat them. Other students, however, fought against the loosening of behavioral guidelines. Some students protested against the Vietnam War; others protested against the protesters.

Though the debates on evangelical and fundamentalist campuses centered on uniquely evangelical questions, they could not escape the changing context of American higher education. As we saw in Chapter 6, in the years since the end of World War II new assumptions hardened about what it took to be a "real" college or university. At the end of the war, too, the GI Bill sent millions of new students flooding onto America's college campuses, including evangelical and fundamentalist ones. By the late 1960s, rising incomes and the baby boom helped keep the postwar enrollment explosion going. In many ways, established evangelical and fundamentalist schools found themselves growing by leaps and bounds in the new environment of postwar higher education. However, even the most established and well-known schools couldn't rest on their reputations. A hungry new group of evangelical and fundamentalist colleges and universities were established in the 1960s and 1970s, catering to the flood of new students and tuition dollars. To survive, every college or university had to come to grips with the new unwritten rules of higher education. For fundamentalist and evangelical schools to survive, they also had to cope with the changing mores of conservative evangelicalism. Evangelical schools worked hard to prove that they had not abandoned the fundamentals of the faith. Fundamentalist schools tried to prove that their staunch unyielding commitments were the only guarantee of an authentically Christian education.

## *Hey Hey Ho Ho*

On college campuses across the nation, some of the fiercest protests concerned the escalating war in Southeast Asia. Compared with the violent antiwar sentiment at some mainstream schools, the atmosphere at some evangelical colleges might have seemed conservative, apathetic, or simply blithely unaware. As one alumnus of Multnomah Bible School in Portland, Oregon, later remembered, "It was as if the protests weren't happening at all. We were so absorbed in our little world."[5]

On other campuses, however, students and administrators leaped headlong into the cultural politics of war protests. At Bob Jones University, for example, students, alumni, and administrators raised their voices in favor of America's soldiers and against the antiwar protesters. In 1966 and again in 1970, students conducted letter-writing campaigns to express their support for American troops and for an aggressive American military policy in Southeast Asia.[6]

The top leadership, likewise, spared no rhetorical excess in its condemnation of war protesters and the liberal attitudes that had encouraged them. Perhaps most memorably, Bob Jones Jr. tongue-lashed antiwar students in the immediate aftermath of the shootings at Kent State University. With four students dead at the hands of nervous National Guard members and many more wounded, some commentators—even those who did not agree with the protesters—felt that the crackdown had gone too far. Not Bob Jones Jr. The day after the shootings, President Jones used his weekly chapel talk to denounce the protesters in provocative terms. The protesters, Jones said, "should have been shot." The country as a whole was better off without them. College campuses and administrators had a duty to dole out merciless punishment to students who flouted the most basic proprieties of church and society. The blame, Jones continued, was not with the National Guard but rather with

> ungodly professors who have taught those kids the wrong kind of ideology, parents who haven't had the guts to rear those kids right and teach them some discipline and the value of money, and the preachers who have given them stones for bread and have encouraged violence and lawlessness.[7]

Whereas some administrators and school leaders pandered to a dissipated and slovenly post-Christian morality, Jones promised, his school would always stand for stern, uncompromising enforcement of traditional values.

If there were any glimmers of dissent or even of apathy among BJU students, faculty, or alumni, no trace has survived in the archival record. Officially, the school community embraced President Jones's take-no-prisoners approach to school discipline. To emphasize their continuing official endorsement of school policy, in early 1970 the alumni association issued a statement of support. Too many schools—even conservative evangelical schools—had allowed themselves the sinful luxury of moral laxity, the alumni claimed. For the alumni of BJU, the raucous and violent protests represented the predictable effects of neo-evangelical reformism. The association resolved:

> Whereas, we note the tragic results of tolerant, soft-core administrators who are permitting the breakdown of principles and policies which in years past brought pride to students and alumni; and Whereas many graduates of these restless institutions are shocked and stand in disbelief at destruction of buildings, property, discipline, and moral integrity . . . we declare our continued allegiance and loyalty to the school.

The BJU Alumni Association sided proudly with BJU's top leadership, in spite of "unwarranted attack by the Neo-Evangelical forces and liberals."[8]

Most other evangelical and fundamentalist schools—even resolutely conservative ones—experienced a more divided campus sentiment about Vietnam, just as they had about the propriety of the neo-evangelical reform movement. At Moody Bible Institute in 1968, for instance, 54 percent of students supported a more aggressive bombing campaign in Southeast Asia, compared with only 21 percent at higher-education institutions nationwide.[9]

Some MBI students wanted their conservative evangelical school to take a stronger stand against the perception that all college students opposed the war. Student Dave Broucek wrote in the pages of the student newspaper that he was "more than just a little disgusted with student 'anti' demonstrations that grab all the headlines." Like President Nixon, Broucek wrote, he believed that a "silent majority" of Americans—young and old—hoped and prayed for a measured, dignified withdrawal from Vietnam. Radical leftist students, Broucek warned, thought they fought for freedom, but in reality they only created "furrows of division among Americans."[10]

MBI's administrators agreed that thoughtful evangelicals should support American policy in Vietnam. President William Culbertson announced in a chapel talk that Christian pacifism certainly deserved respect. However, he added, speaking a couple of days before a planned nationwide protest, the Moratorium to End the War in Vietnam, it was also a Christian duty to support duly elected leaders and to fight communism at every opportunity. "We would not be," Culbertson concluded, "among those who would give encouragement to the enemy, nor would we discourage our own men."[11]

At Biola, too, campus sentiment seemed split. In late 1968 and early 1969, student editors of the *Chimes* protested mildly against US policy in Southeast Asia. Todd Lewis worried that too many patriotic Christians gleefully threatened to bomb Vietnam back into the stone age. A more Christian policy, a truly evangelical policy freed from the accretions of fundamentalist small-mindedness, Lewis argued, would mean caring more deeply for all victims of war, whatever country they hailed from.[12]

Biola president Samuel Sutherland did not approve. He quietly and privately urged Lewis to write another column, one that clarified Biola's support for American policy.[13] Lewis pushed back, quietly and privately.[14] His fellow student editor, Bob Guernsey, did so loudly and publicly. In his next column, Guernsey condemned Biola's administration and student body both, the former for high-handed, unchristian militarism, the latter for "sheep-like" acquiescence.[15] Sutherland kicked Guernsey out for the rest of the academic year.[16]

At Gordon College, student antiwar sentiment quickly met with student counterprotests. In early 1968, for example, a group of students published a short antiwar editorial in the student newspaper.[17] One of their angry fellow students took to the pages of the *Tartan* to fight back. "My immediate reaction," this student wrote, "was that of disgust! . . . I question your sense of loyalty and most of all your sense of duty."[18]

## *The Times They Are A-Changin'*

As students, faculty, alumni, and administrators wrestled with questions of war, evangelicalism, protest, and campus proprieties, they had a keen sense that their schools represented something distinctly different from the mainstream and pluralist campuses that were racked by wave after wave of student protest. As one conservative fundamentalist student group at Biola complained to President Sutherland, Biola's campus must not be allowed to echo to the "popular beat of the day."[19] Students and administrators who hoped for greater political conservatism and greater religious fundamentalism insisted that their fellows respect their unique status as evangelical collegians.

For instance, Pete Schwepker, in 1965 the editor of Biola's student paper, was delighted to have one of his editorials picked up and run in the *Chicago Tribune* and the conservative journal *Human Events*. In the editorial, Schwepker had warned that too many Americans seemed to believe that the "typical college student" was "intelligent, mature, and completely immoral . . . . a Socialist." Such impressions, Schwepker wrote, ignored the fact that the majority of students really lived much more conservative lives. Most college students, like most Americans, "work hard for a living, go to church, follow a code of morals and ethics and study hard." Students at all kinds of schools, Schwepker argued, actually tended to be far more traditional and conservative than most newspapers implied.[20]

Some Biola students tried to step out of their conservative evangelical comfort zone and confront leftist students head on. One Biolan, Norman Goss, reported on his experiences during a year at the University of California at Berkeley. As he put it, he had been "a Biolan in the midst of rebels." He had a difficult time bridging the culture gap between his Biola background and that of the Berkeley students. He hoped to "witness to these people," but he couldn't find an easy way to speak to them about the saving power of Jesus Christ. After all, he discovered, the Free Speech Movement activists at Berkeley "believed as firmly in their beliefs as I believe in mine." It was imperative for all Biola students to share their unique evangelical light with earnest but mistaken leftists, Goss argued. Biolans might be frankly and happily "indoctrinated in our education," Goss wrote, but too many Biolans remained safely ensconced in the friendly evangelical confines of Biola's campus. If they wanted to make a real difference, they needed to exert an evangelical influence at mainstream universities as well.[21]

At Gordon, some students worried that their fellows did not appreciate their difference from stereotypical left-wing student protesters. "Hippies," one Gordon student proclaimed, were nothing but morally conflicted, drug-abusing "slobs."[22] Other Gordon students agreed that they must not simply mimic mainstream college foolishness. *Tartan* editor Lenore Weiss, for example, hoped they could "build on what we know Gordon should represent." In other words, Gordon students must embrace Gordon's evangelical tradition as a school with an unyielding statement of faith. Otherwise, Gordon would swirl helplessly in the tides of left-wing trendiness, copying a "profitless syncretism with constant criticizers whose only pride is their absolute non-acceptance of absolutes." Yet Weiss recognized that many Gordon students wanted to make their school more like non-evangelical ones. Even many *Tartan* readers seemed to want the paper to "imitate a smutty underground sheet." Such meaningless modishness, Weiss argued, missed the point entirely. Gordon College, Weiss hoped, should take pride in its status as a different sort of school, with a markedly different sort of student.[23]

Even at schools that would never be confused with left-wing enclaves, students and administrators worked to define themselves in stark distinction to mainstream trends. In 1975, for example, as the fledgling Lynchburg Baptist College became Liberty Baptist College (it would become Liberty University in 1985), students were warned that they must not imitate the styles of non-fundamentalist schools. As their college catalogue explained, "Students are expected generally to avoid anything which tends to identify them in their own, or someone else's mind, with the youth counter-culture of modern society."[24]

In spite of such stern warnings, students at evangelical colleges and universities did tend to mimic trends at non-evangelical schools. Time and again, students protested against strict rules, hoping to push their campuses to look and feel more like mainstream ones. Their protests could take innumerable forms, from surreptitious rule-breaking to organized petitioning. At many campuses, the sense of widespread rule-breaking became nearly absurd. For instance, one anonymous administrator told an evangelical journalist that he found more illicit copies of *Playboy* in dorm rooms than copies of Christian magazines. Overall, alumni guessed that anywhere between one-third and two-thirds of their fellow students rebelled in some way against campus rules and regulations, especially the traditional ban on attending movies. A survey of Moody Bible Institute graduates from the era found that most of the rebellion concerned non-religious rules. MBI rebels, that is, tended to embrace rules about daily prayer, Bible reading, street evangelism, and chapel attendance. They tended to flout—quietly and in a way that seemed remarkably mild by the campus standards of the sixties—rules against movie attendance, card playing, dancing, and other lifestyle regulations.[25]

Even on the campus of Bob Jones University, administrators offered students a little wiggle room when it came to traditional rules and regulations, as long as it did not clash with the Joneses' ideas about the proper definition of fundamentalism. As late as 1965, Bob Jones Sr. assured a concerned parent that the school would never slacken its rules for appropriate gendered appearances. No woman on BJU's campus, Jones promised, would ever wear short hair. As Jones put it, "a woman is supposed to look like a woman."[26] Just as male students wore shirts and ties, women wore long skirts or dresses. Ten years later, however, Jones's grandson Bob Jones III conceded that sometimes "slacks and pantsuits" were appropriately modest, appropriately feminine attire for women. The rule, the younger Jones decided, was that women should dress modestly at all times. If that could be done with something besides long skirts and dresses, then there was nothing theologically wrong with that.[27]

There was also nothing theologically wrong with beards, Bob Jones III decided. Christ Himself wore one, after all. Nevertheless, no male student on BJU's campus would be allowed to have a beard. Why not? As Jones put it, "They are still associated with people who have an avante gard, rebellious, nonconformist type of spirit about them." In other words, Bob Jones University banned beards not on fundamentalist grounds but rather on conservative, patriotic, cultural grounds. Long hair on men was a different matter entirely. As the Joneses defined it, fundamentalism itself required short hair for men. In 1975, Bob Jones III reassured a nervous inquirer, "Of course, we take a strong Biblical position against long hair." According to the idiosyncratic definition of fundamentalism on the BJU campus, the rule against beards was simple administration; the one against long hair for men was a fundamentalist requirement.[28]

## *Brave Sons and Daughters True*

At other campuses, too, sixties-style conflicts about hippies, free speech, and lifestyle rules were always argued in the language of evangelical or fundamentalist tradition. At Wheaton, where the neo-evangelical reform had been midwifed and welcomed, student rebels fought for greater freedom from the school's traditional restrictions. When they did so, they did not use the language of secular college rebels, but rather that of a unique mix of neo-evangelical and higher-education reformism. Wheaton's student rebels presented their protests as part of an evangelical reformation of a stultifying and unwholesome fundamentalist mindset, a higher-ed reformation that had become a necessary prerequisite to any authentic liberal arts education.

For their part, Wheaton's administrators cautiously welcomed some forms of student activism, even if students veered into politically charged territory. And administrators always encouraged changes that would strengthen Wheaton's reputation as an academically elite institution. What they could not condone or even appear to condone were students' implied denunciations of fundamentalism itself. True, Wheaton may have become the flagship college of the neo-evangelical reform. Its leaders, however, sought to maintain Wheaton's reputation as a "safe" school to which fundamentalist parents could send their children without concern.

In the early 1960s, the atmosphere on Wheaton's campus was so tense that a seemingly minor provocation sparked a major firestorm of controversy. In 1962, students published a gently satirical unofficial student newspaper, *Brave Son*. The name poked fun at one of current president Raymond Edman's favorite descriptions of the Wheaton student body, "brave sons and daughters true." Student reformers did not engage in the language or tactics that would bring so much attention to secular, leftist free-speech reformers such as Mario Savio at the University of California, Berkeley. Instead, Wheaton's free-speech rebels framed their protests as a neo-evangelical appeal for more authentic Christianity against the mindless strictures of fundamentalism.

For example, student writer Glen Watts protested against fundamentalism's intellectually stultifying traditions. Education in too many evangelical colleges, Watts argued, represented nothing more than fundamentalism's "negativisms, clichés, and basic inferiority complex." Students were not taught to think for themselves, Watts charged, but rather were "herded down an educational ramp and out into the world more like cattle than men." Watts encouraged Wheaton students to fight for a more truly evangelical education, a more truly Christian vision. As he put it, the solution was to be found not in more empty "talk about Christ, but [in] an encounter with Him."[29]

The editors and writers of *Brave Son* were not the only Wheaton students to fight for evangelical free speech. Adding fuel to the fire were the provocative tactics of student editor Wes Craven at the student literary magazine *Kodon*. Craven, who went on to enormous mainstream success as the director of the *Nightmare on Elm Street* horror movies, insisted that his magazine would be "controversial." In order for evangelicals to produce decent literature at all, Craven argued, they must be free of any "party-line" attitude. They must overcome the intellectual limitations of fundamentalist tradition and be guided only by "the criteria and boundaries of artistry." In Craven's opinion, "the Fundamental Christian world, and more specifically Wheaton, is sadly short of its potential, and far behind its contemporaries."[30] In order to shake it up and catch up, Craven included two stories he knew would challenge the traditions of Wheaton's prudish fundamentalist past. In one, an unmarried teenage girl wrestled with the moral ambiguity of her pregnancy. In another, a white woman pondered her sexual attraction to an African American man.

If Craven thought these stories would unleash a whirlwind, he was right. *Brave Son* was banned. Control of *Kodon* was removed from student editors, and the magazine's publication was eventually suspended.[31] A mortified President Edman scrambled to reassure outraged alumni that the tone of the magazine did not have official approval. *Kodon,* Edman wrote to interested parties, had veered from its earlier "approved" status and therefore had been suspended.[32]

Board member Herman Fischer responded with a vitriolic denunciation of the tone and spirit of *Kodon.* Craven, Fischer fulminated, had taken cowardly refuge behind evangelical-sounding phrases. Fischer was personally offended by Craven's condemnation of "fundamental Church culture." Fischer insisted that real Christianity, real evangelicalism, had no need to write about "human degradation," since the Bible was entirely clear about humanity's essentially degraded condition. Craven's bad-faith error, Fischer insisted, was to "speak of artistically portraying degradation," because that was merely a "contradiction in terms."[33]

In the short term, the administration managed to shut down Wheaton's evangelical free-speech movement. Yet both Craven and the *Brave Son* editors managed to fire a few parting shots. In an interim edition of *Kodon,* sent to press before the administration ruled to remove student leadership, Craven again blasted the presumptions of fundamentalism. Too many Wheaton students and too many fundamentalists in general, Craven wrote, "feel we have the answer to everything in Christianity. This is not so."[34] He insisted that his protest was not against true evangelical Christianity but rather against the accreted falsehoods of fundamentalism. "We are not rebelling against Christianity," Craven claimed, "but against make-believe."[35]

The student editors of *Brave Son,* too, attempted a brief and ill-fated revenge. In March 1963, a group of five students distributed an independent newsletter on campus, *Critique.* This self-financed publication attacked

Wheaton's tradition of force-feeding fundamentalist verities down students' throats. In one article, Philip McIlnay blasted President Edman for misunderstanding the basic premises of both true Christianity and a true liberal-arts education. Edman had come to him, McIlnay reported, to insist that Wheaton must retain its ability to reassure evangelical parents of its continuing fidelity to fundamentalist tradition. "This college," Edman reportedly told McIlnay, "will be a place Christian parents can send their children to with the confidence that their faith will be established and not shaken."[36] Edman and other leaders, McIlnay charged, failed to grasp the true nature of real Christian education. "We must note," McIlnay wrote, "that the 'protective' approach proscribes the natural freedom of man to seek truth where he will . . . . Christian education must exist in the free atmosphere of such a perspective or we will have no choice but to reject Christian education."[37]

For their parts, McIlnay and his co-editor, Jack Hommes, apparently misunderstood the combustible nature of Wheaton College in 1963. Both students were suspended for a full year. Technically, they had broken no school rules, because none existed to cover such a situation. Nevertheless, the administration kicked them out for "insubordination." Some faculty members protested—privately and after approving the suspensions—that such a penalty was woefully out of proportion to the crime. Students who drank alcohol or engaged in sexual misconduct, Professor Gerald Hawthorne reminded the administration, had been suspended for a week or two. Did Wheaton really want to punish students so severely for thinking critically and writing candidly about central issues of evangelical culture?[38]

For Wheaton's top administration, the answer was an anxious yes. In order to remain attractive to students from the wider conservative evangelical community—including families that had embraced the idea of a neo-evangelical reform as well as those who remained committed to the notion of fundamentalism—Wheaton had little choice but to clamp down hard on any suggestion of institutional wobbling. Wheaton's free-speech rebels had not only challenged Wheaton's delicate artistic sensibilities. They had forced the administration to take drastic action to prove that the school had not abandoned the basic cultural verities that had inspired the movement toward fundamentalist higher education since the 1920s.

In each burst of student protest, Wheaton's leaders had to consider the strict scrutiny that fundamentalists would be applying to their every move. In all the cases, new president Hudson Armerding walked a fine line. He supported evangelical reforms, especially when students claimed they needed them in order to have a "real" liberal-arts college experience. On the other hand, Armerding always went out of his way to reassure traditionalist alumni, parents, faculty, students, and administrators that none of the sixties-style reforms ever threatened Wheaton's status as an unyieldingly orthodox evangelical institution.

For their part, conservative alumni groups made their concerns clear. In 1964, for example, the Wheaton Alumni Association in Los Angeles hosted a panel discussion about the current state of their alma mater and its likely future direction. Influential alumni had been reading the student newspaper with increasing anxiety. They noted that students had been agitating for a relaxation of the "Wheaton Code." Would the school give in to sixties-style student protests and abandon its evangelical tradition? As always, the implied threat was clear: if administrators gave in to student demands, they could kiss vital alumni donations goodbye.[39]

For the next several years, Wheaton's administrators wrestled with questions of change. Could they allow students to put on plays? Could they loosen the dress code? The behavioral rules? Student rebels and their supporters among the faculty and alumni pushed for commonsense evangelical reform. They wanted Wheaton to abandon the empty and theologically meaningless rules that only served to alienate students from real evangelical religion. Moreover, they demanded a real liberal arts education, one that did not sequester them needlessly from provocative ideas. Such ideas, after all, were the heart and soul of real higher education. At the same time, conservatives warned that helter-skelter change would leave Wheaton in the same pathetic state as earlier generations of once-Christian schools. A shake-up of traditional rules could lead down the slippery slope of secularization. Even many seemingly straightforward administrative decisions, then, carried decades of fundamentalist baggage that administrators felt obliged to handle with extreme caution.

In 1965, for example, one of newly appointed President Armerding's first decisions was to allow dramatic productions on campus. As long as those plays promoted the traditional evangelical aims of Wheaton, Armerding announced, they should be welcomed. After all, drama was a respected and sophisticated art form. Wheaton students deserved to have it included in their liberal arts education.[40] He did not make the decision on a whim. Drama had been banned from campus as part of Wheaton's embrace of fundamentalist morality. Abandoning the ban could be seen as an abandonment of fundamentalism itself. Due to the potential sensitivity of the question, a committee had been meeting for more than a year to discuss potential changes in the ban on drama. They wanted to allow drama to be studied on campus, but they worried it would degenerate into worldly, immoral entertainment. In the end, the committee suggested that plays could be studied as art, but not performed as shows. Nothing of any immoral character could be allowed. The plays studied could have no "extensive and expensive props" to turn the heads of students.[41]

As with the loosening of the ban on drama, student rebels succeeded at Wheaton when they convinced administrators that traditional rules were not theologically necessary and that those same rules kept students from getting an authentic higher education. In late 1966, for instance, a group of polite protesters requested an end to the enforcement of Wheaton's thick book of student lifestyle rules. It seemed ridiculous in 1966 for students to be barred from watching movies, smoking, and drinking. In order to be formed as evangelical adults, students insisted, they must be allowed to take responsibility for their own lifestyle choices. As the student leaders put it, they were embarrassed to tell their friends at other schools about their old-fashioned rules. They felt as if they were not experiencing the freedom that they believed must accompany real higher education.[42]

As always, President Armerding moved slowly. He appointed a committee to examine the issue; its charge was to determine what evangelical principles were at stake. Change must not be made simply to keep up with changing norms at mainstream schools. Wheaton, Armerding insisted, must never "passively . . . reflect our culture but actively seek to lead and inform it."[43] Campus conservatives such as registrar Enock Dyrness harrumphed that the spirit of change in the air was precisely why the student rules must remain. Due to the "deterioration taking place in our evangelical churches," Dyrness lamented, it was more important than ever for evangelical institutions such as Wheaton to remain steady.[44] Student leaders pushed back. Politely but firmly, student protesters including future star historian Mark Noll insisted that Wheaton's behavioral rules needed to be reexamined.[45] To shield sincere evangelical students from the most basic moral choices, students argued, might lead to a scandalous stunting of young minds.

In the end, Wheaton did revise its decades-old pledge. Just before the start of the school year in 1967, Armerding announced the careful new approach. Students were still prohibited from drinking, smoking, card playing, and movie attendance. But instead of the language of simple prohibition, the new standards of conduct emphasized student moral responsibility. Henceforth, Wheaton students were enjoined to "cooperate constructively" in the evangelical project of the college. They were always to "exhibit Christian conduct." They still must observe the traditional behavioral rules while on campus, but those rules were only part of a broader goal. Students pledged to "take maximum advantage of the educational opportunities" at the school, "in harmony with both academic and non-academic goals." Those goals, the new rules stated, were ultimately about achieving each student's "maximum personal development." It was now the students' responsibility, the rules made clear, to always monitor their behavior. And that behavior must always promote students' "commitment to Christ and to the purposes of Wheaton College."[46] The new pledge, Armerding insisted, was not a loosening of rules but rather a welcome recognition that real evangelical religion required students to embrace good conduct, not merely submit to it.

In case any worried parent thought that Wheaton had abandoned its commitment to fundamentalist campus traditions, Armerding took pains to reassure them. In 1971, he promised parents that Wheaton still bucked the trends of mainstream higher education. Secular colleges, Armerding claimed, celebrated the death of in loco parentis rules. Not Wheaton. In spite of the new language of its student pledge, Armerding's Wheaton promised to avoid the trap of "a shallow permissiveness." At Wheaton, Armerding insisted, students "should be disciplined and corrected" when necessary. In every case, biblical norms of behavior would reign supreme. And in every case, the school administration would continue to shoulder the responsibility for determining the limits of that behavior.[47]

## *The Left Coast*

Armerding's conservative, reassuring tone could be heard from top administrators at all the schools in the evangelical and fundamentalist network. Someone listening only to Biola president Samuel H. Sutherland might think his campus was blissfully free of leftist student radicalism in 1969. There were no "militant organizations" at Biola such as Students for a Democratic Society (SDS) or the Black Student Union, Sutherland assured the evangelical and fundamentalist communities. Moreover, unlike the scenes at raucous secular schools, Sutherland promised, "progress and change at Biola College will continue to be achieved through an orderly rather than a destructive process."[48]

To someone who spent any amount of time on campus, however, it would quickly have been clear that Biola's students waged the same sorts of sixties campaigns as had Wheaton students. They wanted greater freedom from unnecessary fundamentalist rules. And they wanted a real college education, not just dictation from dusty old fundamentalist textbooks. Just as did President Armerding at Wheaton, Sutherland had good reason to cover up any whisper of slackening fundamentalist fervor at his institution. Just as did Wheaton, Biola needed to remain attractive for fundamentalist students and their tuition dollars, and Sutherland energetically policed his school's image.

Sutherland's claim that there was no SDS or Black Student Union activism on his campus might have been correct, but Biola's students protested in their own ways about issues important to them. Mostly they pushed for a relaxation of their traditional lifestyle rules. They hoped for a loosening of their strict curfew.[49] They wanted greater access to TVs in dorm rooms.[50] And they hoped for more influence over their clothing choices.[51]

Student rebels scored some wins and some losses. By 1969, men and women were allowed to wear Bermuda shorts on campus.[52] But women

FIGURE 7.1 "Only 20 minutes please"
Biola's good-natured rebels plead for wiggle room. *Biola Chimes*, May 1, 1964. Courtesy Biola University Archives.

were never allowed to wear short skirts. In the spring of 1968, one bold group of fashion protesters were suspended for one week each for refusing to change out of their short skirts.[53]

Why, student protesters asked, were they still required to abide by outdated lifestyle rules? In the fall of 1968, the student council sat down with President Sutherland, Dean Richard Chase, and three other administrators. The rules, student leaders charged, were only in place to soothe fundamentalist fuddy-duddies who donated to the alumni fund. If they were really for the glory of God, as President Sutherland insisted, then why weren't students allowed to choose their rules for themselves? Wasn't that sort of individual communion with God the heart and soul of real evangelical Christianity?[54]

Biola's top administrators were happy to talk, but they continued to enforce most of their traditional rules without apology. As always, their goal was to maintain the perception in the evangelical and fundamentalist communities that their campus was a safe space, both theologically and behaviorally. Not only did they hasten to punish students for rule violations, but they also took pains to publicize their continuing dedication to such rule enforcement. For example, one student was expelled in 1966 for homosexuality, having "admitted to at least twenty-five homosexual acts." The problem, as President Sutherland saw it, was that the student threatened to weaken Biola's reputation as a stridently pure school. In spite of prayer interventions, the student could not seem to stop. Not only that, but the student was actively "broadcasting this type of information far and wide"—according to Sutherland, the expelled student used his job as a night watchman to distribute some sort of illicit publications. For all these reasons, Sutherland concluded that he could show no mercy. To Sutherland, there seemed to be a stark and obvious contrast between a safe campus and one that included homosexual students. As Sutherland concluded, "Honestly now, would you want a son or daughter of yours to come to a school where any known aggressive homosexual is allowed freely to pursue his activities?" For Sutherland, simply asking the question in those terms revealed how utterly impossible it was to allow a homosexual student to remain on campus.[55]

Another student was expelled in 1971 for less dramatic infractions of the lifestyle rules. He left campus after being grounded. He walked loudly and provocatively through the hallways of a women's dorm. He faked attendance at a missionary conference. And, worst of all, he repeatedly put up a "vulgar sign" on his dormitory room door. The student, administrators warned, not only broke the rules but also created an environment in which other students had a harder time obeying the rules. The principle was the same, whether students disobeyed due to sexual identity, sixties-style rebellion, or simple immature hijinks. Biola's administrators could change the rules when it made sense, but they could never allow even the vaguest implication that their school was not a safe environment for fundamentalist students.[56]

Just as on Wheaton's campus, the battles at Biola were fought not only in terms of sixties-style liberation but also in the language of the fundamentalist-evangelical feud. One group of seminary students petitioned President Sutherland for greater punctiliousness in enforcing both the campus lifestyle rules and the campus's fundamentalist traditions. The two things, after all, were inextricably tied together, at least in the eyes of these conservative seminarians. Too many female students, the seminarians complained, openly flouted the rule on skirt length. Some earnest male students, they warned, could no longer study due to the distracting "excessive bodily exposure of Biola girls." The rules on female dress, moreover, were not merely a whim but rather a doctrinal necessity, based on biblical insistence on female modesty.[57]

Biola's campus, the seminarians protested, must take steps to preserve its fundamentalist character. Too many students were mouthing the empty phrases of the secular sixties, calling themselves "progressive, democratic Americans" instead of Christians. The school needed to invite more speakers with an explicit "conservative political philosophy." More important, some of Biola's recent liberalizations were obvious "danger signs" that the school might be on the edge of the neo-evangelical "heresy" that had done in many "great schools of the past." In every case, the school needed to actively safeguard its "strong doctrinal position" in order to prevent an all-too-common "deterioration" away from fundamentalist certainties.[58]

One seminarian warned that Biola faced a stark choice: either it could recommit itself to its best fundamentalist principles, or it could relax into "neo-evangelicalism's pseudo-Christianity." He urged Sutherland to correct the "malady" of campus conferences that included non-fundamentalist speakers and ideas. In the dark days of 1969, this fundamentalist warned, the world needed more than ever a college that "will ring a clear, clarion call to evangelize the world in obedience to Christ's command."[59]

Biola's rebels fought back. Not only did they insist on sensible relaxations of senseless rules on clothing and behavior, but they also insisted that their rebellion represented true evangelical Christianity. In 1968, for example, students published a short-lived independent newspaper, the *Catacomb*. They were tired, they wrote, of being treated like a "spiritually degenerated minority" for their advocacy of neo-evangelical reform.[60] In some ways, Biola's rebels agreed with Biola's fundamentalists: both sides thought that politics, lifestyle, and religion were all connected. In the rebels' opinions, though, Biola needed a healthy shake-up of all three. For example, one student urged conservative Biolans to view the war in Vietnam as a Christian issue, not an American one. The true evangelical position was to oppose war—to love the Vietnamese, not to kill them.[61] All in all, the *Catacomb* insisted on student freedom, antiwar politics, and evangelical reform.

At Biola, such sixties-style evangelical rebels fought an uphill battle. The local and national fundamentalist community scrutinized campus goings-on with a feverish intensity. Time and again, President Sutherland insisted that his administration would allow no diminution of its commitment to strident fundamentalism. For example, in 1969 one local resident complained that a recent copy of the official student newspaper contained a questionable advertisement for "Me-n-Ed's Pizza Parlor." In the ad, a cartoon depicted a jolly-looking customer enjoying pizza and swinging a frothy mug of beer. Not only that, the outraged local fundamentalist complained, but the restaurant claimed it was a popular destination for Biola students. Did Biola really allow—or even encourage—its students to drink beer?[62] The complainant was assured that the ad was a horrible oversight and that it would be remedied right away.[63]

The local fundamentalist gadfly was not the only one watching Biola. The same year, the fundamentalist newsletter *Blu-Print* picked up a story in the *Chimes* about a student visiting a local brewery.[64] Predictably, President Sutherland received reams of mail from outraged fundamentalists nationwide, many with no personal connection to the school. Could it be true, the concerned writers asked, that Biola had really abandoned its fundamentalist roots to such a drastic degree? Sutherland did not take such accusations lightly. He cranked out personal letters in response to each and every inquiry. The article in *Blu-Print* was half right, Sutherland explained. Yes, the student had written openly about visiting a brewery. What the *Blu-Print* article failed to mention was that the student had been disciplined harshly. Biola, Sutherland assured concerned fundamentalists, remained committed to its strict fundamentalist roots, both in its religious doctrine and in its behavioral expectations.[65]

For fundamentalists, such questions were always tied inextricably to popular images of sixties-style protests. Sutherland never failed to defend his school's reputation as a unique higher-education haven from such happenings. When an article appeared in a local newspaper, for example, implying that Biola's students included "long-haired men with bare feet and shoddy clothes . . . . [and l]ong-haired, lookalike girls with fluorescent lipstick and mini-skirts," Sutherland took action. He wrote a furious reply to the editor. Biola's students never adopted this sort of hippie uniform. If the reporter had seen "any of this element" on Biola's campus, Sutherland insisted, they must have come from "somewhere else."[66]

Sutherland's vigilance was not merely a personal quirk. In order to survive as an institution, Biola—like other fundamentalist and evangelical colleges—had no choice but to protect its reputation as a safe school for fundamentalist and evangelical students. Any rumor that Biola had strayed, Sutherland knew, could easily dry up the supply of new students with their tuition dollars. And such rumors flew with predictable rapidity through the networks of fundamentalist publications and organizations. They did not have to be true to have enormous influence among fundamentalist parents.

Alumni attitudes, too, could save or kill the school. If conservative donors felt their dollars would fuel sixties-style protests and neo-evangelical reform, they might hesitate to open their checkbooks. In 1970, Biola sent potential alumni donors a fundraising plea that reassured readers of Biola's continuing dedication to its fundamentalist roots. Biola, the school promised, did not merely buck recent campus trends. It had turned itself into a new kind of institution, a frankly anti-sixties missionary training school. Too many headlines recently, the letter explained, had been "frightening." They were full of news about "hippies," "demonstrations," and "mini-skirts" among other "noise and new things." All too often, campuses chattered about "flower-power, black-power, atomic power, student power." The only "power" that really mattered, donors read, was "the explosive power of the Word of God [that] created headlines at BIOLA in the 60's." While other colleges veered wildly into protests and meaningless novelty, Biola remained staunchly committed to training a new generation of missionaries. Such dedication wasn't cheap. The students at Biola lacked adequate classrooms. They needed "investments like yours" in order to continue to spread God's "Message to [a] Frustrated World."[67]

## *Maybe We Do Need a Weatherman*

All the schools in the family of evangelical and fundamentalist institutions shared similar concerns. At Gordon College, for example, in 1968 student protesters insisted, "We want to be treated like real college students."[68] In their view, that meant sit-ins and shake-ups of fundamentalist religion and rulebooks. As at other schools, Gordon's administrators rushed to reassure conservatives that any such protests did not represent the true evangelical spirit of the school. For instance, President Forrester assured one worried correspondent that the few "unfortunate rebels" were only "about one percent of the total student body." Forrester promised he had "no intention to tolerate these things."[69] Another administrator similarly condemned Gordon's "rebels and nonconformists" and noted that "steps were taken to correct the situation."[70]

In Chicago, Moody Bible Institute students made similar demands. In 1970, for instance, student council president Don Wipf declared his support for relaxation of the school's lifestyle rules in the pages of the *Moody Student*. Rules were good, Wipf agreed, but "a person will not mature nor be able to face today's world if he is not free to make choices."[71] At MBI, however, plenty of students disagreed. One student insisted that she did not want to change the rules. She only wanted to submit to "God's Word and let it change me."[72] The editor of the student paper agreed. Though it was frustrating at times to be held to seemingly inconsistent rules, he wrote, maturity came not from rebellion but from obedience. The best thing for students to do, he thought, was to "work more on changing our attitudes than on changing the rules."[73]

As at all schools, students weren't the only ones pushing their school to resist the trends of the college sixties. Fundamentalists around the country pressed MBI to remain a stalwart leader on the side of uncompromisingly fundamentalist higher education. As the unofficial leader of the network of Bible institutes and Bible colleges, MBI had always had an enormous influence. And during the sixties, some fundamentalist school administrators worried about that influence. President B. Myron Cedarholm of Maranatha Baptist Bible College in Wisconsin, for instance, shared his concerns with MBI president William Culbertson. Cedarholm fretted about "Moody's direction these days," and told Culbertson that it wasn't just him. "All across this nation," Cedarholm warned, "many folks are wondering about Moody." Too many great fundamentalist schools, he explained, had relaxed into devilishly liberal student rules and damnably ecumenical evangelical doctrine. Cedarholm named names: "Northfield, Providence, Wheaton, Biola, Westmont, Fuller, Denver Seminary, etc." All of them had once been reliably fundamentalist schools, but all of them had slid into theological and cultural slackness. The neo-evangelical heresy snuck in quietly, by degrees, Cedarholm warned, and "it frightens us." His plaintive appeal could have come from fundamentalist school leaders around the country. "If Moody goes and no longer stands true," he asked, "what chance is there for any school to stand?"[74]

## *The Greatest Generation*

Of course, by the time Cedarholm expressed his concerns, evangelical and fundamentalist school administrators had more to worry about than just the growing divide between the branches of their conservative evangelical family. Moody Bible Institute was not only evangelical but also an evangelical institution. And, as did all of its fellows in the growing family of evangelical and fundamentalist institutes, colleges, seminaries, and universities, MBI in 1971 confronted a landscape of higher education that had become starkly different from anything that had come before. Like all colleges, evangelical schools experienced a boom in attendance that stretched resources and forced drastic rethinkings of campus priorities. Between 1960 and 1972, the percentage of evangelicals who attended college tripled.[75] The evangelical sixties, then, were not merely a row between neo-evangelicals and fundamentalists for the soul of conservative evangelical faith. They were not only a string of battles between stodgy hardliners and hippie protesters. They did not merely mark out the shifting front lines in America's continuing culture wars. In addition to all those things, the sixties experience at evangelical colleges—just as at all sorts of schools nationwide—represented an institutional reshuffling in the face of a momentous demographic shift.

By the early 1960s, Americans were attending college in record numbers. Higher education, which had still been viewed in the early part of the twentieth century as an elite endeavor, became a mass experience in new ways. To satisfy this demand, a crop of new schools emerged. Like all schools, evangelical and fundamentalist institutions experienced a double pressure. First, the new numbers of students prompted administrators to expand to fit everyone in. Such expansions were never simple and never an obviously good investment. After all, tight-fisted administrators had to wonder if the student boom would last. They wondered if expenditures on new facilities were wise investments or a foolish squandering of scarce campus resources. Second, competition from new schools put existing schools in an uncomfortably novel position, competing for students against a dizzying array of fledgling institutions. For fundamentalist and evangelical schools, that competition often took on the flavor of the continuing feud between branches of the conservative evangelical family. New fundamentalist schools hoped to lure students from evangelical institutions with promises of rigorous enforcement of fundamentalist tradition. And new evangelical schools offered more and better intellectual experiences, freed from the baggage of fundamentalist pasts.

In order to understand these changes, we need to back up a couple of decades to the end of World War II. Evangelical and fundamentalist schools participated in the boom caused by the end of the war and the surprisingly popular Servicemen's Readjustment Act. The act, known universally as the GI Bill, offered demobilizing war veterans a chance at a college degree. Vets could have all school expenses covered up to $500 per school year, plus monthly living stipends. Depending on their length of service, veterans could have one to four years of school paid for.[76]

Not every provision of the GI Bill lived up to its promise. For example, African American vets in the South had a tightly restricted number of racially segregated schools to which they could apply.[77] And those schools often had extremely limited financial resources and weren't able to accommodate the burst of new applicants.[78] For all vets, too, as historian Lizabeth Cohen has argued, the GI Bill achieved "much less social engineering than it promised and has been given credit for." Usually, those vets who had the most chance at a college education before the war benefited the most from the opportunities afforded by the GI Bill.[79]

In spite of all those important caveats, however, it is difficult to overstate the impact of the GI Bill on American higher education as a whole. The program turned out to be far more popular than anyone had dreamed. A total of 51 percent of all World War II veterans took advantage of the program, totaling roughly 7.8 million people. Just over two million of those vets went to colleges, universities, or seminaries, while the rest enrolled in non-collegiate training programs. This flood of new students utterly transformed college and university campuses. By 1947, veterans made up just under half (49 percent) of college students.[80] Schools of all sorts scrambled to keep up with this flood of new students, and a burst of new schools emerged to offer veterans the kinds of post-secondary education they clamored for.

Plenty of those returning veterans clamored for a fundamentalist or evangelical education. There is no way to gauge the numbers of students for whom the war served as a religious awakening, but many likely combined the trauma of war with the opportunities of the GI Bill to change their lives. At Bob Jones College alone, returning vets bombarded the school with stories of their foxhole conversions and their hopes to use the GI Bill to make good on their wartime religious commitments.[81]

We can't know how many veterans turned to religion due to the stresses of combat, but we can see that the GI Bill changed the population at fundamentalist and evangelical colleges in drastic ways. At Pepperdine University in California, for example, the GI Bill sent 700 new students to a school that had previously registered only about 1,300 total.[82] At Wheaton, the GI Bill expanded student enrollment from 1,193 students in 1941 to 1,524 in 1946.[83] And the most ardently fundamentalist school in the network may also have been among the most drastically affected by the GI Bill: Bob Jones College exploded from only 455 students in 1941 to 1,585 in 1946.[84] That sort of exponential growth put BJC far ahead of the dramatic growth also seen on many non-evangelical campuses. Rutgers University in New Jersey, for instance, grew from 7,000 students before the war to 16,000 in 1948. Stanford expanded from 4,800 to 7,200. And the University of Minnesota leaped from a student population of 14,986 in 1940 to 27,103 in 1946.[85] Though the growth in absolute numbers at these non-religious schools was much larger, the proportions were often similar to the kinds of dramatic expansions at many evangelical and fundamentalist schools.

At Bob Jones College, the changes from the new tripling of student enrollment led to some drastic changes. Perhaps most notably, the school expanded from a "college" to a "university" in 1947. It also moved from its cramped campus in Cleveland, Tennessee, to its current home in Greenville, South Carolina.[86] Many conservative evangelical and fundamentalist school administrators balked at the theological implications of accepting so many government-funded students. As a rule, most schools found no problem taking new government-funded students, but many refused to take government money directly.[87]

In practice, however, even the staunch fundamentalists at Bob Jones College were willing to define fundamentalism to suit their institutional purposes. When the potential bonanza of the postwar GI Bill became clear, for example, Bob Jones Sr. insisted that there was absolutely no reason to refuse certain forms of government largesse. As leading BJC administrator R. K. Johnson later remembered, Jones told him in 1946 to go to the federal district office in Atlanta and get whatever he could. "If we were entitled to it," Johnson remembered Jones telling him, "then I must never stop until we got what we went after." In the end, BJC accepted fifty federal trailers and seven barracks-style housing units to cram all their new students into.[88]

Bob Jones was not the only fundamentalist to recognize the potential for growth in the postwar years. In the years and decades to come, fundamentalists established a new crop of schools to satisfy the new demands. Institutions such as Tennessee Temple University (1946), Grace College in Indiana (1948), Baptist Bible College in Missouri (1950), Midwestern Baptist College (1953), Indiana Baptist College (1955), Central Baptist Theological Seminary in Minnesota (1956), Clearwater Christian College (1966), Maranatha Baptist Bible University (1968), Liberty University (1970), and Pensacola Christian College (1974) offered fundamentalist students and families an ever-expanding network of schools offering firmly fundamentalist higher education. In addition, students looking for an evangelical school that embraced the neo-evangelical reforms could find a similarly growing menu of options. Moreover, as we saw in Chapter 6, the sprawling network of conservative evangelical "institutes" and "Bible colleges" continued to transform itself in those same decades into "colleges" and "universities." All in all, the possibilities for evangelical higher education grew by leaps and bounds between the end of the war and the emergence of the campus sixties. The new schools, as well as the old ones, usually promised degree programs that would prepare students for careers, and all of them offered an evangelical environment—however they defined it—that would safeguard students and encourage them along the path to salvation as well as to professional success.

It is difficult to measure this burst of expansion precisely, but we can get a sense of its scope from a few sources. First, from among the 117 North American members of the Council for Christian Colleges and Universities in 2016, 21 were founded between 1940 and 1960, and another 15 came between 1960 and 1980. Just as the numbers of Americans in general and evangelicals in particular who attended college grew dramatically, so did the numbers of evangelical and fundamentalist schools competing for those students and their tuition dollars.[89]

The archives of some schools provide a closer look at the ways evangelical schools experienced this new world of competition. With its roots at the beginning of the twentieth century, Biola had gotten used to its privileged spot as California's premier evangelical institution. By the 1960s, its leaders realized that they had suddenly emerged into a very different world. Biola's crosstown evangelical rival, Asuza Pacific, had become a serious competitor for the same group of students.

Asuza Pacific had begun life in 1899 as the Training School for Christian Workers. In 1939, to keep up with the changing expectations of higher education, it expanded its academic program and changed its name to Pacific Bible College. A merger in 1965 created Asuza Pacific College. Only in 1981 would it become Asuza Pacific University.[90] Biola's leaders watched Asuza's growth with barely concealed anxiety. In the spirit of evangelical brotherhood, Biola president Samuel Sutherland encouraged Asuza president Cornelius P. Haggard in the wake of Haggard's 1966 heart attack. Haggard needed to be careful about his health, Sutherland urged, as evangelicals needed him and his leadership skills. Sutherland had heard "glowing reports" of Haggard's ability to improve Asuza's campus and academic offerings. "Please progress at a little slower pace over there," Sutherland concluded awkwardly; "we don't want to be left far behind in our Bible college program."[91]

Meanwhile, among themselves, Biola's top leaders gnashed their teeth at Asuza's growth. They speculated that Asuza's success must have come from a combination of administrative hocus-pocus and theological pandering. After all, Asuza's tuition was not any lower, but they offered more money in scholarships, especially to athletes. And Asuza's recruiters did not insist that those athletes come from evangelical homes. Moreover, Asuza's hungry administrators seemed to make more personal contact with potential students.[92] Sutherland agreed that he had been "too complacent" about the competitive threat posed by Asuza. He had thought that Asuza's frank neo-evangelical embrace of the "NAE doctrinal position" would cost it students from the fundamentalist camp. Yet many students seemed actually to prefer Asuza's "more lenient" neo-evangelical campus rules. Sutherland wasn't "pressing the panic button" yet, he reported, and he wasn't willing to ease up on Biola's student rules just to woo students. But he did think his school needed to do a better job of selling itself. The rules had changed, Sutherland noted, and Biola had to change along with them.[93]

Biola's leaders weren't the only ones alarmed by the new competitive landscape of 1960s evangelical education. In 1967 Wheaton's administrators received a similar shock. They had been accustomed to dealing with overwhelming numbers of applicants. In 1967, however, administrators struggled to understand an alarming drop in student inquiries. In 1964, 8,528 potential freshman had requested information about their college.

By 1967 that number plummeted to only 6,403,[94] with just 1,101 actual applicants.[95] Numbers rebounded somewhat in the ensuing years, with 1,376 applicants in 1968,[96] rising to 1,519 in 1975.[97] Such numbers represented a new institutional reality for the administrators of Wheaton College. Just as did other established evangelical institutions, they realized they could no longer rely on a captive market of ambitious, intelligent conservative evangelical students. They had to compete with a growing number of conservative evangelical colleges and universities, and they had to prove that they were still a safe school for all conservative evangelical students.

Like admissions officers everywhere, Wheaton's bureaucrats looked frantically for reasons for their sudden drop in applications. And like admissions officers everywhere, they found a long list of likely suspects. For example, in 1966, Wheaton enforced for the first time new requirements for high school graduation among applicants. Admissions director Charles Schoenherr wondered if Wheaton's history of strict admissions standards had begun to deter iffy applicants. He mused that Wheaton's weak athletic teams might be dissuading qualified applicants. Schoenherr also had worries unique to Wheaton's evangelical/fundamentalist history. He fretted that Wheaton might be losing out to both new and established fundamentalist schools.[98]

In 1966, the admissions office reported that more and more potential Wheaton students were likely applying to and attending other evangelical colleges.[99] Conservative evangelical students and parents had a much wider range of schools from which they could pick. They might prefer a school that was closer to home. They might like to find a college that more closely reflected their own denominational traditions. And, of course, they might feel strongly that they must go to a school that had clung more firmly to the traditions of separatist fundamentalism. As a leader of the neo-evangelical reform, Wheaton's leaders worried that they had lost out to both new and old fundamentalist competitors. Could it be, Schoenherr asked President Armerding in a 1966 memo, that Wheaton had an "image" problem among its conservative evangelical constituency? "To what extent," Schoenherr wondered, "have rumors about Wheaton going 'liberal' hurt?"[100]

## *Walking the Line*

Not only Wheaton's leaders but administrators at all the conservative evangelical schools asked themselves similar questions. Indeed, the defining struggle of the evangelical sixties on campus might not have been about the war in Vietnam, the push for relaxed rules, or even the ferocious conflicts over race, racism, and civil rights that we'll explore in Chapter 8. To understand the evangelical sixties, we need to put all those battles into the context of the ongoing feud between fundamentalists and evangelicals. Biola's leaders worried that Asuza Pacific might be winning the fight for students by frankly adopting neo-evangelical reforms. Wheaton worried that its reputation for "going 'liberal'" had similarly cost it students who didn't like those same reforms. Moody Bible Institute supporters fretted that the fundamentalist outpost had lost its backbone. Nervous new-evangelical alumni threatened to hold back donations if schools didn't openly repudiate their fundamentalist traditions, just as fundamentalist alumni everywhere threatened to do the same if schools didn't stick by their fundamentalist roots.

At all the schools, even ones that had most fervently embraced liberal and neo-evangelical reforms, administrators tried to reassure fundamentalist and conservative evangelical supporters that they remained true. Every reform, every change was always plausibly deniable. When Gordon College and Wheaton loosened up their student rules, for example, leaders always insisted that such changes represented merely clarifications of traditional evangelical thinking. President Armerding at Wheaton, for instance, left the official student rules in place even as he approved a new set of behavioral guidelines. To student protesters, he could claim that Wheaton had recognized their sensible demands. To conservative alumni, parents, and trustees, he could honestly say that the student rules remained in place and his school had never stopped acting in loco parentis.[101]

At the same time, those schools that continued to embrace fundamentalist traditions did so ever more stridently, in an effort to differentiate themselves from those that had stepped into the suspect territory of neo-evangelical reform. When Bob Jones Jr. denounced antiwar protesters, for example, he blamed not only leftist politics in general but also the "ungodly professors" who had snuck into so many formerly fundamentalist schools.[102] Bob Jones University promised to stand out from both antiwar protests and the "Neo-Evangelical forces and liberals" that seemed to encourage them.[103]

Such fundamentalist/evangelical hostility shaped the evangelical sixties, but it did not create them out of whole cloth. As we've seen, students at evangelical colleges and universities were keenly aware that they attended different sorts of schools. For some, that was a lamentable problem, and they yearned to be treated like "real college students."[104]

For others, the goings-on at mainstream schools were stark warnings, sad displays of what could happen if students abandoned their evangelical certitudes. Why didn't more evangelical students, some asked, recognize the blessings of their unique schools, instead of stupidly mimicking the foolish "publicity seeking rebels," those "misguided and misinformed college students who carry on demonstrations"?[105]

Yet despite the fact that evangelical and fundamentalist students felt different, evangelical and fundamentalist colleges actually participated wholeheartedly in the transformations that swept over American higher education in the period. The tidal wave of new students—and of new types of students—that entered colleges and universities in the wake of World War II hit fundamentalist campuses just as hard as non-fundamentalist ones, sometimes even harder. And the landscape of fundamentalist higher education changed in similar ways to that of mainstream schools. New schools popped up, offering a new array of collegiate experiences. In addition to offering local campuses, junior colleges, and a dizzying array of professional and liberal arts programs, the new world of evangelical and fundamentalist higher education offered students a more precise match to their own religious identity. Some students chose new schools that shared their denominational background. Others chose schools that promoted themselves as the truly fundamentalist option, while yet others decided on an evangelical school that had more aggressively ditched its fundamentalist past.

Just as school administrators at all sorts of institutions wrung their hands at the quandaries of the campus sixties, so evangelical and fundamentalist school leaders walked a difficult line. In every case, they vigorously policed the public image of their schools. And in every case, they worried that potential students might dismiss their campus as too strict, or too lenient; too worldly, or too isolated. In order to survive as an evangelical or fundamentalist institution during the turbulent sixties, administrators had to confront the new realities of both the world of American higher education and the world of American evangelicalism.

# 8

## *Is the Bible Racist?*

*I am not a Negro hater. But I am just so much for Christ and the Bible that I am not willing for anybody to turn me or turn Christian institutions away from the main thing in order to please the modernists and the communists and the agitators.*

—FUNDAMENTALIST PUNDIT JOHN R. RICE, 1970[1]

### *Enter the Taxman*

No one likes the Internal Revenue Service. Collecting taxes is a thankless job. But when the IRS tried in the 1970s and 1980s to withdraw tax-exempt status from Bob Jones University and other racially segregated fundamentalist schools, fundamentalists responded with a fury that took even other conservative evangelicals by surprise.

Racism and racial segregation at fundamentalist and evangelical colleges and universities had a long and complicated history. For most of the twentieth century, government regulators turned a blind eye to frankly discriminatory policies at private schools. In 1970, however, the IRS announced a new plan: any school that seemed to discriminate by race could no longer claim tax-exempt status.[2] After years of suits and appeals, the leaders of Bob Jones University made their case at the highest court in the land. They lost. In 1983, the U.S. Supreme Court voted eight to one to revoke BJU's tax-exempt status.[3]

By this point, it might come as no surprise to readers that such external pressure failed to turn the Bob Joneses from their segregationist course. Instead of changing policies, the Joneses trumpeted their beleaguered racial segregationism as a key tenet of what it meant to be a true fundamentalist institution. BJU's battle against desegregation generated a great deal of political heat throughout the 1970s and 1980s, as we'll explore in more detail in Chapter 9. In this chapter, we'll look at the ways changing ideas about civil rights and racial equality forced fundamentalist and evangelical schools to discuss openly questions of race, racism, and segregation. Not only the Bob Joneses but white evangelical and fundamentalist school leaders across the country had long struggled with a deeply conflicted legacy of race and racism in their institutions. As always, such questions became tangled inextricably with the never-clear boundaries of evangelicalism and fundamentalism itself. Should evangelical schools embrace their long anti-racist history? Or did true fundamental religion require steadfast segregationism in the face of increasing mainstream sentiment to the contrary? At the same time, the hushed-up history of white racism at evangelical colleges offers another example of the ways cautious school administrators felt trapped by the institutional necessities of higher education. Especially at the more ecumenical evangelical schools, many top leaders sympathized with student and faculty civil rights activism. But administrators panicked that protests and rumors of protests might scare away tuition-paying students.

## *New Schools, New Vision*

Bob Jones University wasn't the only school on the desegregation hot seat in the 1970s. At the time, a new burst of evangelical and fundamentalist K-12 schools had appeared across the country, promising to protect Christian kids from the terrible trends in American public education. Many of them were accused of being nothing more than "segregationist academies," havens for white families who were desperate to avoid any whiff of desegregation.[4] Just as BJU led the fight to protect their right to segregate, so did it play a leading role in preparing teachers, principals, and textbooks for the new fundamentalist schools. And BJU was by no means alone. For decades, evangelical and fundamentalist colleges, universities, and institutes had been the hubs and leaders of Christian education in K-12 schools.

Throughout their existence, as we saw in Chapter 6, fundamentalist institutions of higher education had viewed teacher training as one of their primary missions. In many cases, those teachers were being prepared to teach in church-affiliated Sunday schools, or perhaps in missionary settings around the world. The drive to teach teachers spurred one of the first attempts to organize evangelical higher education into something resembling an accrediting agency. As we saw in Chapter 5, beginning in 1931, the Evangelical Teacher Training Association offered a variety of certifications for teachers.[5] Although ETTA's certifications may have been valuable within the circle of evangelical and fundamentalist schools, they meant nothing in the wider world of public school teacher certification. In order to win state approval to offer certificates for teaching in public schools, evangelical and fundamentalist colleges were required to jump through the same elaborate hoops as mainstream institutions. For most, teacher training was such an important part of their institutional mission that they expended a great deal of time and effort to earn and maintain the right to award state teacher certifications. Even Bob Jones College, the anti-accreditation stalwart, didn't blink at state supervision of its teacher-training courses. As early as 1934, Bob Jones College's teacher education program was approved by the state board of education in Tennessee.[6] When Bob Jones College moved to South Carolina in 1947 and became Bob Jones University, the school wooed state regulators to gain approval to issue South Carolina teaching certificates.[7]

Similarly, Wheaton College worked hard to earn accreditation of its teacher-training program in 1959 from the National Council for Accreditation of Teacher Education.[8] Other schools, such as Biola, had a much more difficult time. The California state board of education turned Biola down in 1952. In order to earn state approval to issue teaching certificates, state administrators explained, Biola needed to "change and strengthen the program of the institute."[9] Biola, state regulators decided, suffered from both its "specialized character" and its lack of library facilities.[10] President Samuel Sutherland thought he smelled a secular rat. State inspectors, he charged, accused the creationist institution of lacking basic training in science. Balderdash, Sutherland scoffed. Other non-fundamentalist colleges offered similar programs and were allowed to issue teaching certificates.[11] Undaunted, Sutherland turned to political allies for help. He complained to influential conservative state senator Nelson Dilworth that the board of education was giving Biola the "run-around."[12] Could Senator Dilworth help Biola overcome official "prejudice"?[13] Dilworth, one of California's most prominent Red-hunters, promised to take a "positive personal interest" in every application for teacher certification from a Biola graduate. It was imperative, Dilworth agreed, that more teachers in public schools receive the sort of conservative religious training on offer at schools like Biola.[14] In the end, the state agreed to issue certifications to Biola graduates as long as they did their student teaching through an approved program such as the one at a nearby campus of California State University.[15]

In the 1950s, it made sense for Biola to take such extraordinary measures to issue state-recognized teaching certificates. After all, many of the graduates of its teacher education programs planned to teach in public schools. It was not until the 1970s that independent nondenominational evangelical and fundamentalist K-12 schools began to proliferate in staggering numbers. Of course, such schools had a longer history. Some Protestant groups, such as a variety of Lutheran and Reformed churches, had always maintained separate private schools.[16] And interdenominational fundamentalists had often encouraged independent elementary and secondary schools. By the early 1960s, one organization of such schools, the National Association of Christian Schools, claimed 215 members across the country.[17]

It was only in the 1970s, however, that the "Christian day school" movement really took off. It is notoriously difficult to get a precise count of the number of these new schools. As we've seen, throughout the twentieth century many fundamentalist pastors and church leaders prided themselves on their fierce independence. They steadfastly refused to be yoked to any unequal partners, so the tally of schools that joined national associations will always be smaller than the total number of fundamentalist schools. Even if we look only at the membership rolls of those national groups, however, the growth rate of the networks still seems extraordinary. One study found that four evangelical and fundamentalist school networks—the evangelical National Association of Christian Schools, the fundamentalism-friendly American Association of Christian Schools, the evangelical Association of Christian Schools International, and the Christian Reformed–affiliated Christian Schools International—more than doubled in size between 1971, when they served 159,916 students in the United States, and 1977, when they served 349,679.[18] By 1992, after the National Association of Christian Schools folded, the three remaining networks claimed to include 4,337 member schools, teaching 776,649 students.[19]

Certainly, many of these schools consisted of nothing more than a few children gathered uncertainly in a church basement. Many of them existed for only a few years, as congregations caught up in the enthusiasm for authentically evangelical or fundamentalist education rushed too quickly into establishing their own schools. Even the most established and durable of these private schools, however, faced a daunting set of challenges.[20] Critics derided them as nothing more than segregationist academies.[21] Even sympathizers disagreed about basic questions: Should evangelicals and fundamentalists really pull their children from mainstream public schools? Or should they remain as "salt and light" in increasingly secular public institutions? And what kind of teaching should go on in evangelical and fundamentalist schools? Should Christian teachers embrace the newer forms of classroom instruction, loosely gathered under the name "progressive education"? Or should they adopt a stern, authoritative role? All these questions roiled the fledgling network of Christian day schools. Time and again, colleges and universities became the forum in which these difficult questions were hashed out.

## *Kicking God into the Classroom*

By the early 1980s, Liberty Baptist College was growing from a tiny Baptist college to an ambitious fundamentalist university. Like all fundamentalist universities, Liberty saw itself as a leader in shaping and nurturing the network of evangelical and fundamentalist K-12 schools. School leaders from around the country made the trip to Lynchburg, Virginia, to find reliably fundamentalist teachers for their new schools. It made sense for principals to travel from Illinois, upstate New York, and even Hawaii, as nowhere else could they find so many eager new teachers who presumably shared their educational vision. In 1982, for example, Liberty Baptist College could offer interviews with eight hundred students in its teacher-ed programs. When principals came to recruit, Liberty bent over backward to help, arranging job interviews and informing students of the job opportunities.[22] By the early 1980s, Liberty administrators estimated that a full 90 percent of their teaching graduates worked at private evangelical and fundamentalist schools, but Liberty remained committed to offering state teaching certification for those who planned to teach in public schools.[23]

The older fundamentalist universities had long prepared teachers to work primarily in public schools. When the numbers of private fundamentalist and evangelical schools exploded in the 1970s and 1980s, administrators at those schools found themselves on the defensive. Bob Jones University, for example, had always sent significant numbers of its graduates into public school teaching.[24] By the middle of the 1980s, Bob Jones III—who had inherited the presidency in 1971—found himself on the receiving end of harsh accusations from fundamentalist K-12 school administrators nationwide. Writing from the Mississippi state association of fundamentalist private schools, Bob Dalton blasted BJU's support for public school teaching, and he asked incredulously how any truly fundamentalist university could send graduates to teach in public schools.

Everyone knew the terrible state of public education, with its "drug supermarkets . . . witchcraft . . . socialist propaganda, and . . . . anti-Christ philosophy." Dalton was flabbergasted that any self-identified fundamentalist university "would have anything to do with such a system let alone seek its imprimatur of state-certification."[25]

For his part, Bob Jones III defended BJU's long tradition of preparing public school teachers. As long as fundamentalist teachers were "free to have their testimony and leave their impact," Jones argued, they could have a bigger missionary influence in public schools than in fundamentalist private ones. Private fundamentalist schools were a great blessing, Jones agreed, but they were not the only places fundamentalist college graduates could teach.[26]

Wheaton, too, endured accusations that it did not support the growing network of private Christian schools. Like Bob Jones University, Wheaton had a long tradition of sending its graduates into public school education. By the 1970s, leaders of the Christian school movement peppered Wheaton's leaders with bitter complaints. In 1976, for example, one Wheaton alumnus who ran a private evangelical school complained, "It has grieved me for years that my own alma mater does not endorse the Christian school movement . . . and does not have the burden to train teachers for the Christian school movement specifically."[27]

Wheaton's leaders tried to refute these accusations. They insisted that they did endorse the Christian school movement and that they did encourage their graduates to think of careers in those private schools. Time and again, Wheaton administrators in the 1970s claimed that more than half their teacher-ed graduates went on to teach in private Christian schools.[28] In Wheaton's case, however, the accusations from private school leaders had some basis in fact. A little digging in the education department's archives shows that in both 1976 and 1979, at least, the overwhelming majorities of Wheaton's future teachers completed their student-teaching assignments in public schools. In 1976, only two out of fifty-six Wheaton students were placed in private Christian schools. In 1979, only one was.[29] Wheaton's administrators may have really believed, as one put it in 1976, that "we *are* concerned about the Christian school movement in the US."[30] Nevertheless, Wheaton's long years of training teachers for state certification and work in public schools left their mark. Just as its evangelical character was sometimes accused of straying too far from fundamentalist certainties, so its teacher-training program was seen as being too friendly to secular public schools.

In the 1970s and 1980s, teacher educators at evangelical and fundamentalist schools worried about more than just the public/private school question. They also wondered what kind of teachers they hoped to produce. Should Christian teachers use child-centered, progressive classroom methods? Or should they stick to traditional authoritarian styles? Perhaps not surprisingly, Wheaton's education department had long favored the progressive approach. Between 1952 and 1975, Mary and Lois LeBar ran Wheaton's Christian education department. The LeBar sisters themselves had been educated at Moody Bible Institute and Wheaton, but while earning their doctorates in education at New York University, they imbibed the progressive ideas of John Dewey and other secular educational theorists and translated them into evangelical terms. True evangelical education, the LeBars believed, did not mean listening passively to lectures. If Christian teachers wanted to win souls, their students had to do more than recite platitudes. Real Christian education meant more than imparting information to students. It meant changing students' lives. For decades, the LeBars stamped Wheaton's teacher education program with this progressive educational philosophy.[31]

Wheaton was not alone in promoting a progressive vision for true Christian education. The education school at Bob Jones University, too, believed that good teachers did more than simply lecture to docile students. Just as the LeBars shaped Wheaton's education program, so Walter G. Fremont pushed BJU toward a non-traditional pedagogy. Fremont, who served as dean of the BJU School of Education from 1953 to 1990, and his allies at the university insisted that fundamentalist teachers must avoid the traps of authoritarian teaching and rote memorization. Such methods might seem productive, Fremont argued, but in the long run students didn't really learn much that way.[32]

Too many fundamentalist teachers, the BJU faculty insisted, believed that traditional methods were the best. Students in too many fundamentalist schools and Sunday schools were expected to sit quietly and memorize dry lists of who begat whom. The BJU faculty, on the other hand, argued that real Christian education "must also include the higher levels of comprehension, conviction, and application if Christian attitudes and values are to be implanted in the student and expressed in his life."[33] Teachers trained at Bob Jones University were encouraged to engage students in thoughtful discussions, to take field trips, and to "be flexible so you can seize the 'teachable moment.'" Teachers were to help students build conceptual networks, not just banks of memorized facts. BJU writers encouraged teachers to "make learning purposeful—solve real-life problems with real-life tools."[34]

Other fundamentalist teacher educators disagreed. In the early 1970s, two BJU alumni, Arlin and Beka Horton, accused their alma mater of straying from proper fundamentalist education. When Walter Fremont and his colleagues taught their students to use progressive teaching methods, the Hortons charged, they inadvertently encouraged loose morals and less learning. Bob Jones III wasn't convinced. He continued to support Fremont's ideas about true fundamentalist teacher training. Unfazed, the Hortons implemented their vision of proper education at their own school, Pensacola Christian College (PCC), and in their own publishing house, A Beka Book. At PCC, aspiring teachers learned that they must always maintain authoritarian control of their classrooms. Real learning, the Hortons believed, should take a traditional form, with teachers in every classroom leading students in recitation and memorization drills.[35] As one PCC writer argued, "standing foursquare for traditional education" was sometimes unpopular with students, but it was the only way to teach successfully. True fundamentalist education, the Florida fundamentalists insisted, meant insisting on "Biblical discipline" in the classroom.[36]

The pedagogical goings-on inside evangelical and fundamentalist K-12 classrooms did not attract much attention among outsiders. On the other hand, accusations of racism and segregationism did. The timing of the explosion of new private schools seemed difficult to explain any other way. Throughout the late 1960s and early 1970s, federal courts ruled again and again that local leaders must act to break up segregated schools. Evangelical and fundamentalist school founders usually insisted that their new schools had nothing to do with race, but such claims can be hard to take at face value since so many of them opened just as desegregation plans went into effect.[37]

In some cases, white school founders made no attempt to disguise their segregationist motivation. In Adams County, Mississippi, for example, a new state policy insisting on mandatory busing led sixteen of seventeen Baptist churches in the area to open a new private school for white evangelical children. One local white pastor remembered that the effort was explicitly part of his community's "violent reaction" to busing and school desegregation.[38] As did the leaders of Bob Jones University, some of these K-12 school founders explicitly defended their racial segregationism in theological terms. For example, in 1954 the Cameron Baptist Church in Cameron, South Carolina, resolved, "In integrating the races in schools, we foster miscegenation, thereby changing God's plan and destroying His handiwork."[39] Many conservative white evangelicals, like the ones in Cameron, tied their racial beliefs directly to their religious ones.[40]

Much more common, however, were implied and coded appeals to segregationism. When fundamentalist writer Jerry Combee warned, for instance, that "the public schools have grown into jungles," readers could fill in the heavy racial implications of the warning.[41] And when white evangelicals fled public schools in droves just as their local schools were desegregating, the reason was clear. As Louis Lucas, the chief counsel for the plaintiffs in Memphis's school desegregation suit, quipped wryly, "The interest in God generated by busing is phenomenal. It's amazing how many people opposed to busing have their kids riding buses to private schools."[42]

## *The Most Segregated Hour in America*

Like Lucas, many contemporary observers assumed that white evangelicals and fundamentalists were like so many non-evangelical white people in the United States—whether they admitted it or not, they harbored deep racist convictions. Observers unfamiliar with the history of evangelicalism and evangelical education might not have known of the longer, more complicated history of racism among white evangelicals. Many fundamentalist schools, for example, were founded as explicitly anti-racist missionary institutions. Only as their leaders became more comfortable as part of the landscape of American higher education did they impose racist and segregatory policies. Of course, we need to be careful to understand white evangelical anti-racism as it really was. Much of the anti-racism of fundamentalist institutions in the early twentieth century was larded with unapologetically ethnocentric assumptions about nonwhite people. And many of the anti-racist policies of these schools never went beyond a profoundly condescending urge to uplift nonwhite Christians. Nevertheless, the segregationism of fundamentalist and evangelical schools in the latter half of the century was not a simple holdover from earlier times. Rather, evangelical and fundamentalist thinking about race and religion had experienced a unique career that only made things more complicated in the 1960s and 1970s, when racists, anti-racists, fundamentalists, and evangelicals all pulled up bits and pieces from their own checkered history to argue that their position was the true Christian one.

As the school with the longest evangelical history, Wheaton College had the most dramatic past as a racially integrationist institution. Unlike the newer crop of fundamentalist schools, Wheaton College had been founded by radical abolitionists such as Jonathan Blanchard, its first president. In the nineteenth century, President Blanchard actively encouraged African Americans to attend. He boarded them in his house and argued publicly in favor of interracial marriage.[43]

Before it became Biola University, the Bible Institute of Los Angeles also emphasized its otherworldly focus. In 1913, founder Lyman Stewart insisted that his new school would admit students "without reference to race, color, class, creed, or previous condition." At Biola as at Wheaton, in those early days many radical white evangelicals understood their mission to range beyond mere social conventions and worldly prejudices.[44]

Even in the Deep South, white evangelical schools sometimes taught their students to embrace the scorn of their fellow whites in their zeal to reach across racial lines with their Gospel message. At least, that was the way one student at South Carolina's Columbia Bible College remembered it. The school itself was for white students only during the 1930s. However, just as at all Bible colleges, Columbia students were required to preach the Word to every potential listener. And when they did, some of them saw for the first time the terrors of lynchings and chain gangs. As William Barnett recalled, it was a "traumatic experience" to see firsthand the brutality of segregationism in South Carolina. As white evangelicals fanned out from Columbia Bible College into "black churches . . . schools and Sunday school classes," Barnett remembered, they were "looked at cross-eyed" by angry segregationist whites.[45]

While Barnett was experiencing a racial epiphany that would be echoed decades later by a new generation of white civil rights activists, attitudes about race and racism were undergoing a decided shift on most fundamentalist college campuses. At Wheaton College, by the 1930s administrators had become "none too eager" to admit African American students, as Michael Hamilton has noted.[46] At Moody Bible Institute, too, African Americans were officially welcomed in the 1930s, but the school's leaders insisted that every African American student have a white faculty supervisor. Moreover, MBI administrators kept secret their cross-racial admission policy. By 1938, put simply, they did not want the general public to know that their school admitted African Americans.[47]

Why not? It is a difficult question to answer, because most white fundamentalists in the 1930s maintained a studied silence on the issue. We have a few clues, however. In the case of President Buswell at Wheaton, for example, we saw in Chapter 3 that he maintained a single-minded focus on increasing the social and academic reputation of his school. Above all, Buswell hoped to improve the reputation of fundamentalism by turning Wheaton into an impeccably respectable college. In 1939, Buswell awkwardly suggested that admitting African Americans would threaten that respectability in the eyes of leaders of American higher education. In one case, for instance, Buswell discouraged an African American woman from applying, since it would cause "social problems." He didn't want to say so publicly—likely because he was well aware of his school's strident anti-racist history—but he did mumble his way through the imposition of a new segregationism on Wheaton's campus.[48]

Other fundamentalist schools imposed similar racial policies in the decades to follow. In 1952, for example, Moody Bible Institute dean of education S. Maxwell Coder reported that he had broken up an interracial couple. The students had not been told that their relationship was sinful, but they been asked repeatedly not to allow themselves to be seen together. The concern, Coder explained, was that such a couple might "give rise to criticism" of the school itself. Coder worried that the "racial problem involved" with their relationship would cause resentment of the school and its evangelism. In other words, the leaders of MBI did not think that there was any theological basis for white racism and segregation, but they no longer dared to put their religious cross-racialism ahead of their desire for institutional respectability among their white peers.[49]

At Wheaton in the 1950s, nonwhite students did not have many social options. One interracial couple was punished in the early 1950s for their relationship. Nor was it easy for white Wheaton students to have any social contact at all with students from other races. By one estimate, only about 1 to 2 percent of Wheaton's student body was nonwhite in the 1950s and early 1960s, and about half of those nonwhite students came from abroad.[50] As one white student from that era remembered, ironically the only racially integrated club on campus was the Dixie Club, for southern students.[51]

Just as it would at non-evangelical campuses, the emergence of the civil rights movement in the middle of the twentieth century profoundly shook up evangelical colleges. Most often, students—both white and African American—found allies among the faculty and administration in their quest to push their institutions toward greater racial equality. And, just as at non-evangelical institutions, administrations often responded with a mix of timid reform, hesitant rhetoric, and anxious apologetics. Unlike those at secular schools, though, evangelical civil rights protesters could draw on a long history of evangelical anti-racism. They could push their schools to greater equality not only as a matter of social justice but also as a matter of evangelical ethics. However, as self-consciously conservative institutions, evangelical and fundamentalist schools often witnessed a good deal of counterprotest as well. Some students saw racial segregation as an important part of their schools' evangelical character.

## *Go Tell It on the Mountain*

As historians such as Daniel K. Williams and Molly Worthen have argued, by the mid-1960s white evangelicals and fundamentalists had often joined other white Americans in a broad shift in attitude about race and racism. Though they may not have become as profoundly anti-racist as some activists may have hoped, many fundamentalists did seek, as Williams put it, "to distance themselves from the overt racism that had characterized their churches."[52] As Worthen concluded, "the moderate middle" of white evangelical Protestantism in America seemed to have "experienced a genuine change of heart about the meaning of skin color."[53]

Students, faculty, administrators, and alumni of fundamentalist and evangelical institutions certainly went through some sort of change. But the process was never pretty. Many cautious, conservative, or simply racist voices stymied any change in schools' racial policies. As in all things, administrators worried that their institutions might lose students if they were seen to be straying outside the nebulous boundaries of proper evangelical behavior. At Moody Bible Institute, for example, things changed between 1952 and 1965. By 1965, interracial dating and marriage were no longer banned, but neither were they embraced or encouraged. In 1965, President William Culbertson offered a painfully awkward explanation of MBI's new policy. On the one hand, Culbertson wrote, interracial dating and marriage were absolutely acceptable from a religious perspective. Nothing in the Bible could be construed to forbid it or even discourage it. Nevertheless, Culbertson cautiously warned, there were enormous "sociological problems" involved. In the end, Culbertson believed, the most important factor was that both parties in any marriage must "know the Lord." Yet Culbertson was emphatically unwilling to proclaim this belief loudly and proudly. Even in 1965, MBI would allow interracial dating, but only layered with a profound ambivalence.[54]

That sort of ambivalence was common on evangelical campuses even as most white evangelicals moved in fits and starts toward the idea that racial equality was an important part of their evangelical beliefs. As always, both sides insisted that their views were the proper Christian views on the matter. In 1957, for example, the editor of Biola's *King's Business* magazine ignited a controversy with a pro-integration editorial. Editor Lloyd Hamill blasted the segregationism on display at the time in Little Rock, Arkansas. Like Billy Graham, Hamill insisted, real Christians must fight worldly racism in every way they could. "No Spirit-controlled Christian," Hamill argued in language calculated to hit home with evangelical and fundamentalist readers, "can escape the solid fact that all men are equal in God's sight . . . . [I]t is . . . the plain teaching of the Bible."[55] And Hamill did more than just preach anti-racism. The offices of the *King's Business*, he wrote, had employed African American journalism student Earnestine Ritter for almost a year.[56]

Reaction came fast and furious. The *King's Business* received bagfuls of angry letters from fundamentalist and evangelical segregationists. A few letter writers celebrated the forceful articulation of evangelical egalitarianism, but for every supporter, about ten opponents attacked Hamill's stance as naive, wrongheaded, and, most important, non-Christian.[57] As was so often the case, Biola's leaders recoiled at the sound of controversy. As President Samuel Sutherland explained in a private letter to Billy Graham, Hamill was sacked immediately due to "the very foolish letters he wrote and statements which he made."[58]

By the mid-1960s, things had changed at Biola. Just as it did on evangelical and non-evangelical campuses across the country, by 1964 sentiment had shifted considerably in favor of civil rights activism. Students actively and openly argued that real evangelical Christianity required unyielding racial egalitarianism. In early 1964, for example, student editor Dave Shimeall argued in the pages of the student newspaper that segregation was "an indictment against the Christian Church." Many white evangelicals, Shimeall granted, even prominent leaders, opposed civil rights activism. Some others made vague anti-racist statements but never backed them up with action. The true evangelical, Shimeall wrote, must do more than mouth "clichés and pious phrases." The real evangelical must get out and do something, Shimeall argued. He or she must engage "in 'works' to go with our faith."[59]

In 1964, Biola's spread-out evangelical community tolerated Shimeall's arguments, but it was by no means united in agreement. The next year, new student editor Wes Reeves took the student newspaper in a very different direction. Calls for legal equality were all well and good, Reeves wrote, but if evangelicals valued "lasting freedom," they must always support the right of Mississippi's government to impose segregationist laws. Too many Americans, Reeves lamented, mixed up "individual inequality" with unfreedom. In order to remain truly free, Reeves argued, civil rights activists must recognize that society would always include inequality.[60]

By the mid-1960s, President Sutherland no longer felt obliged to kick out students who voiced pro-civil-rights sentiments. He no longer felt able to impose racial segregation as the unofficial policy of his school. But he also quietly encouraged Reeves to continue his states' rights campaign. "All of our students," Sutherland told Reeves, could benefit from this conservative, anti-civil-rights message. "Do some more of this," Sutherland concluded. "It is extremely wholesome." By encouraging segregationist student voices, Sutherland was able to bolster his school's conservative reputation without having to make any overt statement himself.[61]

Like President Sutherland at Biola and President Culbertson at Moody Bible Institute, sensitive administrators at other evangelical colleges moved timidly as evangelical sentiment shifted. At Wheaton College, for example, administrators asked a faculty committee to investigate the state of racism and anti-racism at their mostly white school. When the committee pushed a little harder and faster than administrators hoped, it met with a predictably cautious response.

The committee included Gordon S. Jaeck, Lamberta Voget, Alvin Moser, David Winter, James Murk, and rising-star anthropologist James O. Buswell III, son of the former Wheaton president. Their report pulled no punches. Wheaton had been founded as an explicitly and actively anti-racist evangelical school, the authors noted. But, lamentably, African Americans had later been discouraged from attending. Once on campus, most African American students had been socially segregated. What had changed? White evangelicals, the committee argued, had strayed from their true theological roots and been swayed by merely worldly social mores. As an evangelical institution, the faculty authors believed, Wheaton needed to remedy this situation. The school should actively recruit nonwhite faculty and students. The campus must be made friendlier to nonwhite students from the United States and around the world. Wheaton College should use its influence to make the nearby town of Wheaton more racially just. And, perhaps most controversially, the faculty authors insisted that dating and marriage rules had to be made equal for all students, across the race line.[62]

Wheaton's top administrators blanched. The dean of the graduate school, Merrill C. Tenney, told President Edman privately that he supported the goal of a more racially just and balanced campus, but—as always—he worried first and foremost that any bold move might threaten Wheaton's reputation among evangelical and fundamentalist families. "Will some of the parents of our students," Tenney asked, "regard a tacit approval of inter-racial marriage as a danger to their children?"[63] Edman apparently thought they would, for he buried the report.[64] Anti-racist sentiment was well and good, top leaders agreed. But nothing could be allowed to threaten Wheaton's reputation as a safe school for conservative evangelical and fundamentalist students.

Unfortunately for Edman and Tenney, Wheaton's community included evangelicals who felt just as strongly about their anti-racism as the administrators did about the need to keep that anti-racism quiet. Instructor James Murk took his vision of evangelical anti-racism directly to the student body. Without the approval of the rest of the faculty committee, Murk published an essay in the student newspaper that repeated much of the original faculty report. "As a Christian college," Murk declared, Wheaton had the ability to exert "a powerful and constructive impact on our evangelical churches."[65] There was no doubt, he argued, what the true Christian position on race relations should be. "Prejudice," Murk wrote, "is sin."[66] There were no "biblical or theological grounds" for racial prejudice.[67]

Though it seemed radical to Wheaton's top administrators in 1962, Murk's position grew more and more influential on Wheaton's campus throughout the 1960s. By late 1968, some of Wheaton's nonwhite students had organized themselves into the Black and Puerto Rican Students of Wheaton College. As did non-evangelical students at colleges across the country, these activists wanted their school to initiate academic programs in African and Latin American studies. Unlike students at secular schools, they wanted those programs to have a distinctly evangelical nature. As the group explained in a short list of demands submitted to Wheaton's administration, they wanted, in essence, "a Christian education relevant to our cultural heritage." The students wanted more nonwhite faculty, more nonwhite students, and an acknowledgment that evangelical religion had never been the province of white Christians alone.[68]

When administrators dithered, students acted. African American student leader Ron Potter gave a blistering chapel talk in which he blasted the racial insensitivity of white evangelicals in general and of Wheaton's administration in particular. The response of those white evangelicals,

Potter charged, was nothing but "pitiful."[69] Some white students agreed. One described his dismay at the "blatant racism practiced on our own campus." Wheaton must do something drastic, he believed, to rid itself of the "dirty white rag of racism."[70]

As always, President Hudson Armerding hoped to defuse the tension and solve any problems quietly and privately. He asked Potter to come to his office for a one-on-one talk.[71] Instead, Potter promised to bring along a half dozen friends and sympathizers, and to publicize their conversation.[72] In the end, Armerding pushed forward a bolder reform than he probably would have liked. He had long sought to hire more African American faculty members, but he lamented that the "competition for the qualified black professor is intense."[73] Nevertheless, by the beginning of 1971 Wheaton's administrators had devoted themselves to making many of the changes demanded by student activists. They had hired at least one additional African American faculty member, and they had added new courses such as Black Americans in American Society, Urban Sociology, and People of Africa.[74]

Yet the official position of Wheaton College on civil rights questions remained almost comically awkward. Perhaps the most striking example of this awkwardness was the tortuous career of *Freedom Now* on Wheaton's campus. In the late 1960s, this evangelical civil rights magazine enjoyed enormous popularity among Wheaton students. Its editor was the popular professor John Alexander, who had brought his brand of white evangelical anti-racism to Wheaton in 1966. Wheaton paid Alexander's salary, yet the campus bookstore wasn't allowed to stock *Freedom Now* openly on its shelves. Instead, copies were kept surreptitiously under the counter. Students could buy it only if they asked for it by name.[75]

This kind of please-no-one compromise led Alexander to quit in dismay in 1970.[76] Yet Wheaton's painfully hesitant racial reforms were not accidents; they did not result merely from personality quirks of top administrators or long-embedded racial prejudices. Rather, as with all the schools in the evangelical and fundamentalist family, during the 1960s and 1970s Wheaton's leaders were trapped in an impossible position. Many of them personally desired greater racial egalitarianism at Wheaton. And many of them believed that they needed more racial equality in order to maintain their position as a respectable intellectual institution. Yet they dared not do anything that might cause fundamentalists and evangelicals to accuse them of breaking the unwritten rules of evangelical life. Wheaton's administrators wanted to support civil rights activism, but they also absolutely needed to be able to deny any charges that Wheaton was a hotbed of civil rights activism.

Wheaton's tentative progress toward greater racial sensitivity was echoed at other evangelical schools. Gordon College initiated a new program in Afro-American history, taught by a newly recruited African American faculty member.[77] The school also initiated a formal Racial Affairs Program.[78] Just as at Wheaton, Gordon's moves had been accelerated by student activism. At Gordon, for example, student activists had brought Jonathan Kozol to campus in early 1969 to speak. Kozol's books about the shockingly unequal treatment of African American students in Boston's public schools had shaken many white readers out of their naive optimism about race in America. If white Gordonites would only "honestly listen" to Kozol's harrowing tales of racial inequality, student activists believed, they could no longer claim convenient ignorance of their evangelical imperative to work for racial justice.[79]

The drive for greater racial inclusion and equity was not limited to the campuses of Gordon and Wheaton alone. By the end of the 1970 school year, school administrators flocked to conferences like the one held on the campus of Eastern Nazarene College in Massachusetts. Their goal was to hash out ways they could improve the experiences of "black Bible students."[80]

## *Southern Pride*

Of course, plenty of school leaders pointedly stayed home. Especially among those institutions that saw themselves as faithful adherents to the fundamentalist side of the conservative-evangelical family, the drive for greater racial integration was often viewed as yet another anti-Christian perversion. At first, fundamentalist leaders such as Bob Jones Sr. simply adopted the racial positions of their white friends and neighbors. Over time, however, Jones and his university transformed racial segregationism into a theological imperative. Once Jones had defined racial segregation as a key tenet of real fundamentalist religion, BJU found itself tied to a theological segregationism that was rapidly losing adherents, even among conservative white fundamentalists.

As the civil rights movement heated up in the mid-1950s, Bob Jones Sr. articulated what he considered to be an enlightened and moderate position on race and integration. Desegregation, Jones told a correspondent, would hurt African Americans. The real solution could only be found in a fair but segregated public square. If the two races were integrated, the "sound orthodox Christian" faith of most "colored people" would be threatened.[81] A few years later, Jones explained again that good "born-again Christian people" of every race were indeed "all one in Christ." But that unity, Jones thought, was only for "a heavenly group." On earth things were different. True, Jones conceded, "colored people have not always been treated right, and it is too bad." When racial "agitators" fought for civil rights and racial integration, however, the worst victims would be those African Americans themselves.[82]

It was only in 1960 that Bob Jones Sr. articulated the position that defined his school's staunch segregationism for decades to come. BJU printed and distributed in pamphlet form his sermon titled "Is Segregation Scriptural?" No one should think, Jones repeated, that some races were superior and some inferior. God created every race, and every good Christian was equal in God's eyes. But civil rights activists went wrong when they assumed that this sort of religious egalitarianism could translate into worldly integrationism. God intended for each race to live in its own way, in its own place. Too many modern Americans, Jones argued, were sinfully trying to "disturb the established order." In their zeal for justice, they missed the central theological point of real Christianity. "God," Jones explained, "never meant to have one race."[83]

Over and over, Jones insisted that his segregationism was not due to any knee-jerk racism. Of course, he repeated, good Christians came from every race. The missionary drive so central to Jones's vision of fundamentalism assumed as much. Each race, though, was meant to be separate; each race was meant to be segregated. Integration activism—what Jones called "racial disturbance"—was not part of God's plan. The Bible, Jones explained, gave real Christians a crystal-clear explanation of God's thinking. God meant for each race to prosper on its own. "When people come along and say, 'Well God is the Father of everybody,' they are wrong . . . . That is a Satanic lie," he preached.[84] Good Christians could come from every race, but every race must remain true to its own version of God's plan. Mixing up the races with intermarriage and excessive cross-racial socializing, Bob Jones insisted, was not only unwise but also positively evil.

As with all things in the world of Bob Jones University, once Bob Jones Sr. elevated racial segregationism into an institutional and scriptural absolute, it became very difficult for the school to change course. As mainstream thinking shifted among white people during the 1960s and 1970s, even among conservative southern white evangelicals and fundamentalists, what had once seemed to be mainstream and even progressive racial thinking turned into a relatively extreme segregationist vision. Nevertheless, the school that Bob Jones Sr. founded stuck to his decree, even as that choice forced the school into a lonelier and lonelier position.

Throughout the 1960s, as other evangelical and fundamentalist schools shifted their positions on sensitive racial questions such as interracial dating and marriage, Bob Jones University treated such ideas as anathema. In 1963, for example, Bob Jones Jr. castigated evangelicals who fought for greater civil rights. Such "rascals in clerical garb," Jones wrote, besmirched the name of true Christianity by "join[ing] hands with anarchists in mob violence and law breaking." In contrast, Jones explained, his school trained young people to "stand for the fundamental principles of Constitutional Americanism."[85] Privately, the younger Jones continued to insist on his father's vision of fundamentalist segregationism as God's true plan. No one was against the "negroes," Jones insisted. But traditional southern segregationism was clearly correct. In northern cities, where "we have the races mixed up in large numbers," Jones wrote, "we have trouble." That trouble was proof that the drive for integration went against God's will. No one at BJU, Jones repeated, was "anti-Negro," not even those who insisted that their white children never mix with African American children. True Christians, however, like all true Americans, realized that "intermarriage of the races is not God's plan."[86]

As other fundamentalist and evangelical schools moved awkwardly toward greater racial egalitarianism in the 1970s, Bob Jones University stuck to its segregationist guns. Even the leaders of BJU sensed the changing times, though. They did not change their policies much, but by 1971 the leaders of BJU explained those policies in increasingly defensive tones. In 1971, for instance, in a formal statement, new president Bob Jones III explained that his school did not admit "Negro students." The worry, Jones wrote, had always been the same. Such students might violate the principles of fundamentalist religion as Bob Jones Sr. had defined them. If they were to date or marry across the race line, such nonwhite students would be expelled. In the political climate at the time—what Jones called "the present agitation and left-wing pressures"—expelling an African American student would be seen as proof of BJU's racism. In other words, to avoid charges of racism, Bob Jones University would not admit African American students.[87]

However, as a token of its commitment to its idiosyncratic principles, BJU also allowed one married African American to enroll briefly in a Bible class. However, that student was an employee, not a regularly admitted student.[88] It was not until the end of the school year in 1975 that the school grudgingly agreed to admit African American students. When it came to interracial dating and marriage, though, Bob Jones III repeated his threat: any students who dated across the color line would be summarily expelled.[89]

That convoluted nod to racial integration did not change BJU's basic position. Throughout the era, BJU took extraordinary measures to prevent its students from having the merest whiff of interracialism. In 1980, for example, BJU cut its formal ties with a local Baptist church. The white pastor, Walter Handford, stood accused of admitting an interracial couple into his congregation. Without hesitation, BJU's director of ministerial training concluded that no BJU student pastors could possibly work there.[90]

As it did in all things, BJU distinguished itself by its unswerving devotion to its own idiosyncratic definition of fundamentalism. Once Bob Jones Sr. declared the Bible to be against interracial marriage, the university paid any cost—cut itself off from any friend—in order to remain true to that declaration. For the rest of the twentieth century, BJU clung to the position laid down by its founder: segregation of the races was a biblical truth, a foundational belief of true fundamentalism.

Predictably, disagreements about race and racial integration became wrapped up in continuing tensions between schools. By the 1970s, for example, members of the nationwide BJU community looked in horror at the racial integrationism of Wheaton College. One Illinois fundamentalist praised the staunch segregationism at BJU. BJU's leaders, he wrote, "have stood firmly on the Word of God in denying integration of the races." His local school, Wheaton College, had gone down the woeful road of neo-evangelicalism and racial integrationism. On Wheaton's campus, he wrote, interracial relationships were actually encouraged. As proof, he clipped an article from the local Wheaton paper about two young missionary students. They planned a trip to a southern mission school together. The young man was African American, and the young woman was white. "How utterly revolting," the fundamentalist concluded. Yet such "sinful practices" were a predictable result of Wheaton's "disobedience to the written word of God."[91]

The Bob Joneses agreed heartily. Bob Jones III wrote to his Illinois fundamentalist friend that he, too, was "astounded by the blasé acceptance of the relationship of this boy and girl." It was another sign that Wheaton had gone down the sorry path of compromise.[92] Bob Jones Jr. also vented his spleen against Wheaton as a sobering example of what might happen if truly fundamentalist schools waffled on the question of racial integration. Jones accused Wheaton's president of actually bragging about his students "participating in so-called freedom marches in Mississippi." Those students, Jones wrote, appeared no different from "the worst kind of hippies and drop-outs." The false-minded drive for worldly approval in the realm of racial integration, Jones believed, was just one symptom of Wheaton's utter spiritual collapse. In language calculated to pierce the heart of any evangelical or fundamentalist school administrator, he insisted that Wheaton was "not in any sense any longer to be regarded as an institution that is anything more than 'somewhat religious.'" He would rather "send my kid to the University of Chicago (as foul as that is)" than to a merely evangelical school like Wheaton, with its racial relaxation. False schools like Wheaton, Jones concluded, were worse than non-Christian schools, because they "make a pretense that they do not live up to."[93]

By the 1970s and 1980s, however, BJU's fundamentalist racial segregationism had separated it from more than just the evangelical Wheaton College. As one evangelical journalist quipped, BJU's policy on integration had made it a question of "Bob Jones versus everybody." Even other self-professed fundamentalist schools in the South no longer agreed that racial segregation had any place in fundamentalist life. Liberty Baptist College, for example, in 1982 proudly claimed two hundred African American students out of a total student body of three thousand.[94] And just as did evangelical colleges, Liberty made at least some effort to make those students feel welcome. By the 1980s, for instance, the school had established a Black Student Fellowship to give students a safe space to organize and socialize.[95]

Of course, we should not assume that white fundamentalists at Liberty or elsewhere had suddenly adopted the staunch evangelical anti-racism of activists like John Alexander. Nor should we even assume too glibly that evangelical schools such as Gordon and Wheaton had extinguished all traces of deeply embedded racial stereotypes and prejudices. Institutionally, however, most evangelical and fundamentalist colleges and universities changed their official and unofficial policies on race and racism. By the late 1960s and early 1970s, most schools had taken steps to improve the racial climate on their campuses. They had recruited and hired more African American faculty; they had established clubs and organizations for nonwhite students; they had initiated academic programs in African studies; and they no longer punished students for civil rights sentiments or activism.

By the end of the 1970s, Bob Jones University stood out—not alone, but increasingly isolated. BJU's leaders stuck to the segregationism that Bob Jones Sr. had described in 1960. When criticized, BJU and its allies retreated to positions familiar since the battle over neo-evangelicalism in the 1950s. Yes, lots of schools would waver, but fidelity to segregation meant fidelity to fundamentalism, to real Christianity, they claimed. To the Bob Joneses, reform of racial policies was just another sinister example of the dangers of reformism in general.

Some fundamentalists praised BJU's steadfast devotion to an increasingly unpopular position. John R. Rice, for example, praised BJU as the true home of Christian higher education. BJU's segregationism was more proof of the school's fearless fidelity. He was not, Rice wrote, "a Negro hater." He was simply such an ardent fundamentalist that he was "not willing for anybody to turn me or turn Christian institutions away from the main thing in order to please the modernists and the communists and the agitators." What was more, any so-called Christians who wanted "the agitation and the revolution" of civil rights activism should not be considered real Christians at all.[96]

Other fundamentalists disagreed. In 1970, the leaders of Moody Bible Institute decided they could not be publicly associated any longer with this sort of racial segregationism. They canceled an invitation for Rice to be a prominent speaker at their upcoming annual Founder's Week conference. Culbertson wrote repeatedly to Rice to explain the decision, telling Rice how much he admired him and asserting that he never had disagreed for a moment with Rice's "insistence on the fundamentals." Like Rice, every member of the Moody Bible Institute community was "glad to affirm our allegiance to the Lord and to His Word."[97] However, Rice's public endorsement of BJU's segregationism had shifted the focus to the question of race. If Rice spoke at MBI, Culbertson explained, it would give "the impression that the Institute agrees with your views in this regard. This cannot be."[98]

## *Great-Grandchildren of Ham*

Like MBI's break with John R. Rice, most schools were willing to risk offending prominent fundamentalist leaders in order to avoid the charge of segregationism. And, just as at MBI, student and alumni activism usually pushed the integrationist program, often in the face of significant foot-dragging on the part of anxious administrators. At every school, the students, faculty, administration, and alumni all insisted that their positions were the true evangelical ones, the true fundamentalist ones. Unlike at many mainstream schools, all parties involved were able to pull up bits and pieces from the complicated history of race and racism in American evangelicalism to make their arguments. Civil rights activists could claim with justification that evangelicals had always led the charge for racial justice. And cautious administrators could point with equal justification at their schools' long fights for mainstream respectability. Raucous and radical civil rights activism, they worried, would threaten that hard-won status.

By the 1970s, these issues became complicated even further by the explosive growth of a new network of fundamentalist and evangelical K-12 schools. Many of these schools had their roots in the drive to integrate public schools racially. If public schools were no longer to be reliably segregated, many white evangelicals rushed to open new private schools that would be. On occasion, the fight against racial integration at these K-12 schools became part and parcel of the same fight at Bob Jones University, as we'll see in Chapter 9. But the new schools also looked to the network of fundamentalist higher-ed institutions to fulfill their more prosaic needs. Who would train their teachers and principals, and how? Who would write suitably fundamentalist and evangelical textbooks? Where could K-12 school administrators go for the sorts of conferences and training that all schools relied on?

No one doubted for a moment that the network of evangelical and fundamentalist colleges and universities was the proper place to debate those issues. Just as with questions of race and racism, though, different schools offered different visions. In every case, the durable ambiguities about the definition of fundamentalism laid down in the 1920s made every question subject to endless evangelical debate. Student activists pushed for more racial egalitarianism. Conservative alumni and trustees threatened to yank their funding. Parents wondered if college X or university Y was still trustworthy. Faculty activists published thoughtful exposés about the history of racism among white evangelicals. Unreconstructed white supremacists and unapologetic civil rights activists both insisted that their views represented true evangelical Christianity. And all the while, school leaders found themselves in yet another seemingly unresolvable dilemma. They knew they must keep their schools unquestionably within the boundaries of real fundamentalism or evangelicalism, yet they also knew that those boundaries were changing rapidly during the 1960s and 1970s. In spite of their presumptive role as the intellectual centers of evangelicalism and fundamentalism, most institutions of higher education did not lead the way when it came to changing ideas about race and racism. Rather, colleges and universities became forums at which debates about these changing ideas took place, with their top leaders only slowly and often grudgingly going along with changes that had become the new standard for evangelical and fundamentalist institutions.

# 9

# *Learn One for the Gipper*

*We believe in America.*

—PRESIDENT PIERRE GUILLERMIN, Liberty Baptist College, 1980[1]

## *College on a Hill*

The builders hadn't even finished the walls. Liberty Baptist College was expanding so quickly that even the most illustrious guests held press conferences in half-completed rooms. In October 1980, Republican presidential candidate Ronald Reagan didn't seem to mind. Reagan told his evangelical and fundamentalist audiences exactly what they wanted to hear. He promised that he would use the Oval Office as a pulpit to preach a renewed moral vision for the United States. The country had gone wrong, Reagan told the Liberty crowd, when it turned its back on its religious values, when it "expelled God from the classroom" and from public life.[2]

As Reagan preached to his fundamentalist choir, pundits and politicians frothed about what they often called a "new Christian right."[3] Some poll-watchers and scholars took Jerry Falwell's boasts at face value. They accepted the idea that the entrance of Liberty's founder into party politics marked a new—or dramatically renewed—political activism among conservative evangelicals and fundamentalists.[4] As we'll see in this chapter, the truth was a more complicated affair. Something did happen in the 1970s and the 1980s, but it was not the much-ballyhooed return of evangelicals to political activism.

At institutions of higher education, certainly, fundamentalists and evangelicals had never retreated from political involvement, although they always argued over the proper distinctions between religious advocacy and political activism. Intellectuals often insisted that they put their religion first and shunned the dirty world of politics, yet since the 1920s fundamentalist and evangelical colleges and universities had remained political places, places that showed a decided lean toward political and cultural conservatism. As the twentieth century progressed, the ongoing feud between evangelical and fundamentalist sides of the family tended to take on political tones, with fundamentalists insisting on conservative politics and evangelicals more open to a broader spectrum of political views.

In most cases, the kind of conservatism that dominated these campuses shared the peculiar political tension inherent in American evangelicalism, what historian George Marsden has aptly called the "establishment-or-outsider paradox."[5] Throughout the twentieth century, white conservative evangelicals shared a proprietary feeling about America. They considered themselves the embodiment of true American values. They saw their schools as reflecting the promise of real America, "our" America, rightfully Christian America.[6] At the same time, however, ever since the 1920s evangelicals were convinced that their proper role as America's moral guardians had been—and was being—usurped by sinister secularists and woefully misguided liberals. When political activism succeeded, evangelicals often celebrated the triumphant revival of true American values. When it failed, as it often did, they took bitter satisfaction in their prophesied role as righteous remnants holding out against a sinful society.

To make things even more confusing, evangelical and fundamentalist thinkers and pundits in every generation often talked as if this long-established tension was something dramatically new. Rather than viewing themselves as continually embroiled in mainstream politics, sometimes winning and sometimes losing, evangelicals tended to describe each victory or loss as a major watershed in Christian history. With every new political setback, pundits exclaimed that God had been kicked out of America once and for all. And every new victory promised to have saved America for all time. Predictably, such rhetoric inflated the perceived stakes of evangelical and fundamentalist political activism, just as it led to misleading notions about the real relationship between evangelicals, fundamentalists, and conservative politics.

This durable and often unconscious tension within American evangelicalism reinforced the traditionally tense state of affairs at fundamentalist and evangelical colleges and universities. Schools were expected to be islands of true Americanism. Yet even as fundamentalist college students rallied on capitol steps around the nation, extravagantly clad in stars, stripes, and "I Love America" kitsch, students, faculty, and administrators wondered about their proper role in the public sphere.[7] Were campuses meant to be headquarters of a campaign to take back America? Were they instead to remain enclaves of the real Christian America, living museums of an imagined patriotic past? Or was there maybe another option, with evangelical schools welcoming earnest Christians of a wide variety of political beliefs?

At the same time, evangelical and fundamentalist schools wrestled with yet another perennially fraught issue: what should they think about evolution? As we saw in Chapter 3, during the first half of the twentieth century fundamentalist campuses were rife with debate about the proper vision of creationism. Everyone agreed that God had created, as the Bible testified. But how? Believers in a young earth and a recent instantaneous creation contended with advocates of long creative ages and with believers in a yawning gap between God's creative acts.

By the 1950s, this tense and often tumultuous creationist debate took on new urgency. It had to. By that time, mainstream scientists had worked out some of the kinks in Darwin's proposed mechanism of evolution. A new explanation of speciation, the "modern evolutionary synthesis" or "neo-Darwinism," had won over the mainstream scientific community. Though evolutionary science remained just as contentious as ever—certainly just as rough-and-tumble as the debates between creationists—by and large the mainstream scientific community had agreed on the outline and portent of their new understanding of the ways species came to be.[8]

Fundamentalists were confronted with a new evolutionary dilemma: they had to either come to terms with the new mainstream consensus or repudiate it utterly. Evangelical scientists argued for a renegotiated truce with mainstream science. They insisted that evolutionary science—properly understood—was also God's science. Real Christianity and real creationism meant understanding real science in its true beauty and complexity. Fundamentalist scientists offered a different answer. Just as the first generation of fundamentalists in the 1920s had invented a new vision of an ancient orthodoxy, a new generation of fundamentalist creationists insisted on a radical form of science as a litmus test for true fundamentalism. To be sure, as we saw in Chapter 3, their argument wasn't new. But its popularity was. As more and more fundamentalists worried about the new influence of evolutionary ideas, a new generation of young-earth activists managed to achieve a staggering new popularity among fundamentalists. Only young-earth creationism, they insisted, was real creationism. Anything else was an apostasy, a world-pleasing liberalism that greased the path to perdition.

This creationist stand-off put fundamentalist and evangelical institutions in a doubly difficult dilemma. Though their mainstream detractors often called them "anti-science," no fundamentalist or evangelical institution could ever really turn its back on science. To attract students, all schools—evangelical and fundamentalist alike—needed to offer more than true religion. They needed to promise the best modern educations, and that included the best understanding of modern science. Even schools that proudly repudiated mainstream evolutionary science always insisted that their young-earth science was better and more modern than the benighted biases of mainstream evolutionary science. And evangelical schools that considered more openly the ideas of mainstream scientists insisted just as loudly that their research made them better creationists and better Christians, not worse ones.

As always, while scholars tested the boundaries of fundamentalist and evangelical belief, school administrators tried their best to muddle through in the middle. Just as they had with the question of Billy Graham and the neo-evangelical revival, school leaders took great pains to reassure everyone in the broader conservative-evangelical community that their schools remained true. As we'll see in the explosive case of Russell Mixter, even the most academically ambitious neo-evangelical schools could not afford to alienate their fundamentalist clientele entirely.

## *The Evangelical Oracle on Evolution*

By the 1950s, evangelicals and fundamentalists looked for satisfying answers to their new creationist dilemma. Did real Christians need to turn their backs on mainstream science? Or was there a more nuanced approach? Wheaton's Russell Mixter said there was. And, as we'll see in this section, by the late 1950s he assumed—with good justification—that the evangelical academy supported him. As he learned to his chagrin, however, school administrators had more to worry about than intellectual legitimacy. Mixter woefully misunderstood the intense and cross-cutting pressures on his school when it came to the touchy questions of evolution and creation.

It wasn't that Mixter didn't know Wheaton. He had joined its faculty way back in 1928, after his own days as a Wheaton student.[9] As a student, Mixter had studied under Wheaton's first generation of fundamentalist scientists, S. J. Bole and L. A. Higley.[10] And it wasn't that Mixter didn't understand the competing visions of proper creationism. Professors Bole and Higley both endorsed the notion of a long gap between God's creative acts. Yet, like all of Professor Bole's students, Mixter also read about other varieties of creationist belief, including George McCready Price's notions of a young earth and a literal catastrophic worldwide flood. Indeed, Mixter himself experienced a youthful enthusiasm for Price's vision of a rigorous fundamentalist creationism that refused to kneel at the altar of modern scientific thinking.[11]

It didn't last. As Mixter completed graduate degrees at Michigan State University and the University of Illinois, he came to acknowledge the legitimacy of mainstream scientific ideas about the age of the earth and the development of species. Like all evangelical and fundamentalist scientists in his generation, he was pushed into an uncomfortable intellectual position. He didn't like either of the two most obvious options: he did not want to reject mainstream science entirely and take theological shelter in the young-earth creationism of George McCready Price and his followers, nor could he reject fundamentalist religion entirely and embrace secular mainstream scientific thinking. Instead, Mixter embraced and shaped a third evangelical option in the idea of "progressive creation."[12] Throughout the 1940s and 1950s, Mixter taught this vision of creationism at Wheaton. In this understanding, God created each type of plant and animal, intervening repeatedly, directly, and miraculously to will each new kind into existence. Over long time periods, however, those kinds of species evolved by mechanisms such as natural selection.[13]

Mixter did more than just teach his vision of true creationism to Wheaton's students. As a leader of the American Scientific Affiliation, he hoped to define new boundaries for evangelical creationism itself. The roots of the ASA went back to 1941, when William Houghton of Moody Bible Institute called for a meeting of leading fundamentalist scientists in the hope that a new Society for the Correlation of Science and the Bible would help fundamentalists overcome their rocky relationship with mainstream science.[14]

Throughout the 1940s, the ASA became the forum in which creationist thinkers debated the proper limits of fundamentalist thought. Could fundamentalists and evangelicals accept the idea of an ancient earth? Did the mainstream scientific ideas of natural selection and other evolutionary mechanisms contradict the plain teaching of the Bible?[15] For their part, Russell Mixter and his "inner circle" of ASA leaders at Wheaton pushed hard for a new evangelical engagement with mainstream science.[16]

And, just as mainstream scientists debated ideas about evolution with vigor and often venom, the ASA experienced moments of dramatic academic confrontation as it tried to define clear boundaries for creationism. In 1948, for example, the ASA conference at Calvin College in Michigan featured a heated back-and-forth between geochemist (and Wheaton alumnus) J. Laurence Kulp and Calvin botanist Edwin Y. Monsma. Kulp's impeccable mainstream academic credentials gave him unique status among the evangelical scientific community. With his Ph.D. from Princeton and his faculty berth at Columbia, Kulp's ideas about science carried great weight. And Kulp did not hesitate to make his case in the strongest language possible. The great antiquity of humanity and of the earth, Kulp's conference paper reasoned, seemed beyond reasonable doubt. When Monsma protested, Kulp rejected Monsma's young-earth assumptions as "foolishness."[17]

The ASA remained divided. One audience member praised Monsma's young-earth bravery. It was the "most sound and fundamental" presentation in the ASA's history, this audience member concluded, because "it is based upon the word of God."[18] The general drift of the ASA, however, seemed to be in favor of Kulp's vigorous rejection of young-earth ideas. As historian Ronald L. Numbers put it, many ASA members "were ready to follow Kulp in boldly shedding the trite fundamentalist apologetics of the past."[19]

Among the boldest of these ASA leaders was Russell Mixter. As Kulp did in the field of geology, Mixter viewed some of the ideas of mainstream biological science as both intellectually undeniable and theologically unobjectionable. By the late 1950s, Mixter's activism within the ASA had turned him into what one scholar has called "the evangelical oracle on evolution."[20] At the ASA's 1957 annual meeting on the campus of Gordon College, for example, Mixter presented a paper in which he argued that evolutionary processes were part and parcel of a progressive creation.[21] In 1959, Mixter edited a new ASA publication, *Evolution and Christian Thought Today*. The book, published on the centenary of Darwin's *Origin of Species*, collected new evangelical ideas about the proper boundaries of creationism by authors such as Walter Hearn, J. Frank Cassel, and James O. Buswell III, son of Wheaton's former president. At the time, Hearn taught at Iowa State College in Ames, while Cassel and Buswell were members of Wheaton's faculty. Like Mixter, many of the authors assumed that true evangelical thinking must include room for mainstream scientific ideas about the evolutionary ways in which species developed.[22]

Mixter could be excused for thinking that such ideas had the institutional support of Wheaton College. He had been joined in his work, after all, by his Wheaton colleagues Cassel and Buswell. And his school took pains to defend Mixter against suggestions of heterodoxy. In early 1960, for example, David Roberts, Wheaton's director of public relations, wrote an angry complaint to Biola's president, Samuel Sutherland. Biola's magazine, the *King's Business*, had included an unfair review of *Evolution and Christian Thought Today*, Roberts argued. The review suggested that Mixter was an "evolutionist," but Roberts insisted Mixter was a "convinced creationist."[23]

Moreover, Wheaton president V. Raymond Edman had seemed satisfied in 1960 when Mixter explained his position. No one at Wheaton, Mixter said, taught atheistic or even theistic evolution, and his idea of "progressive Creation" was squarely within the bounds of true creationism, true evangelical thought.[24] Mixter's colleagues in other departments backed him up. Kenneth Kantzer in the Bible department and Samuel Schultz in the Christian education department assured Edman that no one on the faculty taught anything "unbiblical and suspicious."[25]

Despite the anxiety emanating from Edman's office, Mixter and his faculty allies felt in 1960 that they had the support of their school. After all, Wheaton had agreed to host a conference on *Evolution and Christian Thought Today* in a few months, and the meeting would bring to campus many of the volume's authors. With his long history at Wheaton and his extensive experience contending with rival creationists, Mixter no doubt expected the conference to spark some controversy. He seems to have misunderstood, however, how combustible the atmosphere was on Wheaton's campus.

When Mixter's ASA colleagues took the podium in February 1961, they pushed their evangelical audience to reconsider their assumptions about the proper relationship between evangelical belief and mainstream science. Walter Hearn, for example, chastised head-in-the-sand fundamentalist scientists. "If you were under the impression that evolution was about to blow over," he remarked, "I think you've misread the weather signs!" Cassel, too, pleaded with evangelical Christians to "stop shadow-boxing" and "finger-pointing" and accept the contributions of mainstream science. Buswell enjoined the conference to recognize "true scientific progress" from the mainstream science of human evolution, to ditch the worn-out "straight jacket of certain interpretations of Scripture which ran headlong into conflict with factual scientific data."[26]

Such attitudes may have carried the day among ASA members, but they remained intensely provocative among the wider evangelical and fundamentalist public. It didn't take long for President Edman to hear directly from outraged fundamentalists. One local Baptist pastor who had attended the conference complained that Hearn and Cassel had openly flouted the notion that the book of Genesis should be read literally. Worse, not one member of Wheaton's faculty had spoken out against such ideas. Leaving "such uncontested statements before the student body," the local pastor warned, opened Wheaton to "all types of misinterpretation of the Bible," undermined the school's status as an authentically evangelical institution, and ran "contrary to beliefs held by the college since its founding."[27]

## *Friends and Foes*

Edman could not have been surprised by this sort of reaction. He had been dealing with the fundamentalist rumor mill for years in regard to Mixter's and Wheaton's teachings about evolution. On Wheaton's campus, Edman had long fielded complaints about Mixter from trustee David Otis Fuller. Fuller had been on the board since 1933. He viewed his role as that of a fundamentalist stalwart, actively opposing every whisper of liberalism in culture, politics, and theology.[28] His denomination, the General Association of Regular Baptist Churches, had represented since the 1930s an unapologetically fundamentalist option for conservative Baptists. By the 1950s, Fuller had become disillusioned with Wheaton's piecemeal accommodation with neo-evangelicalism. And since at least 1957, Fuller had fixed his gimlet fundamentalist eye on the work of Russell Mixter. As historian Michael Hamilton has noted, Fuller suspected Mixter of "covertly teaching evolution to Wheaton undergraduates."[29]

It was not only powerful trustees that Edman worried about, however. As always in the world of fundamentalist higher education, the close cross-connections between leaders and institutions led to deep and powerful currents of rumors, counter-rumors, and incessant allegations of untrustworthiness. By the end of 1960, for example, Edman tried to stop the rumor-mongering of influential fundamentalist Charles J. Woodbridge. Edman had heard through the grapevine that Woodbridge had been making disparaging comments about Wheaton to various fundamentalist audiences, hinting that Wheaton now taught evolution. During his sermons, for example, Woodbridge allegedly liked to "throw up his arms and shrug his shoulders so that the whole congregation sagged with the obvious feeling that Wheaton has now gone down the drain of liberalism."[30] Edman confronted Woodbridge and demanded an explanation.[31]

This sort of damage control was about more than just mending Edman's personal relationship with Woodbridge. As always, Edman worried about Wheaton's continuing ability to attract students. According to evangelical rumor, Woodbridge had warned some high schoolers that "Wheaton now teaches evolution." Edman and his inner circle fretted that this sort of whisper campaign could "only have a harmful effect upon Wheaton's recruitment program."[32]

After Mixter's 1961 conference, these fundamentalist whispers turned into shouts. Writing in John R. Rice's widely read fundamentalist newspaper *Sword of the Lord*, Walter Handford warned readers that Wheaton now openly taught evolution. It was a "sad, sad day," Handford lamented, when "one of the best-known Christian colleges" fell into such lamentable heresy.[33] In spite of Edman's protests to the contrary, Handford claimed, Wheaton had done nothing to distance itself officially from the evolutionary ideas on offer at the conference. Faculty members such as James O. Buswell had argued that his evolutionary ideas represented nothing but an improved fundamentalist doctrine, but Handford disagreed. "No strong fundamentalist today," Handford warned readers of *Sword of the Lord*, could possibly agree with the evolution-friendly vision of Wheaton's conference.[34] Phil Jackson of Fuller's fundamentalist GARBC denomination alerted his readers that Wheaton had pernicious "'soft spots' in the faculty of the science department." In spite of Wheaton's alarming friendliness to evolution, Jackson warned GARBC parents, "many of your GARBC young people continue to go there, and we do have a responsibility to help protect them!"[35]

Not surprisingly, Wheaton's fundamentalist rivals at Bob Jones University helped spread the word of Wheaton's alleged evolutionary declension. When fundamentalists asked BJU administrators about Mixter's conference, BJU's leaders referred them to Harold P. Warren. Warren was the fundamentalist pastor of the First Baptist Church of Wheaton. He had attended the 1961 conference and was eager to share his outrage at the evolutionary goings-on. He told concerned fundamentalists nationwide that he and his church no longer gave money to the school. In the good old days, Pastor Warren explained, Wheaton had been admirably open to a "strong, fundamentalist type of sin-judging messages." No longer. Mixter and his evolutionary views were only the tip of the evangelical iceberg. In general, Warren warned, Wheaton's campus now embraced only a "cold, intellectual, proud resistance" to fundamentalism and real creationism.[36]

In the face of such swirling rumors and outright accusations, Edman scrambled to shore up Wheaton's reputation as a reliably creationist school. His confidant Harold Lindsell worked to convince the "Christian public" that fundamentalist critics like John R. Rice were "not to be trusted."[37] Edman himself undertook a rigorous inquisition into faculty attitudes. He wanted to be able to offer a firm and fundamentalist-friendly repudiation of the incessant rumors that Wheaton now taught evolution. Edman reminded faculty members that questions would continue to be raised "by our friends (and by our foes)." He hoped the faculty would agree to reassert their belief in the school's doctrinal statement, "without mental reservation." Did they believe unflinchingly that God created the universe? Did they believe the account in Genesis 1–3 to be true? Most of all, did they "believe and teach that Adam and Eve were real human beings, the first to be created"?[38]

In the world of 1960s creationism, Edman's carefully worded request carried heavy evangelical implications. The school's original statement of belief, dating from Wheaton's embrace of fundamentalism in 1920s, insisted only that faculty members "believe that man was created in the image of God."[39] To attempt, as Edman hoped in 1961, to beef up Wheaton's creationist credentials by insisting on a real, historical Adam and Eve was an innovation. Back in the 1920s, even the sternest, most uncompromising fundamentalists could find no cause for complaint in Wheaton's vague official definition of creationism. By the 1960s, however, fundamentalists like Fuller demanded a change, because they hoped it would edge out any creeping tendencies to accommodate mainstream evolutionary thinking. But Wheaton's faculty disagreed. In response to Edman's circular letter, twenty-one faculty members instead signed copies of Wheaton's original statement of belief.[40]

Even when prodded by Edman, a faculty committee offered only a similarly unapologetic statement of their evangelical beliefs about evolution and creation. "The principle for the evangelical Christian is clear," the committee concluded. Whenever the Bible speaks, "the Christian must stand firmly by what it says."[41] In the case of the age of the earth, however, there was no conflict between the Bible's plain teaching "and those scientific theories which allege that the world may be as old as five billion years." Real Christian belief, real creationist belief, could include a variety of entirely legitimate interpretations. In either case, there was no need to throw out scientific progress in order to remain devotedly Christian.[42]

Such assertions were not enough. Under pressure from Fuller on the board of trustees and fundamentalist sentiment nationwide, Edman rammed through an amendment to the school's official doctrine. No one at Wheaton, Edman continued to insist, taught "that a man's body came up from a single cell by evolutionary process and that at some point in time, that creature received a spiritual nature by the creative act of God." Edman acknowledged that some evangelicals, "not here at Wheaton but elsewhere," tended to "water down the phrase, 'created in the image of God.'" When Wheaton's faculty agreed that humanity was "created in the image of God," Edman insisted, they endorsed real creationism, not evolutionary thinking. In order to reassure anxious creationists, Wheaton would henceforth insist on a clearer statement from its faculty. It would not technically change its original statement, but it would add the following attachment:

> By Article IV of its "Standards of Faith," Wheaton College is committed to the Biblical teaching that man was created by a direct act of God and not from previously existing forms of life; and that all men are descended from the historical Adam and Eve, first parents of the entire human race.[43]

Edman rushed to explain to Wheaton's detractors that this change proved once and for all Wheaton's dedication to the new orthodoxy of creationism. He chastised fundamentalist gossips for spreading "inaccuracies" about Wheaton's position on evolution, and assured all and sundry that his school "stand[s] unswervingly for the faith once delivered to the saints."[44]

The faculty overwhelmingly disliked the change, but most held their noses and signed the new doctrinal statement. Even Mixter signed. From his perspective, the new clarification was unpleasant but not doctrinally objectionable. It did not insist on a young age for the earth. It did not even force Wheaton's scientists to agree to any specific interpretation of the meaning of the creative days in Genesis, or to the length of time since God's creation of Adam and Eve.[45]

Other faculty members protested more vigorously. Stanley Parmenter resigned from his position as chair of the science division. He was disgusted, he told Edman, by Fuller's display of fundamentalist rancor. Fuller had fomented anti-Wheaton sentiment among fundamentalists from outside the Wheaton community. Fuller never listened to faculty input, only to non-expert "people of doubtful judgment." Worst of all, Fuller "singled out" Mixter for a "long, vicious attack" that did not even pretend to consider Mixter's real ideas. Instead, Mixter was made a whipping boy for the many imagined sins of evangelical science. The new statement of faith, Professor Parmenter concluded, was "a rebuff . . . and a serious affront" to Mixter and the faculty. Parmenter and Fuller agreed on one thing: insisting on belief in a real, historical, directly created Adam and Eve implied a fundamentalist limit on the extent of mainstream scientific influence among Wheaton's faculty. The new doctrinal addendum may not have insisted on a young earth or a real worldwide flood, but it did signify a fundamentalist-friendly attitude toward scientific investigation.[46]

Evangelical scientists weren't the only ones to be left dissatisfied. In spite of the new doctrine, Edman had continued difficulty reassuring fundamentalists that Wheaton remained a safely creationist school. In 1962, the mother of a current Wheaton student expressed her concern about the "very disturbing reports about Wheaton" she was hearing through the fundamentalist grapevine. On two different occasions she had "heard that the college is growing liberal." Specifically, she reported, "some-one said they teach evolution at Wheaton." She was on the verge of panic, she told Edman. She read with dismay what John R. Rice wrote in *Sword of the Lord*: that Wheaton no longer honored fundamentalist heroes such as William Bell Riley, William Jennings Bryan, and Harry Rimmer. "What grieves me most," she concluded, "is that our daughter may lose her faith at Wheaton. Is this possible?"[47]

Not in the slightest, Edman assured her. No one at Wheaton "believes or teaches evolution." Every member of the faculty was "a fully persuaded creationist." For proof, Edman enclosed the new, fortified statement of faith. Wheaton continued to honor its fundamentalist friends such as William Bell Riley and honorary alumnus Harry Rimmer. In fact, Edman wrote, all faculty members at Wheaton, like Riley and Rimmer, were "convinced fundamentalists."[48]

It's difficult to imagine President Edman writing such things with an entirely clear conscience. Indeed, he even asked the Wheaton mother not to show his letter to her fundamentalist friends.[49] More than anyone, Edman was aware of the divisions among Wheaton's faculty, trustees, and alumni. The main reason Edman agreed to a new doctrinal statement, however, was precisely so that he could reassure fundamentalist parents and pundits. Whatever his own beliefs about evolution and creation, fundamentalism and evangelicalism, Edman needed to be able to assure potential students that his school would protect their faith. By 1961, that necessity put his school in an intensely awkward position. Evangelical scientists largely recognized the value of some parts, at least, of mainstream evolutionary science. Any authentic Christian testimony, they agreed, needed to come to terms with the intellectual claims of an ancient earth and of changing species over long stretches of time. By 1961, however, large segments of the fundamentalist and evangelical public disagreed. By that date, a resurgent insistence on ideas about a young earth came to be seen by many as absolute requirements for true Christian belief. Fundamentalist creationists, as we'll see in the next section, insisted on new, unbreachable intellectual safeguards to protect authentic belief. As did trustee David Otis Fuller at Wheaton, fundamentalists hoped that their insistence on a young earth and a recent, literal, special creation of humanity could protect the faith of new generations of fundamentalist students.

## *Genesis Flood Watch*

Like the split between neo-evangelicals and fundamentalists, the splits between various sorts of creationists were never clean or simple. Russell Mixter himself continued to insist that his work remained part of true fundamentalism, not any part of a compromise with evolution or a move toward the "new evangelicals."[50] In spite of such claims, however, young-earth creationists often separated themselves from Mixter's ASA and other suspiciously neo-evangelical organizations. David Otis Fuller, for example, quit his position on Wheaton's board of trustees in 1963. He began warning his fundamentalist Baptist brethren to send their children elsewhere.[51] Longtime ASA members such as Walter Lammerts left in 1963 to start the Creation Research Society. Along with young-earth colleagues such as theologian John Whitcomb Jr., Lammerts believed the ASA no longer respected young-earth thinking.[52]

Much as Russell Mixter and his evangelical colleagues had electrified their audiences with their new fervor about the possibility of a progressive creationism that was both better science and better religion, so young-earth creationists rallied around new champions. Most compelling was the 1961 publication of John Whitcomb Jr. and Henry Morris's young-earth blockbuster, *The Genesis Flood.* The book sold tens of thousands of copies in the 1960s, but not because its ideas were new. Its insistence on a literal recent worldwide flood that explained most of the apparent age of the earth had been promoted since the first decade of the 1900s by George McCready Price. Fundamentalist scientists and intellectuals had long debated the merits of "flood geology." By and large, however, fundamentalists in the first half of the twentieth century weren't convinced.[53]

As mainstream evolutionary science made stronger and stronger claims and as some evangelical thinkers seemed swayed by those claims, Whitcomb and Morris offered a new argument for the old idea of a young earth. Earlier generations of fundamentalists—like the leaders who cobbled together Wheaton's original statement of faith—had seen no reason to insist on a young earth. As mainstream science advanced, though, Whitcomb and Morris believed Christianity needed a new floodwall to protect authentic belief, true modern orthodoxy. Just as the first generation of fundamentalists in the 1920s created a new vision of orthodoxy to counter the new theology so popular among liberals, so too did *The Genesis Flood* argue for a new creationist orthodoxy. In both cases, fundamentalists insisted that their innovations were not new, but rather ancient truths. If Christians truly respected the Bible as the "verbally inspired and completely inerrant Word of God," Whitcomb and Morris argued, they needed to adopt without reservation the obvious meaning of the Book of Genesis.[54]

And when fundamentalists did so, they did not need to worry that they were closing their minds to the best modern science. True, Whitcomb and Morris wrote, evolutionary science had won "widespread acceptance," but in fact there was only "a small amount of actual scientific evidence in favor of it!"[55] Mainstream science and foolish evangelical thinkers who accepted it, Whitcomb and Morris explained, had been blinded by "evolutionary basis and bias."[56]

As institutions like Wheaton struggled to explain that progressive creationism was still real creationism, young-earth creationists insisted that only one idea could truly protect and promote real Christian belief. Throughout the 1960s and 1970s, young-earth creationists insisted that mainstream science offered merely a smoother road to damnation. At one debate on Wheaton's campus in 1974, for example, Henry Morris sought to convince Wheaton's faculty that young-earth ideas represented the only scientific path to salvation. By then, the school had moved more decisively away from young-earth thinking. Wheaton's faculty scientists worried, Morris thought, that "flood geology was such an embarrassment . . . that they had to dissociate themselves altogether from creationists who held such views, lest they turn students and other scientists away from Christianity."[57] Morris tried to tell skeptical Wheaton scientists, in contrast, that "literal creationism and flood geology . . . was receiving far more attention and winning far more converts on university campuses than the compromising positions of theistic evolution and progressive creation had ever been able to do."[58] In spite of his best efforts to enlighten them, Morris warned, Wheaton's science faculty insisted on maintaining an alarmingly relaxed attitude toward the meanings of the Book of Genesis. Worst of all, thought Morris, Wheaton's scientists disrespected the plain meaning of Genesis, yet they all assured Morris that they remained "creationists."[59]

To Henry Morris and his fundamentalist sympathizers, such compromise could not be tolerated. "True creationists," Morris insisted, agreed that a young-earth interpretation was what "Scriptures plainly teach." Yet, pathetically and frighteningly, schools like Wheaton continued to mislead the creationist public. They continued to claim the mantle of good science, real Christianity, and authentic creationism when they had, in reality, abandoned all three. Why? To Morris, progressive creationists and theistic evolutionists had sold their Christian birthright for a mess of mainstream scientific pottage. They believed foolishly, Morris charged, that "acceptance in the academic world requires [them] to believe in evolution."[60]

What was an evangelical or fundamentalist parent to do? Real Christians, Morris insisted, should be wary about their school choices. After all, he wrote, many evangelical colleges, even "the most highly respected schools have compromised with evolutionism to an alarming degree." As Morris saw it, the problem for fundamentalist parents and students was that many schools sold themselves as authentic creationist institutions when in fact they taught non-young-earth ideas. Too many colleges, he charged, fudged this important tenet of true belief for mere "promotional purposes."[61] Morris pleaded with fundamentalist and evangelical families not to be fooled by the false talk of progressive creationism. There was no such thing. Only by insisting that faculty accept the "straightforward Biblical teaching of a completed recent creation and worldwide flood" could parents and churches trust institutions of higher education.[62]

At schools that considered themselves fundamentalist stalwarts, Morris's brand of young-earth exceptionalism carried a great deal of weight. Just as schools such as Wheaton continued to insist that real evangelical belief could include a variety of ideas about creation and evolution, schools on the fundamentalist side of the family scrambled to spell out their devotion to an exclusively young-earth variety of creationism. Schools such as the new Liberty Baptist College elaborately and meticulously articulated their uncompromising young-earth beliefs. In the increasingly competitive world of evangelical higher education, fundamentalist colleges like

Liberty hoped to increase their market share by piling on guarantees of their unimpeachable young-earth credentials.

The doctrinal statements of Liberty in the 1970s, for example, tried to exclude even the vaguest doubt about its vigorous young-earth creationism. No other creationist ideas would be tolerated—not day-age models, not gaps, and not any kind of progressive creation. All of the teachers in its affiliated elementary and secondary schools, for example, signed a painstakingly specific and detailed statement about their creationist beliefs. Liberty-affiliated teachers, it explained, must "believe in the Genesis account of creation . . . literally, and not allegorically or figuratively." Liberty's teachers disavowed any notion that human development might have been "a matter of evolution or evolutionary change of species." There had been no "interminable periods of time." Every kind of plant and animal was "made directly." The "days" of Genesis were exactly that, and there was no gap between the creations. In short—according to the official statement of belief, at least—no teacher at Liberty's affiliated schools would adopt any notions of creationism other than Henry Morris's young-earth variety.[63]

## *The Most Dangerous Man in America*

Jerry Falwell and the other leaders of Liberty hoped that planting a flag for young-earth creationism would secure their fundamentalist reputation. As Wheaton and other evangelical schools moved further away from fundamentalist verities, schools such as Liberty used young-earth creationism as another way to prove to the fundamentalist public that their school would never—could never—slide into suspicious compromise with mainstream science and mainline theology. Of course, that was not the only ambition of the new fundamentalist college. As President Pierre Guillermin put it in 1982, his school hoped to be "the Notre Dame of the Christian world athletically and the Harvard of the Christian world academically."[64]

In 1982, such inflated claims seemed, at best, overly optimistic. Certainly Falwell's hilltop campus had grown rapidly, from Lynchburg Baptist College in 1971 to Liberty Baptist College in 1975; it would become Liberty University in 1985. In the school's first few decades, things on campus seemed to be moving fast. One alumnus recalled with rosy-hued nostalgia the rocky early days of the school, when he and other "preacher boys" had no classrooms in which to meet, so they prayed and sang on "the old trash dump road above the present campus." Looking back from

1991, it seemed hard to remember a time when Liberty University's ever-expanding campus lacked such basic amenities.[65] Still, in the early 1980s Liberty Baptist College remained more of a future promise than a present certainty.

The implied promise was about more than just higher education. Liberty's founder, Jerry Falwell, electrified fundamentalists and mainstream politicians alike in the 1970s by leaping into electoral politics. He declared his political movement to be the start of a new revival in American politics and society, the reclaiming of America's promise. Not every fundamentalist was pleased with Falwell's declarations. From Bob Jones University, Bob Jones Jr. blasted Falwell as "the most dangerous man in America today."[66] Not, pointedly, because Falwell's upstart school rivaled BJU's role as the leading intellectual citadel of uncompromising fundamentalism. Rather, Jones accused Falwell of joining unwisely with non-fundamentalists in his new organization, Moral Majority.

Whether they loved it or hated it, fundamentalists tended to assume Falwell's leap into partisan politics was something radically new, part of a "New Christian Right." Many observers thought fundamentalists had separated themselves from political activism since the trials of the 1920s and that Falwell's headfirst plunge into electoral politics represented a radical break with this fundamentalist tradition. From Lynchburg, Liberty's fundamentalists actively promoted this sincerely held myth. For example, Liberty's Ed Hindson insisted in 1981 that his school and his politics represented what he called "the resurgent Fundamentalist Phenomenon." The liberal experiment of the 1960s, Hindson argued, had failed miserably. It was time for fundamentalists to shed their admirable disdain for political activism. Fundamentalists, led by the God-fueled power of Liberty Baptist College, had a chance to take back America. If and only if fundamentalists returned to politics, Hindson explained, they could make a change for the better. A tottering America could be led by "a few thousand highly committed and thoroughly trained young people" into a political revival that could fulfill America's Christian promise.[67]

For the most part, even the most skeptical observers and scholars tended to accept Liberty's imagined past. Instead of seeing Liberty's claims as part of the perennial political tension among American evangelicals—the "establishment-or-outsider paradox" of American fundamentalism[68]—observers agreed that fundamentalists had withdrawn from political activism since the 1930s. Instead of seeing Falwell's claims as part of a long-running evangelical debate about the proper balance between political activism and high-minded separatism, contemporary politicos generally took Liberty's pronouncements at face value. Fundamentalists really had retreated from political activism since the 1930s, they asserted. Until the 1970s, in this telling, fundamentalists had built separatist institutions, staunchly refusing to truck with the dirty world of politics. The emergence of a New Christian Right, one scholar concluded, required fundamentalists to break "their separatist taboos against engaging in politics."[69]

Happily, historians such as Daniel K. Williams have put this widely held myth to rest. Something did change about evangelical politics in the 1970s, but it was not that evangelicals and fundamentalists were engaging with mainstream political campaigns for the first time since the 1930s. Rather, as Williams explained,

> evangelicals gained prominence during Ronald Reagan's campaign not because they were speaking out on political issues—they had been doing this for decades—but because they were taking over the Republican Party. It was an event more than fifty years in the making.[70]

When Liberty Baptist College invited Ronald Reagan to campus in 1980, it did not mean that fundamentalists had emerged from a long self-imposed political hibernation. On the contrary. Since the 1920s, on every political issue, in every decade, fundamentalists wrote letters, buttonholed candidates, and raised funds. Jerry Falwell's alleged leap into politics was really only a leap into the arms of the Republican Party.

Not only Falwell and his beloved Liberty University but fundamentalism as a whole had never retreated from public life. As historian Matthew Sutton has argued convincingly, the "rise-fall-rebirth" story told by Falwell and accepted by so many historians and observers simply doesn't match the historical record.[71] Fundamentalists had never retreated into their churches and slammed the doors shut. As Sutton put it, fundamentalists' "agenda was always about more than correct theology; it was also about reclaiming and then occupying American culture."[72]

Certainly on the campuses of fundamentalist colleges, institutes, and universities there had never been a meaningful withdrawal from the wider society. True, there had always been talk of withdrawal; there had always been debates about the proper public role of a Christian. And there had been endless discussions about the current state of mainstream society and politics. Had America become irredeemably sinful, a modern Sodom rooting blindly in its own godless excess? Or did the United States represent the last, best chance of Christianity? The evangelical and fundamentalist answer to both questions was almost always yes.

Yet no matter their opinion on these perennially difficult questions, students, faculty, and administrators alike had always sought influence in mainstream politics and culture. They cultivated and maintained tight and productive relationships with leading conservative politicians. They actively contributed to the conservative side of causes such as the midcentury crusade against communism. Campus leaders advocated signature conservative policies, such as a smaller federal government. And, as nonfundamentalist intellectuals proposed a new fusion of conservative traditions in the middle of the century, prominent voices at fundamentalist and evangelical colleges cheered them on. Of course, fundamentalist higher education was no more monolithic politically than it was in any other way. As historian David Swartz has shown, a vocal "moral minority" always pushed for an evangelical leftism, especially as the culture wars of the 1960s swept over fundamentalist and evangelical campuses.[73] And, as the divisions between evangelical schools and fundamentalist ones grew more and more pronounced at the end of the century, evangelical campuses tended to be more open to a wider spectrum of political positions. Even among the most fervent neo-evangelical reformers, however, a strong penchant for doctrinal conservatism often translated into a conflicted embrace of conservative political and cultural themes.

## *An Unafraid College*

From the very beginning, fundamentalist scholars and school founders had vigorously embraced a self-image as politically active culture warriors. And in most cases, their politics took a decidedly conservative tone. From Moody Bible Institute, President James M. Gray insisted in 1928 on the need for fundamentalists to use every political weapon at their command to promote fundamentalism-friendly public policies. When MBI's radio station came under political pressure, for example, Gray came out swinging. "The time for fighting has begun," Gray intoned ominously. If MBI's lawyer was not powerful enough to protect the school's rights, Gray insisted, then the school should enlist the political support of allies such as Missouri senator James M. Reed. There was no doubt in Gray's mind that his institution must engage with mainstream politics. Retreat and withdrawal, Gray reasoned, would compromise his school's missionary testimony.[74]

J. Gresham Machen, the donnish public face of 1920s fundamentalism, also took an active role in conservative cultural politics. In 1924, for example, he joined the Sentinels of the Republic, a group dedicated to "maintain[ing] the fundamental principles of the American Constitution." Machen donated his time, influence, and cash to the organization, hoping to limit the growing influence of the federal government, to fight the spread of communism, and "to help preserve a free republican form of government in the United States."[75]

Among the next generation of fundamentalist intellectuals, even the most ardent neo-evangelical reformers often remained politically and culturally conservative. As George Marsden has explained about the founders of the neo-evangelical flagship Fuller Seminary, all were "Republicans of the sort who supported Robert A. Taft."[76] In the 1940s and early 1950s, as Fuller's leaders articulated the need for a new, "progressive Fundamentalism with a social message," that message included many of the key themes of conservative political activism.[77] Fuller's founders and students wanted a new, open evangelicalism, but they also ferociously opposed communism. They courted conservative leaders of big business. They admired free-market thinking. And most of them called themselves conservatives. Among Fuller students between 1950 and 1952, a full two-thirds thought of themselves as "conservative." Another tenth claimed to be "very conservative." Only three of that early group of fifty students labeled themselves "liberal" or "very liberal."[78]

At schools that condemned the neo-evangelical reform, the connections to conservative politics and ideas were even tighter. At Bob Jones University, conservative politicians and culture warriors had always been campus regulars. At the school's groundbreaking ceremony in its first Florida location in 1926, for example, Alabama governor Bibb Graves turned over a symbolic shovelful of earth and praised Bob Jones Sr.'s fight against "godless education."[79] By the early 1950s, BJU had leaped into the emerging world of conservative anti-communism. The school made itself into an institutional hub of the movement by hosting events such as annual "Americanism" conferences. These affairs brought to campus conservative anti-communist activists such as Billy James Hargis and Dan Smoot. In 1962—long before fundamentalists had supposedly emerged from their imagined retreat from mainstream cultural politics—Bob Jones Jr. insisted that such political activism was a natural part of fundamentalist religion. "A good, Bible-believing Christian," Jones insisted, "is by nature a good, patriotic American."[80] The graduates of Bob Jones University, he repeated in 1963, were meant to spread forth across the land to "stand for the fundamental principles of Constitutional Americanism."[81] In some cases, such conservative political evangelism was institutionalized. In the 1964 presidential election, for example, BJU faculty and staff took a group of students on a bus tour of the South, promoting Barry Goldwater as the fundamentalist choice.[82]

BJU had maintained tight connections to other conservative politicians for years. Not surprisingly, perhaps the closest bonds were with South Carolina senator Strom Thurmond. Thurmond's impassioned segregationism and his strategic conservative switch from the Democratic Party to the Republican Party in 1964 mirrored the political instincts of many BJU leaders. Thurmond had long had ties to BJU, speaking to appreciative campus audiences as early as 1950.[83] Longtime administrator Gilbert Stenholm shared a particularly close bond with the conservative senator, even officiating at Thurmond's second wedding in 1968.[84] Thurmond assured Stenholm that Thurmond would always be eager to help BJU "in any matter with the Federal Government."[85] And Stenholm assured Thurmond of BJU's loyalty to Thurmond's political vision. As Stenholm put it, BJU was "a conservative, patriotic university desiring to render a service for the Lord and for the country."[86] By 1969, years before fundamentalists supposedly emerged from political exile, Stenholm was comfortably chumming around with his friend in the U.S. Senate, lamenting the vicissitudes of "some of us conservative Republicans."[87]

The embrace of conservative politics and cultural themes was not limited to the Southern campus of Bob Jones University. As far back as the 1930s, Wheaton's leaders cultivated the college's reputation as a flag-waving, traditional, patriotic institution. In 1935, for example, President Buswell proudly advertised his school as a uniquely "unafraid college . . . one college where parents can send their children without any fear of their being inoculated with any 'isms but Americanism and Christianism."[88] Buswell's successor, V. Raymond Edman, maintained Wheaton's status as a bulwark of conservative patriotic anti-communism. In a 1948 promotional letter, for example, President Edman warned the wider Wheaton community that "American education is besieged by Communist betrayers." In such trying times, Edman reassured Wheatonites, their beloved school "stands steadily and unqualifiedly for the Christian and American way of life."[89] Like many of his fundamentalist contemporaries, Edman assumed—for publicity purposes at least—that fundamentalist values were American values and vice versa.

The connection seemed especially true when those values were stacked up against the perceived threat of communism. At every school throughout the middle of the twentieth century, fundamentalists and evangelicals actively pursued the "political demonology" of the anti-communist movement.[90] Students in Moody Bible Institute's Christian Education Club, for example, listened to desperate warnings about "Reds' creeping tentacles."[91] At Fuller Seminary in California, students in Harold Lindsell's Critique of Communism class in 1961 were asked in their final exams to write an essay describing their "own plan of action as an answer to Communism." For full credit, they could "show what specific steps [they] would take in order to meet this danger."[92]

Of course, the midcentury anti-communist impulse was broad and diverse, including liberal anti-Stalinist labor unionists as well as right-wing paranoiacs.[93] The anti-communist themes embraced by the leaders of fundamentalist and evangelical colleges tipped toward the latter. During his tenure at Fuller Seminary, for example, Harold Lindsell collected reams of anti-communist literature from conservative activists such as Fred Schwarz.[94] At Bob Jones University, Gilbert Stenholm's files bulged with his collection of right-wing anti-communist newsletters. From official pronouncements of the House Un-American Activities Committee to homemade mimeographed newsletters, Stenholm actively gathered everything he could find about the communist menace to Christianity and the American way of life.[95]

The leaders of fundamentalist institutions also tended to agree on the dangers of a bloated and expanding federal government. As we saw in Chapter 7, schools often did not hesitate to accept federal largess in the post–World War II years. But they insisted that they would not take any federal aid that included even the faintest whiff of government influence. For example, from Moody Bible Institute, President William Culbertson proudly declared that his school had "never considered applying for government funds." The dangers were simply too great. Culbertson warned of the "government pressures and controls" that would inevitably follow.[96] At nearby Wheaton College, President Edman assiduously studied the issue of federal aid to higher education.[97] Into the 1970s, Wheaton insisted that it "steadfastly guards its independence from federal funding." No Wheaton student received federal funding. The school itself would accept no federal funding. The danger, Wheaton's leaders believed, lay in the inevitable "government interference" that would come with any federal money.[98]

As a self-consciously conservative "fusion" movement emerged in the middle of the twentieth century, influential voices at fundamentalist and evangelical schools bought in. Conservative pundits and intellectuals such as William F. Buckley Jr. and Frank Meyer argued that conservatives must unite, whether they believed in a smaller government, a stauncher anti-communism, or an effete traditionalism as laid out by thinkers such as Edmund Burke.[99] This conservative intellectual movement appealed to many fundamentalists. Students, faculty, and administrators devoured movement magazines such as *National Review* and *Human Events*.[100] Some students insisted that this emerging "movement" conservatism was a natural home for conservative evangelicals. In the pages of Biola's student newspaper, for example, editor Wes Reeves argued in 1965 that any thinking Christian should read Buckley's *National Review* and recognize the need for conservative culture-war activism.[101]

As they did in all things, ardent school-watchers around the country subjected the ideological goings-on on campus to relentless fundamentalist scrutiny. In every decade, at every school, administrators rushed to reassure worried fundamentalists that their schools remained true to a traditionalist, patriotic conservatism that ranged far beyond theological doctrine. In 1947, for example, MBI's Culbertson reassured an anxious donor from Nashville that his school would always remain "glad to take our stand for the old-fashioned kind of Americanism."[102] Similarly, in the early 1960s, an angry alumnus excoriated current Wheaton president V. Raymond Edman for allowing Arnold Toynbee to speak on campus. After all, the man fumed, Toynbee "all but calls himself a communist."[103] In Massachusetts, anti-communist activist Rosalind Woods Guardabassi threatened to cut off her donations and expose the insufficient anti-communist zeal of Gordon College. "I used to think of Gordon College as a patriotic Christian Center," Guardabassi wrote to President Forrester in 1967. "I hope it still is!"[104]

It was not only conservative patriotic anti-communism that riled activists. In 1969, Biola president Samuel Sutherland hastened to reassure donors and alumni that Biola's students were indeed political conservatives. True, a student had written a letter in the student newspaper endorsing Democratic presidential candidate Hubert Humphrey. The student body as a whole, Sutherland assured Biola supporters, was at least 80 percent Republican. There were some "wonderful students who are Democrats," but Sutherland did not support such affiliations; rather, he explained, it was strategic common sense to allow the Democratic students to remain at school in the hope that Biola could educate them out of their misguided, childish political liberalism.[105]

## *God's Own Party*

By the late 1960s, when Sutherland explained his plan to wean left-leaning evangelical students from their political folly, there was absolutely nothing new about political thought and activism on fundamentalist and evangelical campuses. Fundamentalist and evangelical college communities had always been political places; students, faculty, and administration had always actively participated in mainstream politics. And, as at Biola, those politics always tipped decisively toward a deep cultural conservatism. But something did change by the 1970s. Like Sutherland, more and more fundamentalist and evangelical school leaders made tighter and tighter connections between their traditional conservative political ideology and their exclusive support for the Republican Party. Political dissenters were tolerated—like the lonely Humphrey supporter on Biola's campus—but by the 1970s the trend was clear. The vehicle for conservative public activism was becoming the Republican Party.

At some schools—the ones that tended to embrace the neo-evangelical reform with the most openness and enthusiasm—the connections between conservative evangelical religion and conservative politics remained more open to debate and dissent. At schools that remained more attached to fundamentalist attitudes, on the other hand, party politics came to seem like an intrinsic part of conservative religion. As usual, not all fundamentalists agreed on what that meant in practice. At the staunchly fundamentalist campuses of Bob Jones University and Liberty Baptist College, for example, leaders were not at all united about how to be Republicans.

At Bob Jones University, the embrace of the GOP sometimes seemed like something dramatically new. The Bob Joneses, like many evangelists, had long insisted that they were above politics. They were interested in winning souls, they claimed, not wrangling votes. What they usually meant by that, though, was that they would not stoop to mere partisan politics; they would not embrace one party or another in their unrelenting political activism. In 1969, for example, Bob Jones Jr. told a friend that he was thoroughly "opposed to party politics . . . on principle." He voted for the right person, not the right party. But he and his school never remained aloof from voting and politics as a whole. At the same time that he claimed to be opposed to politics, Jones assured his friend that he was "urging our students to remember how their senators voted when the next election comes up in their state."[106]

At times, Bob Jones Jr.'s experience as a fundamentalist controversialist served him badly in the world of partisan politics. In the 1976 presidential election, Jones had come to agree that religious leaders could and should be partisan political activists. As he put it, preachers "should denounce what's spiritually and morally wrong, and if that means getting into politics, so be it." As he waded into the 1976 election, Jones lashed out at Democratic candidate Jimmy Carter, calling him a "foul-mouthed, double-crossing hypocrite, a complete phony." But he also viciously attacked the Republican candidate, calling Gerald Ford's wife, Betty Ford, "a plain slut."[107]

The politics favored by Jerry Falwell's Liberty Baptist College didn't differ much from the conservative ideas of the Bob Joneses, but Falwell's activists tended to fight for them with smiles on their faces and cheerful music in the background. Throughout the late 1970s and early 1980s, Liberty's leaders offered GOP leaders their substantial support, as long as those politicians embraced Liberty's vision of conservative American values. One of Liberty's greatest political weapons was its student body. Unlike the shoot-from-the-hip fundamentalist style of Bob Jones Jr., Jerry Falwell understood something about the cultural politics of finesse. So, for example, while Jones threatened and fulminated, Falwell sent "fine, young Christian student[s]" to hand-deliver promotional material to members of the U.S. Congress.[108]

Those Christian students had been trained in the art of GOP politics. Students at Liberty Baptist College learned that real Christianity, real fundamentalism, meant a certain sort of political activism. At Liberty in the 1970s and early 1980s, the ever-present politics of cultural conservatism had become the partisan politics of GOP influence peddling. And in case anyone misunderstood the connection, students were required to attend training conferences to make it clear. As Liberty students read in one political conference description, "Sessions are required and attendance will be taken. Students will not be allowed to leave campus without written permission."[109] In the early 1980s, Liberty students could also attend the Institute of Applied Politics, in which experienced conservative politicians such as former Arizona representative John Conlan taught them how to "make a positive impact on American government."[110] And Liberty students barnstormed America's state capitols, singing about their love for America.[111] Meanwhile, Jerry Falwell himself buttonholed conservative politicians, smilingly but ruthlessly eliminating wiggle room. Senators and representatives had to declare their "conservative, pro-family" values or go without Falwell's support.[112]

And that support, Falwell insisted, was enormous. He claimed the backing of "the vast majority of Americans" in his political crusade.[113] It was not as clear, however, whether Falwell could claim the support of other fundamentalists. As Falwell reached out to non-fundamentalist conservatives with his Moral Majority organization, other fundamentalists blanched. It might be entirely legitimate to collaborate with non-fundamentalists for non-religious purposes, but some fundamentalists thought that Falwell's overtures to conservative Catholics and mainline Protestants went entirely too far. For example, by the end of the 1970s, Falwell's more-established rivals at Bob Jones University spared no rhetorical excess in their condemnation of Falwell's brand of fundamentalist politics. As Bob Jones III declared in 1979, "Jerry Falwell does not deserve to be called a Fundamentalist."[114] The BJU alumni association, too, expressed its "disgust" with Jerry Falwell's presumed leadership of politicized fundamentalism. Such scrambling for control of the GOP, the alumni accused, was a "weak, embryonic New Evangelical position."[115]

As the father had done when confronted with Billy Graham's revival successes, so the son confronted Jerry Falwell's political ambitions in no uncertain terms. Bob Jones Jr. held long, agonizing personal meetings with Falwell to hash out their differences. According to Jones, Falwell insisted that he was a fundamentalist and that Liberty was indeed a fundamentalist school.[116] The two men could not agree, however, on the extent to which a true fundamentalist could collaborate with non-fundamentalists. Just as his father had accused Billy Graham in the 1950s, Bob Jones Jr. insisted that Falwell's inclusive conservatism would lead inexorably to heresy and spiritual contamination. By the middle of 1980, Jones had washed his hands of Falwell. The Liberty leader, Jones charged, had "no sense of integrity and ethics." Falwell might "loudly proclaim [him]self a Fundamentalist," Jones said, but there was no religious leader of any stripe who was "more crooked, unethical, and deceptive."[117]

## Bob Jones University v. United States

The fundamentalist rivalry between Bob Jones University and Liberty Baptist College did not drive either school out of partisan politics. In the late 1970s and early 1980s, both communities continued to connect their long-standing conservative political activism to the fortunes of the Republican Party. With the electoral triumph of Ronald Reagan in 1980, their support was put to the test. As the case of Bob Jones University's bitter fight for tax exemptions makes clear, fundamentalist colleges were often at the center of political storms. Someone who listened only to the rhetoric of Bob Jones III might think that his school got into politics and out again as its political fortunes whipsawed from triumph to defeat. In fact, however, BJU and other fundamentalist and evangelical schools had always been and would always be involved in political horse-trading.

As we saw in Chapter 8, the most explosive and contentious political issues on the campuses of many fundamentalist schools in the 1970s were those of racial desegregation and tax-exempt status. Under the Carter administration, the Internal Revenue Service put new rules in place to determine tax exemptions. It would no longer be enough for a college to insist that its admissions were open to any student. If a school had no significant minority enrollment, it was required to prove that it actively recruited minority students. If schools—including elementary and secondary schools as well as colleges and universities—could not enroll at least 20 percent of the school-age population in their communities, they would be classified as segregatory institutions, not eligible for tax exemption.[118]

The political response was enormous. Outraged fundamentalists flooded Congress and the IRS with hundreds of thousands of letters.[119] As conservative operative Paul Weyrich famously argued, the issue of tax exemptions for segregated evangelical schools packed more political punch than did "abortion, school prayer, or the ERA."[120]

The leaders of the GOP took notice. The Republican Party platform in 1980 declared the party's plan to "halt the unconstitutional regulatory vendetta launched by Mr. Carter's IRS commissioner against independent schools."[121] Candidate Ronald Reagan's campaign literature declared that Reagan "opposes the IRS's attempt to remove the tax-exempt status of private schools by administrative fiat."[122]

And fundamentalists reciprocated. At least in part, evangelical and fundamentalist support propelled Reagan to electoral victory in 1980.[123] For a while, BJU's support of Reagan seemed to have paid off. For his part, President Bob Jones III crowed in 1981 that his school had triumphed. "The power to tax," Jones wrote to the extended BJU community, "is indeed the power to destroy." By mobilizing the political might of fundamentalism, BJU had managed to jerk back the chain of "certain bureaucrats" who had targeted the school unfairly.[124]

In 1982, the Reagan administration threw out the reviled IRS policy, which meant that BJU and other schools could maintain their tax exemption without pursing active desegregation policies. President Reagan, however, didn't seem to understand how that action would intersect with the politics of racial segregation. When twenty lawyers resigned in protest from his Justice Department, Reagan quickly reversed himself.[125]

The leader of BJU did not take the reversal lightly. Bob Jones III called President Reagan "a traitor to God's people."[126] The time had come for Jones to take his fundamentalist supporters and quit the GOP, he said. As Jones put it, "It might be good for us to stay away from the polls and let their ship sink."[127] But BJU did not give up on its legal case. It pursued its case for religious liberty all the way to the U.S. Supreme Court, finally losing with an eight-to-one decision in May 1983.[128]

It is tempting to understand the case of *Bob Jones University v. United States* as an example of the ways fundamentalists entered mainstream politics, only to retreat back to their churches and campuses when things didn't go their way. That description, after all, was the way fundamentalist leaders such as the Bob Joneses and Jerry Falwell talked. Backing a certain candidate, Bob Jones Jr. had explained, meant "getting into politics."[129] And turning their back on the traitorous Ronald Reagan meant leading "God's people" back out.[130]

Such talk, however, was itself only a political ploy. Obviously, withdrawing votes is just as political an act as writing letters or busing supporters to polling places. Long before its fight with the IRS, the BJU community had been engaged with mainstream politics. And long after BJU lost its case, BJU leaders and students would continue to be engaged in culture-war politics. Indeed, BJU's threatened withdrawal of support for Reagan earned BJU some scraps of influence in the Reagan White House. President Reagan was not willing or able to back BJU's segregatory practices publicly, but he could and did appoint George Youstra of the BJU faculty to serve as an undersecretary of education.[131] President Reagan might not have supported BJU as much as the Bob Joneses would have liked, but Reagan did appoint William Rehnquist—the only Supreme Court justice to have voted in favor of BJU—to be chief justice of the Supreme Court.[132]

For Bob Jones Jr., who by 1982 was serving as BJU's chancellor, Reagan's flip-flop in the IRS case was unforgivable. As he told a top BJU administrator, Reagan had "double-crossed and betrayed us." At the same time, however, Jones bragged about his continuing close connections at the top levers of political power. Reagan might have surrounded himself with "rascals and 'liberals,'" Jones wrote, but Reagan also included a Bob Jones University alumnus on his staff. That loyal grad fed Jones a steady diet of inside information and gossip. Even as Jones blasted the "vicious blacks on the staff" in the Reagan administration, he claimed to enjoy his own special insider's access to the goings-on in Washington.[133]

## *The Same Old Christian Right*

The battles at Bob Jones University in the early 1980s were certainly political. Like other conservative evangelicals and fundamentalists, the leaders of BJU mobilized in favor of Republican Party candidates and expected political rewards. And when those rewards were not quite as fulsome as the Bob Joneses hoped, they fulminated angrily against Reagan and other GOP leaders. But those fulminations never represented a withdrawal from political activism. Rather, they were only the latest example of the long-standing political tradition among conservative evangelicals. For generations, the campuses of evangelical and fundamentalist colleges had been hotbeds of political thought and activism. When political campaigns succeeded, evangelicals and fundamentalists talked as if they were part of a widespread political revival, as if they were getting into politics. When such campaigns failed, fundamentalist school leaders talked as if they were a righteous beleaguered remnant, as if they were shaking the political dust from their feet and walking away. In fact, however, the campuses of evangelical and fundamentalist schools had always been and would always be intensely political places.

And, as ever, questions of politics and political influence remained inextricably bound up with other questions of proper Christian belief. Evangelicals wondered if they could vote for progressive political causes. They wondered, too, if they might consider mainstream ideas about science. Even the most insightful and involved insiders had trouble predicting how their schools would behave. As the turbulent case of Russell Mixter showed, evangelical scientists might claim the confidence of their colleagues, yet not the support of their anxious institutions. Young-earth creationism became a new generation's test for fundamentalist schools, a new way to define ancient orthodoxy and to divide true fundamentalism from false evangelicalism. And school administrators, even at schools that had embraced the neo-evangelical reform, tried hard to remain attractive to students from all sides of the conservative-evangelical family.

In every case, every variety of creationist thought insisted that it was the real creationism, that it taught both the best science and the best religion. After all, visions of creationism represented more than just schools of thought. They often represented brick-and-mortar schools, schools that could never admit to offering either lower-quality science or lower-quality religion. Every college, every institute, every university, and every seminary always insisted that it offered the very best in modern thinking and the very best in religious purity. If a school such as Wheaton College moved away from young-earth thinking, it did so with a cautious stutter step, always reassuring members of the broad evangelical public that it offered students both the best science and the purest faith. And if the leaders of Liberty Baptist College embraced young-earth creationism as the sole acceptable type of creationism, they also promoted their school's abundant offerings as the very best modern scientific education.

They had to. By the 1960s, as we've seen, evangelical and fundamentalist school leaders were keenly aware of the intense competition they faced from one another. A fundamentalist school might trumpet its impeccable young-earth doctrine, while an evangelical institution might brag about its mainstream scientific credentials, but both types of schools always insisted that they offered students a modern scientific education that would nurture and protect true Christian faith.

# *Epilogue*

## SANDALS OF THE EVANGELICAL MIND

*Yes, when I call "fellow humans who happen to be Muslims [or Jews or atheists] my brothers and sisters" I am standing in full agreement with the Wheaton College statement of faith.*

—TENURED WHEATON POLITICAL SCIENCE PROFESSOR LARYCIA HAWKINS, December 17, 2015[1]

*Thankful the embattled leaders @WheatonCollege are putting theological integrity over political correctness. Pray God will help them.*

—BOB JONES UNIVERSITY PRESIDENT STEVEN PETTIT, December 19, 2015[2]

### *The More Things Change . . .*

Thanks to a research grant from the Spencer Foundation, I spent the 2014–2015 school year buried in the archives of six of the schools that feature so prominently in these pages: Wheaton, Gordon, Biola, Moody, Bob Jones, and Liberty. Every once in a while, I came up for air. When I did, I noticed how very similar in some ways the campuses were to my home campus, but yet at times how strikingly different. For example, if you took away the warm weather and sunshine, the scene outside the library at Biola might have been the scene outside the library at Binghamton University or the University of Wisconsin. The students were dressed in identical non-uniforms: jeans, flip-flops, and carefully slovenly T-shirts. They seemed to spend their time in similar ways: skateboarding, playing guitar, and chatting. They carried the same ubiquitous coffee mugs and smartphones. But when you walk around Biola's campus you can suddenly come face-to-face with a huge mural of Jesus, thirty feet tall. And when you browse through the curriculum library at Biola you can read US history textbooks that explain the origins of Native Americans as part of the fallout from the collapse of the tower of Babel.[3] You won't find such things on the walls of my campus or in my school's textbook library.

Things at Liberty University, too, can seem very similar to those on any other university campus, if maybe a little—or a lot—nicer. The school's leaders, after all, have won the higher-education lottery, investing at the right time in the possibilities of online education.[4] And they have plowed that money into brick-and-mortar facilities.[5] The archives room, for example, is tastefully decorated and gently lit, with several large tables open to researchers. The school employs a full-time archivist and a small army of smiling student assistants. More impressive to most visitors, probably, is the all-year snowboarding hill built at great expense into the nearby hillside. (A friendly fundamentalist student told me it was made of something like Velcro, except both fake snow and snow board had only the hooked side. The combination allows boarders to slide down, no matter how hot the weather.) It could seem just like any other booming elite university campus. After a little while, however, you start to notice a strange sound, a sound you wouldn't hear on secular campuses: everywhere on campus, there is Christian contemporary music piped out to sidewalks through a mysterious system of hidden speakers. It serves as an ever-present aural reminder that Liberty is meant to be a different type of school.

My experiences as I traveled from my public university to evangelical and fundamentalist schools could likely have been repeated in nearly any decade of the twentieth century. Though its leaders and students often thought of themselves as something distinct, something different, "Fundamentalist U" has always been inextricably part of America's system of higher education. As we've seen time and time again in these pages, evangelical and fundamentalist institutions of higher education have always faced the same challenges as have other schools. By the middle of the century, for instance, schools all scrambled to adopt standardized admission and graduation requirements. Schools almost all scrimped and sacrificed in order to meet the demands of accreditors. Schools all worried about keeping their students safe. And schools all struggled to pay for it all.[6]

The schools in the fundamentalist and evangelical family have been no different. Nor have the schools in this book been able to keep aloof from the seismic shifts that transformed all colleges and universities. They boomed in the aftermath of the GI Bill. They rocked in the revolutions

FIGURE E.1 "Should I give to the alumni fund?"
A desperate plea familiar to every college and every alum. This one came from Wheaton College, 1947. Courtesy of Archives, Buswell Library, Wheaton College.

and counterrevolutions of the sixties. And these days, just as small secular liberal arts colleges such as Sweet Briar totter on the brink of financial collapse, so too do many fundamentalist schools.[7]

And yet Fundamentalist U has not been just another college or university. Some aspects of life on these campuses have always been and continue to be distinctive. The focus on training missionaries has not abated, for instance, nor has the perennial family feud between neo-evangelicals and fundamentalists. At all the campuses of evangelical and fundamentalist schools, unique battles continue over strict lifestyle rules for students and strict doctrinal beliefs for faculty members. Perhaps most important, yet hardest to put a finger on, is that the schools in this extended and fractious fundamentalist family continue to be subjected to endless external scrutiny. Preachers, pundits, and parents all scour the pages of evangelical and fundamentalist newspapers and websites for any hint that their schools are going soft—however they might define "soft" at the moment. Evangelicals and fundamentalists still expect more from evangelical schools. Throughout all the confrontations and divisions that have raged on these campuses across the twentieth century, there has always been and continues to be a hard-to-define sense among evangelicals and fundamentalists that these are somehow "our" schools, even when they can never quite agree on who "we" are or should be.

In some ways, the twentieth-century history I dug up in the basement archives of these schools can seem worlds away from the vibrant twenty-first-century campus life going on in the quads above. In this century, for example, Bob Jones University has apologized for its racist, segregationist past. It proudly boasts of its accreditation. It even has sports.[8] Maybe most shocking for those who know the history, BJU president Steve Pettit recently paid a friendly visit to Wheaton's campus, the first time in more than a generation that a BJU president had done so.[9]

## . . . *The More They Stay the Same*

The new warmth between BJU and Wheaton is part and parcel of the same durable tensions that have always racked evangelical higher education. The thaw in school relations, after all, came at the same time as a tenured political science professor at Wheaton, Larycia Hawkins, was informed that the college had initiated termination procedures against her. Professor Hawkins had announced that she planned to wear a hijab in solidarity with Muslim women worldwide. After all, Hawkins wrote, Muslims, Jews, and Christians all worshiped the same God.[10]

The specific issue was new, but the pattern was as old as fundamentalism itself. Some faculty members and students protested Hawkins's proposed firing. Some alumni supported it. Outraged evangelical celebrities denounced Wheaton's administrators for both tolerating and not tolerating such notions among its faculty; for example, BJU's president, Steve Pettit, lauded Wheaton's brave commitment to "putting theological integrity over political correctness."[11]

Wheaton's administration dithered. They announced the termination, then they withdrew it, then they announced it again, until finally they announced that they had worked out a settlement with Professor Hawkins under which she would leave amicably.[12]

As had happened repeatedly in the twentieth century, the Hawkins case provoked so much outcry because it prodded perennial sore spots in evangelical higher education. Were her statements really outside the vague boundaries of evangelical orthodoxy? Was she subject to extra scrutiny because she was an African American woman? Could a real college sack a tenured professor over an expression of belief? As we've seen throughout this book, the vagaries of fundamentalism meant that professors at fundamentalist and evangelical colleges have always been subjected to stern and sometimes ferocious scrutiny. Professor Hawkins was only the latest example of the unresolved tensions at the core of evangelical and fundamentalist higher education.

Nor was her case the only one. College-watchers like me experienced a dizzying sense of déjà vu in the goings-on at Bryan College in 2014. Under pressure from creationist pundits such as Ken Ham, Bryan's leaders changed the school's statement of faith. Just as Wheaton College had done under similar pressure in 1961, Bryan College would henceforth require faculty to believe in a real, literal, historical Adam and Eve as the progenitors of the human race.[13]

Predictably, the school community was divided. Some students and alumni protested the decision. Others praised it. Two professors successfully sued the school for changing a school charter that expressly stipulated it would never be changed.[14] The controversy provoked mass resignations; many administrators, nearly half the trustees, and about twenty other employees left in disgust.[15] Insiders and outsiders alike were left with unanswered questions: Why would President Stephen Livesay make such an intensely unpopular move? Why would he insist on tightening a doctrine that many thought was already tight enough? Like all evangelical college presidents, Livesay found himself squeezed by the merciless realities of American evangelical higher education. In order to stay alive, schools need tuition-paying students. And in the twenty-first century, just as in the twentieth, the disapproval of fundamentalist pundits can spell doom. If Ken Ham pronounced Bryan to be soft on evolution, creationist students and their families might go elsewhere. Like all his predecessors throughout the twentieth century, Livesay found himself between a rock and a hard place.[16]

At every school in the network, patterns laid down in the early decades of the twentieth century continued to drive events in the twenty-first. At Bob Jones University in late 2014, for example, investigators blasted BJU's woeful mishandling of charges of sexual abuse.[17] The committee's findings would come as no surprise to those familiar with BJU's history.

First, the committee concluded that students who reported sexual assault or abuse were often dismissed as "gripers." Ever since Bob Jones Sr. denounced complainers as disloyal in the 1920s, voicing dissatisfaction has been the quickest ticket off campus. As a consequence, many victims felt discouraged; they felt as if there was no one to whom they could turn for help. Second, the committee accused BJU administrators of incredible ignorance of state law and mainstream practice when it came to cases of sexual abuse and assault. One school leader, for example—the campus leader in charge of handling student abuse reports—was unaware of state mandatory-reporting laws. Such official ignorance might seem astounding, but it made sense in the light of BJU's practice of valuing loyalty over nearly every other quality. Long before school leadership passed out of the Jones family, the school had put frantic emphasis on loyalty, not expertise.[18] One rose through the ranks at BJU because of impeccable loyalty, not because of impeccable credentials or experience.

## *Fundamentalist U*

In some ways, these recent controversies seem new. BJU, for example, never would have thought to invite outside investigators to its campus during the twentieth century. And no female African American tenured professor had ever before faced Professor Hawkins's dilemma, since she was the first female African American tenured professor at Wheaton. But although the specific details of each case differ, the pattern has remained the same.

There has never been a clear definition of the boundaries of fundamentalism or evangelicalism and the campuses of colleges, universities, seminaries, and Bible institutes have often been the places at which those boundaries were endlessly debated. It has been too easy for historians to read the careful ponderings of fundamentalist intellectuals about the proper definition of "new evangelical" or "fundamentalist," about creationism and science, about sexuality and racism, and assume that those definitions answered the questions once and for all. In fact, as we've seen over and over again, fundamentalist and evangelical institutions offered not one definition but many. At many schools, administrators hoped to keep the boundaries as wide and as fuzzy as possible, in order to attract as many students as possible and to keep their reputations as "safe" schools for fundamentalist and evangelical students.

And it has not only been the "fundamentalist" part of Fundamentalist U that has been unclear. American higher education as a whole has always been in flux, and it still is. There have never been simple, satisfying answers to some basic questions. What is the purpose of higher education? Is it professional training? Personal growth? Intellectual exploration? Social networking? It has always been all these things, and more. The schools in this book have added new elements to those questions, but they have never disputed the validity of the questions themselves or the vagaries of the answers. For example, fundamentalist and evangelical colleges promised to prepare students to be doctors and lawyers, but also to be missionaries and Sunday-school teachers. They promised personal growth, but always in secure evangelical and fundamentalist directions. Schools advertised their intellectual excellence, but made sure it was always guided by distinctly evangelical intellectual traditions. And finally, evangelical and fundamentalist schools offered a social experience that would shape students' lives and future families in reliably religious ways.

In short, if we want to understand either fundamentalism or higher education, we need to see that they have always been in a state of awkward tension. The exigencies of institutional life have shaped fundamentalism, pulling together sides of a family that often seemed determined to splinter apart. And fundamentalism has changed the landscape of American higher education, offering students and their families a way to experience higher education without enduring the presumed secular bias of mainstream colleges and universities. In every case, in every decade, at every school, students, alumni, faculty, parents, administrators, and nosy neighbors scrambled to figure out how to remain true to evangelical belief and true to the demands of higher education, even as the definitions of both kept changing.

# *Research Appendix*

Those of us who try to make sense of fundamentalism face a dilemma: how can we study something if none of us is entirely clear on what that something is? As I began the research for this book, I struggled to establish a working definition of the type of schools on which I would focus. I needed to impose some boundaries on the inherently amorphous family of fundamentalist colleges, seminaries, institutes, and universities without doing damage to the historical realities. My goal had to be something more tightly focused than simply "conservative religious" colleges, or even "conservative Protestant" ones, or even "conservative evangelical Protestant" schools.

For starters, I limited my reach to interdenominational evangelical Protestant schools that identified as part of the fundamentalist movement in some way, at some point of time. To put it another way, I focused on schools that used words like "we" and "us" when they talked about fundamentalism in the 1920s, 1930s, and 1940s, not "they" and "them."

Due to limitations of time, space, and resources, I did not focus as closely on denominational colleges, though as historians such as Darren Dochuk, Bethany Moreton, Christopher Gehrz, Michael S. Hamilton, and others have shown, many of them contributed significantly to conservative evangelical higher education in a variety of ways.[1] I also didn't look at other sorts of religious schools, though they certainly had some similar experiences and shared some of those experiences with the leaders of the evangelical collegiate network.

Instead, I faced the challenge of including a wide enough section of this unique school network to see beyond the particularities of any one school or of any one type of school, yet keeping a tight enough focus that I could speak in something other than vague generalities. Thanks to a generous grant from the Spencer Foundation, I spent the academic year 2014–2015 traveling to the archives of schools in this network. I had to decide which schools to begin with, which schools to focus on. Sometimes external factors dictated my choices. For example, I tried to visit Bryan College in Tennessee, but those archives were not open to outside researchers. I hoped to visit Tennessee Temple University, but it closed abruptly.

Of the archives I could visit, I had to allot my time and effort carefully. If I couldn't get to the archives of every college that thought of itself as fundamentalist, I wanted at least to be sure I visited schools that represented the diversity among the network of interdenominational conservative evangelical schools. I wanted schools from all around the country. I also wanted schools that represented the Bible institute/Bible college tradition, graduate seminaries, and the liberal arts college/university path. Of course, I absolutely needed to study schools that represented both the continuing self-identified "fundamentalist" tradition as well as those fundamentalist schools that moved to a self-identification as "neo-evangelical" or simply "evangelical."

In practice, I ended up with a sort of flagship approach. I favored schools that had a history going back at least to the 1920s. And I spent my time first in the archives of schools that had a wider influence in the network. As an added benefit, those schools tended to be the ones that also had the largest archival collections. Each of the schools whose archives I visited in person satisfied more than one of my desirable categories.

I was also interested in schools I didn't visit in person. Bryan College, for example, has made its yearbooks and other periodicals available online, and I read such sources avidly. More important, many of the schools that considered themselves part of this fundamentalist/evangelical network were well represented in the archives of the schools I was able to visit. School leaders corresponded tirelessly with one another and hashed out the meanings of higher education and specifically of fundamentalist higher education at all the schools, not just the ones whose archives I dug into. Students compared schools in this network as they decided where to go to college. Alumni and interested fundamentalist bystanders actively compared the goings-on at these institutions to one another. Was Westmont College becoming too liberal? Or not liberal enough? Should Messiah, Bethel, Taylor, or Seattle Pacific be part of the nascent Christian College Consortium? Did Pensacola Christian College represent true fundamentalism? How could Bible institutes across the country—from Philadelphia to Multnomah—learn from bigger schools such as Moody Bible Institute to chart their own path from "institute" to "college" to "university"? And did they want to?

I also spent time with the rich trove of periodicals emanating from the world of conservative evangelical Protestantism. Titles such as *Christianity Today, Sword of the Lord, Christian Beacon, Searchlight, Christian Fundamentals in School and Church, Moody Monthly, Our Hope, King's Business,* and *Sunday School Times* all included a wealth of information and debate about evangelical higher education as a whole, not just about the schools I visited.

As with all research, the more I uncovered, the more I wanted to dig. New questions kept popping up, some of which have been addressed by historians and other scholars, but many of which have not. For example, what has been the experience of evangelical students at non-evangelical colleges? How have evangelical schools worked with or learned from other religious schools, such as Catholic ones? What

**Table A.1**

| | Moody Bible Institute | Wheaton College | Gordon College | Dallas Theological Seminary (visited in 2008) | Westminster Theological Seminary (visited in 2009) | Biola University | Liberty University | Bob Jones University |
|---|---|---|---|---|---|---|---|---|
| Southern | | | | 📖 | | 📖 | 📖 | 📖 |
| Eastern | | | 📖 | | 📖 | | | |
| Western | | | | | | 📖 | | |
| Midwestern | 📖 | 📖 | | | | | | |
| Fundamentalist | | | | 📖 | 📖 | | 📖 | 📖 |
| Evangelical | 📖 | 📖 | 📖 | | | 📖 | | |
| Bible institute | 📖 | | 📖 | | | 📖 | | |
| Founded 1920s or before | 📖 | 📖 | 📖 | 📖 | 📖 | 📖 | | 📖 |
| Seminary (as the main focus of my archival research) | | | | 📖 | 📖 | | | |

has it been like to be a non-evangelical student at a staunchly evangelical school, or to be a student from one of the smaller denominations? What long-term effect has attendance at a conservative evangelical college had on students as they've moved on to families and careers?

In this book, I have asked a different set of questions. I've tried to examine not only the ways these fundamentalist colleges, universities, seminaries, and institutes have helped define the meanings of evangelicalism but also the ways they've shaped the wider network of American higher education. I've wondered about the experiences of students at these schools as well as the experiences of faculty and administration. How have these colleges been unique, and how have they fallen in line with dominant trends in American education and culture? Given that these have been the leading institutions of conservative evangelicalism, I've tried to uncover just what it meant to them across the twentieth century to be both "conservative" and "evangelical," when those terms have themselves undergone enormous transformations.

## SELECT ARCHIVAL SOURCES

### *Archive Collections*

Archives of the Billy Graham Center, Wheaton, Illinois
- Elisabeth Howard Elliot Papers
- John Abram Huffman Sr. Papers
- Harold Lindsell Papers

Biola University Archives, La Mirada, California
- J. Richard Chase Papers
- Samuel Sutherland Papers

Bob Jones University Archives, Greenville, South Carolina
- Fundamentalism File
- W. O. H. Garman Papers
- Gilbert Stenholm Papers
- "Turner Box": copied files collected by Dr. Daniel L. Turner for his *Standing Without Apology: The History of Bob Jones University* (Greenville: BJU Press, 1997), encompassing administrative files as well as correspondence to and from school leaders including Bob Jones Sr., Bob Jones Jr., and Bob Jones III

Dallas Theological Seminary Archives, Dallas, Texas
- Lewis Sperry Chafer Papers

Gordon College Archives, Wenham, Massachusetts
- President's Office Papers, 1918–1969
- Nathan Robinson Wood Papers

Liberty University Archives, Lynchburg, Virginia
- Jerry Falwell Papers

Pierre Guillermin Papers
Student Affairs Papers
Moody Bible Institute Archives, Chicago, Illinois
William Culbertson Papers
Faculty Rules Collection
James M. Gray Papers
William Houghton Papers
Student Discipline Collection
Student Life Collection
Student Records Collection
Westminster Theological Seminary Archives, Philadelphia, Pennsylvania
J. Gresham Machen Papers
Wheaton College Archives, Billy Graham Center, Wheaton, Illinois
Hudson T. Armerding Papers
J. Oliver Buswell Papers
V. Raymond Edman Papers
Student Publications File

### *Student Newspapers and Yearbooks*

*Announcements* (Liberty University)
*The Biolan* (Biola University)
*Biola Alumni Annuals* (Biola University)
*Brave Son* (unofficial—Wheaton College)
*The Broadcaster* (Gordon College)
*Bryan Blueprint* (Bryan College)
*Bryan Life* (Bryan College)
*The Catacomb* (unofficial—Biola University)
*Chimes* (Biola University)
*The Collegian* (Liberty University)
*The Commoner* (Bryan College)
*Critique* (unofficial—Wheaton College)
*Crucible* (unofficial—Wheaton College)
*The Eight* (unofficial—Moody Bible Institute)
*The Evangelical Student* (copies in Machen Papers, Westminster; Chafer Papers, Dallas)
*Evangelical Theological College Bulletin* (Dallas Theological Seminary)
*Hypernikon* (Gordon College)
*Kodon* (Wheaton College)
*Liberty Baptist College Newsletter* (Liberty University)
*The Liberty Republican* (Unofficial—Liberty University)
*Little Moby's Post* (Bob Jones University)

*Moody Memo* (Moody Bible Institute)
*Moody Student* (Moody Bible Institute)
*The Newsette* (Bryan College)
*Tartan* (Gordon College)
*The Trumpet* (Liberty University)
*Wheaton Record* (Wheaton College)

### *Oral Histories*

Archives of the Billy Graham Center, Wheaton, Illinois
- William John Barnett
- Wayne G. Bragg
- Margaret L. Clapper
- Paul A. Contento
- Vincent Leroy Crossett
- Jesse Wilbert Hoover
- John Abram Huffman
- Melvin David Suttie
- Paul Dean Votaw
- Elizabeth Howard Warner

Bob Jones University Archives, Greenville, South Carolina
- Garland Babb
- Jim Bellis
- Bud Bierman
- Stewart Custer
- John Dreisbach
- Bill Fulton
- Coretta Grass
- William Liverman
- Joan Mulfinger
- Joyce Parks

# *Notes*

ABBREVIATIONS USED IN THE NOTES

| | |
|---|---|
| AP | Hudson Armerding Papers, Wheaton College Archives, Wheaton, Illinois |
| BGC | Archives of the Billy Graham Center, Wheaton, Illinois |
| BJUFF | Bob Jones University Fundamentalism File, Bob Jones University, Greenville, South Carolina |
| BP | J. Oliver Buswell Papers, Wheaton College Archives, Wheaton, Illinois |
| CP | William Culbertson Papers, Moody Bible Institute Archives, Chicago, Illinois |
| EEP | Elisabeth Elliot Papers, Collection 278, Archives of the Billy Graham Center, Wheaton, Illinois |
| EP | V. Raymond Edman Papers, Wheaton College Archives, Wheaton, Illinois |
| FP | Jerry Falwell Papers, Liberty University Archives, Lynchburg, Virginia |
| GP | James M. Gray Papers, Moody Bible Institute Archives, Chicago, Illinois |
| GSP | Gilbert Stenholm Papers, Bob Jones University Archives, Greenville, South Carolina |
| HLP | Harold Lindsell Papers, Collection 192, Archives of the Billy Graham Center, Wheaton, Illinois |
| POP | President's Office Papers, Gordon College Archives, Wenham, Massachusetts |
| SP | Samuel Sutherland Papers, Biola University Archives, La Mirada, California |
| SRC | Student Records Collection, Moody Bible Institute Archives, Chicago, Illinois |
| TB | "Turner Box": copied files collected by Dr. Daniel L. Turner for his *Standing Without Apology: The History of Bob Jones University* (Greenville: BJU Press, 1997). Bob Jones University Archives, Greenville, South Carolina |

## INTRODUCTION

1. *Wheaton College v. Burwell*, 573 US (2014).
2. Evan Allen, "Gordon College Leader Joins Request for Exemption to Hiring Rule," *Boston Globe*, July 4, 2014.
3. Jeb Bush, "Liberty Commencement 2015," May 9, 2015, https://www.youtube.com/watch?v=QzQyu5Sp2b8 (accessed May 29, 2015).
4. Daniel K. Williams, *God's Own Party: The Making of the Christian Right* (New York: Oxford University Press, 2010), 191.
5. Virginia L. Brereton, *Training God's Army: The American Bible School, 1880–1940* (Bloomington: Indiana University Press, 1990), xviii.
6. David Gibson, "Bob Jones University Questions 'Fundamentalist' Label," *HuffPost Religion*, November 21, 2011.
7. See Kathryn Lofton, "Commonly Modern: Rethinking the Modernist-Fundamentalist Controversies," *Church History* 83 (March 2014): 141–144.
8. George Marsden, *Reforming Fundamentalism: Fuller Seminary and the New Evangelicalism* (Grand Rapids, MI: Eerdmans, 1987), 162.
9. See, for example, T. M. Luhrmann, *When God Talks Back: Understanding the American Evangelical Relationship with God* (New York: Knopf, 2012).
10. Molly Worthen, *Apostles of Reason: The Crisis of Authority in American Evangelicalism* (New York: Oxford University Press, 2014), 38–39.
11. See Darren Dochuk, *From Bible Belt to Sun Belt: Plain-Folk Religion, Grassroots Politics, and the Rise of Evangelical Conservatism* (New York: Norton, 2011), 113, 129–133, 209–222; Bethany Moreton, *To Serve God and Wal-Mart: The Making of Christian Free Enterprise* (Cambridge, MA: Harvard University Press, 2009), 163–168.

## CHAPTER 1

1. A. A. Baker, *The Successful Christian School: Foundational Principles for Starting and Operating a Successful Christian School* (Pensacola, FL: A Beka Book Publications, 1979), 34.
2. See, for example, B. Gray Allison, "The American Campus as a Spiritual Force," *Christianity Today*, May 10, 1968, 5; Baker, *The Successful Christian School*, 34; Samuel L. Blumenfeld, *Is Public Education Necessary?* (Old Greenwich, CT: Devin-Adair, 1981), 15.
3. John R. Thelin, *A History of American Higher Education* (Baltimore: Johns Hopkins University Press, 2004), 20–23.
4. Roger L. Geiger, *The History of American Higher Education: Learning and Culture from the Founding to World War II* (Princeton, NJ: Princeton University Press, 2015), 1.
5. George M. Marsden, *The Soul of the American University: From Protestant Establishment to Established Nonbelief* (New York: Oxford University Press, 1994), 41.

6. Geiger, *History of American Higher Education*, 5.
7. Marsden, *Soul of the American University*, 52.
8. Quoted in Geiger, *History of American Higher Education*, 28.
9. Marsden, *Soul of the American University*, 61.
10. Geiger, *History of American Higher Education*, 3.
11. John Corrigan, "Catholick Congregational Clergy and Public Piety," *Church History* 60 (June 1991): 210–222.
12. Geiger, *History of American Higher Education*, 21.
13. Ibid., 49–50.
14. Ibid., 29–30.
15. Jeremiah Day et al., *Reports on the Course of Instruction in Yale College* (New Haven, CT: Hezekiah Howe, 1828), in *Liberal Education for a Land of Colleges: Yale's* Reports *of 1828*, ed. David B. Potts (New York: Palgrave Macmillan, 2010), 7. Emphasis in original.
16. Susan B. Carter and Claudia Goldin, eds., "Table Bc523-536—Enrollment in Institutions of Higher Education by Sex, Enrollment Status, and Type of Institution: 1869–1995," *Historical Statistics of the United States, Millennial Edition Online* (Washington, DC: US Bureau of the Census, 2006). By way of contrast, only 2.3 percent of the same age group (18–24-year-olds) were enrolled in colleges in 1904; 6.7 percent in 1925; 14.7 percent in 1948; 23.8 percent in 1959; 35.8 percent in 1970, and 56.6 percent in 1995.
17. Geiger, *History of American Higher Education*, 79.
18. Marsden, *Soul of the American University*, 240.
19. Geiger, *History of American Higher Education*, 126.
20. Ibid., 275, 384, 481.
21. Ibid., 136–138. This Timothy Dwight IV should not be confused with his grandson Timothy Dwight V, who led Yale between 1886 and 1899. The younger President Dwight also presided over institutional innovations, such as turning Yale College into Yale University. See Julie A. Reuben, *The Making of the Modern University: Intellectual Transformation and the Marginalization of Morality* (Chicago: University of Chicago Press, 1996), 71–72.
22. Quoted in Potts, ed., *Liberal Education for a Land of Colleges*, 24.
23. Ibid., 339.
24. See Reuben, *The Making of the Modern University*, 4, 61–73; see also Andrew Jewett, *Science, Democracy, and the American University: From the Civil War to the Cold War* (New York: Cambridge University Press, 2014).
25. Geiger, *History of American Higher Education*, 281–307; Thelin, *A History of American Higher Education*, 75–83.
26. Laurence R. Veysey, *The Emergence of the American University* (Chicago: University of Chicago Press, 1965), 2.
27. Geiger, *History of American Higher Education*, 316.
28. Quoted in Reuben, *Making of the Modern University*, 91.

29. The first Ph.D. granted in the United States was at Yale in 1861. See Roger L. Geiger, *To Advance Knowledge: The Growth of American Research Universities, 1900–1940* (New York: Oxford University Press, 1986), 4.
30. Quoted in Marsden, *Soul of the American University*, 221.
31. Geiger, *History of American Higher Education*, 326.
32. David P. Setran, *The College "Y": Student Religion in the Era of Secularization* (New York: Palgrave Macmillan, 2007), 3–4.
33. Geiger, *History of American Higher Education*, 365–376, quotation on 375.
34. See, for example, Adam R. Nelson, *Education and Democracy: The Meaning of Alexander Meiklejohn, 1872–1964* (Madison: University of Wisconsin Press, 2001), 45–49. Dean Meiklejohn tried hard to limit the anti-democratic influence of professionalized sports at Brown, to no effect.
35. James Burrill Angell, *The Old and the New Ideal of Scholars: A Baccalaureate Address Delivered June 18, 1905* (Ann Arbor: University of Michigan Press, 1905), 3.
36. Jon H. Roberts and James Turner, *The Sacred and the Secular University* (Princeton, NJ: Princeton University Press, 2000), 21–22.
37. Jewett, *Science, Democracy, and the American University*, 10.
38. Ibid., 13.
39. Roberts and Turner, *Sacred and Secular University*, 70.
40. Andrew Dickson White, *The Cornell University: What It Is, and What It Is Not* (Ithaca, NY: Cornell University Press, 1872), 20.
41. Ibid., 24–27.
42. Marsden, *Soul of the American University*, 115.
43. White, *The Cornell University*, 28.
44. Ibid., 3.
45. Ibid., 27.
46. Ibid., 3.
47. Harold Bolce, "Blasting at the Rock of Ages," *Cosmopolitan*, May 1909, 665.
48. Ibid., 669.
49. Ibid., 670.
50. Andrew Dickson White, *The History of Warfare Between Science and Theology in Christendom* (New York: D. Appleton, 1896); *Seven Great Statesmen in the Warfare of Humanity with Unreason* (New York: Century, 1910).
51. Thelin, *A History of American Higher Education*, 157–158.
52. George Marsden, *Reforming Fundamentalism: Fuller Seminary and the New Evangelicalism* (Grand Rapids, MI: Eerdmans, 1987), 214.

## CHAPTER 2

1. J. Frank Norris, "A Mother's Son," *Searchlight*, May 12, 1921, 2. This apocryphal quotation proved popular among fundamentalist activists. It was picked up, for instance, by anti-evolution leader T. T. Martin in his book *Hell and the*

*High School: Christ or Evolution, Which?* (Kansas City, MO: Western Baptist Publishing, 1923), 155.

2. George S. May, "Des Moines University and Dr. T. T. Shields," *Iowa Journal of History* (July 1956): 225–226; Adam Laats, *Fundamentalism and Education in the Scopes Era: God, Darwin, and the Roots of America's Culture Wars* (New York: Palgrave Macmillan, 2010), 130–131.
3. William Bell Riley, "Editorial," *Christian Fundamentalist* (December 1927): 31; William Bell Riley, "The Redemption of Des Moines University," *Christian Fundamentalist* (August 1927): 6; J. Frank Norris, "A Modern Miracle," *Fundamentalist* (June 24, 1927): 8–9; "Educated—What For?," *King's Business*, May 1928, 269–270.
4. May, "Des Moines University," 197, 201–205, 211–213; Laats, *Fundamentalism and Education in the Scopes Era*, 131.
5. See William R. Hutchison, *The Modernist Impulse in American Protestantism* (Cambridge, MA: Harvard University Press, 1976).
6. See Brendan M. Pietsch, *Dispensational Modernism* (New York: Oxford University Press, 2015), 12; see also Matthew Avery Sutton, "New Trends in the Historiography of American Fundamentalism," *Journal of American Studies* 51 (2017): 235–241.
7. Timothy E. W. Gloege, *Guaranteed Pure: The Moody Bible Institute, Business, and the Making of Modern Evangelicalism* (Chapel Hill: University of North Carolina Press, 2015), 163.
8. George M. Marsden, *Fundamentalism and American Culture: The Shaping of Twentieth Century Evangelicalism, 1870–1925*, 2nd ed. (New York: Oxford University Press, 2006), 173–175.
9. William V. Trollinger, *God's Empire: William Bell Riley and Midwestern Fundamentalism* (Madison: University of Wisconsin Press, 1990), 163.
10. J. Frank Norris, in *Searchlight*, October 26, 1923, 1.
11. See, for example, Frederick Lewis Allen, *Only Yesterday: An Informal History of the Nineteen-Twenties*, 2nd ed. (New York: Harper and Bros., 1959, orig. 1931), 171; William F. Leuchtenberg, *The Perils of Prosperity, 1914–1932*, 2nd ed. (Chicago: University of Chicago Press, 1993, orig. 1958), 224; Norman F. Furniss, *The Fundamentalist Controversy, 1918–1931* (New Haven, CT: Yale University Press, 1954), 178–181.
12. Joel A. Carpenter, *Revive Us Again: The Reawakening of American Fundamentalism* (New York: Oxford University Press, 1997), 3.
13. The first historical look at fundamentalism was Stewart G. Cole's *History of Fundamentalism* (Westport, CT: Greenwood Press, 1931). Cole damned fundamentalists as a "cult" (304, 306) led by "disturbed men" (251) whose religious fervor reflected a "psychotic condition" (250). An influential article by H. Richard Niebuhr in the 1931 *Encyclopedia of Social Sciences* supported this contention ("Fundamentalism," in *The Encyclopedia of the Social Sciences*, ed. Edwin R. A. Seligman, 526–527 [New York: Macmillan, 1931]). Niebuhr declared that

fundamentalism came from an older, more rural America. It resulted from an unhealthy and outdated "static" social environment, one sure to give way to the steamroller of modernity. In 1954, Norman Furniss essentially endorsed this limited definition in his book, *The Fundamentalist Controversy, 1918–1931* (New Haven, CT: Yale University Press, 1954).

A newer generation of historians, themselves often from evangelical backgrounds, overturned these shortsighted definitions. In *The Roots of Fundamentalism: British and American Millenarianism, 1800–1930* (Chicago: University of Chicago Press, 1970), Ernest R. Sandeen defined fundamentalism as a movement based in the theology of premillennialism. In articles and his 1980 book, *Fundamentalism and American Culture: The Shaping of American Evangelicalism* (New York: Oxford University Press), George M. Marsden agreed that premillennial theology was an important distinctive element of fundamentalism, but insisted that fundamentalism had always included a broader array of religious, cultural, and intellectual themes. (See also Marsden, "Defining Fundamentalism," *Christian Scholar's Review* 1 [Winter 1971]: 141–151, and Sandeen, "Defining Fundamentalism, A Reply to Professor Marsden," *Christian Scholar's Review* 1 [Spring 1971]: 227–232. And see George M. Marsden, *Fundamentalism and American Culture: The Shaping of American Evangelicalism*, 2nd ed. [New York: Oxford University Press, 2006], 199–228.) Marsden's nuanced definition inspired a burst of scholarly studies of fundamentalism in all its cultural complexity, including Carpenter, *Revive Us Again*; Trollinger, *God's Empire*; Virginia L. Brereton, *Training God's Army: The American Bible School, 1880–1940* (Bloomington; Indiana University Press, 1990); and a host of others, including the author's own *Fundamentalism and Education in the Scopes Era*.

Some historians have insisted on the need for a narrow definition for fundamentalism, because in the words of Joel Carpenter, "more generic usage obscures more than it illumines" (*Revive Us Again*, 4). Carpenter was especially leery of commentators who slapped a "fundamentalist" label on any and all conservatives or conservative Protestants. As he argued, "Labelling movements, sects, and traditions such as the Pentecostals, Mennonites, Seventh-day Adventists, Missouri Synod Lutherans, Jehovah's Witnesses, Churches of Christ, black Baptists, Mormons, Southern Baptists, and holiness Wesleyans as fundamentalists belittles their great diversity and violates their unique identities" (4).

Religious distinctions are certainly vital, but they are not enough. As Carpenter also noted, fundamentalism was more than just theology; it was "a way of life with a subculture to sustain its doctrinal distinctives" (*Revive Us Again*, 3). Recently, historian Matthew Sutton has similarly argued that we can understand fundamentalism as "radical apocalyptic evangelicalism," but we must always remember that the fundamentalist "agenda was always about more than correct theology" (*American Apocalypse: A History of Modern Evangelicalism* [Cambridge, MA: Harvard University Press, 2014], 3, 130).

To comprehend fundamentalism as it was lived in institutions of higher education, doctrinal distinctives matter, but they can't tell the whole story. After all, we can't tell a fundamentalist college from other sorts of colleges based only on such theological considerations. Fundamentalist colleges were not merely schools that taught a single, clearly defined fundamentalist theology. For one thing, as devotedly interdenominational institutions, their theology was eclectic and willfully unsystematic. Moreover, they incorporated into their guiding principles a range of broadly conservative notions about culture, politics, and society along with their conservative evangelical theology. For the leaders, faculty, students, and alumni of those schools, such things became an important part of what it meant to be a fundamentalist, of what it meant to have gone to a fundamentalist school.

As historian Timothy E. W. Gloege has argued recently, at fundamentalist schools such as Moody Bible Institute, fundamentalism was more than a set of "manifestos and theological propositions." Rather, its "life force was its corporate evangelical framework," which worked more like a set of "unexamined first principles—as common sense." Fundamentalism is better understood as a certain "grammar" than as a checklist of religious beliefs (*Guaranteed Pure*, 3).

For all these reasons, we will be wise to stick with a broad and inclusive understanding of fundamentalism. If we hope to make sense of the ways fundamentalist students, school leaders, and observers contended endlessly over whether or not a particular colleges was truly fundamentalist, we need to acknowledge that claims about true fundamentalism could not be checked against traditional authorities, because fundamentalism itself represented something new. Nor could fundamentalism ever be defined once and for all by theological creeds alone, because those creeds themselves were open to endless dispute and were accompanied by vague but vital conservative attitudes toward society, knowledge, politics, and America.

14. *Congressional Record*, 69th Congress, 1st Session, LXVII—Part 5, 5748.
15. J. H. Ralston, "Our Monthly Potpourri," *Moody Bible Institute Monthly*, April 1925, 371–372; Neil Staebler and John S. Diekhoff, "Religion at Michigan," *Michigan Chimes*, March 1925, 28–29, 57.
16. J. Gresham Machen, "What Fundamentalism Now Stands For," *New York Times*, June 21, 1925.
17. "Blanton, Thomas Lindsay," Texas State Historical Association, https://tshaonline.org/handbook/online/articles/fbl17 (accessed September 28, 2015).
18. "House Rebukes Zioncheck," *Seattle Post-Intelligencer*, April 21, 1936. Included in Digital Collections, Washington State University Library, Wallis and Marilyn Kimble Northwest History Database (accessed September 28, 2015).
19. *Congressional Record*, 69 Congress, 1 Session, LXVII—Part 5, 5748; see also Willard B. Gatewood Jr., ed., *Controversy in the Twenties: Fundamentalism, Modernism, and Evolution* (Nashville, TN: Vanderbilt University Press, 1969), 321–326.

20. *Congressional Record*, 69th Congress, 1st Session, LXVII—Part 5, 5748.
21. Staebler and Diekhoff, “Religion at Michigan.”
22. Ralston, “Our Monthly Potpourri,” 371–372.
23. Machen, “What Fundamentalism Now Stands For”; Machen, “What Fundamentalism and Evolution Stand For,” *Literary Digest*, July 11, 1925, 31–32.
24. J. Gresham Machen to R. S. Kellerman, October 7, 1924; Machen Papers, Montgomery Library Archives, Westminster Theological Seminary, Philadelphia.
25. Machen to F. E. Robinson, n.d.; Machen Papers.
26. J. Gresham Machen and Charles P. Fagnani, “Does Fundamentalism Obstruct Social Progress?,” *Survey Graphic* 5 (July 1924): 427.
27. Machen to Albert Sidney Johnson, May 25, 1925; Machen Papers.
28. Machen to Albert Sidney Johnson, June 30, 1925; Machen Papers.
29. “Dr. Machen Declines the Presidency of Bryan University,” *The Presbyterian* 97 (July 7, 1927): 8–9.
30. Maynard Shipley, “Evolution Still a Live Issue in the Schools,” *Current History* 27 (March 1928): 801.
31. *King’s Business*, January–June 1925, 90.
32. Curtis Lee Laws, “Editorial Notes and Comments,” *Watchman-Examiner* 13 (August 20, 1925): 1071.
33. James M. Gray, “The Sacred Cow of Evolution,” *Moody Bible Institute Monthly*, January 1929, 225; Alfred Fairhurst, *Atheism in Our Universities* (Cincinnati: Standard Publishing, 1923), 84, 92; T. T. Martin, *The Evolution Issue* (Los Angeles: n.p., 1923), 38–39.
34. Straton in “Hails Rising Spiritual Tide,” *New York Times*, August 27, 1925; Winrod in “Start World Fight Against Evolution,” *New York Times*, May 9, 1927.
35. J. Frank Norris, *Searchlight*, January 13, 1922, 1.
36. Willard B. Gatewood Jr., *Preachers, Pedagogues, and Politicians: The Evolution Controversy in North Carolina, 1920–1927* (Chapel Hill: University of North Carolina Press, 1966), 193 (“foreigners”), 154 (“damn Yankee”), 167 (“Northerners”).
37. Leonard Moore, *Citizen Klansmen: The Ku Klux Klan in Indiana, 1921–1928* (Chapel Hill: University of North Carolina Press, 1991), 15–16, 18.
38. Harbor Allen, “Supreme Kingdom’s Campaign,” *Christian Fundamentals in School and Church* 8 (October–December 1926): 51.
39. Ibid.
40. Maynard Shipley, *The War on Modern Science: A Short History of the Fundamentalist Attacks on Evolution and Modernism* (New York: Knopf, 1927), 48.
41. Ibid., 44.
42. Adam Laats, “Monkeys, Bibles, and the Little Red Schoolhouse: Atlanta’s School Battles in the Scopes Era,” *Georgia Historical Quarterly* 95, no. 3 (Fall 2011): 384–386.

43. H. L. Mencken, "Fundamentalism: Divine and Secular," in *The Bathtub Hoax and Other Blasts and Bravos from the Chicago Tribune*, ed. Robert McHugh, 123–124 (New York: Knopf, 1958).
44. "Huxley Shocked by Fundamentalism," *Current Opinion*, March 1, 1925, 339.
45. "The Menace of Fundamentalism," *The Independent*, May 30, 1925, 114.
46. "What Is a Fundamentalist?," *Forum* 76 (December 1926): 861.
47. Gatewood, *Controversy in the 'Twenties*, 309.
48. Curtis Lee Laws, Editorial, *Christian Fundamentals in School and Church* 7 (October–December 1925): 66–67.
49. Shailer Mathews, "Ten Years of American Protestantism," *North American Review* 217 (May 1923): 591.
50. "The College and Fundamentalism," *The Independent*, June 20, 1925, 114.
51. Machen had studied at Johns Hopkins University, Princeton, Princeton Seminary, and the German universities of Marburg and Gottingen. See C. Allyn Russell, *Voices of American Fundamentalism: Seven Biographical Studies* (Philadelphia: Westminster Press, 1976), 148.
52. Bob Jones Sr., *The Perils of America, or, Where Are We Headed?* "from a sermon delivered at the Chicago Gospel Tabernacle, March 5, 1934" (n.p., n.d.), 35.
53. T. T. Martin, *Hell and the High School: Christ or Evolution, Which?* (Kansas City, MO: Western Baptist Publishing, 1923), 155. Martin seems to have picked up and slightly misquoted this story from J. Frank Norris, "A Mother's Son," *Searchlight*, May 12, 1921, 2.
54. James H. Leuba, *The Belief in God and Immortality: A Psychological, Anthropological and Statistical Study*, 2nd ed. (Chicago: Open Court, 1921); William Jennings Bryan, *The Menace of Darwinism* (Louisville, KY: Pentecostal Publishing, [1919?]), 32; James H. Leuba to William Jennings Bryan, May 16, 1925; Bryan Papers, Library of Congress.
55. Charles A. Blanchard, "Report of Committee on Correlation of Colleges, Seminaries and Academies," *God Hath Spoken* (Philadelphia: Bible Conference Committee, 1919), 19–20.
56. George W. McPherson, *The Crisis in Church and College* (Yonkers, NY: Yonkers Book, 1919); Fairhurst, *Atheism in Our Universities*; Laats, *Fundamentalism and Education in the Scopes Era*, 49.
57. See Irvin G. Wyllie, "Bryan, Birge, and the Wisconsin Evolution Controversy, 1921–1922," *Wisconsin Magazine of History* 35 (1951–52): 294–301; Laats, *Fundamentalism and Education in the Scopes Era*, 50–52.
58. "William Jennings Bryan, "The Modern Arena," *The Commoner*, June 1921, 3.
59. Laats, *Fundamentalism and Education in the Scopes Era*, 50–54, 121–123, 125–126.
60. Curtis Lee Laws, "What Have We a Right to Expect from Our Schools?," *Watchman-Examiner*, October 12, 1922, 1293.
61. Gatewood, *Preachers, Pedagogues, and Politicians*, 32.

62. Ibid., 37.
63. Laats, *Fundamentalism and Education in the Scopes Era*, 55–56.
64. J. Frank Norris, "Great Rejoicing! 100 Percent of Baylor Faculty Sign Creedal Statement Which Is 100% for Fundamentalism," *Searchlight*, November 28, 1924, 1.
65. John D. Hannah, "Social and Intellectual Origins of the Evangelical Theological College," Ph.D. diss., University of Texas at Dallas, 1988, 174.
66. *Evangelical Theological College: First Annual Announcement, 1924–1925* (Dallas: Evangelical Theological College, 1925), 5; Hannah, "Social and Intellectual Origins of the Evangelical Theological College," 159.
67. Laats, *Fundamentalism and Education in the Scopes Era*, 181–182.
68. Lewis Sperry Chafer to Arno C. Gaebelein, November 13, 1923; Accession 2006–18, L. S. Chafer Correspondence, Box 12, Individual Correspondence G Through K, File 23, Arno Gaebelein, President's Office Papers, Archives, Dallas Theological Seminary, Dallas, Texas.
69. Ibid.
70. Lewis Sperry Chafer to Robert Dick Wilson, December 20, 1923, Accession 2006-18, Box 16, File 23, President's Office Papers, Archives, Dallas Theological Seminary.
71. Rollin T. Chafer, "Superiority Complex of Teachers of Naturalism," *Evangelical Theological College Bulletin* 7 (June 1931): 2–4.
72. Virginia Lieson Brereton, *Training God's Army: The American Bible School, 1880–1940* (Bloomington: Indiana University Press, 1990), 71.
73. Gene A. Getz, *MBI: The Story of Moody Bible Institute* (Chicago: Moody Press, 1969), 71; Gloege, *Guaranteed Pure*, 154.
74. James Findlay, "Moody, 'Gapmen,' and the Gospel: The Early Days of Moody Bible Institute," *Church History* 31 (September 1962): 322–335.
75. Robert Williams and Marilyn Miller, *Chartered for His Glory: Biola University, 1908–1983* (La Mirada, CA: Biola University Press, 1983), 35; Gloege, *Guaranteed Pure*, 192.
76. A. B. Simpson, "Missionary Training Colleges," *Christian Alliance* 1 (May 1888): 76, quoted in Brereton, *Training God's Army*, 55.
77. Williams and Miller, *Chartered for His Glory*, 16.
78. Cited in Brereton, *Training God's Army*, 81.
79. Williams and Miller, *Chartered for His Glory*, 15.
80. Brereton, *Training God's Army*, 79–82.
81. Roger L. Geiger, *The History of American Higher Education: Learning and Culture from the Founding to World War II* (Princeton, NJ: Princeton University Press, 2015), 272–273.
82. Ibid., 302.
83. A. J. Angulo, *William Barton Rogers and the Idea of MIT* (Baltimore: Johns Hopkins University Press, 2009), 86–89.

84. Geiger, *The History of American Higher Education*, 307–308.
85. Virginia Lieson Brereton, "Protestant Fundamentalist Bible Schools, 1882–1940," Ph.D. diss., Columbia University, 1981, 304 n. 31.
86. Nathan R. Wood, *A School of Christ* (Boston: Gordon College of Theology and Missions, 1953), 10.
87. Typescript of Culbertson biography—n.d., n.p., CP; also Members of the Pastors Course to James M. Gray, July 27, 1931, CP.
88. May, "Des Moines University and Dr. T. T. Shields," 199.
89. William Bell Riley, "The Redemption of Des Moines University," *Christian Fundamentalist* 1 (August 1927): 6.
90. May, "Des Moines University and Dr. T. T. Shields," 204.
91. M. Grier, "Fundamentalism's Newest Fortress," *School and Society* 26, no. 14 (July 2, 1927): 15.
92. May, "Des Moines University and Dr. T. T. Shields," 211.
93. Ibid., 212.
94. Ibid., 217.
95. Ibid., 220.
96. Ibid., 226.
97. Ibid., 226–229.
98. William Bell Riley, "William Jennings Bryan University," *Christian Fundamentals in School and Church* 7 (October–December 1925): 52.
99. Laats, *Fundamentalism and Education in the Scopes Era*, 132.
100. LaDonna Robinson Olson, *Legacy of Faith: The Story of Bryan College* (Hayesville, NC: Schoettle, 1995), 49–50.
101. Ibid., 147–148.
102. Ibid., 147.
103. Trollinger, *God's Empire*, 163.
104. Olson, *Legacy of Faith*, 147.
105. James M. Gray, "Editorial Notes," *Moody Bible Institute Monthly*, April 1921, 347; Curtis Lee Laws, "Fundamentalism from the Baptist Viewpoint," *Moody Bible Institute Monthly*, September 1922, 15.
106. See, for example, Gloege, *Guaranteed Pure*, 185.
107. Sandeen, *Roots of Fundamentalism*.
108. Laats, *Fundamentalism and Education in the Scopes Era*, 132–135.
109. Charter, *Bob Jones College Annual Bulletin* 3 (April 1929), BJU Catalogue File, Bob Jones University Archives, Greenville, South Carolina; Bob Jones Sr., *Original Intentions of the Founder* (Greenville, SC: Bob Jones University, 1960), BJU Pamphlet File, Bob Jones University Archives.
110. Bob Jones Sr., *Bob Jones Magazine* 1 (June 1928): 3.
111. Mark Taylor Dalhouse, *An Island in the Lake of Fire: Bob Jones University, Fundamentalism, and the Separatist Movement* (Athens: University of Georgia Press, 1996), 40–41.

112. Bob Jones to "Friend," n.d.; Box HC 20/24, Folder: Bob Jones College, Crown Point, FL, Letters to New Students; Bob Jones University Archives.
113. Daniel L. Turner, *Standing Without Apology: The History of Bob Jones University* (Greenville, SC: Bob Jones University Press, 1997), 38–39.
114. Jones, *Perils of America*, 35.
115. Ibid., 7.
116. Bob Jones Sr., *WHY . . . Bob Jones University Was Founded; WHY . . . It Has Made So Many World-Wide Contacts in So Short a Time; WHY . . . It Does Not Hold Membership in a Regional Educational Association* (n.p., n.d. [likely 1949]), BJU Pamphlet File, Bob Jones University Archives.
117. Hudson Armerding to Campus, November 15, 1965; Box 19, Folder 14; AP.
118. Turner, *Standing Without Apology*, 89.
119. J. Oliver Buswell, "Review of *Bob Jones' Revival Sermons*," *Bible of Today* (April 1949): 216–217; clipping in TB, Folder: Buswell, James Oliver.

## CHAPTER 3

1. Joseph Free to Bob Jones Sr., May 25, 1938; TB, Folder: Mr. Joseph Free.
2. Michael S. Hamilton, "The Fundamentalist Harvard: Wheaton College and the Continuing Vitality of American Evangelicalism, 1919–1965," Ph.D. diss., University of Notre Dame, 1994, 53.
3. Roger L. Geiger, *The History of American Higher Education: Learning and Culture from the Founding to World War II* (Princeton, NJ: Princeton University Press, 2015), 494.
4. Mark Taylor Dalhouse, *An Island in the Lake of Fire: Bob Jones University, Fundamentalism, and the Separatist Movement* (Athens: University of Georgia Press, 1996), 148.
5. Hamilton, "Fundamentalist Harvard," 37.
6. Timothy Weber, *Living in the Shadow of the Second Coming: American Premillennialism, 1875–1982* (Chicago: University of Chicago Press, 1987), 238.
7. Joel A. Carpenter, *Revive Us Again: The Reawakening of American Fundamentalism* (New York: Oxford University Press, 1997), 133–135.
8. Harry J. Albus, "Christian Education Today," *Christian Life* 10 (September 1948): 26, 46. Cited in Carpenter, *Revive Us Again*, 21.
9. Department of Education, *Biennial Survey of Education, 1938–1940* (Washington, DC: General Printing Office, 1944), 7. Cited in Roger L. Geiger, *To Advance Knowledge: The Growth of American Research Universities, 1900–1940* (New York: Oxford University Press, 1986), 250.
10. *Evangelical Theological College Bulletin* 2 (June 1926): 6–7; Rudolf Albert Renfer, "A History of Dallas Theological Seminary," Ph.D. diss., University of Texas at Austin, 1959, 314.
11. Hamilton, "Fundamentalist Harvard," 32.

12. Adam Laats, *Fundamentalism and Education in the Scopes Era: God, Darwin, and the Roots of America's Culture Wars* (New York: Palgrave Macmillan, 2010), 135–138.
13. Dalhouse, *Island in the Lake of Fire*, 46–47.
14. Daniel L. Turner, *Standing Without Apology: The History of Bob Jones University* (Greenville, SC: Bob Jones University Press, 1997), 35, 57; Dalhouse, *Island in the Lake of Fire*, 44.
15. Dalhouse, *Island in the Lake of Fire*, 47.
16. Hamilton, "Fundamentalist Harvard," 50.
17. Geiger, *To Advance Knowledge*, 161.
18. Leo V. Tepley, M.D., to Whom It May Concern, February 8, 1933; Box 13: Denver Bible Institute; Correspondence, BP. Please note that all the correspondence cited in this section comes from this same box, Folders 4–8. Names that did not become part of the public record have been replaced by pseudonyms to protect privacy. Changed names have been marked with an asterisk.
19. Clifton L. Fowler to "Brother Ted," July 25, 1933.
20. Deacons of the Church to Mrs. Angie L. Fowler, May 5, 1933.
21. Thomas M. Hopkins, M.D., statement, n.d.
22. Thomas M. Hopkins, M.D., to Whom It May Concern, January 5, 1936.
23. Clifton Fowler to J. Oliver Buswell, February 21, 1936; Buswell to Fowler, February 27, 1936.
24. R. G. McQuilkin to Clarence H. Benson, March 2, 1936; Paul W. Rood to Fowler, March 25, 1936; Will H. Houghton to Fowler, March 25, 1936; Fowler to Buswell, April 22, 1936.
25. J. Oliver Buswell, circular letter, August 1936; R. G. McQuilkin to Clarence H. Benson, March 2, 1936.
26. Fowler to Buswell, April 22, 1936.
27. R. G. McQuilkin to Clarence H. Benson, March 2, 1936.
28. Buswell to committee, August 15, 1936.
29. Buswell letter to Denver-area fundamentalist leaders, August 1936.
30. Charles Rose,* typescript testimony, n.d.
31. Frank Inbrell,* typescript testimony, n.d.
32. T. L. Grace* to Buswell, August 20, 1936.
33. M. S. Jansma* to Buswell, August 20, 1936; Carlton Rose to Buswell, August 20, 1936; R. L. Upright to Buswell, August 26, 1936.
34. Stanley Skivington, open letter, n.d.; Herbert Nelson* to Buswell, September 16, 1936.
35. M. S. Jansma* to Buswell, August 20, 1936; R. L. Upright* to Buswell, August 26, 1936; Stanley Skivington, open letter, n.d.; Jerry C. Boston to Buswell, September 10, 1936.
36. Carlton Rose* to Buswell, August 20, 1936.
37. Harriet Stafford* to Pearl Salinas,* May 14, 1936.

38. "Excerpts of Threats and Derogatory Statements Made by Mrs. Angie L. Fowler," n.d., signed by Pearl Salinas,* June 24–26, 1936.
39. W. C. Notworth* to Buswell, August 15, 1936.
40. R. N. Hoffman to Buswell, September 4, 1936; see also Ernest Safer* to Buswell, September 29, 1936.
41. Buswell to Loveless, September 18, 1936.
42. Kirk to Buswell, September 22, 1936.
43. Houghton to Buswell, August 31, 1936.
44. S. V. Norton* to Houghton, October 2, 1936.
45. Reginald Patterson* to W. R. Elliot, October 8, 1936.
46. Buswell to W. R. Elliot, October 21, 1936.
47. "Preliminary Report," December 1936.
48. James Guswell* to Buswell, May 15, 1937.
49. Loveless to Buswell, May 20, 1937.
50. Houghton to Buswell, May 28, 1937.
51. Fowler to Buswell, January 4, 1937; Fowler to Buswell, January 6, 1937.
52. Turner, *Standing Without Apology*, 64.
53. Ibid., 83.
54. Dalhouse, *Island in the Lake of Fire*, 46.
55. Turner, *Standing Without Apology*, 46.
56. Ibid., 49.
57. Bob Jones Sr. to Ruth Flood, August 6, 1937; Pastor of First Baptist Church of Lynn Haven, FL, to Bob Jones Sr. TB, Folder: Miss Ruth Flood.
58. Bob Jones Jr. to "Floodie," August 31, 1936; TB, Folder: Miss Ruth Flood.
59. Flood to Bob Jones Sr., August 4, 1937; TB, Folder: Miss Ruth Flood.
60. Bob Jones Sr. to Flood, August 6, 1937; TB, Folder: Miss Ruth Flood.
61. Ruth Flood to Emma Washburne, June 16, 1938; TB, Folder: Miss Ruth Flood.
62. Bob Jones Jr. to Marjorie Foster, June 11, 1938; TB, Folder: Marjorie Foster.
63. Marjorie Foster to Bob Jones Jr., n.d.; TB, Folder: Marjorie Foster.
64. Bob Jones Sr. to Dorothy Seay, December 16, 1936; TB, Folder: Miss Dorothy R. Seay.
65. Seay to Bob Jones Sr., August 21, 1936; TB, Folder: Miss Dorothy R. Seay.
66. Bob Jones Sr. to Seay, December 16, 1936; TB, Folder: Miss Dorothy R. Seay.
67. Ibid.
68. Joseph Free to Bob Jones Jr., August 13, 1937; Free to Bob Jones Sr., May 25, 1938; TB, Folder: Mr. Joseph Free.
69. Free to Bob Jones Sr., May 25, 1938; TB, Folder: Mr. Joseph Free.
70. Bob Jones Sr. to Joseph Free, May 23, 1938; TB, Folder: Mr. Joseph Free.
71. Bob Jones Sr. to Seay, May 26, 1938; TB, Folder: Miss Dorothy R. Seay.
72. Typescript of questions with student answers; TB, Folder: Miss Dorothy R. Seay.
73. Bob Jones Sr. to Seay, May 26, 1938; TB, Folder: Miss Dorothy R. Seay.

74. Bob Jones Sr. to Joseph Free, May 23, 1938; TB, Folder: Mr. Joseph Free.
75. Free to Bob Jones Sr., May 25, 1938; TB, Folder: Mr. Joseph Free.
76. Ibid.
77. Ibid.
78. Anonymous, "Accent on Sin," *American Mercury* 51, no. 201 (September 1940): 16–23; quotations from 18 ("certain perverse adolescent relish") and 19. See also Turner, *Standing Without Apology*, 73.
79. Turner, *Standing Without Apology*, 64.
80. Bob Jones Jr. to Bureau of Appointments, University of Michigan, Ann Arbor, June 13, 1938; TB, Folder: Mr. Joseph Free.
81. Turner, *Standing Without Apology*, 65.
82. Dalhouse, *Island in the Lake of Fire*, 72.
83. Hamilton, "Fundamentalist Harvard," 30–31.
84. J. Oliver Buswell to "Friends," June 2, 1942; Press release, "National Bible Institute Presidency," April 24, 1941; Buswell to Bob Jones Jr., May 2, 1941; TB, Folder: Buswell, James Oliver.
85. Hamilton, "Fundamentalist Harvard," 54.
86. Interview with William John Barnett, May 30, 1995; Collection 248, BGC.
87. Interview with Paul Dean Votaw, March 4, 1980; Collection 105, BGC.
88. Hamilton, "Fundamentalist Harvard," 72.
89. Ibid., 48.
90. J. Oliver Buswell, open letter, February 2, 1940; Box 1, Folder 5, BP.
91. Hamilton, "Fundamentalist Harvard," 48–49.
92. Ibid., 75.
93. Report from Chicago Alumni Group to board of Trustees, n.d., Box 1, Folder 5, BP.
94. See, for example, Geiger, *History of American Higher Education*, 494–497.
95. Hamilton, "Fundamentalist Harvard," 73.
96. Virginia Jones, open letter, December 11, 1939; Box 26, Folder 10, BP.
97. Ivan Rose to Buswell, n.d.; Box 26, Folder 10, BP.
98. Student evaluation forms for Ethics and Theism; Box 26, Folder 10, BP.
99. Interview with Vincent Leroy Crossett, November 16, 1984; Collection 288, BGC.
100. Faculty questionnaire, June 17, 1939; Box 1, Folder 5, BP.
101. "An Alumnus" [L. A. Higley] to H. A. Ironside, February 11, 1939; Box 18, Folder 4, BP. Emphasis in original.
102. "An Alumnus" [L. A. Higley] to William McCarrell, n.d.; Box 18, Folder 4, BP.
103. Hamilton, "Fundamentalist Harvard," 77.
104. Memo, Meeting of Executive Council, December 8, 1938; Box 1, Folder 5, BP.
105. George Kirk to Ted M. Benson, January 31, 1940; Box 1, Folder 5, BP.
106. Hamilton, "Fundamentalist Harvard," 77.
107. George Kirk to Ted M. Benson, January 31, 1940; Box 1, Folder 5, BP.

108. "An Alumnus" [L. A. Higley] to William McCarrell, n.d.; Box 18, Folder 4, BP.
109. Charles A. Blanchard, "Report of Committee on Correlation of Colleges, Seminaries and Academies," *God Hath Spoken* (Philadelphia: Bible Conference Committee, 1919), 19–20.
110. Lowell H. Coate, "Further Suggestions About the New Scholarship," *Moody Bible Institute Monthly*, August 1923, 563–564.
111. Clarence H. Benson, "Our Monthly Potpourri," *Moody Bible Institute Monthly*, August 1927, 583.
112. *Bob Jones College Annual Bulletin* 3 (April 1929), BJU Catalogue File, Bob Jones University Archives.
113. James M. Gray, "Editorial Notes," *Moody Bible Institute Monthly*, August 1926, 557.
114. Turner, *Standing Without Apology*, 334 n. 43.
115. Editors of *Sunday School Times* to "Friends," September 18, 1946; Box 3, Folder: S, 1945–1952, Gen'l Correspondence, Folder 4, POP, 1945–1959.
116. George McCready Price, "Modern Problems in Science and Religion," *Moody Bible Institute Monthly*, February 1921, 255–257.
117. Leander S. Keyser, "God or Matter, Creation or Evolution, Which?," *Moody Bible Institute Monthly*, April 1923, 353–355.
118. Mabel E. Kerr, "Why Not Be Up-to-Date?," *Moody Bible Institute Monthly* 23 (April 1923): 336.
119. James M. Gray, "The Sacred Cow of Evolution," *Moody Bible Institute Monthly*, January 1929, 225.
120. James M. Gray to Reuben Torrey, October 14, 1925; folder: Correspondence 1920–1925, GP.
121. Interview with William John Barnett, May 30, 1995; Collection 248, BGC.
122. Interview with Jesse Wilbert Hoover, October 7, 1985; Collection 319, BGC (Mixter). Interview with Melvin David Suttie, January 18, 1985; Collection 293, BGC (Leedy).
123. "Betty" to "Dearest Folks," October 21, 1945; Box 3, Folder 4, EEP, 1941–1987, Collection 278, BGC.
124. Buswell to Charles G. Trumbull, May 7, 1927; Box 25, Folder 12, BP.
125. J. Oliver Buswell, "The Length of the Creative Days," *Christian Faith and Life* 41 (1935): 120.
126. Numbers, *The Creationists*, 123, 129.
127. Ibid., 131–132.
128. Ibid., 76.
129. Harry Rimmer, "Modern Science and the Youth of Today" (1925), in *The Antievolution Pamphlets of Harry Rimmer*, ed. Edward B. Davis (New York: Garland Publishing, 1995), 462.
130. Ibid., 474.
131. Wood to Rimmer, October 19, 1936; Box 2, Folder: Correspondence: R, POP, 1918–1944.

132. Wood to Rimmer, January 8, 1937; Box 2, Folder: Correspondence: R, POP, 1918–1944.
133. Christopher M. Rios, *After the Monkey Trial: Evangelical Scientists and a New Creationism* (New York: Fordham University Press, 2014), 42.
134. Numbers, *The Creationists*, 180–181.

## CHAPTER 4

1. Anne Williams Warwick, *Tides: Growing Up on St. Andrews Bay* (Panama City, FL: Boyd Bros. Printing, 1984), 122.
2. Elisabeth Elliot to "Dearest Folks," June 16, 1948; Box 3, Folder 8, EEP, 1941–1987, Collection 278, BGC.
3. Polly Weaver, "Pursuit of Learning . . . and the Undaily Male," *Mademoiselle*, January 1958, 80; cited in Beth L. Bailey, *From Front Porch to Back Seat: Courtship in Twentieth-Century America* (Baltimore: Johns Hopkins University Press, 1988), 44.
4. Warwick, *Tides*, 96.
5. Bailey, *From Front Porch to Back Seat*, 85.
6. Virginius Dabney, *Mr. Jefferson's University: A History* (Charlottesville: University of Virginia Press, 1981), 471.
7. A. J. Angulo and Leland Graham, "Winthrop College in the Sixties: Campus Protests, Southern Style," *Historical Studies in Education*, Fall 2011, 117.
8. Paul K. Conkin, *Gone with the Ivy: A Biography of Vanderbilt University* (Knoxville: University of Tennessee Press, 1985), 640.
9. Charles Blankenship to R. K. Johnson, November 3, 1953; TB, Folder: Ted Mercer et al.
10. Interview with Vincent Leroy Crossett, November 16, 1984; Collection 288, BGC.
11. See, for example, Ernest R. Sandeen, *The Roots of Fundamentalism: British and American Millenarianism, 1800–1930* (Chicago: University of Chicago Press, 1970).
12. Warwick, *Tides*, 121.
13. Elisabeth Elliot to "Dearest Folks," October 8, 1944; Box 3, Folder 3, EEP. Emphasis in original.
14. Edward "Eddie" Kindstedt to his mother, February 11, 1941; Box 20/24, Folder: Bob Jones College, Cleveland, TN, Dr. Bob Jones Jr., Letters, 1941, Edward Kindstedt.
15. Ibid. Emphasis in original.
16. Roger L. Geiger, *The History of American Higher Education: Learning and Culture from the Founding to World War II* (Princeton, NJ: Princeton University Press, 2015), 85.
17. Helen Lefkowitz Horowitz, *Campus Life: Undergraduate Cultures from the End of the Eighteenth Century to the Present* (New York: Knopf, 1987), 24, 31, 37.
18. Daniel L. Turner, *Standing Without Apology: The History of Bob Jones University* (Greenville, SC: Bob Jones University Press, 1997), 208.

19. Warwick, *Tides*, 127.
20. Michael S. Hamilton, "The Fundamentalist Harvard: Wheaton College and the Continuing Vitality of American Evangelicalism, 1919–1965," Ph.D. diss., University of Notre Dame, 1994, 190.
21. Interview with Elizabeth Howard Warner, November 15, 1978; Collection 75, BGC.
22. Interview with William John Barnett, May 30, 1995; Collection 248, BGC. Barnett attended Wheaton between 1937 and 1939.
23. Elisabeth Elliot to "Dearest Folks," October 8, 1944; Box 3, Folder 3, EEP.
24. Interview with Paul Dean Votaw, March 4, 1980; Collection 105, BGC. See also interview with Jesse Wilbert Hoover, October 7, 1985; Collection 319, BGC.
25. Undated copy of *The Broadcaster*, Box 1, Folder: Correspondence: B, POP, 1918–1944.
26. Hamilton, "Fundamentalist Harvard," 194.
27. Samuel H. Sutherland to Roy Sprague, May 19, 1953; Folder: Chimes, The, Student Newspaper Publication Biola, SP.
28. Samuel H. Sutherland to Elizabeth McCullough, March 8, 1954; Folder: Chimes, The, Student Newspaper Publication Biola, SP.
29. Turner, *Standing Without Apology*, 45.
30. Samuel Sutherland, "Christian Activities Committee," November 19, 1952; Folder: Faculty Reports and Misc., SP.
31. Turner, *Standing Without Apology*, 41.
32. *Hypernikon* (student yearbook), 1951. Gordon College library, Wenham, Massachusetts.
33. Interview with Elizabeth Howard Warner, November 15, 1978; Collection 75, BGC.
34. Betty Howard to "Dearest Folks," September 14, 1944; Box 3, Folder 3, EEP.
35. Betty Howard to "Dearest Folks," October 8, 1944. Box 3, Folder 3, EEP.
36. *Hypernikon*, 1951.
37. W. R. Hale [Superintendent of Men], "Life at Biola," *The Chimes*, March 1940, 2.
38. James D. Edwards to Harry O. Engstrom, December 13, 1960. TB, Folder: Student Life.
39. Kathryn Louise Oliver to J. Oliver Buswell, n.d. (c. September 1926). Box 6, Folder 6, BP.
40. Buswell to Oliver, September 21, 1926; Box 6, Folder 6, BP.
41. Betty Howard to "Dearest Folks," November 12, 1944; Box 3, Folder 3, EEP.
42. Student Records, Box 1, Folder 9; Moody Bible Institute Archives, Chicago, Illinois.
43. Clara F. Fairbanks to Samuel H. Sutherland, May 11, 1942; Folder: "F" Correspondence (General) File #1, SP.
44. Samuel H. Sutherland to Fairbanks, May 20, 1942; Folder: "F" Correspondence (General) File #1, SP.
45. Enock C. Dyrness to J. Oliver Buswell, April 3, 1929. Box 26, Folder 9, BP.

46. Interview with Wayne G. Bragg, May 9, 1980; Collection 96, BGC.
47. Betty Howard to "Dearest Folks," September 12, 1944; Box 3, Folder 3, EEP.
48. Betty Howard to "Dearest Folks," September 14, 1944; Box 3, Folder 3, EEP.
49. Interview with William John Barnett, BGC.
50. Betty Howard to "Dearest Folks," October 8, 1944; Box 3, Folder 3, EEP.
51. Lee Wiens, "Why Should Wheaton 'Bs' Beat Us?," *Moody Student*, March 23, 1945, 2.
52. Turner, *Standing Without Apology*, 40–41.
53. Bob Jones Jr. to Jim Walton, August 10, 1976; TB, Folder: Bob Jones Sr., Jr., III, and Few Deans (attitude-position on certain subjects).
54. J. Oliver Buswell, "Review of *Bob Jones' Revival Sermons*," *Bible of Today*, April 1949, 216–217; clipping in TB, Folder: Buswell, James Oliver.
55. The archival files at Bob Jones University offer several examples of such concerns. See, for example, Samuel Meyersburg to Bob Jones Jr., March 11, 1953; Carolyn Diveley to Bob Jones Jr., April 16, 1962; Jim Walton to Bob Jones III, n.d.; TB, Folder: Bob Jones Sr., Jr., III, and Few Deans (attitude-position on certain subjects).
56. Bob Jones Sr. to Mr. and Mrs. Henry P. Stover, May 19, 1955; TB, Folder: Bob Jones Sr., Jr., III, and Few Deans (attitude-position on certain subjects).
57. Interview with Vincent Leroy Crossett, November 16, 1984; Collection 288, BGC.
58. "What a Nightmare!," *Moody Student*, November 28, 1941, 1.
59. *Hypernikon*, 1951.
60. William Culbertson, "Chapel Talk," February 24, 1947; Box 1, Folder: Culbertson, Wm. Policies While at MBI, CP.
61. Helen Lefkowitz Horowitz, *Campus Life: Undergraduate Cultures from the End of the Eighteenth Century to the Present* (New York: Knopf, 1987).
62. Christopher P. Loss, *Between Citizens and State: The Politics of American Higher Education in the Twentieth Century* (Princeton, NJ: Princeton University Press, 2012), 36–38.
63. Memo to William Culbertson from Bernice Van Baren, March 29, 1950; Box 1, Folder: Culbertson, Wm. Policies While at MBI, CP.
64. Typescript: *The Gordon Handbook*, n.d. [likely c. 1941–1945, mentions these "war years"], 11; Box 3, Folder: Gordon College, POP, 1918–1944.
65. Ibid., 12.
66. Ibid.
67. Ibid., 13.
68. Gerald F. Hawthorne to Peter Veltman, August 26, 1966; Box 42, Folder 10, AP.
69. Bob Jones Sr. to Billy T. Gower, May 1, 1953. TB, Folder: Student Life.
70. Circular letter, Editors of *Sunday School Times* to "Friends," September 18, 1946; Box 3, Folder: S, 1945–1952, Gen'l Correspondence, Folder 4; POP, 1945–1959.
71. T. Leonard Lewis to Editors *of Sunday School Times*, September 20, 1946; Box 3, Folder: S, 1945–1952, Gen'l Correspondence, Folder 4; POP, 1945–1959.

72. Phillip E. Howard [editor of *Sunday School Times*] to Lewis, March 26, 1946; Box 3, Folder: S, 1945–1952, Gen'l Correspondence, Folder 4; POP, 1945–1959.
73. Samuel H. Sutherland to Alice Squires, May 8, 1958; Folder: Chimes, The, Student Newspaper Publication Biola, SP.
74. "A Grieved Donor of a Quarter of a Century," to Samuel H. Sutherland, n.d., [envelope postmarked May 16, 1958]; Folder: Chimes, The, Student Newspaper Publication Biola, SP.
75. Samuel H. Sutherland to Alice Squires, May 8, 1958; Folder: Chimes, The, Student Newspaper Publication Biola, SP.
76. Interview with Vincent Leroy Crossett, BGC.
77. William E. Brusseau, "Letter to the Editor," *Moody Student*, November 8, 1946, 2.
78. Corinne R. Smith to V. Raymond Edman, July 23, 1951; Box 3, Folder 20, EP.
79. Spiritual Life and Standards Committee, "Open Letter to the Wheaton Family," June 4, 1947; Box 3, Folder 20, EP.
80. C. David Weyerhauser to William Culbertson, January 1960, cited in George Marsden, *Reforming Fundamentalism: Fuller Seminary and the New Evangelicalism* (Grand Rapids, MI: Eerdmans, 1987), 204.
81. Turner, *Standing Without Apology*, 38–39.
82. Interview with William John Barnett, BGC.
83. Interview with Paul Dean Votaw, BGC.
84. Front Matter, *Biola Chimes*, March 1938, 1.
85. Ralph Parce to James M. Gray, October 6, 1934; Box 2, Folder 13, SRC.
86. Harold L. Lundquist to James M. Gray, October 17, 1934; Box 2, Folder 13, SRC.
87. Elizabeth Dilling to James M. Gray, November 2, 1934; Box 2, Folder 13, SRC.
88. Ralph Parce to Socialist Party of Wisconsin, November 12, 1934; Box 2, Folder 13, SRC.
89. Ruby A. Jackson, Memo, October 14, 1940; Box 2, Folder 13, SRC.
90. Will Houghton, Memo, December 30, 1941; Box 2, Folder 15, SRC.
91. Blanche B. Breckenridge, Memo, July 6, 1938; Box 2, Folder 15, SRC.
92. Hamilton, "Fundamentalist Harvard," 188–189.
93. Fuller to Edman, June 2, 1949, File of Trustees Minutes, July 11, 1949, cited in Hamilton, "Fundamentalist Harvard," 189. Emphasis in original.
94. Interview with Wayne G. Bragg, BGC.
95. Arthur I. Hart to T. Leonard Lewis, November 28, 1950; Lewis to Hart, December 13, 1950; Box 1, Folder: H, 1945–1952, General Correspondence, Folder 1, POP, 1945–1959.
96. Hamilton, "Fundamentalist Harvard," 209.
97. William Liverman interview, Bob Jones University Archives, Greenville, South Carolina.
98. Superintendent James W. Davis to John Roy, April 25, 1932; Box 2, Folder 8, SRC.
99. John Roy to James W. Davis, April 26, 1932; Box 2, Folder 8, SRC.

100. D. L. Foster to Carl Roy, June 24, 1932; Box 2, Folder 8, SRC.
101. James W. Davis, Memo, June 11, 1932; Box 2, Folder 8, SRC.
102. James W. Davis to Mr. and Mrs. Edward T. Lloyd, February 20, 1932; Box 2, Folder 8, SRC.
103. James W. Davis to Ruby A. Jackson, October 28, 1932; Box 2, Folder 8, SRC.
104. Ruby A. Jackson, Memo, June 29, 1933; Box 2, Folder 8, SRC.
105. Ruby A. Jackson, Memo, May 28, 1930; Box 2, Folder 9, SRC.
106. A. F. Broman, Memo, October 21, 1948; Box 2, Folder 14, SRC.
107. James W. Davis, "Statement Concerning Benjamin Kolton," February 21, 1934; Box 2, Folder 8, SRC.
108. James W. Davis to MBI Faculty, July 25, 1931; Box 2, Folder 9, SRC.
109. Blanche B. Breckenridge, Memo, November 21, 1938; Box 2, Folder 15, SRC.
110. Hamilton, "Fundamentalist Harvard," 209.
111. Bailey, *From Front Porch to Back Seat*, 85.
112. Betty A. DeBerg, *Ungodly Women: Gender and the First Wave of American Fundamentalism*, new ed. (Atlanta: Mercer University Press, 2000), 12, 43, 45, 49, 128.
113. Margaret Lamberts Bendroth, *Fundamentalism and Gender, 1875 to the Present* (New Haven, CT: Yale University Press, 1993), 52, 86–87.
114. Robert Williams and Marilyn Miller, *Chartered for His Glory: Biola University, 1908–1983* (La Mirada, CA: Biola University Press, 1983), 16.
115. Hamilton, "Fundamentalist Harvard," 136.
116. Bendroth, *Fundamentalism and Gender*, 98–100.
117. Hamilton, "Fundamentalist Harvard," 109, 216.
118. Dean of the Faculty to Helga Bender, October 27, 1937; Box 1, Folder: Applications for Positions, POP, 1918–1944.
119. Bob Jones to "Friend," n.d.; Box HC 20/24, Folder: Bob Jones College, Crown Point, FL, Letters to New Students.
120. Samuel H. Sutherland to Mrs. H. F. Gilbert, March 12, 1958; Folder: "F" Correspondence (General) File #2, SP.
121. Elisabeth Elliot to "Dearest Folks," October 3, 1944; Box 3, Folder 3, EEP.
122. Elisabeth Elliot to "Dearest Folks," October 9, 1945; Box 3, Folder 4, EEP.
123. Elisabeth Elliot to "Dearest Folks," May 5, 1946; Box 3, Folder 5, EEP.
124. Bailey, *From Front Porch to Back Seat*, 13.
125. Interview with Paul A. Contento, December 9, 1992; Collection 472, BGC.
126. Warwick, *Tides*, 121.
127. Ibid., 122.
128. Bob Jones Sr. to Julia Atkinson, July 21, 1928; Box HC 20/24, Folder: Bob Jones College, Crown Point, FL, Letters to New Students.
129. Turner, *Standing Without Apology*, 44.
130. Interview with Paul A. Contento, BGC.
131. *Booklet: Supplement to Men's Student Handbook*, n.d. [likely 1948 or 1949, the date William Culbertson took over as president,]; Folder: Students, CP.

132. *Student Information Booklet, 1938–1940,* 14. Hedley J. Parker Scrapbook, Student Life Collection, Moody Bible Institute Archives.
133. John R. Rice, "Editor Visits Bob Jones College," *Sword of the Lord,* June 8, 1945, 5.
134. *Student Information Booklet, 1938–1940,* 15.
135. Ibid., 14.
136. See Box 1, Folder 3, SRC.
137. Typescript: *The Gordon Handbook,* 17.
138. *Booklet: Supplement to Men's Student Handbook,* n.d.; CP.
139. Samuel H. Sutherland to Charles Mayes, April 16, 1948; Folder: Student Problems, SP.
140. William Liverman interview, Bob Jones University Archives.
141. Warwick, *Tides,* 123. Emphasis in original.
142. Ibid.
143. Elisabeth Elliot to "Dearest Folks," n.d.; Box 3, Folder 4, EEP.
144. Elisabeth Elliot to "Dearest Folks," November 26, 1944; Box 3, Folder 3, EEP.
145. Samuel H. Sutherland to Charles Mayes, April 16, 1948; Folder: Student Problems, SP.
146. "The Gong," *Biola Chimes,* April 1939, 4.
147. Elisabeth Elliot, www.elisabethelliot.org (accessed February 26, 2016).
148. Elisabeth Elliott to "Dearest Folks," n.d. [1947]; Box 3, Folder 6, EEP.
149. Elisabeth Elliot to "Dearest Folks," June 16, 1948; Box 3, Folder 8, EEP.
150. Elisabeth Elliot to "Dearest Folks," September 27, 1948; Box 3, Folder 9, EEP. Emphasis in original.
151. Ibid.
152. "What I Look for in a Christian Young Woman," *Moody Student,* November 30, 1945, 3.
153. Ibid.
154. "What I Look for in a Christian Young Man," *Moody Student,* November 30, 1945, 3.
155. Ibid.
156. "What I Look for in a Christian Young Woman," *Moody Student,* December 14, 1945, 4.
157. "What I Look for in a Christian Young Man," *Moody Student,* November 30, 1945, 3.
158. William Liverman interview, Bob Jones University Archives.
159. Margaret A. Nash and Jennifer A. R. Silverman, "'An Indelible Mark': Gay Purges in Higher Education in the 1940s," *History of Education Quarterly* 55 (November 2015): 441–459.
160. Will Houghton to Oliver Buswell, August 31, 1936; Box 13, Folder 7, BP.
161. P. W. Philpott to Will Houghton, October 2, 1936; Box 13, Folder 7, BP.
162. Joshua Gravett to Clifton Fowler, n.d.; Box 13, Folder 4, BP.

163. Undated statement from Dr. Hopkins, Box 13, Folder 5, BP.
164. V. C. Oltroggee to Oliver Buswell, August 20, 1936; Box 13, Folder 6, BP.
165. Rose Encinas, ed., "Excerpts of Threats and Derogatory Statements Made by Mrs. Angie L. Fowler," n.d.; Box 13, Folder 5, BP.
166. Samuel H. Sutherland to Al Salter, November 9, 1942; Folder: Student Problems, SP.
167. Samuel H. Sutherland to R. S. Beal, February 22, 1955; Folder: Student Problems, SP.
168. David Cooper to Miss Soubirou, April 16, 1951; Folder: Student Problems, SP.
169. Biola University, "A Statement Concerning David Cooper," April 19, 1951; Folder: Student Problems, SP.
170. Matthew Welde to Bob Jones Sr., July 16, 1953; TB, Folder: Ted Mercer et al.
171. Nash and Silverman, "'An Indelible Mark,'" 446.
172. Interview with Paul Dean Votaw, BGC.

## CHAPTER 5

1. Bob Jones Sr. to Billy Graham, January 17, 1956; TB, Folder: Billy Graham.
2. William Martin, *A Prophet with Honor: The Billy Graham Story* (New York: Harper Collins, 1992), 66.
3. Bob Jones Sr. to Billy Graham, April 5, 1951; Bob Jones Sr. to William Franklin Graham (Sr.), January 6, 1937; TB, Folder: Billy Graham.
4. Bob Jones Sr. to William Franklin Graham (Sr.), January 11, 1937; TB, Folder: Billy Graham.
5. Marshall Frady, *Billy Graham: A Parable of American Righteousness* (New York: Simon and Schuster, 2006), 98.
6. Bob Jones Sr. to William Franklin Graham (Sr.), January 7, 1937; TB, Folder: Billy Graham. See also Martin, *Prophet with Honor*, 70.
7. See Grant Wacker, *America's Pastor: Billy Graham and the Shaping of a Nation* (Cambridge, MA: Harvard University Press, 2014).
8. Historian George M. Marsden has quipped that the easiest way to define evangelicals in mid-twentieth-century America was as "anyone who likes Billy Graham." See George M. Marsden, *Understanding Fundamentalism and Evangelicalism* (Grand Rapids, MI: Eerdmans, 1991), 6.
9. George Marsden, *Reforming Fundamentalism: Fuller Seminary and the New Evangelicalism* (Grand Rapids, MI: Eerdmans, 1987), 147.
10. Marsden, *Reforming Fundamentalism*, 162.
11. Paul K. Jewett to Board of Trustees, "Memorandum Regarding Sabbatical Program for Fuller Theological Seminary," n.d.; Box 4, Folder 8, HLP.
12. Michael S. Hamilton, "The Fundamentalist Harvard: Wheaton College and the Continuing Vitality of American Evangelicalism, 1919–1965," Ph.D. diss., University of Notre Dame, 1994, 157.

13. Ibid., 160.
14. Bob Jones Sr., Chapel Talk, March 4, 1941, cited in Daniel L. Turner, *Standing Without Apology: The History of Bob Jones University* (Greenville, SC: Bob Jones University Press, 1997), 63.
15. Turner, *Standing Without Apology*, 146.
16. Ibid., 149.
17. Bob Jones Sr. to "Fellow Workers," September 1955; GSP.
18. Bob Jones Sr. to B. G. Osipoff, June 3, 1938; TB, Folder: Dr. and Mrs. B. G. Osipoff.
19. Bob Jones Sr. to "Fellow Workers," September 1955; GSP.
20. Response to a Westmont College Survey, August 23, 1965; Box 1, Folder: Education: Higher, Special Questionnaires, Studies, 1965, POP, 1964–1965.
21. J. F. Wellemeyer Jr., ed., *Compensation on the Campus: Case Studies of College and University Faculty Compensation Practices* (Washington, DC: Association for Higher Education, National Education Association, 1961), 82.
22. Ibid., 458.
23. "1969–70 Salary and Rank," Folder: Faculty, J. Richard Chase Papers, Biola University Archives, La Mirada, California.
24. "A Survey of Salaries Paid for Part Time Instruction in Colleges/Universities of the Greater Los Angeles Area 1968–1969," Folder: Faculty, Chase Papers.
25. Irene S. Larson, "Unique" [typescript memoir], n.d., Miscellaneous Materials File, Liberty University Archives, Lynchburg, Virginia.
26. Christopher Jencks and David Riesman, *The Academic Revolution* (New York: Doubleday, 1968), 18.
27. For examples, see Ellen Schrecker, *Many Are the Crimes: McCarthyism in America* (Princeton, NJ: Princeton University Press, 1999), 212, 277–278, 366, 404.
28. See Neil Gross, *Why Are Professors Liberal and Why Do Conservatives Care?* (Cambridge, MA: Harvard University Press, 2013). See also Adam Laats, "Persecution and the Conservative Academic," *I Love You but You're Going to Hell* (blog), December 22, 2012; and Laats, "The Social Sciences Need More Conservatives!," *I Love You but You're Going to Hell* (blog), February 24, 2015.
29. James M. Gray, Memo, March 19, 1926; Folder: Correspondence, 1926–1931, GP.
30. "Be Ye Separate," *Moody Memo*, July 11, 1947, 2.
31. Samuel H. Sutherland to Faculty, November 20, 1952; Folder: Faculty Reports and Misc., SP.
32. Hamilton, "Fundamentalist Harvard," 161.
33. V. Raymond Edman to Robert Baptista, August 29, 1966; Box 2, Folder 1, EP.
34. Marsden, *Reforming Fundamentalism*, 247.
35. Paul E. Toms to Harold Lindsell, November 30, 1978; Box 5, Folder 3, HLP.
36. Gilbert Stenholm to Bob Jones III, January 22, 1968; Folder: Administrative correspondence, GSP.

37. Gilbert Stenholm to Dr Bob's [*sic*, i.e., to Bob Jones Jr. and Bob Jones III], August 27, 1975; Folder: Administrative Correspondence, GSP.
38. C. Gregg Singer to Roger Voskuyl, July 13, 1948; Box 3, Folder 13, EP.
39. Harvey Crouser, "Confidential Report to the President," December 7, 1949; Box 3, Folder 13, EP.
40. Herman A. Fischer to Charles Farah Jr., August 3, 1948; Box 3, Folder 13, EP.
41. W. H. Griffith Thomas, "Report of Committee on Resolutions," *God Hath Spoken* (Philadelphia: Bible Conference Committee, 1919), 12; Edman to Board Members, Memorandum, December 11, 1961; Box 3, Folder 2:1, EP. In this memo, Edman explained the history of the annual statement of faith. The school had adopted the World's Christian Fundamentals Association statement as its own in 1926. The school would change it again in 1961 in order to tighten its meanings of creationism, as we'll explore in Chapter 9.
42. C. Gregg Singer to Board of Trustees, January 8, 1948; Box 3, Folder 13, EP.
43. Ibid.
44. C. Gregg Singer to the Board of Trustees, April 29, 1948; Box 3, Folder 13, 1945–1967, EP.
45. V. Raymond Edman to Norman Burns, October 14, 1948; Box 9, Folder 10, EP. See also Edman to Singer, August 18, 1948; Box 9, Folder 10, EP.
46. V. Raymond Edman, Public Statement, typescript, n.d.; Box 3, Folder 13, EP. Emphasis in original.
47. C. Gregg Singer to Roger Voskuyl, July 13, 1948; Box 3, Folder 13, EP.
48. Mark Taylor Dalhouse, *An Island in the Lake of Fire: Bob Jones University, Fundamentalism, and the Separatist Movement* (Athens: University of Georgia Press, 1996), 74.
49. Ted Mercer and Karl Keefer claimed that "up to seventy" (Keefer) or "more than seventy" (Mercer) faculty members had left at the end of the 1952 school year. See Karl Keefer to Fellow Faculty, July 10, 1953; Folder: Mercer, Ted, Bob Jones University Fundamentalism File (BJUFF); Ted Mercer, *An Additional Statement to the Alumni and Board of Trustees of Bob Jones University* (n.p., August 1953), 9. Bob Jones University in-house historian Dan Turner claimed that fifty-three more faculty members left at the end of the 1953 school year. See Turner, *Standing Without Apology*, 157. Bob Jones Sr. claimed that only twenty-three faculty members left in 1953. See Bob Jones Sr. to Matthew Welde, August 15, 1953; TB, Folder: Mercer/Keefer.
50. Bob Jones Sr. to Bob Jones Jr., June 15, 1953; TB, Folder: Mercer/Keefer.
51. Bob Jones Sr., Statement, typescript, June 19, 1953; Folder: Mercer, Ted, BJUFF.
52. Bob Jones Sr. to "Friend," July 2, 1953; Folder: Mercer, Ted, BJUFF.
53. Bob Jones Sr. to Mrs. Homer Cox, June 20, 1953; TB, Folder: Ted Mercer et al. Emphasis in original.
54. Alice Mercer to Matt Welde, August 12, 1953; TB, Folder: Ted Mercer et al.
55. Matthew Welde to Bob Jones Sr., July 16, 1953; TB, Folder: Ted Mercer et al.

56. Charles Blankenship to R. K. Johnson, November 3, 1953; TB, Folder: Ted Mercer et al.
57. Bob Jones Sr. to Bob Jones Jr., June 15, 1953; TB, Folder: Mercer/Keefer.
58. Bob Jones Sr. to Mrs. Homer Cox, June 20, 1953.
59. Ted Mercer, *A Statement Concerning My Dismissal from Bob Jones University* (n.p., July 1953), 4.
60. Ibid., 5.
61. Ibid., 6.
62. Ibid.
63. Ibid., 7.
64. Ibid., 9.
65. Ibid., 13.
66. Ibid., 12.
67. Ibid., 8.
68. Ibid., 14.
69. Ted Mercer, *An Additional Statement to the Alumni and Board of Trustees of Bob Jones University* (n.p., August 1953).
70. Ibid., 3–4.
71. Ibid., 5.
72. Ibid., 4.
73. Ibid., 10.
74. Ibid.
75. Ibid., 18.
76. Karl E. Keefer to Bob Jones Jr., June 24, 1953; Folder: Mercer, Ted, BJUFF.
77. Karl Keefer to Fellow Faculty, July 10, 1953; Folder: Mercer, Ted, BJUFF.
78. Bob Jones Sr. to Matthew Welde, August 15, 1953.
79. Alice Mercer to Matt Welde, August 12, 1953. Emphasis in original.
80. Doreene Holmes to Alumni, August 8, 1953; Folder: Bob Jones University—Alumni Association, GSP.
81. Gilbert Stenholm to Alumni, August 8, 1953; Folder: Bob Jones University—Alumni Association, GSP.
82. James D. Edwards to Alumni, August 8, 1953; Folder: Bob Jones University—Alumni Association, GSP.
83. R. K. Johnson to Alumni, August 8, 1953; Folder: Bob Jones University—Alumni Association, GSP.
84. Mercer, *A Statement Concerning My Dismissal from Bob Jones University*, 13.
85. Mercer, *An Additional Statement*, 7.
86. Ibid., 9.
87. Roy I. Mumme to Mercer, August 5, 1953; TB, Folder: Mercer/Keefer.
88. Bob Jones Sr. to Wilbert Welch, June 29, 1953; Box HC 20/24, Folder: Bob Jones U Greenville—Letter Dr. Bob Jones Sr.—Wilbert Welch 1952, 53, 1967.

89. Alex Green, "T.C. Mercer, from Bob Jones to Bryan," *Bryan Triangle*, April 19, 2012, http://www.bryantriangle.com/archives/2012/t-c-mercer-from-bob-jones-to-bryan (accessed May 3, 2016).
90. Turner, *Standing Without Apology*, 158.
91. Bob Jones Sr. to "Fellow Workers," September 1955; GSP. Emphasis in original. There was an identical letter from 1954 in Stenholm's papers as well.
92. Ibid.
93. Darren Dochuk, *From Bible Belt to Sun Belt: Plain-Folk Religion, Grassroots Politics, and the Rise of Evangelical Conservatism* (New York: Norton, 2011), 212.
94. Carl F. H. Henry, *The Uneasy Conscience of Modern Fundamentalism* (Grand Rapids, MI: Eerdmans, 1947), xx.
95. Joel A. Carpenter, *Revive Us Again: The Reawakening of American Fundamentalism* (New York: Oxford University Press, 1997), 141–160.
96. Bob Jones Sr. to E. G. Zorn, July 23, 1943; Bob Jones University Archives, cited in Dalhouse, *Island in the Lake of Fire*, 62.
97. Carpenter, *Revive Us Again*, 145.
98. Ibid., 145–147.
99. Ibid., 150.
100. Dalhouse, *Island in the Lake of Fire*, 65.
101. J. Carl, "Readers Say," *United Evangelical Action* (August 1, 1947): 23.
102. Bob Jones Sr. to R. L. Decker, May 16, 1949; Bob Jones University Archives, cited in Dalhouse, *Island in the Lake of Fire*, 66.
103. Dalhouse, *Island in the Lake of Fire*, 73; Turner, *Standing Without Apology*, 166.
104. Marsden, *Reforming Fundamentalism*, 146.
105. Hamilton, "Fundamentalist Harvard," 45.
106. Marsden, *Reforming Fundamentalism*, 165.
107. Bob Jones Sr. to W. F. Graham, January 6, 1937; TB, Folder: Billy Graham.
108. Billy Graham to Bob Jones Sr., December 11, 1947; TB, Folder: Billy Graham.
109. See, for example, Bob Jones Sr. to Billy Graham, December 19, 1949; Billy Graham to Bob Jones Sr., December 28, 1949; Billy Graham to Bob Jones Sr., October 23, 1950; Bob Jones Sr. to Billy Graham, October 25, 1950; TB, Folder: Billy Graham.
110. Bob Jones Sr. to Billy Graham, April 5, 1951; TB, Folder: Billy Graham.
111. Billy Graham to Bob Jones Sr., June 3, 1952; TB, Folder: Billy Graham.
112. Bob Jones Sr. to Billy Graham, December 30, 1953; TB, Folder: Billy Graham.
113. See, for example, Bob Jones Sr., to "Friend," March 6, 1957; TB, Folder: Billy Graham.
114. Bob Jones Sr. to Billy Graham, January 17, 1956; TB, Folder: Billy Graham.
115. Bob Jones Jr. to Ralph W. Mitchell, November 7, 1956; TB, Folder: Billy Graham.
116. William Culbertson to Bob Jones Jr., June 12, 1958; Folder: Moody Bible Institute, BJUFF.

117. Miss [Name Blacked Out] to Bob Jones Jr., March 2, 1959; Folder: Moody Bible Institute, BJUFF.
118. William Culbertson to Bob Jones Jr., June 23, 1959; Folder: Moody Bible Institute, BJUFF.
119. Dalhouse, *Island in the Lake of Fire*, 86.
120. Marsden, *Reforming Fundamentalism*, 192.
121. Calvin Veltman, "Farewell to Fundamentalism," *Wheaton Record* 85 (January 10, 1963): 2.
122. Marsden, *Reforming Fundamentalism*, 146.
123. Edward J. Carnell, *The Case for Orthodox Theology* (Philadelphia: Westminster Press, 1959), 113.
124. Interview with John Abram Huffman, April 14, 1988; Collection 389, BGC.
125. See Marsden, *Reforming Fundamentalism*, 146, 162. From Fuller's perspective, and Marsden's, the emergence of a more ecumenical evangelical identity marked a "decisive break" (146) and an "irreparable breach" (162) with Fuller's fundamentalist roots.
126. George W. Dollar, *A History of Fundamentalism in America* (Greenville, SC: Bob Jones University Press, 1973), 283–284.
127. Ibid., 284–285.
128. Ibid., 285.
129. William C. Ringenberg, *The Christian College: A History of Protestant Higher Education in America* (Grand Rapids, MI: Eerdmans, 1984), 173.
130. Ibid., 180.
131. Ibid., 182.
132. Ibid., 184.
133. Ibid., 186.
134. Timothy L. Smith, "Introduction: Christian Colleges and American Culture," in *Making Higher Education Christian: The History and Mission of Evangelical Colleges in America*, ed. Joel A. Carpenter and Kenneth W. Shipps (Grand Rapids, MI: Christian University Press, 1987), 3.
135. Carl Henry, "What Is Fundamentalism?," *United Evangelical Action*, July 16, 1966, 303.
136. Dollar, *A History of Fundamentalism in America*, 285.
137. William Culbertson to L. Nelson Bell, May 12, 1955; Box 7, Folder: Correspondence with and About Billy Graham, CP.
138. William Culbertson to Bob Jones Sr., November 27, 1957; Folder: Moody Bible Institute, BJUFF.
139. William Culbertson to Down Howard, December 8, 1959; Box 6, Folder: Questions Answered: N, CP.
140. William Culbertson to Joseph D. Moesta, January 11, 1962; Box 6, Folder: Questions Answered: N, CP.
141. William Culbertson, Press Release, typescript, February 27, 1962; Box 7, Folder: Correspondence with and About Billy Graham, CP.

142. Billy Graham to William Culbertson, June 21, 1958; Box 7, Folder: Correspondence with and About Billy Graham, CP.
143. William Culbertson to Samuel H. Sutherland, July 3, 1968; Box 7, Folder: Correspondence with and About Billy Graham, CP.
144. Typescript of Culbertson biography—n.d., n.p.; Box 1: Folder, Culbertson, biography, CP.
145. "Billy Graham Committee Meeting," June 24, 1965; Box 1, Folder: Graham, Billy, Crusade Boston 1964, POP, 1964–1965.
146. James Forrester to Billy Graham, July 9, 1964; Box 1, Folder: G, POP, 1964–1965.
147. William C. Fleming to James Forrester, May 20, 1966; Box 2, Folder: F, 1966, POP, 1966–1969.
148. John R. Alexander to James Forrester, June 9, 1967; Box 1, Folder: A, 1966, POP, 1966–1969.
149. James Forrester to John R. Alexander, June 21, 1967; Box 1, Folder: A, 1966, POP, 1966–1969.
150. Marsden, *Reforming Fundamentalism*, 146.
151. Harold Ockenga to Joan Bauer Smith, August 20, 1969; Box 3, Folder: S, 1969, POP, 1966–1969.
152. Sanford L. Fisher to Mary E. Margerum, November 17, 1969; Box 2, Folder: F, 1969, POP, 1966–1969.
153. Paul R. Jackson, "Wheaton College," in "Special Information Bulletin," November 15, 1961; Folder: Wheaton College, GSP.
154. Bob Waggoner to Bob Jones Jr., September 4, 1963; TB, Folder: Wheaton College.
155. Bob Jones Jr. to Mr. and Mrs. Edward E. Bowers, September 4, 1968; TB, Folder: Wheaton College.
156. V. Raymond Edman to Irene Miller, August 1, 1962; Box 4, Folder 3, EP.
157. Richard W. Anderson to V. Raymond Edman, n.d. [Edman's reply is dated February 5, 1963]; Box 6, Folder 11, EP. Emphasis in original.
158. Memo, May 29, 1964; TB, Folder: Wheaton College.
159. H. G. Faulkner to Bob Jones University, January 8, 1970; TB, Folder: Wheaton College.
160. Bob Jones III to Joshua Ekpikhe, April 30, 1973; TB, Folder: Wheaton College.
161. Kathy Martin, Memo, July 24, 1974; TB, Folder: Wheaton College.
162. Bob Jones Sr. to Harold Lindsell, May 4, 1950; Box 30, Folder 5, HLP.
163. Kathy Martin, Memo, July 24, 1974; TB, Folder: Wheaton College.
164. Samuel Sutherland to LaRoy Anderson, February 20, 1970. Folder: A Correspondence (General), SP.

## CHAPTER 6

1. Ad for Sudan Interior Mission, *Moody Student*, March 10, 1967, 6.
2. For a list of Bible schools with founding dates, see Virginia Lieson Brereton, *Training God's Army: The American Bible School, 1880–1940* (Bloomington, IN: Indiana University Press, 1990), 71–77.

3. William C. Ringenberg, *The Christian College: A History of Protestant Higher Education in America*, 2nd ed. (Grand Rapids, MI: Eerdmans, 2006), 157; see also "About University of Northwestern," https://www.unwsp.edu/web/about/1902-1947 (accessed April 11, 2016).
4. Bryan LaPlaca, "Shelton College, Local Forges, and 'Back in the Day' Back in the Day," NorthJersey.com, February 15, 2010, http://www.northjersey.com/news/shelton-college-local-forges-and-back-in-the-day-back-in-the-day-1.206262?page=all (accessed April 11, 2016).
5. "Nyack History," Nyack College, http://www.nyack.edu/content/History (accessed April 11, 2016).
6. "Our History," Cairn University, http://cairn.edu/about/history (accessed April 11, 2016).
7. "History," Multnomah University, http://www.multnomah.edu/about/history (accessed April 11, 2016).
8. Roger L. Geiger, *The History of American Higher Education: Learning and Culture from the Founding to World War II* (Princeton, NJ: Princeton University Press, 2015), 481, 532; see also Marc VanOverbeke, *The Standardization of American Schooling: Linking Secondary and Higher Education, 1870–1910* (New York: Palgrave Macmillan, 2008).
9. Molly Worthen, *Apostles of Reason: The Crisis of Authority in American Evangelicalism* (New York: Oxford University Press, 2014), 51.
10. Samuel H. Sutherland to Allen Fast, May 15, 1957; Folder: "F" Correspondence (General) File #1, SP.
11. William Houghton to Crowell, Christiansen, Culbertson, Stockburger, and Hitt, n.d.; Folder: Dr. Houghton Letters From, Houghton Papers, Moody Bible Institute Archives, Chicago, Illinois.
12. "What About Your Son or Daughter?," *Moody Monthly*, July 1938, 560.
13. J. Oliver Buswell, "President of Wheaton College Writes a Word to Biola Students," *Biola Chimes*, February 1939, 1.
14. Clarence C. Mason Jr., "How to Choose Your School," *Sunday: Pleasurable Reading for Today's Christian Home*, April 1948, 39–40.
15. Leith Anderson, "'Moody Bible College'" *Moody Student*, October 23, 1964, 2.
16. Russ Lapeer, "Bible College Issue," *Moody Student*, November 6, 1964, 2.
17. H. C. Crowell, memo [penned in at top, "Early 1959"]; Box 1, Folder: Culbertson, Wm. Policies while at MBI, CP.
18. Typescript of Culbertson biography, n.d. Box 1, Folder: Culbertson, biography, CP.
19. See, for example, *The Evangelical Student* 1 (April 1926): 2. The authors claim that their League of Evangelical Students enrolled members in thirty-two schools, including two colleges or universities, fifteen seminaries, and fifteen Bible colleges or institutes.
20. Maxwell Coder, "What Next for Junior?," *Moody Monthly*, June 1960, 18.

21. S. A. Witmer, "The Paradox in Bible College Education," in *S. A. Witmer, Beloved Educator*, ed. Timothy M. Warner, 33–35 (Wheaton, IL: n.p., 1970). Quoted in Ringenberg, *The Christian College*, 167.
22. *Campus Life, 1981–1982: Guide to Christian Colleges*. Folder: Colleges & Bible Institutes, GSP.
23. Kenneth Gangel, "The Bible College: Past, Present, and Future," *Christianity Today*, November 7, 1980, 36.
24. Perry V. Jenness to Oliver Buswell, August 17, 1936; Box 13, Folder 6, Buswell BP.
25. *Campus Life, 1981–1982 Guide to Christian Colleges*. Folder: Colleges & Bible Institutes, GSP.
26. Paul S. Liechty to Registrar, Fuller Seminary, March 21, 1950; Box 30, Folder 5, HLP.
27. Robert H. Heckart to John Huffman, August 16, 1955; Box 5, Folder 10, Huffman Papers, Collection 389, BGC.
28. Huffman to Heckart, September 5, 1955; Huffman Papers.
29. Interview with William John Barnett, May 30, 1995; Collection 248, BGC.
30. University of Illinois Registrar's Office, "Final Rating of Wheaton College," January 16, 1925; "Student Recruitment" file; Blanchard Papers, Wheaton College Archives.
31. Ibid.
32. Michael S. Hamilton, "The Fundamentalist Harvard: Wheaton College and the Continuing Vitality of American Evangelicalism, 1919–1965," Ph.D. diss., University of Notre Dame, 1994, 93.
33. Ibid., 90–94.
34. Leonard Lewis to Manuel C. Avila Jr., May 21, 1951; Box 1, Folder A, 1945–1952, POP, 1945–1959; Hudson Armerding to Board of Trustees, January 30, 1957; Box 1, Folder: Armerding, Hudson T., POP, 1964–1965.
35. Samuel Sutherland, "Biola Is Accredited!," *King's Business*, February 24, 1961, 6–7.
36. See, for example, *Christianity Today*, December 8, 1967, 33.
37. *Lynchburg Baptist College Newsletter* 1, no. 1 (July 1, 1974); copy in Folder 13:4, Series 4, Folder 1, Box LU 13:4, Box 5, Liberty University Archives, Lynchburg, Virginia.
38. Diana Knutson, "The Miracle on Liberty Mountain," April 26, 1982, 9; copy in Folder LU 13–7: Series 2, Folder 1, Liberty University Archives.
39. Brereton, *Training God's Army*, 143.
40. Ringenberg, *The Christian College*, 165–166.
41. Douglas A. Barcalow, "Continuing Education in the Bible College Movement: A Historical Study of Five Institutions," Ed.D. diss., Northern Illinois University, 1986, 123.
42. Ringenberg, *The Christian College*, 166–167.
43. Quoted in Ringenberg, *The Christian College*, 167.

44. Mark Taylor Dalhouse, *An Island in the Lake of Fire: Bob Jones University, Fundamentalism, and the Separatist Movement* (Athens: University of Georgia Press, 1996), 42.
45. Press release, June/July 1939; Box HC 20/24, Folder: Bob Jones College, Cleveland, TN, Ensembles Press Releases, 1939–4, Bob Jones University Archives, Greenville, South Carolina.
46. Bob Jones Sr. to Ellis Fuller, December 17, 1947; Box HC 20/24, Folder: Southern Baptist Theological Seminary, Correspondence with, Bob Jones University Archives.
47. Bob Jones Sr. to Harold Lindsell, May 4, 1950; Box 30, Folder 5, HLP.
48. Dalhouse, *Island in the Lake of Fire*, 4.
49. Harry Teat to Bob Jones Jr., August 13, 1942; Box HC 20/24, Folder: Bob Jones College, Cleveland, TN, Letters Bob Jones Jr—Harry Teat, 1937–1942, Bob Jones University Archives.
50. Bob Jones Sr. to Registrar, June 19, 1942; Box HC 20/24, Folder: Southern Baptist Theological Seminary, Correspondence with, Bob Jones University Archives.
51. Bob Jones Sr. to SBC Seminary, Attn. Hugh Peterson, September 7, 1942; Box HC 20/24, Folder: Southern Baptist Theological Seminary, Correspondence with, Bob Jones University Archives.
52. Turner, *Standing Without Apology*, 165.
53. Ellis Fuller to Bob Jones Sr., January 1, 1948; Box HC 20/24, Folder: Southern Baptist Theological Seminary, Correspondence with, Bob Jones University Archives.
54. Hudson Armerding to Leonard Lewis, December 6, 1955; Box 1, Folder; Armerding, Hudson T., POP, 1964–1965.
55. Hudson Armerding, "A Study of Needs for a Projected Christian University of 4,000 Students," December 1, 1955; Box 1, Folder; Armerding, Hudson T., POP, 1964–1965.
56. Armerding, "A Christian University and the Authority of Scripture," n.d.; Box 1, Folder; Armerding, Hudson T., POP, 1964–1965.
57. James Forrester to Carl F. Henry, August 31, 1961; Box 1, Folder: H, POP, 1959–61.
58. Carl F. Henry, "Why Not a Federated Campus?," *Christianity Today*, January 19, 1962, 24.
59. Robert S. Lutz, "'National University' Proposed at NAE," *Christianity Today*, May 13, 1966, 47–48; press release: "Wheaton President Proposes Cooperative National University," April 1966; Box 15, Folder 30, AP.
60. Carl F. Henry to James Forrester, September 5, 1961; Box 1, Folder: H, POP, 1959–1961. Henry can't be blamed for not seeing the future. In 1961, the schools may have seemed irreconcilably divided, but in 1985 the two schools combined on Gordon's campus.

61. "A Proposal to the Institute for Advanced Christian Studies," December 3, 1969; Box 15, Folder 20, AP.
62. "Summary of Meeting, Christian College Consortium," January 11, 1971; Box 12, Folder 10, AP.
63. Christian College Consortium, meeting minutes, May 12, 1971; Box 12, Folder 10, AP.
64. James A. Patterson, *Shining Lights: A History of the Council for Christian Colleges and Universities* (Grand Rapids, MI: Baker Academic, 2001), 42, 51. The Christian College Coalition, in turn, would become the Coalition for Christian Colleges and Universities in 1995, then the Council for Christian Colleges and Universities in 1999.
65. Hudson Armerding to John R. Dellenback, October 1, 1980; Box 12, Folder 15, AP.
66. Patterson, *Shining Lights*, 34.
67. Timothy P. Weber, "The Two-Edged Sword: The Fundamentalist Use of the Bible," in *The Bible in America: Essays in Cultural History*, ed. Nathan O. Hatch and Mark A. Noll, 101–120 (New York: Oxford University Press, 1982).
68. W. H. Griffith Thomas, "Report of the Committee on Resolutions," *God Hath Spoken* (Philadelphia: Bible Conference Committee, 1919), 13.
69. "National Survey of Attitudes of Colleges Toward Certain Evangelical Policies, 1919"; Box 2: College-Related, Blanchard Papers, Wheaton College Archives.
70. Bob Jones Sr., *Bob Jones Magazine* 1 (June 1928), 3.
71. Ringenberg, *The Christian College*, 16.
72. Cited in Brereton, *Training God's Army*, 87.
73. Weber, "The Two-Edged Sword."
74. Brereton, *Training God's Army*, 88–89.
75. Brendan M. Pietsch, *Dispensational Modernism* (New York: Oxford University Press, 2015), 80–92.
76. Ibid., 96–123.
77. James M. Gray, *How to Master the English Bible* (Chicago: Bible Institute Colportage Association, 1904).
78. James M. Gray, *Synthetic Bible Studies*, rev. ed. (New York: Revell, 1923), 11.
79. See, for example, Gladys Porter's notes from Alfred Thompson Eade, *The New "Panorama" Bible Study Course: "A Visual Aid to Bible Study": Panorama Study Number 1, "The Plan of the Ages"* (Grand Rapids, MI: Fleming H. Revell, 1947); fragments in Gladys Porter Scrapbook, Student Life Collection, Moody Bible Institute Archives.
80. See Pietsch, *Dispensational Modernism*, 203.
81. Worthen, *Apostles of Reason*, 30, 220–223.
82. Frank Gaebelein to Harold Ockenga, July 28, 1969; Box 2, Folder: G, 1969, POP, 1966–1969.

83. Arthur F. Holmes, *The Idea of a Christian College* (Grand Rapids, MI: Eerdmans, 1975), 15.
84. Holmes, *The Idea of a Christian College*, 56.
85. Ibid., 59.
86. Ringenberg, *The Christian College*, 161.
87. Joel A. Carpenter, *Revive Us Again: The Reawakening of American Fundamentalism* (New York: Oxford University Press, 1997), 177.
88. "What Led Me to Biola," *Biola Chimes*, September 1940, 4.
89. Robert Williams and Marilyn Miller, *Chartered for His Glory: Biola University, 1908–1983* (La Mirada, CA: Biola University Press, 1983), 16.
90. See, for example, *Biola Chimes*, February 1938, 4.
91. See, for example, Hedley J. Parker Scrapbook, 21, Student Life Collection, Moody Bible Institute Archives.
92. Williams and Miller, *Chartered for His Glory*, 96.
93. Ibid., 46–47.
94. Ibid., 71.
95. "Seniors Scan Hope-Filled Horizon," *Biola Chimes*, June 1938, 1.
96. *Activities of Alumni Members*, June 1945; Folder: Alumni, SP.
97. *Alumni Information—Biola College—1962*; Folder: Alumni, SP.
98. Clyde Cook, "Education and Missions: A Divorce?," *King's Business*, December 1969, 26.
99. Virginia L. Brereton, *Training God's Army: The American Bible School, 1880–1940* (Bloomington; Indiana University Press, 1990), 128.
100. Carpenter, *Revive Us Again*, 84.
101. George Marsden, *Reforming Fundamentalism: Fuller Seminary and the New Evangelicalism* (Grand Rapids, MI: Eerdmans, 1987), 84.
102. Turner, *Standing Without Apology*, 203.
103. Ibid., 254–255.
104. *1982 Foreign Missions Emphasis Week*, Folder LU 13-3: series 10, Folder 1, Liberty University Archives.
105. Interview with Paul A. Contento, December 9, 1992; Collection 472, BGC.
106. Interview with Margaret L. Clapper, January 19, 1993; Collection 480, BGC.
107. Interview with Paul Dean Votaw, March 4, 1980; Collection 105, BGC. See also interview with Jesse Wilbert Hoover, October 7, 1985; Collection 319, BGC.
108. Interview with Melvin David Suttie, January 18, 1985; Collection 293, BGC.
109. Interview with Paul A. Contento, BGC.
110. Gladys Porter notebook, "The Progress of World-Wide Missions," 1944; Gladys Porter Scrapbook, Student Life Collection, Moody Bible Institute Archives.
111. Robert Lampson 1931 Recommendation File, SRC.
112. Albert S. Nichols, "Admission Policy of Wheaton College," February 23, 1946; Box 2, Folder 3, EP.

113. See, for example, Assistant Superintendent to Mr. James Simpson, July 15, 1932; SRC.
114. Samuel H. Sutherland to Boyd DeFrance, May 30, 1952; Folder: Student Problems, SP.
115. Darren Dochuk, *From Bible Belt to Sun Belt: Plain-Folk Religion, Grassroots Politics, and the Rise of Evangelical Conservatism* (New York: Norton, 2011), 113, 129; Bethany Moreton, *To Serve God and Wal-Mart: The Making of Christian Free Enterprise* (Cambridge, MA: Harvard University Press, 2009), 166.
116. Dochuk, *From Bible Belt to Sun Belt*, 215, 340; Moreton, *To Serve God and Wal-Mart*, 173–189.
117. Emmett R. Lehman to James Forrester, January 26, 1965; Box 1, Folder: American Studies Program, 1965, POP, 1964–1965; Emmett Lehman to James Forrester, June 21, 1965; Box 1, Folder: American Studies Program, 1965, POP, 1964–1965.
118. Emmett R. Lehman to James Forrester, December 31, 1964; Box 1, Folder: American Studies—Freedom Forum, POP, 1966–1969.
119. Ibid.
120. Carleton Campbell to Forrester, November 5, 1964; Box 1, Folder: American Studies—Freedom Forum, POP, 1966–1969.
121. Forrester to Carleton Campbell, October 27, 1965; Box 1, Folder: American Studies—Freedom Forum, POP, 1966–1969.
122. Program: "The Role of the Christian Educator in Today's World," n.d.; Box 1, Folder: American Studies—Freedom Forum, POP, 1966–1969. Ellipsis in original.
123. Stanley R. Allaby to Leymon W. Ketcham "Deac," February 8, 1966; Box 1, Folder: American Studies—Freedom Forum, POP, 1966–1969.
124. Patterson, *Shining Lights*, 38–39.
125. J. Gresham Machen to F. E. Robinson, n.d.; Machen Papers, Montgomery Library Archives, Westminster Theological Seminary Archives, Philadelphia, Pennsylvania.
126. J. Gresham Machen to E. D. Given, June 28, 1925; Machen Papers.
127. D. G. Hart, *Defending the Faith: J. Gresham Machen and the Crisis of Conservative Protestantism in America* (Grand Rapids, MI: Baker Books, 1994), 58. See also D. G. Hart, *Calvinism: A History* (New Haven, CT: Yale University Press, 2013), 258–264.
128. J. Gresham Machen to Andrew S. Layman, August 6, 1929; J. Gresham Machen to D. Maclean, September 30, 1929, Machen Papers; James M. Gray, "Editorial Notes: Westminster Theological Seminary," *Moody Bible Institute Monthly*, September 1929, 6; Oswald T. Allis, "The New Presbyterian Seminary," *Sunday School Times*, August 31, 1929; J. Gresham Machen, "Westminster Theological Seminary: Its Purpose and Plan," *The Presbyterian* 99 (October 10, 1929): 6–9.

129. Nathan Wood to Loraine Boettner, April 6, 1934; Box 1, Folder: Correspondence B, POP, 1918–1944. See also Loraine Boettner, *The Reformed Doctrine of Predestination* (Grand Rapids, MI: Eerdmans, 1932).
130. William Harry Jellema, "Calvinism and Higher Education," in *God-Centered Living, or, Calvinism in Action,* ed. Clarence Bouma (Grand Rapids, MI: Baker Book House, 1951), 109.
131. Hart, *Defending the Faith,* 164.
132. Hamilton, "Fundamentalist Harvard," 146.
133. Ibid., 147.
134. Ibid., 147–148.
135. Ibid., 150.
136. Ibid., 151–152.
137. J. Calvin, "What True Faith Is," *Tartan,* May 23, 1969, 4.

## CHAPTER 7

1. Wesley Earl Craven, "From the Editor: To the Woman Who Came to My Office and Wept," *Kodon* 17, no. 2 (Winter 1962): 3.
2. On the vagaries of historical memory about the sixties, see Sam Wineburg, "Making (Historical) Sense in the New Millennium," in *Historical Thinking and Other Unnatural Acts: Charting the Future of Teaching the Past* (Philadelphia: Temple University Press, 2001), 232–255. And of course, much of the campus unrest popularly associated with the sixties happened in the early 1970s. For a discussion of the difference between the 1960s and "the sixties," see, for example, Andrew Hartman, *War for the Soul of America: A History of the Culture Wars* (Chicago: University of Chicago Press, 2015), 9–37.
3. Molly Worthen, *Apostles of Reason: The Crisis of Authority in American Evangelicalism* (New York: Oxford University Press, 2014), 63–65; George H. Nash, *The Conservative Intellectual Movement in America Since 1945, Thirtieth-Anniversary Edition* (Wilmington, DE: ISI Books, 2008), 40–42; John A. Andrews III, *The Other Side of the Sixties: Young Americans for Freedom and the Rise of Conservative Politics* (New Brunswick, NJ: Rutgers University Press, 1997); Gregory L. Schneider, *Cadres for Conservatism: Young Americans for Freedom and the Rise of the Contemporary Right* (New York: New York University Press, 1999); Rebecca E. Klatch, *A Generation Divided: The New Left, the New Right, and the 1960s* (Berkeley: University of California Press, 1999).
4. Glenn Arnold, "The Christian Collegian After a Decade of Change," *Christianity Today,* November 3, 1978, 22.
5. Randall Balmer, *Mine Eyes Have Seen the Glory: A Journey into the Evangelical Subculture in America,* 3rd ed. (New York: Oxford University Press, 2000), 133.
6. "BJU Stages Write-in," *BJU Bulletin,* May 1966, 15; "BJU Student Leaders Protest Anarchy," *Voice of the Alumni,* June 1970, 2.

7. Bob Jones Jr., "Chapel Talk," May 5, 1970, typescript; GSP.
8. Resolution passed by BJU Alumni Association, April 2, 1970; Folder: Bob Jones University—Alumni Association, GSP.
9. Michael Jay Sider-Rose, "Between Heaven and Earth: Moody Bible Institute and the Politics of the Moderate Christian Right, 1945–1986," Ph.D. diss., University of Pittsburgh, 2000, 187.
10. Dave Broucek, "Let's End Peaceniks' War," *Moody Student*, November 14, 1969, 2.
11. "Culbertson Chapel Announcement," October 13, 1969; Typescript, Box 1, Folder: Culbertson, Wm. Policies While at MBI, CP.
12. Todd Lewis, "The Times They Are . . . ," *The Chimes*, January 15, 1969, 3.
13. Samuel H. Sutherland to Todd Lewis, January 21, 1969; Folder: Chimes, The, Student Newspaper Publication Biola, SP.
14. Dick Chase to Samuel Sutherland, n.d., Folder: Chimes, The, Student Newspaper Publication Biola, SP.
15. Bob Guernsey, "Why It's So Quiet," *The Chimes*, March 12, 1969, 2.
16. Memo, n.d.; Folder: Chimes, The, Student Newspaper Publication Biola, SP.
17. Andrew Brown, Robert Cruickshank, Ed Vaeni, and Sue Bingham, "A Choice, Not an Echo," *Gordon Tartan*, February 27, 1968, 2.
18. Brian McLamb, "Letter Blasts Vietnam Editorial," *Gordon Tartan*, March 12, 1968, 2.
19. Memo to Samuel Sutherland from Students of Talbot Theological Seminary, n.d.; typescript, Folder: "Brown" (Art) Controversy Correspondence, SP.
20. Peter Schwepker, "Nation Reads Biola Chimes Editorial," *Biola Chimes*, September 16, 1965, 1; Peter Schwepker, "There Are Always Two Sides to Life," *Biola Chimes*, September 16, 1965, 2.
21. Norman Goss, "Biolan in the Midst of Rebels," *Biola Chimes*, October 22, 1965, 2.
22. Editorial, "Hippies Have Sown Seeds of Destruction," *Gordon Tartan*, January 18, 1968, 3.
23. Lenore Weiss, "Editor Speaks Out," *Gordon Tartan*, September 24, 1968, 2.
24. *Lynchburg Baptist College Catalogue 1975–76*, 24; Liberty University Archives, Lynchburg, Virginia.
25. Glenn Arnold, "The Christian Collegian After a Decade of Change," *Christianity Today*, November 3, 1978, 22–26.
26. Bob Jones Sr. to Mrs. Ruth Shuman, June 22, 1965; TB, Folder: Bob Jones Sr., Jr., III, and Few Deans (attitude-position on certain subjects).
27. Bob Jones III to Mrs. Herman Parsons, July 16, 1975; TB, Folder: Student Life.
28. Bob Jones III to P. Kirkpatrick, January 14, 1975; TB, Folder: Student Life.
29. Glen Watts, "The Mumbling Majority," *Brave Son* 1, no. 2 (April 1962): 3–4.
30. Wesley Earl Craven, "A Warning from the Editor," *Kodon* 17, no. 1 (Fall 1962): 3.
31. Michael S. Hamilton, "The Fundamentalist Harvard: Wheaton College and the Continuing Vitality of American Evangelicalism, 1919–1965," Ph.D. diss., University of Notre Dame, 1994, 249–250.

32. V. Raymond Edman to Paul M. Saxton, February 7, 1963; Box 6, Folder 11, EP.
33. Herman A. Fischer to Harry E. Cawood, February 9, 1963; Box 6, Folder 11, EP.
34. Craven, "From the Editor: To the Woman Who Came to My Office and Wept," 4.
35. Ibid., 6.
36. Philip K. McIlnay, "Academics and the Faith," *Critique* 1, no. 1 (March 1963): 1.
37. Ibid., 2.
38. Hamilton, "Fundamentalist Harvard," 251–252.
39. Harold Lindsell to Raymond Edman, February 14, 1964; Box 3, Folder 15, HLP.
40. Hudson Armerding to Campus, November 15, 1965; Box 19, Folder 14, AP.
41. Frank O. Green to the Members of the Drama and Pledge Committee, October 27, 1964; Box 19, Folder 14, AP.
42. Peter Veltman to Armerding, October 20, 1966; Box 42, Folder 10, AP.
43. Armerding memo, July 1, 1966; Box 42, Folder 10, AP.
44. Enock C. Dyrness to Armerding, June 20, 1966; Box 42, Folder 10, AP.
45. Mark Noll to Armerding, May 26, 1966; Box 42, Folder 10, AP.
46. Armerding to faculty and staff, August 26, 1967; Box 42, Folder 10, AP.
47. Armerding, "Parents' Day Chapel Talk," October 30, 1971; Box 53, Folder 74, AP.
48. Memo, "Policy and Procedure Re: Militant Organizations Effect on Biola College Campus," April 10, 1969; Folder: Militant Organizations and their Effect on Biola Campus, SP.
49. "Only Twenty Minutes Please!," *Biola Chimes* May 1, 1964, 5.
50. "Boob Tube O.K.'ed for Girl's Dorm," *Biola Chimes*, February 18, 1966, 1; Linda Smith, "Letter to the Editor," *Biola Chimes*, February 18, 1966, 2.
51. "Council Drafts Resolution on Informal Dress," *Biola Chimes*, February 19, 1969, 2.
52. "Next Year's Cultural Arts Series OK'd," *Biola Chimes*, March 19, 1969, 1.
53. Margaret J. Hart to Lowell and Marie Wendt, April 5, 1968; Hart to Mr. and Mrs. Older B. Anderson, April 5, 1968; Folder: Student Problems, SP.
54. Bob Guernsey, "Council Discusses Policy with Administration," *Biola Chimes*, October 23, 1968, 1.
55. Samuel H. Sutherland to Clyde Narramore, February 8, 1966; Folder: Student Problems, SP.
56. See the extensive correspondence about this student between November 1970 and January 1976; Folder: Correspondence Student (Prior to July 1, 1970), SP.
57. Memo to Samuel Sutherland from Students of Talbot Theological Seminary, n.d.; typescript, Folder: "Brown" (Art) Controversy Correspondence, SP.
58. Ibid.
59. Hugo Lehmann to Samuel Sutherland, May 7, 1969; Folder: "Brown" (Art) Controversy Correspondence, SP.
60. Bill Bascom, "An Explanation . . . ," *The Catacomb*, March 20, 1968, 1. Tellingly, President Sutherland filed his copy of this newspaper in his "Student Problems" file. See SP.

61. Ken Bascom, "To Love Is to Kill," *Catacomb*, March 20, 1968, 2.
62. Roger Dunn to Bob Guernsey, April 21, 1969; Folder: Chimes, The, Student Newspaper Publication Biola, SP.
63. Guernsey to Dunn, April 24, 1969; Folder: Chimes, The, Student Newspaper Publication Biola, SP.
64. Jim Wiese, "Alice's Restaurant," *Biola Chimes*, November 20, 1968, 2.
65. See, for example, Sutherland to Sallie I. Harris, March 17, 1969; Sutherland to Kathy McKean, March 20, 1969; Sutherland to Loren Anderson, March 27, 1969; Folder: Chimes, The, Student Newspaper Publication Biola, SP.
66. Sutherland to Editor, *Anaheim Bulletin*, September 18, 1967; Folder: A Correspondence (General), SP.
67. John M. Isaac to "Friends," February 16, 1970; Folder: A Correspondence (General), SP.
68. P. Andrew Brown, "Apathy on the Way Out?," *Gordon Tartan*, December 10, 1968, 7.
69. James Forrester to Nathan Garnett, December 5, 1967; Box 2, Folder: G, 1967, POP, 1966–1969.
70. George Rideout to Harrison, August 6, 1968; Box 2, Folder: G, 1967, POP, 1966–1969.
71. "Students, Deans to Revise Rules," *Moody Student*, November 20, 1970, 1.
72. Ibid.
73. Mike Farrell, "Are We Fighting the Wrong Fight?," *Moody Student*, December 16, 1970, 2.
74. B. Myron Cedarholm to William Culbertson, January 21, 1971; Box 1, Folder: Correspondence with and about John Rice, CP.
75. David R. Swartz, *Moral Minority: The Evangelical Left in an Age of Conservatism* (Philadelphia: University of Pennsylvania Press, 2012), 16.
76. Keith W. Olson, *The G.I. Bill, the Veterans, and the Colleges* (Lexington: University Press of Kentucky, 1974), 17–18, 29, 43.
77. Sarah Turner and John Bound, "Closing the Gap or Widening the Divide: The Effects of the G.I. Bill and World War II on the Educational Outcomes of Black Americans," *Journal of Economic History* 63 (March 2003): 151.
78. Ibid., 153.
79. Lizabeth Cohen, *A Consumer's Republic: The Politics of Mass Consumption in Postwar America* (New York: Knopf Doubleday, 2008), 156.
80. Suzanne Mettler, *Soldiers to Citizens: The GI Bill and the Making of the Greatest Generation* (New York: Oxford University Press, 2005), 7.
81. Turner, *Standing Without Apology*, 370 n. 40.
82. Darren Dochuk, *From Bible Belt to Sun Belt: Plain-Folk Religion, Grassroots Politics, and the Rise of Evangelical Conservatism* (New York: Norton, 2011), 126.
83. Paul M. Bechtel, *Wheaton College: A Heritage Remembered, 1860–1984* (Wheaton, IL: Harold Shaw, 1984), 165, 184.
84. Turner, *Standing Without Apology*, 370 n. 41.

85. Mettler, *Soldiers to Citizens*, 67.
86. Turner, *Standing Without Apology*, 101.
87. William C. Ringenberg, *The Christian College: A History of Protestant Higher Education in America* (Grand Rapids, MI: Eerdmans, 1984), 210.
88. Turner, *Standing Without Apology*, 101–102.
89. Granted, Council for Christian Colleges and University (CCCU) membership has never been an exact map to schools that identify as evangelical. Many evangelical or fundamentalist schools are not members of the CCCU. And many CCCU members would never think of themselves as part of the family of American evangelical institutions. Plus, schools tend to exaggerate their own histories, so it can be difficult to tell when exactly a school was founded, or when it moved from being an "academy," "normal school," "institute," or other institution to something we might recognize as a modern-style college or university. In addition, today's membership list does not include schools such as Barrington College that have closed their doors. Given all these caveats, from today's CCCU members alone (see "Members & Affiliates," Council for Christian Colleges and Universities, http://www.cccu.org/members_and_affiliates [accessed June 7, 2016]) the list of new evangelical colleges and universities that popped up between 1940 and 1980 stretches to thirty-six schools, nearly a third of current membership. In addition, a quick look at the recommended list of "Creation Colleges" from Answers in Genesis (see "Creation Colleges," *Answers in Genesis*, https://answersingenesis.org/colleges/colleges-and-universities [accessed June 7, 2016]) gives at least another ten schools founded in the same period. A few of these schools are also members of the CCCU, but most are not. Speaking broadly, creation colleges favored by Answers in Genesis tend to lean heavily to the more conservative, more fundamentalist side of the evangelical family.
90. "About APU," Asuza Pacific University, http://www.apu.edu/about/history/timeline (accessed April 11, 2016).
91. Samuel Sutherland to Cornelius P. Haggard, October 14, 1966; Folder Asuza-Pacific College Correspondence, SP.
92. Dr. Bill Bynum to Samuel Sutherland, July 12, 1966; Folder Asuza-Pacific College Correspondence, SP.
93. Samuel Sutherland to Dr. James Christian, July 12, 1966; Folder Asuza-Pacific College Correspondence, SP.
94. Robert O. DeVette to Peter Veltman, September 1, 1967; Box 4, Folder 12, AP.
95. Box 3, Folder 12: Admissions, 1968–69, AP.
96. Box 3, Folder 13: Admissions, 1969–70, AP.
97. Box 3, Folder 19: admissions, 1976–77, AP.
98. Charles W. Shoenherr to Armerding, April 15, 1966; Box 3, Folder 11, AP.
99. Report to the President from the Admissions Office, July 15, 1966; Box 4, Folder 12, AP.

100. Charles W. Shoenherr to Armerding, April 15, 1966; Box 3, Folder 11, AP.
101. Armerding to faculty and staff, August 12, 1967; Box 42, Folder 10, AP; Armerding, "Parents' Day Chapel Talk," October 30, 1971; Box 53, Folder 74, AP.
102. Bob Jones Jr., "Chapel Talk," May 5, 1970, typescript, GSP.
103. Resolution passed by BJU Alumni Association, April 2, 1970; Folder: Bob Jones University—Alumni Association, GSP.
104. P. Andrew Brown, "Apathy on the Way Out?," *Gordon Tartan*, December 10, 1968, 7.
105. Ronald F. Lucas, "Letter to the Editor," *Biola Chimes*, November 5, 1965, 2.

## CHAPTER 8

1. John R. Rice, "The Integration Question at Bob Jones University," *Sword of the Lord*, March 13, 1970, 4.
2. Mark Taylor Dalhouse, *An Island in the Lake of Fire: Bob Jones University, Fundamentalism, and the Separatist Movement* (Athens: University of Georgia Press, 1996), 156.
3. *Bob Jones University v. United States*, 461 U.S. 574 (1983); Dalhouse, *Island in the Lake of Fire*, 155–159; Aaron Haberman, "Into the Wilderness: Ronald Reagan, Bob Jones University, and the Political Education of the Christian Right," *Historian* 67 (2005): 234–253.
4. See, e.g., David Nevin and Robert E. Bills, *The Schools That Fear Built: Segregationist Academies in the South* (Washington, DC: Acropolis Books, 1976).
5. Constitution: Evangelical Teacher Training Association; Folder: Evangelical Teacher Training Association, SP.
6. Daniel L. Turner, *Standing Without Apology: The History of Bob Jones University* (Greenville, SC: Bob Jones University Press, 1997), 67.
7. Dalhouse, *Island in the Lake of Fire*, 132.
8. Minutes, Teacher Education Committee and Education Department, December 7, 1966; Box 19, Folder 24, AP.
9. Joel A. Burkman to Samuel Sutherland, May 15, 1952; File: Education, US, Department of, SP.
10. Roy E. Simpson to Wallace Emerson, January 10, 1952; File: Education: State Department of, File #1, SP.
11. Samuel Sutherland to Aubrey Douglass, February 26, 1952; File: Education: State Department of, File #1, SP.
12. Samuel Sutherland to Senator Nelson S. Dilworth, May 1, 1952; File: Education: State Department of, File #1, SP.
13. Wallace Emerson to Nelson Dilworth, January 14, 1952; File: Education: State Department of, File #1, SP.
14. Nelson Dilworth to Samuel Sutherland, February 4, 1952; File: Education: State Department of, File #1, SP. For Senator Dilworth's role as a leader in California's

purge of suspected communists in schools, see Adam Laats, *The Other School Reformers: Conservative Activism in American Education* (Cambridge, MA: Harvard University Press, 2015), 140, 154, 178.

15. Robert D. Rhodes to J. Burton Vasche, January 27, 1959; Folder: Vasche—State Department of Education, SP.
16. Elizabeth Lewis Pardoe, "Poor Children and Enlightened Citizens: Lutheran Education in America, 1748–1800," *Pennsylvania History* 68, no. 2 (2001): 162–201. Peter P. DeBoer, "North American Calvinist Day Schools," in *Religious Schools in the United States K-12: A Source Book*, ed. Thomas C. Hunt and James C. Carper, 69–95 (New York: Garland Publishing, 1993); Jon Diefenthaler, "Lutheran Schools in Transition," in *Religious Schools in the United States K-12*, ed. Hunt and Carper, 419–443; *Basic Principles of the Christian Schools of America* (Grand Rapids, MI: National Union of Christian Schools, n.d. [1925]); *The Bible and the Christian Schools of America* (Chicago: National Union of Christian Schools, 1925).
17. John F. Blanchard Jr., "Yes, You Can Have a Christian School!," *Moody Monthly*, May 1964, 34–35, 55–60; see also Mark A. Fakkema, "Christian Schools and How to Establish Them," *Christian Life*, September 1947, 20–21.
18. Virginia Davis Nordin and William Lloyd Turner, "More than Segregation Academies: The Growing Protestant Fundamentalist Schools," *Phi Delta Kappan* 61 (February 1980): 391.
19. See Warren S. Benson, "A History of the National Association of Christian Schools During the Period of 1947–1972," Ph.D. diss., Loyola University Chicago, 1975; "1991/1992 School Statistics," Christian Day School File, File #070264, BJUFF.
20. See Adam Laats, "Our Schools, Our Country: American Evangelicals, Public Schools, and the Supreme Court Decisions of 1962 and 1963," *Journal of Religious History* 36, no. 3 (September 2012): 319–334; Adam Laats, "Forging a Fundamentalist 'One Best System': Struggles over Curriculum and Educational Philosophy for Christian Day Schools, 1970–1989," *History of Education Quarterly* 50 (February 2010): 55–83; Adam Laats, "Inside Out: Christian Day Schools and the Transformation of Conservative Protestant Educational Activism, 1962–1990," in *Inequity in Education: A Historical Perspective*, ed. Debra Meyers and Burke Miller, 183–209 (Lexington, KY: Lexington Books, 2009). See also Cary Shaw, "National Trends and a Local Response: A History of the Conservative Evangelical Twin Tiers Christian Academy," Ed.D. dissertation, Binghamton University (SUNY), 2015.
21. Nevin and Bills, *Schools That Fear Built.*
22. Announcement, March 14, 1976; Miscellaneous Materials File: Folder 13:4, Series 4, Folder 4B, Liberty University Archives, Lynchburg, Virginia; Student Affairs notes, November 20, 1981; Student Affairs notes, May 7, 1982, Liberty University Archives.

23. "Liberty Baptist College," typescript announcement, Fall 1982, Miscellaneous Materials File, Liberty University Archives; Summer Scope '80, Miscellaneous Materials File, Liberty University Archives.
24. Turner, *Standing Without Apology*, 201.
25. Bob Dalton to Walter Fremont, April 8, 1986; Folder, Administrative Correspondence, GSP.
26. Bob Jones III to Bob Dalton, April 15, 1986; Folder, Administrative Correspondence, GSP.
27. Roy W. Lowrie to E. Harold Harper, April 26, 1976; Box 19, Folder 30, AP.
28. E. Harold Harper to Roy W. Lowrie, April 29, 1976; Box 19, Folder 30, AP; Cliff Schimmels to John M. Fretz, September 26, 1979; Box 19, Folder 27, AP.
29. "Student Teaching Assignments," Spring, 1976; Box 19, Folder 30, AP; "Student Teaching Assignments for Spring Quarter SY 1979–80," Box 19, Folder 27, AP.
30. E. Harold Harper to Roy W. Lowrie, April 29, 1976; Box 19, Folder 30, AP. Emphasis in original.
31. Michael S. Hamilton, "The Fundamentalist Harvard: Wheaton College and the Continuing Vitality of American Evangelicalism, 1919–1965," Ph.D. diss., Notre Dame University, 1994, 148–149.
32. "And with All Thy Getting . . . ," *Home School Helper*, Autumn 1986, 3.
33. Ronald A. Horton, ed., *Christian Education: Its Mandate and Mission* (Greenville, SC: Journey Forth/Bob Jones University Press, 1992), 20.
34. "Teaching Hints," *Home School Helper*, Summer 1986, 1.
35. See Appendix C: "Philosophy of Pensacola Christian School," in *The Successful Christian School: Foundational Principles for Starting and Operating a Successful Christian School*, ed. A. A. Baker (Pensacola, FL: A Beka Book Publications, 1979), 188. See also Laats, "Forging a Fundamentalist 'One Best System,'" 75–78.
36. Jerry H. Combee, "Human Nature and Christian Education: The Connection Between Discipline, Curriculum, and Methods," in *The Successful Christian School*, ed. Baker, 176 ("biblical discipline"), 185 ("standing foursquare").
37. Nevin and Bills, *Schools That Fear Built*, 2; Gary Orfield, *Public School Desegregation in the United States, 1968–1980* (Washington, DC: Joint Center for Political Studies, 1983), 1–2; Roger Biles, "A Bittersweet Victory: Public School Desegregation in Memphis," *Journal of Negro Education* 55 (Autumn 1986): 479–481.
38. Mark Newman, *Getting Right with God: Southern Baptists and Desegregation, 1945–1995* (Tuscaloosa: University of Alabama Press, 2001), 106.
39. Ibid., 51.
40. Jane Dailey, "The Theology of Massive Resistance: Sex, Segregation, and the Sacred After *Brown*," in *Massive Resistance: Southern Opposition to the Second Reconstruction*, ed. Clive Webb, 151–180 (New York: Oxford University Press, 2005).
41. Jerry H. Combee, "Human Nature and Christian Education," 176.

42. Biles, "A Bittersweet Victory," 481.
43. Hamilton, "Fundamentalist Harvard," 212.
44. Robert Williams and Marilyn Miller, *Chartered for His Glory: Biola University, 1908–1983* (La Mirada, CA: Biola University Press, 1983), 28.
45. Interview with William John Barnett, May 30, 1995; Collection 248, BGC.
46. Hamilton, "Fundamentalist Harvard," 213.
47. Timothy Gloege, *Guaranteed Pure: The Moody Bible Institute, Business, and the Making of Modern Evangelicalism* (Chapel Hill: University of North Carolina Press, 2015), 228.
48. Hamilton, "Fundamentalist Harvard," 213.
49. S. Maxwell Coder to Philip R. Newell, April 1, 1952; SRC.
50. Hamilton, "Fundamentalist Harvard," 215.
51. Interview with Wayne G. Bragg, May 9, 1980; Collection 96, BGC.
52. Daniel K. Williams, *God's Own Party: The Making of the Christian Right* (New York: Oxford University Press, 2010), 92.
53. Molly Worthen, *Apostles of Reason: The Crisis of Authority in American Evangelicalism* (New York: Oxford University Press, 2014), 137. See also Michael O. Emerson and Christian Smith, *Divided by Faith: Evangelical Religion and the Problem of Race in America* (New York: Oxford University Press, 2000), 46–48.
54. William Culbertson to Sam Lin, "Interracial Marriage," November 8, 1965; Box 1, untitled folder, answers to commonly asked questions, CP.
55. Lloyd Hamill, "The Problem of Segregation and the Christian," *King's Business*, November 1957, 6.
56. "Reader Reactions," *King's Business*, December 1957, 8.
57. "Reader Reaction," *King's Business*, February 1958, 9.
58. Samuel Sutherland to Billy Graham, September 10, 1958; Folder: Graham, Billy, Correspondence, Re: Controversy, SP.
59. Dave Shimeall, "Editorial: Segregation: An Indictment Against the Christian Church," *Biola Chimes*, March 20, 1964, 2.
60. Wes Reeves, "Freedom vs. Equality," *Biola Chimes*, February 26, 1965, 2.
61. Samuel Sutherland to Wes Reeves, February 27, 1965; Folder: Chimes, SP.
62. Gordon S. Jaeck to V. Raymond Edman, July 11, 1960; Box 7, Folder 17, EP.
63. Merrill C. Tenney to V. Raymond Edman, July 29, 1960; Box 7, Folder 17, EP.
64. V. Raymond Edman to Executive Council, July 22, 1960; Box 7, Folder 17, EP.
65. James M. Murk, "The Race Question," *Brave Son*, April 1962, 12.
66. Ibid., 11.
67. Ibid., 10.
68. Peter Veltman to Hudson Armerding, November 17, 1968; Box 9, Folder 12, AP.
69. Hudson Armerding to Grover Wilcox, March 12, 1970; Box 9, Folder 12, AP; R. Potter, "The 'Black Problem' Is Your Problem," *Wheaton Record*, February 27, 1970, 4.
70. R. Thomas, "We Discuss Racism as Problem, Ignore Blatant Prejudice," *Wheaton Record*, February 6, 1970, 4.

71. Hudson Armerding to Ron Potter, March 13, 1970; Box 9, Folder 12, AP.
72. Ron Potter to Hudson Armerding, March 17, 1970; Box 9, Folder 12, AP.
73. Hudson Armerding, "Minority Groups," typewritten statement, February 21, 1969; Box 9, Folder 12, AP.
74. Peter Veltman to Hudson Armerding, January 27, 1971; Box 9, Folder 12, AP.
75. David R. Swartz, *Moral Minority: The Evangelical Left in an Age of Conservatism* (Philadelphia: University of Pennsylvania Press, 2012), 38.
76. Ibid.
77. "Afro-American History Offered," *Gordon Tartan*, September 17, 1969, 1.
78. "Editor's Note," *Gordon Tartan*, May 23, 1969, 2.
79. "Editor's Note," *Gordon Tartan*, February 19, 1969, 2.
80. "Smith to Attend Parley on Black Bible Students," *Moody Student*, May 8, 1970, 1.
81. Bob Jones Sr. to Robert L. Larsen, October 28, 1955; TB, Folder: Bob Jones Sr., Jr., III, and Few Deans (attitude-position on certain subjects), Bob Jones University Archives, Greenville, South Carolina.
82. Bob Jones Sr. to Mrs. J. O. Lollis, January 11, 1957; TB, Folder: Bob Jones Sr., Jr., III, and Few Deans (attitude-position on certain subjects).
83. Bob Jones Sr., *Is Segregation Scriptural? Address Given over Radio Station WMUU, Bob Jones University, Greenville, South Carolina, April 17, 1960* (n.p., n.d.), 10.
84. Ibid., 11.
85. Turner, *Standing Without Apology*, 209.
86. Bob Jones Jr. to "Bill," June 27, 1964; Folder: Jones, Bob, 1911–1997 [JUNIOR] Correspondence, BJUFF.
87. Bob Jones III, "A Statement from the Chairman of the Board of Trustees and President of Bob Jones University," typescript, September 10, 1971; Folder: "Policy on Negroes," GSP.
88. Ibid.
89. Turner, *Standing Without Apology*, 227.
90. Richard Rupp to Walter Handford, January 8, 1980; Folder: Administrative Correspondence, GSP.
91. Ralph F. Balog to Bob Jones III, September 27, 1976; TB, Folder: Wheaton College.
92. Bob Jones III to Ralph F. Balog, October 2, 1976; TB, Folder: Wheaton College.
93. Bob Jones Jr. to Jim Walton, April 29, 1975; TB, Folder: Wheaton College.
94. "Bob Jones Versus Everybody: Its Views on Biblical Separation Are Not Shared by Most Conservative Christian Schools," *Christianity Today*, February 19, 1982, 27.
95. "Black Student Fellowship," *Campus Crier*, October 30, 1981; Student Affairs records, Folder 37:10, Series 2, Folder 1b, Liberty University Archives.
96. John R. Rice, "The Integration Question at Bob Jones University," *Sword of the Lord*, March 13, 1970, 4.
97. William Culbertson to John R. Rice, December 30, 1970; Folder: Correspondence with and About John R. Rice, CP.

98. William Culbertson to John R. Rice, December 8, 1970; Folder: Correspondence with and About John R. Rice, CP.

## CHAPTER 9

1. A. P. Guillermin, "The President's Perspective: Welcome to Mr. Reagan, NRB," *President's Newsletter*, October 3, 1980, 1.
2. Howell Raines, "Reagan Is Balancing Two Different Stances," *New York Times*, October 4, 1980.
3. See, for example, Martin E. Marty, "Politics and God's 'Prophets,'" *New York Times*, April 29, 1982; Richard John Neuhaus, *The Naked Public Square: Religion and Democracy in America* (Grand Rapids, MI: Eerdmans, 1984), 5–7.
4. See, for example, George Vecsey, "Militant Television Preachers Try to Weld Fundamentalist Christians' Political Power," *New York Times*, January 21, 1980; Kenneth A. Briggs, "Dispute on Religion Raised by Campaign," *New York Times*, November 9, 1980; Susan Friend Harding, *The Book of Jerry Falwell: Fundamentalist Language and Politics* (Princeton, NJ: Princeton University Press, 2000), 9, 11, 21, 23.
5. George M. Marsden, *Fundamentalism and American Culture*, 2nd ed. (New York: Oxford University Press, 2006), 7.
6. Talk about the United States as "our" country was widespread among evangelicals and fundamentalists throughout the twentieth century. Even those fundamentalists who have been described as retreating from public life between the 1930s and the 1970s often used this sort of language. See, for example, Ray Chamberlin, "Prayer and Bible in Public Schools," *Sword of the Lord*, January 17, 1964, 1, 12; "Who Is Undermining the Constitution?," *Moody Monthly*, October 1964, 1–2.
7. Daniel K. Williams, *God's Own Party: The Making of the Christian Right* (New York: Oxford University Press, 2010), 171; See also John W. Warner to Jerry [Falwell], April 3, 1979; Collection: FAL 5:1–7; Box 1; Series 1, Folder 1, FP, Liberty University Archives.
8. For more on the emergence and new dominance of the modern evolutionary synthesis, see, for example, Edward J. Larson, *Evolution: The Remarkable History of a Scientific Theory* (New York: Modern Library, 2006); Kostas Kampourakis, *Understanding Evolution* (New York: Cambridge University Press, 2014); Adam Laats and Harvey Siegel, *Teaching Evolution in a Creation Nation* (Chicago: University of Chicago Press, 2015).
9. Paul M. Bechtel, *Wheaton College: A Heritage Remembered, 1860–1984* (Wheaton, IL: Harold Shaw, 1984), 125.
10. Michael S. Hamilton, "The Fundamentalist Harvard: Wheaton College and the Continuing Vitality of American Evangelicalism, 1919–1965," Ph.D. diss., Notre Dame University, 1994, 228.

11. Ronald L. Numbers, *The Creationists: From Scientific Creationism to Intelligent Design*, expanded ed. (Cambridge, MA: Harvard University Press, 2006), 195.
12. See, for example, Bernard Ramm, *The Christian View of Science and Scripture* (Grand Rapids, MI: Eerdmans, 1954), 117; Russell Mixter to V. Raymond Edman, November 17, 1960; Box 4, Folder 4, EP.
13. Hamilton, "Fundamentalist Harvard," 229; Numbers, *Creationists*, 196–197.
14. Christopher M. Rios, *After the Monkey Trial: Evangelical Scientists and a New Creationism* (New York: Fordham University Press, 2014), 42–43.
15. See Rios, *After the Monkey Trial;* see also Mark A. Kalthoff, "The New Evangelical Engagement with Science: The American Scientific Affiliation, Origin to 1963," Ph.D. diss., Indiana University, 1998.
16. Numbers, *The Creationists*, 181–182.
17. Ibid., 187.
18. Rios, *After the Monkey Trial*, 51.
19. Numbers, *The Creationists*, 188.
20. Kalthoff, "The New Evangelical Engagement with Science," 635.
21. Rios, *After the Monkey Trial*, 56.
22. Numbers, *The Creationists*, 201.
23. David L. Roberts to Samuel Sutherland, May 23, 1960; Folder: Evolution (Mixter Debate), SP.
24. Russell Mixter to V. Raymond Edman, November 17, 1960; Box 4, Folder 4, EP.
25. Kenneth Kantzer and Samuel J. Schultz to Edman, November 17, 1960; Box 4, Folder 4, EP.
26. Rios, *After the Monkey Trial*, 58–59.
27. Charles E. Harnden to V. Raymond Edman, April 20, 1961; Box 4, Folder 3, EP.
28. Hamilton, "Fundamentalist Harvard," 189–190.
29. Ibid., 230.
30. Harold Lindsell to V. Raymond Edman, December 9, 1960; Box 3, Folder 15, HLP.
31. Charles J. Woodbridge to V. Raymond Edman, November 30, 1960; Harold Lindsell to V. Raymond Edman, December 9, 1960; Box 3, Folder 15, HLP.
32. Harold Lindsell to V. Raymond Edman, November 2, 1960; Box 3, Folder 15, HLP.
33. Walt Handford, "Evolution at Wheaton College," *Sword of the Lord*, June 9, 1961, 1.
34. Ibid., 10.
35. Paul R. Jackson, "Wheaton College," in "Special Information Bulletin," November 15, 1961; Folder: Wheaton College, GSP.
36. Harold P. Warren to Mel Swanson, May 1, 1962; Folder: Wheaton College, GSP.
37. Harold Lindsell to V. Raymond Edman, September 21, 1961; Box 3, Folder 15, HLP.

38. V. Raymond Edman to Bible and Philosophy Department, March 27, 1961; Box 4, Folder 4, EP.
39. V. Raymond Edman, Memo to the Board of Trustees, November 7, 1961; Box 4, Folder 4, EP.
40. Faculty to V. Raymond Edman, May 4, 1961; Box 4, Folder 4, EP.
41. V. Raymond Edman, "Christianity and Science at Wheaton," *Bulletin of Wheaton College*, May 1961, 3; Box 4, Folder 3, EP.
42. Ibid., 5.
43. V. Raymond Edman, Memo to the Board of Trustees, November 7, 1961; see also Edman to Board, Memorandum, December 11, 1961; Box 4, Folder 4, EP.
44. V. Raymond Edman to Friends, November 7, 1961; Box 3, Folder 15, HLP.
45. Hamilton, "The Fundamentalist Harvard," 233.
46. Stanley M. Parmenter to V. Raymond Edman, November 11, 1961; Box 3, Folder 2:1, EP.
47. Irene Miller to V. Raymond Edman, July 23, 1962; Box 4, Folder 3, EP.
48. V. Raymond Edman to Irene Miller, August 1, 1962; Box 4, Folder 3, EP.
49. Ibid.
50. Russell Mixter to Robert T. Ketcham, February 18, 1963; Folder: Creation: Ketcham—Carnell—Buswell—Mixter Correspondence, GSP.
51. Hamilton, "Fundamentalist Harvard," 233.
52. Rios, *After the Monkey Trial*, 64–65.
53. Numbers, *The Creationists*, 213–234.
54. John C. Whitcomb Jr. and Henry M. Morris, *The Genesis Flood: The Biblical Record and Its Scientific Implications*, 8th ed. (Philadelphia: Presbyterian and Reformed Publishing, 1966), xxiv.
55. Ibid., 447.
56. Ibid., 439.
57. Henry M. Morris and Duane T. Gish, eds., *The Battle for Creation: Acts/Facts/Impacts Vol. 2* (San Diego: Creation-Life Publishers, 1976), 16.
58. Ibid., 17.
59. Ibid., 18.
60. Henry M. Morris, "Evolution in Christian Colleges," in *Battle for Creation*, ed. Morris and Gish, 81.
61. Ibid., 80.
62. Ibid.
63. "Doctrinal Statement Lynchburg Christian Schools," n.d., typescript; Series 3, Folder 1, Guillermin Papers, Liberty University Archives.
64. Diana Knutson, "The Miracle on Liberty Mountain," April 26, 1982; General University Materials, LU 13:7-9, Box 2, Folder LU 13-7: Series 2, Folder 1, Liberty University Archives.
65. Barry L. Webster to Dr. Falwell, October 2, 1991; Collection: FAL 5: 1-7; Box 1, Series 2, Folder 1, FP.

66. Williams, *God's Own Party*, 173.
67. Ed Hindson, "Liberalism's Failures Present Opportunities to Conservatives," President's Newsletter, May 19, 1981, 2; Folder: LU 1-1, Series 2, Folder 1F, President's Newsletter, vol. 5: Fall 1983–Spring 1984, Guillermin Papers.
68. Marsden, *Fundamentalism and American Culture*, 7.
69. Harding, *The Book of Jerry Falwell*, 9.
70. Williams, *God's Own Party*, 2, 130, 266.
71. Matthew Avery Sutton, *American Apocalypse: A History of Modern Evangelicalism* (Cambridge, MA: Harvard University Press, 2014), xiii.
72. Ibid., 130.
73. David R. Swartz, *Moral Minority: The Evangelical Left in an Age of Conservatism* (Philadelphia: University of Pennsylvania Press, 2012).
74. James M. Gray to Henry P. Crowell, November 11, 1928; Folder: Correspondence 1926–1931, GP.
75. *Sentinels of the Republic* (n.d.); pamphlet in Machen Papers. See also Carla E. Lucas to J. Gresham Machen, December 13, 1924; Katharine T. Balch to J. Gresham Machen, December 16, 1924; File: 1924–25, Sentinels of the Republic, J. Gresham Machen Papers, Montgomery Library Archives, Westminster Theological Seminary, Philadelphia, Pennsylvania.
76. George Marsden, *Reforming Fundamentalism: Fuller Seminary and the New Evangelicalism* (Grand Rapids, MI: Eerdmans, 1987), 62.
77. Carl F. H. Henry, *The Uneasy Conscience of Modern Fundamentalism* (Grand Rapids, MI: Eerdmans Publishing, 1947), xx.
78. Marsden, *Reforming Fundamentalism*, 154, 156, 207.
79. Mark Taylor Dalhouse, *An Island in the Lake of Fire: Bob Jones University, Fundamentalism, and the Separatist Movement* (Athens: University of Georgia Press, 1996), 39.
80. Ibid., 105.
81. Daniel L. Turner, *Standing Without Apology: The History of Bob Jones University* (Greenville, SC: Bob Jones University Press, 1997), 209.
82. Larry King, "Bob Jones University: The Buckle on the Bible Belt," *Harper's*, June 1966, 51, 53.
83. Typescript of speech by Strom Thurmond, delivered at Bob Jones University, December 14, 1950; Folder: Strom Thurmond, GSP.
84. Strom Thurmond to Gilbert Stenholm, December 31, 1968; Folder: Stenholm—Correspondence—Thurmond, Strom, GSP.
85. Ibid.
86. Gilbert Stenholm to Strom Thurmond, November 4, 1969; Folder: Strom Thurmond, GSP.
87. Gilbert Stenholm to Strom Thurmond, July 26, 1969; Folder; Strom Thurmond, GSP.
88. Clipping in Buswell's files: N. E. Merritt, "An Unafraid College," *The Advisor*, June 12, 1935, 4; Box 21, Folder 18, BP.

89. V. Raymond Edman, "Promotional Letter," n.d. [c. 1948]; Box 3, Folder 14, EP.
90. Michael Paul Rogin, *"Ronald Reagan," the Movie and Other Episodes in Political Demonology* (Berkeley: University of California Press, 1987).
91. "Robnett Warns of Reds' Creeping Tentacles," *Moody Student*, June 8, 1951, 1.
92. Final Exam, Critique of Communism, 1961–1962; Box 4, Folder 18, HLP.
93. See Ellen Schrecker, *Many Are the Crimes: McCarthyism in America* (Princeton, NJ: Princeton University Press, 1998).
94. Box 3, Folder 10, HLP. For Schwarz's crusades, see Darren Dochuk, *From Bible Belt to Sun Belt: Plain-Folk Religion, Grassroots Politics, and the Rise of Evangelical Conservatism* (New York: Norton, 2011), 223–224.
95. Folder: Clippings—Anti-communism, GSP.
96. William Culbertson, "Government Aid"; Box 1, untitled folder, answers to commonly asked questions, CP.
97. Edman collected an exhaustive file of clippings from various sources on the question of federal aid to colleges. His strong feelings on the issue are evident in the emotive and informal notes he made as he read these materials. For example, he scrawled and emphatically underlined "Also agin it" in the margins of one article about federal school aid in a pamphlet from Illinois College, dated summer 1961. See Box 5, Folder 3, EP.
98. *Here We Stand*, n.d. [1980, based on file folder]; Box 10, Folder 3, HLP.
99. George H. Nash, *The Conservative Intellectual Movement in America Since 1945, Thirtieth Anniversary Edition* (Wilmington, DE: ISI Books), xx–xxi, 211–213, 266–283, 543.
100. Weston Reeves, "Political Theory and Theology," *Biola Chimes*, March 26, 1965, 2. See also V. Raymond Edman's [Wheaton] large collection of clippings from *Human Events*, EP; Gilbert Stenholm's [BJU] collection of *Human Events* clippings, GSP. James Forrester of Gordon College also read *Human Events*. See Forrester to Milton I. Wick, January 6, 1966; Box 2, Folder: H, 1966, POP, 1966–1969.
101. Reeves, "Political Theory and Theology," 2.
102. William Culbertson to C. F. Harris, July 28, 1947; Folder: Questions answered: C, CP.
103. James F. Brown to V. Raymond Edman, August 11, 1963; Box 3, Folder 13, EP.
104. Rosalind Woods Guardabassi to James Forrester, September 8, 1967; Box 2, Folder: G, 1966, POP, 1966–1969.
105. Form letter, Samuel H. Sutherland to ________, January 27, 1969. The file includes twenty-six copies of this form letter, but it is not clear how many of them Sutherland actually sent out. Sutherland explained separately in a handwritten note to *Chimes* editor Bob Guernsey that he had received between fifty and sixty complaints about open support for Democrats at Biola. See Folder: Chimes, The, Student Newspaper Publication Biola, SP.
106. Bob Jones Jr. to Winfield Martin, November 24, 1969; Folder: Administrative Correspondence, GSP.

107. Bill Inman, "Evangelist Jones Takes Slap at Betty Ford," *Greenville Piedmont*, October 21, 1976; clipping in Folder: Jones, Bob, 1911–1997—Statements, BJUFF.
108. Charles F. Bennett to Reverend Falwell, May 6, 1980; Series 1, Folder 1, FP.
109. Announcement, *Campus Crier*, February 5, 1982; Student Affairs Papers, LU 37:1-12, Box 1; Folder 37:10, Series 2, Folder 1b.
110. *Summer Scope '80* (n.d., pamphlet); Miscellaneous Materials, Box LU 13:6, Box 2; Folder LU 13-6: Series 1, Folder 2.
111. Announcement sheet, March 26, 1976; Miscellaneous Materials, LU 13:4 Box 5; Folder 13:4, Series 4, Folder 4B. John W. Warner to Jerry, April 3, 1979; Series 1, Folder 1, FP.
112. Robert J. Billings to Jerry Falwell, March 16, 1979; Series 1, Folder 1, FP.
113. George Vecsey, "Militant Television Preachers Try to Weld Fundamentalist Christians' Political Power," *New York Times*, January 21, 1980.
114. Bob Jones III to Truman Dollar, November 20, 1979; Folder: Bob Jones University—Separation, GSP.
115. Bud Bierman to Jerry Falwell, November 19, 1982; Folder: Bob Jones University—Separation, GSP.
116. Bob Jones Jr., confidential memo, n.d.; Folder: Jerry Falwell, GSP.
117. Bob Jones Jr. to Jerry Falwell, July 29, 1980; Folder: Jerry Falwell, GSP.
118. Joseph Crespino, "Civil Rights and the Religious Right," in *Rightward Bound: Making American Conservative in the 1970s*, ed. Bruce J. Schulman and Julian E. Zelizer (Cambridge, MA: Harvard University Press, 2008), 100; Aaron Haberman, "Into the Wilderness: Ronald Reagan, Bob Jones University, and the Political Education of the Christian Right," *Historian* 67 (2005): 239.
119. Crespino, "Civil Rights and the Religious Right," 100.
120. William Martin, *With God on Our Side: The Rise of the Religious Right in America* (New York: Broadway Books, 2005), 173.
121. Haberman, "Into the Wilderness," 240.
122. Ibid.
123. Williams, *God's Own Party*, 192–193.
124. Bob Jones III, form letter, February 19, 1981; Folder: Bob Jones University—Tax Case, GSP.
125. Haberman, "Into the Wilderness," 243–245.
126. Michael Briggs, "Bob Jones Calls Reagan 'Traitor to God's People,'" *Chicago Sun-Times*, March 1, 1982; see also Williams, *God's Own Party*, 197; Haberman, "Into the Wilderness," 146.
127. Briggs, "Bob Jones Calls Reagan 'Traitor to God's People.'"
128. Haberman, "Into the Wilderness," 249.
129. Inman, "Evangelist Jones Takes a Slap at Betty Ford."
130. Briggs, "Bob Jones Calls Reagan 'Traitor to God's People.'"
131. Dalhouse, *Island in the Lake of Fire*, 159.
132. Haberman, "Into the Wilderness," 249.

133. Bob Jones Jr. to W. O. H. Garman, February 1, 1982; Folder: Bob Jones University, W. O. H. Garman Papers, Bob Jones University Archives.

### EPILOGUE: SANDALS OF THE EVANGELICAL MIND

1. Napp Nazworth, "Larycia Hawkins' Theological Statement Following 'Same God' Controversy," *Christian Post*, January 7, 2016. Bracketed text in original.
2. Steve Pettit, Twitter post, December 19, 2015, 9:15 a.m., https://twitter.com/BJUPresident/status/678262271798329346 (accessed January 17, 2016).
3. Michael R. Lowman with Laurel Hicks, George T. Thompson, and the editorial department of A Beka Book Publications, *United States History in Christian Perspective: Heritage of Freedom* (Pensacola, FL: A Beka Book Publications, 1996), 5.
4. Michael McDonald, "God a Click Away as Web Courses Fuel Falwell's College," *Bloomberg*, February 27, 2013.
5. See Adam Laats, "Is Jerry Falwell an Idiot?," *I Love You but You're Going to Hell* (blog), February 5, 2015.
6. *Should I Give to the Alumni Fund?*, Wheaton College, 1947; Box 2, Folder 4: Alumni Association, 1947–1965, EP.
7. Scott Jaschik, "Sweet Briar Survives," *Inside Higher Ed*, June 22, 2016; see also Adam Laats, "Can Fundamentalist Colleges Survive?," *I Love You but You're Going to Hell* (blog), June 7, 2015.
8. See "Statement About Race at BJU," Bob Jones University website, http://www.bju.edu/about/what-we-believe/race-statement.php (accessed November 17, 2016).
9. Kirkland An, "BJU President Comes to Wheaton," *Wheaton Record*, October 22, 2015, 1–2.
10. Nazworth, "Larycia Hawkins' Theological Statement."
11. Steve Pettit, Twitter post, December 19, 2015, 9:15 a.m., https://twitter.com/BJUPresident/status/678262271798329346 (accessed January 17, 2016).
12. Coverage of the case was extensive. See, for example, Jeremy Weber and Ted Olsen, "Wheaton College, Larycia Hawkins to 'Part Ways,'" *Christianity Today*, February 6, 2016. See also Adam Laats, "Elite Wheaton Still a School of a Different Sort," *Chicago Sun-Times*, January 8, 2016.
13. Kevin Hardy, "Bryan College Takes Stand on Creation That Has Professors Worried for Their Jobs," *Times Free Press*, March 2, 2014.
14. Reed Johnson, "Bryan College Settles Lawsuit with Professors," *Herald News* [Dayton, TN], October 10, 2014.
15. Bradford Sample, email communication with author, June 26, 2015.
16. See Adam Laats, "Bryan and the Gray Lady," *I Love You but You're Going to Hell* (blog), May 21, 2015; Adam Laats, "What Would Bryan Do?," *I Love You but You're Going to Hell*, March 17, 2014; Adam Laats, "Ken Ham Is My Guidance

Counselor," *I Love You but You're Going to Hell*, April 11, 2014. See also Ken Ham's rejoinder, "Why I Care Where Your Children Attend College," *Answers in Genesis*, May 10, 2014.

17. GRACE, "Final Report: For the Investigatory Review of Sexual Abuse Disclosures and Institutional Reponses at Bob Jones University," December 11, 2014, https://www.scribd.com/document/249877237/Final-ReportGrace (accessed November 18, 2016).
18. See Adam Laats, "Investigative Report: Sex Abuse at Fundamentalist U," *I Love You but You're Going to Hell* (blog), December 14, 2014.

### RESEARCH APPENDIX

1. On the midcentury enthusiasm for "Christian free enterprise" led by Church of Christ-affiliated schools such as Harding and Pepperdine, see Darren Dochuk, *From Bible Belt to Sun Belt: Plain-Folk Religion, Grassroots Politics, and the Rise of Evangelical Conservatism* (New York: Norton, 2011), 113, 129–133, 209–222; and Bethany Moreton, *To Serve God and Wal-Mart: The Making of Christian Free Enterprise* (Cambridge, MA: Harvard University Press, 2009), 163–168. For a thoughtful collection of essays about higher education among Brethren, Scandinavian Lutheran, and other Pietist groups, see Christopher Gerhz, ed., *The Pietist Vision of Higher Education: Forming Whole and Holy Persons* (Westmont, IL: InterVarsity Press, 2015). For the vital impact of Christian-Reformed-affiliated Calvin College, see Michael S. Hamilton's much-anticipated *Calvin College and the Revival of Christian Learning in America* (Grand Rapids, MI: Eerdmans, forthcoming).

# Index